CATHOLICS IN THE MOVIES

CATHOLICS IN THE
MOVIES

edited by Colleen McDannell

OXFORD
UNIVERSITY PRESS

2008

OXFORD
UNIVERSITY PRESS

Oxford University Press, Inc., publishes works that further
Oxford University's objective of excellence
in research, scholarship, and education.

Oxford   New York
Auckland   Cape Town   Dar es Salaam   Hong Kong   Karachi
Kuala Lumpur   Madrid   Melbourne   Mexico City   Nairobi
New Delhi   Shanghai   Taipei   Toronto

With offices in
Argentina   Austria   Brazil   Chile   Czech Republic   France   Greece
Guatemala   Hungary   Italy   Japan   Poland   Portugal   Singapore
South Korea   Switzerland   Thailand   Turkey   Ukraine   Vietnam

Published by Oxford University Press, Inc.
198 Madison Avenue, New York, New York 10016

www.oup.com

Oxford is a registered trademark of Oxford University Press

Library of Congress Cataloging-in-Publication Data
Catholics in the movies / edited by Colleen McDannell.
  p. cm.
ISBN 978-0-19-530656-9; 978-0-19-530657-6 (pbk.)
1. Catholics in motion pictures.   2. Catholic Church—In motion pictures.
I. McDannell, Colleen.
PN1995.9.C35C38 2007
791.43'68282—dc22   2007013466

9 8 7 6 5 4 3 2 1

Printed in the United States of America
on acid-free paper

*To Brigit Hurdle McDannell and
to all our children, nieces, and
nephews who love the movies*

ACKNOWLEDGMENTS

While all of the individual contributors have had a chance to thank in their end-notes those who helped with their chapters, I would like to take this opportunity to thank everyone who enabled this project to come to fruition. For many years, the Cushwa Center for the Study of American Catholicism at Notre Dame University has provided financial and intellectual support for those of us who study Catholics in the United States. When I approached its director, Timothy Matovina, about a project on Catholics and the movies, he graciously lent the support of the center. That support, combined with a collaborative grant from the American Academy of Religion, enabled us to meet on three beautiful spring days at Notre Dame. It is rare in our business that a group of scholars can gather together in one place and then have an intellectually stimulating conversation as well as a flat-out fun time. The hospitality of Tim and his associate director, Kathleen Sprows Cummings, enabled us to read drafts of each other's chapters, spend time sharing our ideas, and get to know each other. What we found was that working with movies was an engaging way to get at many cultural and social issues from a variety of perspectives. Thank you all for taking time from your own writing projects to work on this one and to then patiently endure my endless editorial requests.

I would also like to acknowledge the support of the University of Utah Research Committee, which enabled me to travel to Beverly Hills and work at the Margaret Herrick Library of the Academy of Motion Picture Arts and Sciences. In addition to gathering materials for the first chapter, I located many of the illustrations reproduced in this volume. The staff members at the Herrick are as accommodating as their facilities are beautiful. I am beginning to understand why film history is a popular scholarly activity.

Jared Anderson read every chapter and made important suggestions about how to get across our ideas to the "average" reader. James T. Fisher and Peter Gardella were involved in the project at various stages, and I also want to thank them for their special contributions. Several of the contributors would like to thank Judith Weisenfeld for her computer skills, which enabled them to pull out images from DVD recordings of the films.

Contents

DARRYL V. CATERINE is an assistant professor at LeMoyne College. He is the author of *Conservative Catholicism and the Carmelites: Identity, Ethnicity, and Tradition in the Modern Church*.

THOMAS J. FERRARO is a professor of English at Duke University. He is the author of *Feeling Italian: The Art of Ethnicity in America* and *Ethnic Passages: Literary Immigrants in 20th-Century America*; he is the editor of *Catholic Lives, Contemporary America*.

TRACY FESSENDEN is an associate professor of religious studies at Arizona State University. She is the author of *Culture and Redemption: Religion, the Secular, and American Literature* and co-editor of *The Puritan Origins of American Sex: Religion, Sexuality, and National Identity in American Literature*.

AMY FRYKHOLM is special correspondent for *The Christian Century*. She is the author of *Rapture Culture: Left Behind in Evangelical America*.

PAULA M. KANE is an associate professor of religious studies and holds the Marous Chair in Contemporary Catholic Studies at the University of Pittsburgh. She is the author of *Separatism and Subculture: Boston Catholicism 1900–1920* and the co-editor of *Gender Identities in American Catholicism*.

JEFFREY MARLETT is an associate professor of religious studies at the College of St. Rose. He is the author of *Saving the Heartland: Catholic Missionaries in Rural America, 1920–1960*.

COLLEEN MCDANNELL is a professor of history and the Sterling M. McMurrin Professor of Religious Studies at the University of Utah. She is the author of

Picturing Faith: Photography and the Great Depression; Material Christianity: American Religion and Popular Culture; The Christian Home in Victorian America; and coauthor of *Heaven: A History;* she is the editor of the two-volume *The Religions of the United States in Practice.*

TIMOTHY J. MEAGHER is an associate professor of history and the director of archives at the Catholic University of America. He is the author of *Inventing Irish America: Generation, Class, and Ethnic Identity in a New England City, 1880–1928* and coeditor of *The New York Irish.*

CARLO ROTELLA is the director of American studies and a professor of English at Boston College. He is the author of *Cut Time: An Education at the Fights; Good with Their Hands: Boxers, Bluesmen, and Other Characters from the Rust Belt;* and *October Cities: The Redevelopment of Urban Literature.*

THERESA SANDERS is an associate professor of theology at Georgetown University. She is the author of *Celluloid Saints: Images of Sanctity in Film* and *Body and Belief: Why the Body of Jesus Cannot Heal.*

ANTHONY BURKE SMITH is an assistant professor of religious studies at the University of Dayton. He is the author of the forthcoming *The Look of Catholics: Religion, Popular Culture and National Identity in Mid-Twentieth-Century America.*

JUDITH WEISENFELD is a professor of Religion at Princeton University. She is the author of *Hollywood Be Thy Name: African-American Religion in American Film, 1929–1949* and *African American Women and Christian Activism: New York's Black Y.W.C.A., 1905–1945.*

CATHOLICS IN THE MOVIES

I

Why the Movies?
Why Religion?

Colleen McDannell

Who doesn't like to go to the movies? Since the beginning of the twentieth century, Americans have been drawn to moving images that flit across a screen. At first, these pictures in motion lasted only a few minutes, but slowly their makers shaped the images into stories of adventure and romance. Sound and color were added to create a multiple sensory experience. We go to the movies for many reasons but perhaps the most obvious is that we enjoy having our emotions engaged by a skilled filmmaker. Good movies allow us to imagine ourselves in new stories; they encourage us to create relationships with the characters we see on the screen. Sitting in a darkened theater with a group of friends and strangers makes this kind of storytelling especially engaging. On an emotional level it might even recall the intensity of listening to tales told on starry nights while gazing at a blazing campfire. Generations of Americans have courted at the movies, taken their buddies to the movies, gone to the movies when profoundly alone. Although watching a movie at home on a television screen (or on an airplane or at the library or on a computer) is not the same, it too can carry us momentarily to a different time and place. Movies draw us into their worlds, and in doing so they touch our innermost thoughts, dreams, and fears. We go to movies to escape, to be entertained, to imagine lives that we can never live. We also learn from the movies. Sometimes we are aware of what they teach, but typically we like them best when the lessons are passed quietly and without note. Many of us imagine life through the movies. They structure our feelings.

As much as movies are about experiences, they are also about communication. Of course movies are made to entertain and to make money. At the same time, they convey ideas. The relationship between reality as we perceive it and the ways that moviemakers represent it is complicated and fluid. Even the silliest comedy presents images of reality—about gender roles, ambition, wealth, the body, our families. Movies convey many different ideas in many different ways. All films, even the wildest science fiction adventures, are a type of "documentary." Made up of layers of ideas about our society, our culture, and our multiple psychologies, movies are shaped by different periods and times. They participate in the era in which they are made but never in a simple or straightforward manner because they play with time. One strand of time is embedded in the plot. Another time is the period when the movie was produced. This time colors the script, alters the music, and shapes the director. Finally, audiences bring with them the times in which they live and thus filter "movie time" through their time. Director Sofia Coppola's *Marie Antoinette* (2006), for instance, is about eighteenth-century royalty, but it is also about contemporary youth culture, leisure, and consumerism. What will audiences feel when they see *Marie Antoinette* in thirty years?

Like language, movies produce, maintain, repair, criticize, and transform reality. Films can collaborate and support what we know already, but they can also debunk what we think is true. Movies make fun of our world while simultaneously making us feel secure living within it. At times, filmmakers purposefully mirror widely accepted values in order to quickly engage viewers. They use "cultural shorthand" or stereotypes so that they can tell their stories without fuss. In this way they reinforce ideas that they assume we all bring to the pictures. At other times, moviemakers begin with what we take as "natural" and then subtly play with our assumptions. Movies provoke reflection, thought, and criticism. We can all point to a movie that "changed" our lives or that got us to think (and feel) in a different way. Moviemakers can harbor hopes of motivating societal change, or they can see their productions as pure entertainment. How audiences will respond to what directors and producers think they have accomplished is equally as complex.

Why Think *about Movies?*

Many of us love going to the movies. We love being entertained. We love the whole moviegoing experience. But doesn't studying movies ruin them? The contributors to this book hope to convince you that thinking about movies can be as enjoyable and exciting as seeing them. We gain a richer experience of viewing when we engage with the ideas embedded in the films we watch. By thinking about movies, we get to linger over the images that captivated or amused us. We get to play over again those moments that struck us as poignant or playful. We get to figure out why we just *hated* that movie: what emotions did it touch (or not touch) that left us feeling empty? Thinking about movies not only creates intelligent moviegoers, it ratchets up the emotional level of experiencing a film. When we look underneath the surface and push beyond the obvious we discover even more feelings and ideas. The ideas and emotions contained in a movie are a part of our cultural environment and can help to reveal manifestations of larger historical and social developments. Thinking about movies deepens our appreciation of the artistry and technological savvy of human creativity. By becoming careful and committed movie observers, we are personally enriched. At the same time we become more sophisticated in our appraisal of the world in which we live. Movies shape our culture and our lives in profound ways. Thinking about movies, looking at them with more intent and awareness, unlocks their hidden charms.

Contributors to *Catholics in the Movies* have chosen films from different decades of moviemaking and laid out what he or she thinks is most important about the film. The chapters are arranged chronologically because we believe that understanding historical change helps us better to uncover the various meanings of movies. Some of the movies are classics that were praised when they appeared in theaters and that continue to amaze and stimulate viewers. A few are no longer well known or did not have wide theater release. We offer interpretations that open up their logic, importance, emotions, and messages. We also are interested in describing *how* a movie "means." How do writers, directors, cinematographers, musicians, and sound engineers create particular meanings? How does the interplay of the visual and the aural stimulate feelings and ideas? Our interpretations reveal the unseen, articulate the intuited, investigate the familiar, deepen reflection, and open thought. We hope that through our thoughtful engagement with the films you will look again at these movies and perhaps alter your first (perhaps too brusque and casual) perceptions.

There are many ways to interpret the cultural expressions of books, artworks, music, or film. You will see that each chapter not only has a unique style, but each contributor approaches his or her movie from a particular angle. They try to say something about the film that is fresh and new. We can look at the inner logic of a movie, analyzing it as a world with its own rules and language. In this interpretation we focus on internal form and argue that meaning lies *within* the frame of the movie screen. Where the director places the actors, how the colors on the screen are balanced, what moves the plot along—these elements provide us the essential clues to understanding what is *really* going on in the film. Outside social forces—like the politics of the filmmaker, the tensions of the era, or the evolution of camera technology—are less important. At other times, interpretations can be extremely sensitive to those very external forces that shape the ideas contained in a movie. When contributor Theresa Sanders discusses *Seven Cities of Gold*, for instance, she finds that the U.S. Supreme Court decision in *Brown v. Board of Education* and America's involvement in the cold war help us to understand the film more than a discussion of camera techniques. Interpretations can also be based on the biographies of the filmmakers, as I show in my chapters on William Peter Blatty's *The Exorcist* and Mel Gibson's *The Passion of the Christ*. The life of a director or writer can shed light on why a film takes on a particular look. As much as formal concerns and historical events shape film, so do the personalities of the people who actually put the movies together.

We should not assume, however, that the statements of the moviemakers about their movies are the best interpretations and so naturally triumph over all other interpretations. The makers of movies provide one voice, not the final voice. Indeed, for much of movie history it was impossible to figure out who was responsible for a film's "idea." In the 1930s and 1940s, when Hollywood studios controlled the production of movies, groups of writers created film stories. For many films one could not isolate nor articulate the intentions of one writer. Scripts were submitted to censors, who made more adjustments, thus adding another influence on the collaborative processes. Producers could keep films from being released or would insist that they be drastically reshaped. By the mid-1960s, some directors had achieved more independence in making films, but even they would admit that what is intended and what is achieved are often not the same. Interpreting what we see in the theater is never clear-cut because the movies—like all cultural expressions—are the result of a variety of intentions. Consequently, we should be careful when listening to the commentaries on DVDs and not assume that these "official" comments are definitive. Considering the intentions of a director or writer should open up more interpretations, not close them down.

The interpretive process gets even more complicated when we consider that the audience carries to the movies its own ideas. Every time we see a movie we get something different out of it. We interpret it differently because our beliefs, values, and society are continually changing. When we see new movies, we think about the old ones in a different light. Unfortunately, our reflections rarely are preserved. We know what the reviewer from the *New York Times* thought about

Dogma (1999) because it was published. The opinions of most of the twenty-somethings who flocked to see it have been lost. Some scholars do, however, seek out the reflections of ordinary people. Amy Frykholm's chapter on *Dogma* uses focus-group interviewing to ferret out the meaning of that film for a small group of people. She explores how individuals see movies from their own cultural and psychological perspectives. From those reflections she makes larger interpretive conclusions. While professional critics may have sophisticated insight into the intentions of the filmmakers, what is exciting about movies is the unpredictable responses they can evoke. Since movies do not communicate in a direct way, any movie can be "misread." However, just as we should not privilege the interpretations of the director, we should also take the audience's responses as only one way of revealing the meanings and ideas of movies.

Movie seeing, just like moviemaking, is an intricate and creative process of making and remaking reality. Thinking about movies allows us not only to experience what the moviemakers intended for us to feel, but to analyze the many different ways that movies "work." In the twenty-first century, watching rather than reading generates our common culture (and fractures it as well). To understand a film is to take into account the individuals who made it, the context in which it was made, its internal logic, and the views of the people who are watching it.

Why Religion?

Historians and film critics look at the movies from many different directions. They ask, for example, how women are represented in certain films and then compare those images with changing notions of femininity and domesticity. Other scholars look at how moviemakers present the working world, thus exploring how Americans think about social mobility and class. Minority and racial communities are depicted on film, and historians chart how those representations have changed over a century of moviemaking. Scholars also look at how certain events have been portrayed at various times by different directors or screenwriters. There are books about film and the Civil War, about film and the frontier, about film and the 1960s. In each of these cases, the focus has been on how critical aspects of our society—race, class, ethnicity, gender, social change—are represented on the screen.

What has been missing from the literature on movies are historical explorations of the place of religion in film. Historians and critics of the movies have forgotten that Americans are the most religious people in the Western world. They go to church, synagogue, and mosque more than Europeans do. Even those who dismiss organized religion and never put a dime in the collection basket tell pollsters that they believe in God, that they pray, and that they hope they will end up in heaven and not hell. Americans enthusiastically buy books like *The Da Vinci Code*, which speculates about the family of the historical Jesus, and they expect their presidents to discuss their personal faith on television. From the colonial Spanish establishment of missions in the New World, to the Quaker condemnation of slavery, to the cross burnings of the Ku Klux Klan, to twenty-first-century debates about the place of religion in public schools, American history has been shaped by religion. While we could simplify our history by reducing religious motivations to merely economic or psychological factors, the reality is that people act on deeply held beliefs and values. One of the things that makes the United States unique in the industrialized world is the continual commitment of its people to organized religious communities. Whether we think this is a good situation or a bad one, we cannot deny the importance of religion to the lives of millions of Americans.

Religion is not merely learned in synagogues, mosques, and churches. The common admission—"everything I know about religion I learned from the movies"—is true for believers as much as for unbelievers. Representing religion in film is as old as the movies themselves. In 1897 on a rooftop in New York City, a camera crew filmed *The Passion Play*, a story of Jesus' suffering and crucifixion. Based on popular plays staged in the Catholic part of Germany, *The Passion Play* was commissioned by the Eden Musée, which was a popular wax museum. Designed to uplift the residents of New York City by bringing historical and literary characters "to life," the Eden Musée unabashedly combined what we now call high and low culture. Its owners began to showcase films soon after the advent of the new entertainment technology. *The Passion Play* was a hit. When most motion pictures were only twenty minutes long, this fifty-five-minute slide/film story of Jesus' last days was the longest "movie" in the United States. It played at the Eden Musée twice daily for three months and then toured the country as a marvel of technological sophistication and religious inspiration.

Some silent filmmakers, as well as many ministers and priests, thought that Bible-based movies could easily bridge the gap between entertainment and devotion. A properly made film—one that was tasteful and pious—could educate and inspire. Once the newness of seeing a "moving picture" wore off though, audiences also wanted dramatic storytelling. Biblical epics became the source for movie spectacles filled with adventure, romance, violence, and scantily clad "pagan" dancers. Cecil B. DeMille invented the biblical extravaganza with *The Ten Commandments* (1923), *King of Kings* (1927), and *The Sign of the Cross* (1932) and then went on to teach later generations what Moses looked like in his 1956 remake of *The Ten Commandments.* Later movies like *Ben Hur* (1958) and *The Greatest Story Ever Told* (1965) provided the images out of which many of us have constructed our mental pictures of Jewish and Christian history. Even the animated *Prince of Egypt* (1998) continued this trend. Consequently, it is not surprising that biblical scholars have concentrated on evaluating the differences between cinematic portrayals of the Bible and the scriptures in their various written forms. Movie images, rather than the words of the King James version of the Bible, now make up our common "biblical language." When what is portrayed on the screen conflicts with the beliefs of particular religious communities, conflicts arise. Both *The Last Temptation of Christ* (1988) and *The Passion of the Christ* (2004) generated considerable conversation, and even boycotts, because of their representations of Jesus.[1]

Christian theologians (those who study Christianity as believers) also explore the Bible through the movies. Instead of focusing on the obvious biblical epics, however, they look for hidden Christian themes embedded in films that are not specifically marked by religious characters or objects. Theologians assume that the Christian story of salvation has universal appeal and so can appear—typically unintentionally—in movies. These scholars locate allegories of Christ or of "redeemer figures" in various Hollywood productions. Films become the modern way of telling parables that relate to Christian values and thus push us to think through the nature of God, the problem of evil, and the question of salvation. Other scholars argue that movies *themselves* are spiritual. Captured within movies are modern myths—fundamentally true stories that help us to articulate our cultural anxieties and desires. They argue that moviegoing (even more than churchgoing) speaks to our deepest concerns, values, and beliefs. Movies tell us what our social values are and how (and if) we should change them. If we want to know what Americans really believe, some scholars argue, then we should study what they see on the screen.

Unfortunately, historians of film and scholars of religion have been less interested in the many other ways that religion appears in movies. The contributors to *Catholics in the Movies* explore what happens when organized religion—not just Bible stories or spiritual themes—enters into a film. While it is fruitful to discuss the mythological power of a film like *Star Wars*, there also needs to be historical examinations of the ways that religious individuals, objects, histories, and settings are represented. We learn about how religion works by watching films, and so we should become aware of how and why films convey particular kinds of information. What happens when religion is inserted into a movie?

Hollywood feature films, for instance, have frequently represented the Protestant minister. In films as divergent as *Miracle Woman* (1931), *Elmer Gantry* (1960),

I.I. Preacher Harry Powell (Robert Mitchum) has had the words "love" and "hate" tattooed on his fingers. *Courtesy of the Academy of Motion Picture Arts and Sciences*

The Apostle (1997), and *Saved!* (2004) the evangelical preacher has been represented as a misguided woman, a con artist, a murderer with a heart of gold, and a well-meaning pastor. Catholic director John Ford made the leader of a congregation of Welsh miners in *How Green Was My Valley* (1941) look more like an Irish priest than a nonconformist minister. Perhaps the creepiest villain of the film noir genre was

1.2. In this scene from *The Jazz Singer* (1927), Jakie Rabinowitz (Al Jolson) gets a hug from his girlfriend, Mary Dale (May McAvoy), as she tries to persuade him to continue his rise to stardom. His mother, Sara (Eugenie Besserer), looks anxiously at the pair. Moisha Yudelson (Otto Lederer) holds two prayer shawls meant as birthday presents for Jakie's father, Cantor Rabinowitz (Warner Oland). *Courtesy of the Academy of Motion Picture Arts and Sciences*

the murderous preacher in *Night of the Hunter* (1955). Movies about religious leaders raise questions about authority, authenticity, faith, charisma, and democracy. Are ministers inspired servants of Christ or corrupt exploiters? Often, the answers to those questions speak eloquently not only to our cultural values but to the specific, historical situation in which Protestants find themselves in America. Movies also give us clues about how non-Protestants view Protestant influence. Looking at where and when religious leaders appear in films—from the Jewish cantor in *The Jazz Singer* (1927), to the Mormon leaders in *Brigham Young* (1940), to the hip Catholic priest in *Keeping the Faith* (2000)—is to examine the various ways that religious authority is understood in American society.

Few religious traditions have not been subjected to the camera. A detective went undercover in an Amish community in *Witness* (1985). Anthony Quinn played a follower of Muhammad in *The Message* (1976), and Denzel Washington stood for the Nation of Islam in *Malcolm X* (1992). In 1981, Hasidic and Orthodox communities of Jews were represented in *The Chosen*. Martin Scorsese was banned from Tibet by the Chinese government for making *Kundun* (1997), a film about the Dalai Lama, and American actor Keanu Reeves starred as Prince Siddhartha in Bernardo Bertolucci's *Little Buddha* (1993). The care that filmmakers take to present religious traditions is uneven, and they pick and choose which parts of a faith community they want to represent. Scholars are quick to uncover the ways that such films misinterpret or even lie about religion, but it is equally important for us to consider the politics behind why a religion might be misread. By looking at religion in movies, we can speculate about what certain groups of people are feeling about religions and what kinds of religious feelings they are having at particular times. To what extent do filmmakers and audiences rely on religious stereotypes, and when do they provide more complicated portrayals of the lives of religious people?

When movies are accused of misreading religious history there can be controversy. Those controversies generate windows into American culture and society— as well as income for the moviemakers. When *The Da Vinci Code* (2006) opened at over 3,700 theaters, it grossed an impressive $77 million domestically and $147 million abroad during its first weekend. Despite being panned by the critics, *The Da Vinci Code* earned more money overseas during those first days than any other American-made movie ever had made. Based on the mega-bestselling book by Dan Brown, the film made claims about Christianity that the author said were historically accurate, but were they? To what extent did *The Da Vinci Code* reinvent a Christian history that spoke to contemporary concerns about the power of religion? Which religious groups mobilized against (or for) the film, and how successful were they?

Early in the twenty-first century, commercial films like *The Da Vinci Code* and *The Passion of the Christ* were box-office hits partly because of their ability to get people talking about religious beliefs, rituals, and history. Equally important, but less studied, are the movies that *religious* people make about religion. Although religious groups can be critical of the film industry, they have also used the movies to get out their own messages of faith. As early as 1918 the Catholic Art Association made *The Transgressor*, a tale about the Catholic working class. In the 1950s the Protestant Film Commission sponsored the production of a series of short movies meant to raise ethical and religious questions. Languishing in the basements of churches, synagogues, seminary libraries, and denominational archives are countless films made to educate believers about the rituals, beliefs, and histories of their communities. While many of these movies have little production value, they have considerable cultural worth as they provide glimpses into how believers see themselves and the world around them.

Religious organizations occasionally make movies that are up to Hollywood standards. A group of Catholic priests, the Paulist fathers, established a film and television production company in 1960. By 1989 Paulist Pictures had made *Romero*, the story of the murdered Archbishop Oscar Romero, who fought for social justice in El Salvador. A major Hollywood studio distributed the film, and it showed in theaters across the country. Paulist Pictures' next movie, *Entertaining Angels: The Dorothy Day Story* (1996), is discussed by contributor Tracy Fessenden. She explores how an unconventional Catholic is turned into a conventional one. What is lost when moviemakers simplify a life?

While conservative Protestants still condemn much of what comes out of Hollywood, increasingly they too are in the moviemaking business. Beginning in the late 1960s, evangelicals began producing feature films as part of their witnessing efforts. By the turn of the century, a host of "family-friendly" movies have engaged viewers with good stories and sophisticated production values. From the casting of Michael York as the Antichrist in *Megiddo: Omega Code II* (2001) to the animated vegetables in *Jonah: A VeggieTales Movie* (2002), film is being used to stimulate the religious imagination and to cement social and political values. Some of these films are produced by Christian media companies, such as the Trinity Broadcast Network. Others are financed by individual filmmakers who seek to engage specific segments of the population. From their studio in Provo, Utah, Kurt Hale and Dave Hunter have created a genre of "Mormon movies" that includes *Churchball* (2006), *Mobsters and Mormons* (2005), *Hometeachers* (2004), *The R M* (2003), and *The Singles Ward* (2002). Denominationally based colleges increasingly support film and media programs to prepare young filmmakers in their craft. Their hope is that, in the future, audiences will have moral alternatives to Hollywood movies. These graduates, such as Brigham Young University alumni Jared and Jerusha Hess, who made the very popular *Napoleon Dynamite* (2004), inhabit the middle ground between commercial Hollywood and Christian media companies.

Feature films move easily between fact and fiction. Another aspect of religious movie culture seeks a more direct engagement with real life. From the stark portrayal of Bible hawkers in *Salesman* (1968), to the stories of gay and lesbian Orthodox and Hasidic Jews in *Trembling before G-d* (2001), documentary filmmakers also create representations of faith communities. These movies seek to present religion not within a fictional narrative but as a "true" expression of "real" people. And yet, as with feature films, documentary filmmakers must edit their footage into a compelling story. Without characters and plot, a documentary is as dry as an encyclopedia article. Even educational videos that are presented as "objective" are expressions of the concerns of their makers. Documentaries, believer-produced feature films, Hollywood studio movies, and independent cinema all represent religious behaviors and beliefs. We need to become aware of how those representations are produced, for what purposes they are made, and how their images influence how we understand religion.

Why Catholics?

Filmmakers have represented many different religions in many different ways. The most sustained cinematic attention, however, has been directed toward Roman Catholicism. Perhaps movie critic (and former altar boy) Roger Ebert best summarized the reason for this attention when he observed that "one of the fascinations of the Catholic Church is that it is the oldest continuously surviving organization in the world."[2] Catholic characters, spaces, and rituals have been stock features in popular films since the silent picture era. An intensely visual religion with a well-defined ritual and authority system, Catholicism lends itself to the drama and pageantry—the iconography—of film. Moviegoers watch as Catholic visionaries interact with the supernatural, priests counsel their flocks, reformers fight for social justice, and bishops wield authoritarian power. As the religion of many immigrants, Catholic characters represent outsider status as well as the "American way of life." Rather than being marginal to American popular culture, Catholic people, places, and rituals are central. At the movies, Catholicism—rather than Protestantism—is *the* American religion.

Catholicism is central to the world of the movies for a variety of reasons. During the golden era of the 1930s and 1940s, Catholic characters represented the immigrant other—a character distinguished from the native-born Protestant American. Moviemakers placed the Irish (and, later, Italians) in the "old neighborhood" where they listened to Catholic priests, sang Catholic hymns, and went to Catholic schools. Catholicism marked these immigrant characters as somewhat foreign and alien but also as profoundly local and American. This urban space was imagined differently from its opposite—the Protestant rural heartland. In the old neighborhood, local space and community life were primary. The music playing in the background was initially "The Sidewalks of New York," which eventually transformed into swing and then into bebop. Movies marked characters as Catholic when they wanted to explore the themes of the loyalty of friends, the

1.3. Paramount Pictures recreated the old neighborhood on its Hollywood lot to look like the busy streets of New York. Here, the studio is filming the opening of *Going My Way* (1944). *Courtesy of the Academy of Motion Picture Arts and Sciences*

power of the family, and the charm of ethnic traditions. The old neighborhood easily became associated with the Catholic parish because in both cases communities impose a set of obligations and responsibilities that the individual cannot fully avoid. Like the Democratic political ward, the parish was represented in movies as an Irish American institution. Parish priests, represented in *Going My Way* (1944) and analyzed by contributor Anthony Smith, became the mediators between Old World traditions and New World innovations.

Whereas the Catholic parish and the political ward were acceptable forms of the ethnic neighborhood, the urban gang was also marked as Catholic. Before World War II, the cities were volatile mixtures of European immigrant groups making their way up the social ladder, African Americans with southern roots, pockets of communities of Asians, and neighborhoods of "established" Americans. Each group—from the Russian Jews to the moneyed WASP factory owners—had its violent ways in the neighborhood. But in silent films and during the golden era of the movies, the Irish and then the Italians were the lords of criminality. By 1924

1.4. During the golden era of the movies, the Irish and then the Italians were the lords of criminality. Catholicism was often associated with profound violence, as Rocky Sullivan (James Cagney) demonstrates to Father Jerry Connolly (Pat O'Brien) in *Angels with Dirty Faces* (1938). *Courtesy of the Academy of Motion Picture Arts and Sciences*

immigration restrictions were complete, yet Jews and Irish Catholics were already making movies. Contributor Thomas Ferraro examines the relationship between the Irish American criminal and the Irish American priest in *Angels with Dirty Faces* (1938). The association in film of Catholicism with profound violence was not merely a trivial moviemaking convention that declined as immigrants assimilated. As contributor Carlo Rotella argues in his essay on *The Godfather* trilogy (1972, 1974, 1990), Catholic rituals contributed to the power of men who "ran" the neighborhood. Even when the old neighborhood was transformed into the Long Island suburbs or—as contributor Timothy Meagher demonstrates in his analysis of *True Confessions* (1981)—into the city of Los Angeles, intense relationships of loyalty, family, and power continue to be marked as Catholic.

Moviemakers tell stories of the old neighborhood because so many movie-goers actually *live* there. By 1930, 20 percent of the U.S. population was Catholic and was heavily concentrated in the cities east of the Mississippi. Over half of the residents of Boston and Chicago, during the full span of the twentieth century, were Catholics. What Catholics saw on the screen during those years had to have some relationship to how they imagined their everyday existence. The urban culture evolved out of a complicated mix of Catholic, Jewish, and African American influences, and this mix served as the foundation for much of the entertainment industry. Jews and Catholics established and ran the vaudeville houses that eventually became the nickelodeons and then the movie theaters. African American entertainments were adopted (or stolen) and adapted for white consumption. Southern migrants, European immigrants, and the children of immigrants became the producers as well as the consumers of the popular culture of an industrializing nation.

Catholics also became the regulators of popular culture. In 1915 the Supreme Court ruled in *Mutual Film Corp. v. the Industrial Commission of Ohio* that the movies were—in effect—more like a hamburger patty than a book. The nation's highest court decided that the movies were a "business, pure and simple" and thus could be regulated. Like meat they could be inspected for purity so that no one would be ingesting the equivalent of pig tummies or mice poop. State and city censorship boards were deemed to be constitutional. In 1922 the trade organization for movies, the Motion Picture Producers and Distributors of America, devised a way for Hollywood to circumvent the restrictions of a variety of censorship boards. In 1930 the members adopted the Production Code, which assured moviegoers, "No picture shall be produced which will lower the moral standards of those who see it."[3] The Production Code, which set out moral standards for movie plots, behaviors, and representations, was composed by a Jesuit priest, Daniel Lord, with the support of Catholic layman Martin Quigley. As Catholics, they were well acquainted with the notion that visual imagery stimulated the imagination—for good or bad. In 1933 another Catholic, Joseph L. Breen, was appointed to see that the Production Code was applied to the scripts that were produced in Hollywood. That same year the Legion of Decency was founded to make sure that average Catholics promised not to watch immoral movies or attend theaters that showed them.

Breen made sure that, in the movies, evil doing was met with the appropriate punishment. Movies were expected to have the top-billed star speak for morality and to respect all lawful authorities. There was to be no cynical contempt for middle-class social standards, no morbid or depressing themes. Divorce was to be presented as a sin, adultery was to be vigorously punished, and modern living (drinking, jazz, married women working) was to be represented as undesirable. Only heterosexual monogamy was to be pictured as normal, and all other forms of sexual attraction were to be eliminated. There could be no romantic interest between those of different races. Costumes had to be modest, and swimming or sleeping in the nude were prohibited. Not only was there to be no bathroom humor, there were to be no bathrooms portrayed in the movies. Even runny noses were considered to be "vulgar."

By the 1930s, Catholics had taken over from Protestants the task of making sure that all movies were "good" movies. This had not always been the case. Earlier in the century, Protestants felt that *they* should possess the power to represent society on the screen and thus to provide positive moral lessons for the masses. Crime and punishment, class and ethnicity, family and romance, should all be portrayed such that they upheld the moral values of middle-class, white Protestants. In her discussion of the silent movie *Regeneration* (1915), Judith Weisenfeld illustrates how early filmmakers represented the Protestant settlement house and its workers as the means of redemption for the wayward Irish Catholic criminal. In these early "problem films," Catholicism contributed to the decline of the city: priests did not condemn drinking, Catholics had too many babies, and Rome ruined Catholics for democracy. Catholicism was associated with the "dark ages" of European monarchies that restricted liberty and free thought. From the perspective of Protestant reformers of the early twentieth century, Catholics just had the wrong values.

By the next decade, however, Protestants were wrangling over exactly which values were important and what kind of institutions should reform America. Conservative Protestants wanted to adhere closely to traditional Victorian sensibilities while liberals preferred more free-ranging modern attitudes. Congregations in the South and Midwest wanted their preachers to condemn sinners while those in the East held that employing sociology and psychology could correct bad behaviors. The failure of Prohibition convinced many social reformers that Protestant ministers could no longer be relied on to shepherd their congregations to do the right thing. New Protestant denominations were being formed by those who rejected modern interpretations of the Bible that stressed it was only a guide to morals and not a textbook for how nature worked. Artists, intellectuals, and writers who had been raised Protestant decided that churchgoing had little relevance to their creative endeavors. By 1928, it seemed that the only thing upon which Protestants could agree was that Catholic Al Smith should not be elected president.

Meanwhile, Catholics were spending their hard-earned pennies on establishing their own institutions. By 1928 immigrants and their children could give birth in Catholic hospitals, place unwanted children in Catholic orphanages, find jobs through their parish priests, play on Catholic sports teams, get married in elaborate neighborhood churches, and find eternal rest in Catholic cemeteries. Through these spiritual, economic, and social institutions, priests and bishops were exerting more and more influence over their parishioners. In 1884 an American council of bishops had determined that all Catholic children must be sent to Catholic schools. An elaborate educational system was developing that would socialize children into a world of distinct rituals, values, and history. While individual Catholics were not shy in challenging the power of their priests, they also knew that they gained much from their parishes. When the clergy did take time out to comment on modern literature or thought, it was to criticize it.

The Catholic clergy, many of whom were middle-class Irish immigrants climbing up the social ladder, eagerly took up the task of policing moviegoing from the Protestants. Who better to regulate the entertainment of immigrants than other immigrants? Neither the Jewish studio owners who made the movies nor the immigrants who went to them wanted a Protestant-dominated federal government to censor the movie industry. Many middle-class Catholics, who once were cultural outsiders, took up the responsibility of promoting "respectability." Irish American Catholics, especially middle class women and priests, claimed the moral high ground vacated by Protestants. In doing so, they hoped to demonstrate their superiority over other urban dwellers that included African Americans, Jews, socialists, as well as fellow Catholic Italians and Poles whose devotional life felt alien to the Irish. By claiming to be the final arbiters and enforcers of morality in filmmaking, Irish American Catholics assumed a powerful place in defining how Americans would see themselves.

Before movie censorship officially ended in the mid-1960s, portrayals of Catholic priests, nuns, rituals, and objects on the screen were checked over to make sure that they were accurate and gave no offense. When Catholic director Alfred Hitchcock made *I Confess* (1953), he had to be very careful that the film met both the moral standards of the Production Code and the rubrics laid out for priests administering the Sacrament of Penance. Both Joseph Breen and a priest/advisor in Los Angeles made sure that the script Hitchcock was using corresponded exactly to Catholic rituals and was free from errors in text or gesture. While the Production Code prohibited any religious leader from being portrayed as a villain or in a comic manner, Breen was especially attentive to Catholic practices. As contributor Paula Kane will explore through *The Song of Bernadette* (1943) Catholics and Jews found themselves together in the movie industry and created a set of American values and practices that spoke to their own position as minority communities in what they perceived to be a Protestant America.

By the 1950s Catholics were no longer on the cultural margins of American society. Their numbers had increased to 25 percent of the population. The GI Bill had enabled many of the children and grandchildren of immigrants to go to college and enter into the professional and managerial classes. Unlike African Americans, who still were excluded from suburban housing because of restrictive covenants and red-lining, white ethnics moved out of the increasingly deteriorating cities. Not surprisingly, the children and grandchildren of the immigrants who ran the nickelodeons and movie palaces would eventually take their places as directors, writers, and actors. Catholics (raised as or converted into) are particularly well represented as directors. The most well known include Mack Sennett, Frank Capra, John Ford, Leo McCarey, John Farrow, Alfred Hitchcock, Martin Scorsese, Francis Ford Coppola, Robert Altman, Brian De Palma, Nancy Sacova, Kevin Smith, John Sayles, Ken Russell, Abel Ferrara, Michael Cimino, Roman Polanski, Edward Burns, Roger Corman, Mel Gibson, and Michael Moore. Some scholars have argued that a "Catholic imagination" can be discerned in some of their films. That imagination stresses the physical and corporeal, plays out the meaning of sin and salvation, attends to social codes and hierarchies, up-ends rigid distinctions between people, and stresses the commonalities among all classes. It is no easy matter, however, to understand the Catholicism of such a diverse group of men and women, much less to find an underlining "Catholic" sensibility in their films. Frank Capra became a Christian Scientist in his later life. John Sayles calls himself a "Catholic atheist." Mel Gibson and Michael Moore both went to Catholic schools and are passionate about their convictions, but what other commonalities can we detect in their films? Rather than trying to discern subtle Catholic footprints in films, in this volume we prefer to look at the more central, direct, and deliberate ways that Catholicism appears in the movies.

As the nature of immigration changed after the Second World War, the aura of Europeanness that surrounded Catholicism also altered. Moviemakers increasingly associated Catholics not with the local community or the old neighborhood, but with the powerfully imperial and cosmopolitan. Catholicism was injected into the movies to stress the significance of international institutions that fought for religion and morality. Like most Americans, Catholics enthusiastically embraced a cold war rhetoric that pitted godless communism against God-fearing capitalism. Unlike most Americans, Catholics were conscious of their coreligionists who lived in countries like Poland, Indochina, and Cuba which had "fallen" to communist regimes. Catholic books and newspapers reported on communist repression throughout the world. This repression was presented as the continuation of the oppression the church had experienced in countries like Mexico and Germany. The international nature of Catholicism, in contrast to Protestantism, made it the perfect choice for moviemakers when they needed a religion to fight the *interna-*

tional spread of communism. In movies as diverse as *The Fugitive* (1947), *Satan Never Sleeps* (1962), and *The Cardinal* (1963), Catholics bring a humane American Christianity into the world of inhumane international atheism. Even the popular *The Sound of Music* (1965) exploits the idea of worldwide Catholicism by having the nuns of Maria's order rescue an aristocratic Christian family from the terror of the Nazi state. In the movies, the religion used to represent religion's fight against godless secularism or communism was usually Catholicism.

When Elia Kazan made *On the Waterfront* (1955) he echoed a cinematic tradition of populist priests drawing their strength from the people they served in the neighborhood. Director Otto Preminger exploited a different source of Catholic power in *The Cardinal* (1963). While the neighborhood provides a healthy environment for vocational nurturance, the parish is only the first stop in a long career trajectory. Priests achieve their real influence not by popular acclaim but through their connection to the hierarchical authority of Rome. The protagonist in *The Cardinal* evolves from a young curate being formed by a grumpy pastor in rural America to being given the "red hat," with all its ensuing spiritual and political power. In the early 1960s this rise to power was not presented as corrupting but rather as the positive end result of a life of devotion and commitment. Nothing permanently inhibits the young priest's rise to glory—not his personal ambition, not the death of his sister when he would not condone her abortion, not the KKK members who beat him for supporting a black parish, not the young Viennese student who falls in love with the manly "priest in disguise." Catholic power is represented as achieved through self-reflection (not self-doubt or blind obedience), cultivated by foreign elites, and directed toward the enforcement of an international order. The movies, along with most of the nation, were caught up in the charisma of their new Catholic president. The election of John F. Kennedy in 1960 had not brought about the downfall of the nation as many had feared. Rather, a young and handsome Catholic male was enabling the country to take its proper place in world affairs.

Movie fascination with Italy, Rome, and the Vatican during the Kennedy years was an inversion of negative nineteenth-century fantasies about Catholicism. What was once thought of as antidemocratic was now admired. Catholics had what Protestants lacked (but desired): a centralized and disciplined authority structure that demanded and provided obedience, a sexuality that could be controlled such that it produced both celibate workers and fertile congregants, a powerful history that reached back two thousand years and across continents, and a set of rituals that vigorously engaged all of the senses in order to generate spiritual ecstasy and communal solidarity. Moviemakers fully exploited the profoundly sensual, visual, and aural character of this Catholic story. With dramatic flare they presented cardinals and popes in robes and lace who never sacrificed their masculine power for their sartorial splendor. Clergy had intense friendships with other men, but their relationships never sullied their heterosexual orientation. Indeed, in this imaginary world women were inconsequential. Catholic leaders expressed their influence within the male world of politics. *The Shoes of the Fisherman* (1968), for instance, contains almost three hours of lavish depictions of the election and coronation of the first Russian pope (he's actually Ukrainian). No one questions his relationship with the young theologian who becomes his friend and assistant. In the final minutes of the movie, the pope (played by Anthony Quinn) succeeds in preventing World War III. Catholic vestments, rituals, traditions, values, and authority structures were fully harnessed by the movies to save the world from evil.

Throughout the cold war era, Hollywood constructed masculine Catholic priests as empowered via their connection to Old World forms of ritual, privilege, and authority. Women, however, were another matter. The cold war years were the years of the nun movies, which ranged from Ingrid Bergman in *The Bells of St. Mary's* (1945), to Audrey Hepburn in *The Nun's Story* (1959), to Elvis Presley's last film, aptly entitled *Change of Habit* (1969). The number of real Catholic sisters in the United States peaked in 1965, and it was their image—not that of the cardinals—that Americans saw on their streets. These women were staffing Catholic schools, running hospitals, serving as overseas missionaries, praying in cloisters, and negotiating with clergymen. Working outside of the home gave many sisters a sense of personal, spiritual, and professional satisfaction. Women were willing to give up husbands and children in order to express their religious commitments by praying and working within the Catholic community.

In the movies, nuns had prescribed roles that moderated their independence and self-fulfillment. In the 1960s, when a man put on the dress of a Catholic priest the garments legitimated and purified his engagement with worldly power. When women wore habits and rosaries, their work became circumscribed and introverted. The influence exerted by nuns was represented at best as bossy and at worst as dictatorial and abusive. In *The Trouble with Angels* (1966), the Mother Superior (Rosalind Russell) spends her time chasing the misbehaving Mary Clancy (Hayley Mills). In *Change of Habit*, Sister Michelle (Mary Tyler Moore) takes off her habit and puts on a skirt in order to work in the clinic with Dr. John Carpenter (Elvis Presley). At the end we are left guessing whether she will return to her convent or run off with the guitar-playing doc. What we do know is that she will not join the "liberated" nuns threatening to reorder the man's world. For women, cold war Catholicism was portrayed as moderating the inde-

1.5. Anthony Quinn plays Kiril Lakota, a Ukrainian bishop who unexpectedly is elected pope in *The Shoes of the Fisherman* (1968). As the cold war progressed, Catholic clergymen were often portrayed as defenders of the international moral order against godless communists. *Courtesy of the Academy of Motion Picture Arts and Sciences*

1.6. Father Chuck O'Malley (Bing Crosby) croons a tune surrounded by the sisters in *The Bells of St. Mary's* (1945). Sister Mary Benedict (Ingrid Bergman), who is playing the piano, exemplifies the restrained independence of Hollywood's representation of Catholic nuns in the postwar years. *Courtesy of the Academy of Motion Picture Arts and Sciences*

pendent spirit rather than facilitating it. This mold was cracking, however, even before the Second Vatican Council (1962–1965). As contributor Jeff Marlett shows in his chapter on *Lilies of the Field* (1963), new relationships were being imagined by Americans, and nuns were used to explore the changes occurring between the races and the genders.

By the time *The Exorcist* (1973) was released, the male-dominated institutions of government, religion, the military, and medicine had lost some of their allure. Americans were filled with anxieties over the choices they were making to liberate women and teens, to take their place as world leaders, to embrace technology, and to rationalize religion. Collective insecurity fueled personal doubt. The devil, as the movie so graphically tells us, had entered our bedrooms. In *The Exorcist*, however, a specifically Catholic approach was used to conquer the demons of doubt and insecurity.

We were able to actually "see" the workings of the devil on film because twenty years earlier an ex-Catholic Italian director had made a film about Catholic hypocrisy that infuriated New York City Catholics. In 1950 Roberto Rossellini's *Il miracolo* (The Miracle) opened at a small art theater in New York City. Barely forty minutes long, it told the story of a simple-minded goat herder who became mysteriously pregnant and was mocked by her fellow villagers before delivering her baby in a local church. Although he had not seen it, the head of New York's archdiocese, Cardinal Francis Spellman, composed a letter to be read at mass at all 400 parishes under his authority, condemning the film as "a despicable affront to every Christian" and "a vicious insult to Italian womanhood."[4] A thousand Catholics picketed the film. They considered the movie sacrilegious because it ridiculed the virgin birth of Jesus and portrayed Catholic villagers as simpletons and hypocrites. The New York state censorship board eventually reversed an earlier ruling and decided that *Il miracolo* was indeed sacrilegious.

Rather than withdraw the imported film from American theaters, its distributor decided to challenge the board's decision. When the case arrived at the Supreme Court in 1952, the justices reversed their earlier 1915 ruling that defined moviemaking as a business that could be regulated. The Court now argued that movies were expressions of ideas and so must be covered under the freedom of speech clause of the Constitution. Just like books and newspapers, movies could not be censored. The Court also concluded that there were no good definitions of "sacrilegious" and so censors were merely "set adrift upon a boundless sea amid a myriad of conflicting currents of religious views, with no charts but those provided by the most vocal and powerful orthodoxies." Therefore, the government "has no legitimate interest in protecting any or all religions from views distasteful to them.... It is not the business of government in our nation to suppress real or imagined attacks upon a particular religious doctrine, whether they appear in publications, speeches, or motion pictures."[5] Despite this ruling, the movie industry continued to enforce the Production Code, but with the retirement of Joseph Breen in 1954, enthusiasm for censorship waned. Younger Americans were challenging the values of their parents. What was once hailed as respectability was now defined as prudery. The whole concept of vulgarity and blasphemy seemed hopelessly narrow-minded and old-fashioned. In 1968 the Motion Picture Association of America developed a rating system to replace the Production Code. A version of that rating system is what currently defines who can and cannot see a film. The makers of *The Exorcist* could explore their understanding of the evils of possession without the worries of censorship.

Changes were also occurring in the ways that Catholics understood their relationship to the movies. In 1957 Pope Pius XII wrote that movies were a "noble art" and that they could potentially benefit humankind.[6] Catholic liberals in the United States took this to mean that movies could now represent adult themes in more sophisticated ways. Catholic laypeople who were going to college were being exposed to modern literature, art, and criticism. Their economic stability enabled them to be more independent from both parish and family pressures. Increasingly, American Catholics were asking their church for a more nuanced understanding of modern arts and of society.

Shifts in American Catholicism were accompanied by changes within the larger church. Between 1962 and 1965 the world's bishops were called by Pope John XXIII to a series of meetings in Rome. They discussed at the Vatican how the doctrine and rituals of the Catholic church might be updated to meet the challenges of the twentieth century. The Second Vatican Council would be a turning point in Catholic history. With the help of influential theologians, the bishops wrote a series of documents that would serve as the guidelines for changing Catholic practice and reinvigorating Catholic beliefs. Latin would no longer be used in the rituals of the church, and priests now said mass in the language of their parishioners. Theologians questioned whether the traditional preoccupation with the supernatural was supportive of a truly Christian lifestyle. Nuns thought about the purposes of their jobs, and many simplified (or eliminated) their habits to make their work easier. Older devotions, like saying the rosary, were devalued. Catholics were encouraged to read the Bible. American churches were pared down to the barest of ornamentation in order to draw the congregation's attention to the celebration of the sacraments. As practices were reevaluated, Catholic material culture was pushed to the periphery of spiritual life.

Simplifying rituals and customs so that people could focus on what was important in them may have been good for practicing Catholics, but it was not good for the movies. Many Catholics had jettisoned their Catholic "look" and were no longer interested in defending devotional traditions or theological dogmatism. The result was that many kinds of Catholic looks flourished in the United States. Movies had never been good at dealing with Catholic diversity because they rely on simple clues to quickly communicate their ideas. However, the end of movie censorship also meant that studios no longer had to match the religion on-screen to that of their clerical advisors. Movie Catholicism did not have to look like the Catholicism imagined by Joseph Breen or the Legion of Decency or like the new understandings of faith articulated in the documents of the Second Vatican Council. Moviemakers could pick and choose from Catholic life and reassemble those elements into something that suited their dramatic needs.

By the 1980s, moviemakers were making up their own Catholic spaces, characters, and objects that corresponded to Hollywood's need for the dramatic, the exotic, and the erotic. Fantasies about Catholicism returned to nineteenth-century themes of secrecy, darkness, murder, institutional corruption, and spiritual cynicism. Priests became symbols of corruption as they tricked their followers and elbowed their ways to the top. In a complete inversion of *The Cardinal*, Christopher Reeve in *The Monsignor* (1982) plays a thieving, murdering priest who funds the Vatican with Mafia money. Jack Lemmon's Father Tim Farley is asked to spy on two seminarians in *Mass Appeal* (1984). In *Agnes of God* (1985) a nun kills her baby. Catholic objects (crucifixes, rosaries, statues) were detached from both pre–Vatican II beliefs and current Catholic practices. They then were associated primarily with the uncontrollable supernatural. In *Sixth Sense* (1999) a little boy who sees the dead protects himself by constructing a tent filled with statues of Jesus, Mary, and the saints. While he goes to a Catholic school (as did the director, M. Night Shyamalan), the woman who gets the wounds of Christ in *Stigmata* (1999) is an unsuspecting, non-Catholic hairdresser. In *The Omen* (1976, 2006), the baby Antichrist is given to unsuspecting parents by a Catholic priest in a Roman hospital. Individuals caught up in this supernatural world use Catholic objects and spaces but not their institutions, communities, or beliefs. Miracles, prophecies, Armageddon, the Antichrist, relics, demons, exorcisms, secret gospels—Catholics supposedly know about such things.

While most mainstream movies conjured up Catholicism when institutional corruption or gothic horror was needed, the 1980s also marked the establishment of independent filmmaking and the small production company. With an eye toward complicated stories and subtle directing, filmmakers began to explore religious impulses with sensitivity and awareness. After actor Susan Sarandon read Sister Helen Prejean's account of her interactions with a death-row prisoner, she prodded her partner, Tim Robbins, to buy the rights to the book and make the film. Robbins then wrote, directed, and produced *Dead Man Walking* (1995), which explored the meaning of Christian love through the actions of a Catholic nun. Both Sarandon and Robbins were raised in Catholic families and the film's male lead, Sean Penn, had a Catholic mother. *Dead Man Walking* was nominated for four Academy Awards with Susan Sarandon winning an Oscar for her portrayal of Sister Prejean. With similar sensitivity but a bit more humor, director Nancy Sacova returned to the old neighborhood in *Household Saints* (1993) to explore the evolution (perhaps devolution) of Italian American piety. Contributor Darryl Caterine considers another low-budget, art-house production in his chapter on *Santitos* (1999). As in *Household Saints*, the protagonist is a young woman who has an intimate relationship with a collection of Catholic saints. These three films—all based on the writings of women and all focusing on women's religious experiences—act as counterbalances to the associations of Catholics with horror and with corrupt institutions.

1.7. Based on a book by Sister Helen Prejean (played by Susan Sarandon), *Dead Man Walking* (1995) sensitively explores the relationships among a nun, a convicted killer on death row (Sean Penn), and the families of both the victim and the perpetrator. Sarandon won an Oscar for her performance as a woman devoted to God and social justice. *Courtesy of the Academy of Motion Picture Arts and Sciences*

In spite of their influence in American politics and culture, representations of white, evangelical Protestantism is rare in commercial moviemaking. *The Apostle* (1998) and *Saved!* (2004) are notable but unique exceptions. Hollywood seems disinterested in the reality that Pentecostal Protestants are more apt to do exorcisms (called "deliverances") than are Catholic priests; "Armageddon" and the "Antichrist" are part of fundamentalists' vocabulary not Catholics', and evangelicals these days buy more Christian material culture than do Catholics. Even given the conservative theology of the present and past popes (Benedict XVI and John Paul II), Catholics tolerate more moral and doctrinal ambiguity than do many Protestants. Conservative Protestants may dominate the religious media but Catholic representations fill the commercial media. When screenplay writer (and Catholic) Brian Helgeland wanted to ratchet up the evil level in *Mystic River* (2003), he placed a bishop's ring on the finger of the pedophile who kidnaps the movie's protagonist. In *Million Dollar Baby* (2004) director Clint Eastwood reflected on the meaning of love and life through a working-class Irish American boxer/coach struggling with his Catholic conscience. Even Mormon director and writer Jared Hess introduced Catholic religious orders into his comedy *Nacho Libre* (2006) when he wanted to illustrate infatuation with the joys of wrestling, the charm of doing good for orphans, and the allure of chaste women. While few critics found his foray into the Mexican countryside as funny as *Napoleon Dynamite*, none were as harsh as the U.S. Conference of Catholic Bishops' film office, which gave it their lowest rating of "morally offensive."[7] The disjuncture between the political reality of evangelicals and the representational power of Catholicism, the continual insertion of Catholic images in films, and the vigorous responses of Catholics to their representations all serve to underscore the point of this book: in the world of the movies, religion is Catholic.

NOTES

1. All dates refer to general U.S. release.
2. Roger Ebert, "Veni, Vidi, Da Vinci," review of *The Da Vinci Code*, 17 May 2006, available at www.rogerebert.com. There seems to be some debate over this claim, with other scholars observing that the Buddhist sangha (community) pre-dates the establishment of the papacy by about 500 years.
3. The Motion Picture Production Code of 1930 (also known as the Hays Code) is reproduced at http://www.artsreformation.com/a001/hays-code.html

4. Marjorie Heins, "*The Miracle*: Film Censorship and the Entanglement of Church and State," *University of Virginia Forum for Contemporary Thought* (28 October 2002), available at http://www.fepproject.org/commentaries/themiracle.html.

5. *Joseph Burstyn, Inc. v. Wilson*, 343 U.S. 495 (1952).

6. *Miranda Prorsus* ("Remarkable Technical Inventions"), 1957.

7. U.S. Conference of Catholic Bishops, Office for Film and Broadcasting, review of *Nacho Libre*, available at http://www.nccbuscc.org/movies/n/nacholibre.shtml.

FURTHER READING

Belton, John. *American Cinema/American Culture*. New York: McGraw-Hill, 1994.

Blake, Richard A. *AfterImage: The Indelible Catholic Imagination of Six American Filmmakers*. Chicago, IL: Loyola University Press, 2000.

Bodnar, John. *Blue-Collar Hollywood: Liberalism, Democracy, and Working People in American Film*. Baltimore, MD: Johns Hopkins University Press, 2003.

Dolan, Jay P. *The American Catholic Experience: A History from Colonial Times to the Present*. Garden City, NY: Doubleday, 1985.

———. *In Search of an American Catholicism: A History of Religion and Culture in Tension*. New York: Oxford University Press, 2002.

Fisher, James. "Alternative Sources of Catholic Intellectual Vitality," *U.S. Catholic Historian* 13 (1995): 83–88.

Forshey, Gerald E. *American Religious and Biblical Spectaculars*. New York: Praeger, 1992.

Franchot, Jenny. *Roads to Rome: The Antebellum Protestant Encounter with Catholicism*. Berkeley: University of California Press, 1994.

Giles, Paul. *American Catholic Arts and Fiction: Culture, Ideology, Aesthetics*. New York: Cambridge University Press, 1992.

Greeley, Andrew. *The Catholic Myth: The Behavior and Belief of American Catholics*. New York: Scribner's, 1990.

Hill, John, and Pamela Church Gibson, eds. *American Cinema and Hollywood: Critical Approaches*. New York: Oxford University Press, 2000.

Keyser, Les, and Barbara Keyser. *Hollywood and the Catholic Church: The Image of Roman Catholicism in American Movies*. Chicago, IL: Loyola University Press, 1984.

Massa, Mark S. *Catholics and American Culture*. New York: Herder and Herder, 2001.

McGinn, Colin. *The Power of Movies: How Screen and Mind Interact*. New York: Pantheon, 2005.

McGreevey, John T. *Catholicism and American Freedom: A History*. New York: Norton, 2004.

Miles, Margaret R. *Seeing and Believing: Religion and Values in the Movies*. Boston: Beacon, 1996.

Monaco, James. *How to Read a Film: The World of Movies, Media, and Multimedia*. New York: Oxford University Press, 2000.

Sklar, Robert. *Movie-Made America: A Cultural History of American Movies*. New York: Vintage, 1994.

Smith, Jeffrey A. "Hollywood Theology: The Commodification of Religion in Twentieth-Century Films," *Religion and American Culture* 11 (2001): 191–231.

Tentler, Leslie Woodcock. "On the Margins: The State of American Catholic History," *American Quarterly* 45 (1993): 104–27.

Tracy, David. *The Analogical Imagination: Christian Theology and the Culture of Pluralism*. New York: Crossroad, 1981.

2

THE SILENT SOCIAL PROBLEM FILM

Regeneration (1915)

Judith Weisenfeld

In 1903 American readers were treated to the publication of Owen Kildare's (1864–1911) memoir, *My Mamie Rose: The Story of My Regeneration*, which was released to critical acclaim. One reviewer characterized Kildare's relation of his life story as offering "a deep and true insight into human nature and human life even in its most untoward conditions, which the story reveals."[1] With tales of gritty tenement life in New York City's Bowery district, lively descriptions of the author's sojourns as a boxer and a member of the Chicory Hall gang, accounts of his travels in Europe and North Africa and of his involvement with the city's famed Tammany Hall political machine, the memoir surely had the makings of a movie. In fact, Kildare's memoir proved so cinematically appealing that studios produced two film versions during the silent era.

The book's path to the screen began in 1908 when a New York theater producer purchased the rights and mounted a stage version titled *The Regeneration*, which also received some strongly positive reviews despite Kildare's disavowal of the stage adaptation. The success of the book and of the stage version made the story appealing to William Fox, who acquired the property and assigned it to one of the studio's newly signed directors, Raoul Walsh. The Fox film, titled *Regeneration*, went into production for release in 1915 with Walsh and Carl Harbaugh adapting the memoir for the screen. The film starred Rockliffe Fellowes and Anna Q. Nilsson. The memoir also served as the basis for another film, Universal's *Fool's Highway* (1924), directed by Irving Cummings and featuring Pat O'Malley and Mary Philbin.[2]

More than simply an adventure story or a tale of the hard life of the early twentieth-century urban ghetto, *My Mamie Rose* is an account of Kildare's spiritual transformation and his success, with the help of a schoolteacher with whom he falls in love, in rising above the "unfortunate moral condition" of his birth.[3] Raoul Walsh's film version of the memoir embraces the urban grittiness of Kildare's experiences and presents an extraordinary snapshot of life in a New York slum in the early twentieth century. More significantly, Walsh's adaptation of Kildare's memoir locates the story of the moral transformation of a poor Irish tenement kid within the broader context of religion, ethnicity, and moral development. Of Irish descent on his father's side and Catholic in upbringing, Walsh makes a strong argument in the film for understanding the moral potential of a character like Owen Kildare to be determined not by his ethnic background, but by his ability to resist the temptations of alcohol and crime, so alluring to many men in his neighborhood. The film similarly argues, against the grain of much popular and academic discourse of its day, that the religion of Irish Catholics as such does not make them a destructive social or political force in America's cities.

Audiences went to the movies to see *Regeneration* in a period in which the state of American cities and the large numbers of impoverished immigrants inhabiting those cities worried many native-born white Protestants. In some cases, this concern manifested itself in attempts to aid the immigrants. Assistance sometimes took the form of attempts by Protestant social reformers to convince Jewish and Catholic immigrants that the religious and cultural values of white Protestants were not only superior to their own but at the very core of what it means to be American. Catholic (and Jewish) leaders struggled to maintain their religious, ethnic, and cultural heritage in the new environment, even as they understood that the poverty, crime, and lack of access to opportunities that characterized the lives of many immigrants needed to be addressed. But, for them, embracing Protestantism was not the answer.

Although much of this debate about how best to address immigrants' needs took place between Catholic and Protestant leaders, American popular culture also contributed. Early film, as an entertainment medium accessible to the masses, reached large numbers of people and had the power to help shape opinions about religion, immigration, and poverty. *Regeneration*'s contribution to this discussion charts a course between Protestant and Catholic approaches to poverty. While not embracing the anti-Catholic rhetoric of much of nineteenth- and early twentieth-century American social reform discourse, Walsh presents an insider's critique of the church that questions the efficacy of its efforts to serve the material needs of its members. In addition, the film promotes conformity to the behavioral standards of the Protestant elite as the path out of poverty. At the same time, *Regeneration* relies heavily on Catholic religious sensibilities in its insistence that social and political forces, rather than a lack of moral strength, contributed to the circumstances of impoverished immigrants. In addition, Walsh mobilizes the unique visual characteristics of film to highlight Catholic belief in the transformative possibilities that result from supernatural appearances of the Virgin Mary. In his rendering on film, Walsh transforms the holy figure of the Virgin Mary into the human character of Marie, who opens up new life possibilities for the film's hero. The result is a dramatic hybrid of Catholic and Protestant sensibilities regarding interactions among religion, ethnicity, and American belonging. Walsh endorses a middle course between the two camps, holding on to aspects of Catholic spirituality and values and looking to American Protestantism for opportunities for progress.

While Walsh was able to put forward a middle way between Catholic and Protestant ways of understanding and addressing urban poverty that appealed to audiences, moved them, and made them think, the course he charted was not an easy one to maintain. Film frequently embraces ethnic and religious stereotypes that many viewers regard simply as innocent entertainment. Many groups, American Catholics among them, have argued otherwise and insisted that movie images have power beyond the theater in that they help to shape viewers' ideas about the world and the people around them. Indeed, just twelve years after the release of *Regeneration*, Irish American Catholics would rise up in protest against the representation of Catholicism and Irish culture in the Metro-Goldwyn-Mayer film *The Callahans and the Murphys*. Presenting Catholicism in film often has had political ramifications, even from the earliest years of moviemaking.

Vanished Artifacts

The rise of moviegoing as entertainment in the first decades of the twentieth century coincided with an unprecedented period of immigration to the United States from Southern, Central, and Eastern Europe. The new arrivals and their children, many of them Catholic, embraced this novel form of recreation with tremendous enthusiasm as it provided working-class people, who had limited

money available for leisure activities, access to entertainment. What they saw on the screen were silent films in which much of the narrative was conveyed through the body language, gestures, and facial expressions of the actors. To today's viewers the acting techniques of silent film may seem unnatural but, for early audiences, the acting was similar to the stage acting of the day, and the exaggerated style also helped to communicate the story in the absence of spoken dialogue. Since there was no dialogue sound in silent films, they also included intertitles, film frames with text that served various functions. Intertitles could be used to introduce characters, represent dialogue, present contextual information for viewers, or to comment on the action on-screen. It was possible, however, to understand and take pleasure in many silent films even if one could not read English. Exhibitors sought to increase viewers' enjoyment of silent films by including live musical accompaniment aimed at representing and enhancing the mood of the action on-screen. Small theaters provided only a piano or organ, while larger theaters might present an entire orchestra. While the musical accompaniment was generally improvised or taken from a compilation of stock movie music, in some cases film studios provided full written scores. The silent film approach of conveying narrative and mood through acting, intertitles, and musical accompaniment remained the standard for the movies from the beginnings of commercial film in the late nineteenth century through the late 1920s, when studios developed the technology to synchronize sound and image. *The Callahans and the Murphys*, released in 1927, was produced at the very end of the silent film era, and thus represents one of the last silent representations of Catholics on film.

In the silent era, film audiences were treated to documentaries, comedies, melodramas, and adventure movies as well as educational and religious films, and they saw these in a variety of venues. They might go to see continuously shown short movies in small converted storefront theaters called "nickelodeons" (they charged a nickel admission) or at larger theaters designed especially for showing motion pictures. Whatever the setting, the stories projected on the movie screens aided immigrants in adjusting to their new environment. Many of the films replayed familiar stories and projected recognizable images on the screen, as well as introducing new ideas and contexts. The sense of Americanness that some immigrant viewers derived from the experience of moviegoing coalesced around the class identity of the majority of early film's audience and helped to bridge ethnic, religious, racial, and gender differences. Working-class white immigrants also joined with Americans from all religious, class, racial, and ethnic backgrounds in their enjoyment of film. By some estimates, in 1920 half of all Americans went to the movies once a week. The moviegoing experience also functioned, then, as a way of introducing American-born viewers to ideas about the cultures of immigrant communities.

Historians interested in thinking about how this new visual medium portrayed Catholic beliefs, practices, and characters find themselves faced with a significant challenge. Almost 90 percent of films released in the 1910s and 80 percent of films released in the 1920s have been lost to nitrate decomposition or combustion of the cellulose film stock with which they were made.[4] Published reviews, newspaper advertisements, coverage of the production process in film trade magazines, and publicity images, however, do provide a tantalizing sense of a large number of motion pictures featuring Catholic characters and settings. Even if the films no longer exist, written accounts of films that are now presumed lost can give us a sense of their stories and of the critical responses of moviegoers. Nevertheless, the absence of the films themselves makes it difficult to analyze the relationship between the visual style of a motion picture and its narrative goals. How a film achieves those narrative goals depends not only on the story and dialogue, but also on what we literally see on-screen. Of course, the difficulty of recovering a full picture of the world of early film applies to a broader range of topics than simply representations of Catholicism, but the fact that silent films often explored class, ethnic, racial, and religious difference makes the loss of so many films that much more regrettable.

Despite the fact that the majority of the movies that early film audiences had available to them appear to have been lost, some films across a range of genres and from a variety of producers have survived. In other cases, important films that were presumed lost have been found, and their recovery helps to enhance our understanding of early movies. *Regeneration* was long assumed to have been lost when, in 1976, a film preservationist was given a partly decomposed print found in a basement in Missoula, Montana. It is a happy accident that the film survived, and in relatively good shape. We are not so lucky with regard to *The Callahans and the Murphys*, of which no print apparently survives. The absence of such a large percentage of silent films makes it difficult to speak definitively about aesthetic trends in early filmmaking or to make an authoritative case that *Regeneration*'s approach to representing Catholics is characteristic of the larger body of movies produced in that period. Even facing all of these difficulties, it is important that we try to take account of early films' addressing of the relationship between religion and ethnicity.

Whether or not we can argue that *Regeneration* is representative of the general approach of early film to presenting Catholics and Catholicism, it is worthy of consideration simply because it is a well-made and affecting film that would likely stand out in any selection of American films from the silent era. Reviews from the period noted positive audience responses to the film and its "masterful direction." Contemporary critics cited *Regeneration* as a powerful work of art. In 1916 *Moving Picture World* selected it as "one of the great American films," and it was added to the National Film Registry in 2000. The Library of Congress selected *Regeneration* for preservation not only because of its rarity as a surviving silent film but also because of its success as film art. In addition, *Regeneration* was the first feature-length film directed by Raoul Walsh, whose career as a Hollywood director spanned fifty years. Walsh not only directed many of the industry's leading stars, but his work ranged across a number of important film genres. He excelled, however, at action films, which he referred to as "dagger, sword, and gun" movies, which tended to feature primarily male actors.[5] His body of work includes such important and popular films as *The Thief of Bagdad* (1924), *The Big Trail* (1930), *Klondike Annie* (1936), *They Drive by Night* (1940), and *High Sierra* (1941). Raoul Walsh was a prolific and innovative director, and *Regeneration* stands as one of his important contributions.

Because the movie was produced when the central visual conventions of American filmmaking were being developed, its aesthetic approach to religion, ethnicity, and social reform merits attention. *Regeneration* provides a useful example of how social concerns and aesthetic sophistication could be combined effectively in silent cinema. The film makes subtle and yet powerful arguments about the relationships between ethnicity and religion and between moral character and fitness for citizenship, and looks at the relative effectiveness of the Catholic church and Protestant settlement house work for urban social reform.

Catholic Context

Regeneration hit the movie screens in a particularly fraught moment of a long history of contention between Catholics and Protestants that had its roots in Europe but took on a unique form in the American context. Since the introduction in sixteenth-century Europe of the religious changes that produced Protestantism, Catholics and Protestants have been critical of each other's institutional and theological approaches to Christianity. Although a host of complex theological, political, and social issues are involved, the main points of contention include Catholics' seeking salvation through the mediation of the Roman Catholic church and Protestants' emphasizing the primacy of faith and the Bible in the individual's road to salvation. Catholics' belief in the ability of material objects to bear supernatural power, in miraculous appearances, and in the intercession of holy beings like the Virgin Mary and the saints has often seemed to Protestants to take individuals away from the core elements of Christianity as represented in the scriptures. Similarly, Protestants interpret Catholics' commitment to the church's clerical hierarchy and religious orders as inserting unnecessary layers between believers and God. For Catholics, the Protestant rejection of the Catholic ritual life and of the church as the appropriate form of organization and authority for believers is itself straying from Christian truth.

In the American context, some Protestants refused to see Catholicism and American democracy as compatible and became increasingly concerned during the late nineteenth and early twentieth centuries about the growing numbers of Catholic immigrants. Nativists—native-born Americans who were opposed to immigration—often characterized Catholicism as fundamentally anti-American and envisioned Irish Catholics and other Catholic immigrants as the pope's army dispatched to destabilize the American democratic system. Popular culture provided especially effective tools for promoting the fear of Catholic conspiracy, and Americans saw the publication throughout the nineteenth century of novels that promoted fear of Catholicism as a subversive force. Throughout the 1870s political cartoonist Thomas Nast advanced this position by making pointed use of images of Irish Americans as lazy, brutish, and subhuman and of Catholic clergy as a predatory force intent on destroying American democracy.

At the same time that American Protestantism contained within it a strand that envisioned Catholicism as religiously, politically, and socially dangerous, it was also the case that some Protestants accepted Catholicism as one of many religious traditions that deserved a place in American life. Indeed, some American Protestants found Catholicism fascinating and this attraction was represented in a variety of forms of literary and popular culture, including the movies. Catholics appeared on-screen from the earliest years of American film and, although movies often used Catholic contexts as the settings for their narratives, religious concerns were rarely central to these stories. Convents, for example, were featured in some early films as plot devices that removed female characters from sexual or other danger, prevented them from entering into unapproved marriages, or simply functioned to get them out of the way. Female characters also sometimes chose to enter convents because their love objects had become unavailable. In *Pieces of Silver: A Story of Hearts and Souls* (1914), a young woman (Helen Gardner) is tricked by her aunt into entering a convent so that the aunt can claim the girl's inheritance. Although the young woman eventually learns the truth, she chooses to become a nun partially because the man she had hoped to marry had become a priest upon finding that she had entered the convent. In the historical drama *Naked Hearts*

(1916), Maud (Francelia Billington) decides to become a nun when she learns the news (which the audience later finds out to be untrue) that her fiancé has been killed in a Civil War battle. She unfortunately takes her vows just before he returns to her. *The Worldly Madonna* (1922) uses the convent as part of the melodramatic story of identical twin sisters (both played by Clara Kimball Young) who have taken very different paths, one into the novitiate and the other into drugs and a career as a cabaret singer. Janet, the novice, agrees to switch places with her sister, Lucy, to protect her after Lucy appears to have committed a crime. In the end, Lucy is vindicated; Janet falls in love and marries a politician; and, in the final twist, Lucy takes the veil in all sincerity. Priests appeared frequently in films as confessors of characters who were often not marked as Catholic in any other way than that they seek out the confidence of a priest. In other cases, the priest was the focus of the drama and functioned as a rescuer or counselor. In *The Parish Priest* (1920), for example, Father John Whalen (William Desmond) is assigned to a small New Jersey parish and devotes himself to fulfilling a dying parishioner's wish that her son marry.[6]

Reforming the Movies, Reforming Society

In addition to locating *Regeneration* in the context of the early history of film portrayals of Catholics, the release of Walsh's film may also be usefully understood in the context of various social reform movements of the late nineteenth and early twentieth centuries. Some of these reforms sought to regulate the behavior of immigrant communities, focusing on crime, alcohol abuse, and child welfare in the urban environment. By the time of the film's release the settlement house, a residential neighborhood center in which the reformers themselves lived, had become a common and accepted approach to aiding the urban poor. Typically, settlement house workers were single, college-educated, Protestant women committed to helping the urban poor obtain education as a way of elevating them out of poverty. Although the founders of most settlement houses envisioned them as secular spaces and did not carry on explicitly religious programs, many settlements did have connections with and derived support from local Protestant clergy. In addition, white Protestant understandings of self, family, and citizen shaped the supposedly secular approach of settlements to social reform.

This same period saw deep concern about the impact of the movies on American society and anxiety about the appeal of moviegoing for young people in particular. In addition to efforts like those pursued by settlement houses, reformers directed their attention to controlling the content of films available for consumption by urban immigrants and other Americans. To counter cultural criticism, film producers worked hard to establish filmgoing as respectable entertainment for middle-class people. Among the various means filmmakers and exhibitors used to accomplish this goal was the production of religious films and so-called social problem films. Studios of the day, including Biograph, Vitagraph, Universal, and Fox, presented audiences with religious subject matter in the hopes of quelling the complaints that the release of other types of movies generated. Early biblical and religious films like Vitagraph's *The Life of Moses* (1909–1910) served these purposes well as their subject matter helped to overcome objections to Sunday exhibitions and to make it acceptable for a broader audience, including women and children, to attend.

As with religious films, social problem films sought to do more than simply entertain. Social problem films presented to early film audiences tales about sexual morality, the dangers of alcohol and drugs, political and economic corruption, labor issues, crime, poverty, and immigration. Some focused on changing individual habits, as in the familiar and often re-presented *Ten Nights in a Barroom* (1897, 1903, 1913, 1921) or Biograph's *A Drunkard's Reformation* (1909), written and directed by D. W. Griffith. Other films addressed broader social questions and aimed not so much at bringing individual behavior in line with middle-class moral standards but at changing larger social systems. The silent era was characterized by the exhibition of many explicitly political films, through which filmmakers attempted to use mass culture to exert social power and influence public discussions.

Early directors like Lois Weber devoted their entire careers to making films that addressed a variety of social problems, including corruption and hypocrisy in Protestant churches. Weber, a Christian Scientist, produced a body of films that she called "missionary films" in which she opposed opium smuggling (*Hop: The Devil's Brew*, 1916), abortion (*Where Are My Children?* 1916), and capital punishment (*The People vs. John Doe*, 1916) and lauded Margaret Sanger's campaign for birth control (*Hand That Rocks the Cradle*, 1917). Despite Weber's strong religious commitments, her films did not steer clear of controversy. *Hand That Rocks the Cradle* was banned in New York City because it advocated the use of birth control. Religious leaders attacked her 1915 allegorical film *Hypocrites*, in which a minister uses the pulpit to rail against the hypocrisy of his congregants, who show little evidence of Christian commitment in their daily lives. Perhaps the most controversial aspect of *Hypocrites* was Weber's inclusion of a nude female allegorical figure, Naked Truth. Weber first shows the figure in a painting within the film, and it later appears to the minister in a vision to help him distinguish between the faithful and the hypocrites. Weber saw herself as both elevating the filmgoing experience to the level of respectable entertainment and performing social service. She told a newspaper reporter, "I'll tell you what I'd like to be, and that is, the editorial page of the Universal Company. My close study of the editorial page has taught me that it speaks with stentorian tones and that its effect is far reaching upon thousands of readers." Weber was convinced that, through film, she could "deliver a message to the world . . . that will receive a ready and cheerful response from the better element of the big general public."[7]

Other significant figures in early film, particularly D. W. Griffith, left large numbers of social problem films among their body of work. Best known for his sentimental championing of the antiblack terrorism of the Ku Klux Klan in *The Birth of a Nation* (1915), Griffith saw film as a powerful tool for social reform. For him, policing and reinforcing racial hierarchy was an important task of the Christian reformer in twentieth-century America. In addition to filmic interventions aimed at reinforcing white supremacy, Griffith took up a host of other issues about modern American life. He explored the destructive aspects of capitalist enterprise in *A Corner in Wheat* (1909), the exploitation of laborers in *The Song of the Shirt* (1908) and *The Lily of the Tenements* (1911), and the experiences of the urban poor in *A Child of the Ghetto* (1910) and *The Musketeers of Pig Alley* (1912). Films like those made by Weber, Griffith, and others that were produced with the intention of functioning as "editorials" formed an important part of the landscape of early cinema and contributed to the work of film producers to enhance the status of the medium. Other filmmakers in the period engaged a similar range of issues in films that were not explicitly part of a social reform agenda but that should be viewed within the broad category of the social problem film. *Regeneration* can be considered a social problem film because of its engagement of important social issues of the day, even though the film did not come into being as the result of the social concerns of a particular director.

It should also be remembered that, even as directors and producers of social problem films identified clear reform goals, these movies often made full use of commonplace ethnic and religious stereotypes. Some movies that sought to expose the havoc created by organized crime or by urban gangs, for example, presented Italian and Irish Americans as inherently criminal. Films that were interested in showing the lives of Chinese immigrants also routinely portrayed Chinese men as inhumane and violent "heathens" who lusted after white women. Movies that focused on Japanese life in America showed Japanese men as sinister, ruthless aggressors and Japanese women as submissive brides. Thus, even in early films in which filmmakers might have intended to encourage awareness or tolerance, viewers often found negative moral evaluations embedded in traditional ways of representing ethnic and religious groups. Notably, one of the most striking elements of *Regeneration* is its attempt to unravel some of these long-standing connections and to explore the ways in which environment, rather than ethnic heritage or religious affiliation, shaped people's life chances.

A Middle Way

Raoul Walsh (1887–1980) was uniquely qualified to direct a film version of Kildare's life story. He had grown up in a family in which his father, Thomas, was deeply committed to Irish nationalism, to progressive causes, and to the Catholic church. Emigrating from Ireland in the late 1870s, Thomas Walsh founded a lucrative clothing business in New York City. He and his business partner, a German Jew, used their wealth to aid poor immigrants and to assist Jewish families to immigrate to the United States. In addition, the elder Walsh formed a close relationship with Archbishop John Murphy Farley and contributed to the church's work with orphans in the city. Raoul Walsh did not seek to follow in his father's footsteps but became enraptured by the theater and the movies at a young age. In his memoir, Walsh noted his father's insistence that his work in the arts should reflect a commitment to progressive causes. He recalled bragging to his father about his role as a Klan leader in the controversial stage play of Thomas W. Dixon's novel *The Clansman*. Thomas Walsh chastised his son, telling him, "You should not feel proud of portraying the part of an infamous bigot, whose organization is anti-Catholic, anti-Jew, and anti-Negro. But as sure as there is a God above us, these hatemongers will one day fade away like leaves falling from the trees in autumn."[8] Walsh did not comment on his father's criticism of his lack of concern with the racism of *The Clansman* and seemed interested only in the opportunities that the stage experience would provide him in advancing his acting career. Although Walsh's account of his life leaves the question of the impact of his father's politics unexplored, a close reading of his adaptation of Owen Kildare's memoirs in *Regeneration* reveals the influence of his early life on the film's understanding of the relationships among ethnicity, religion, and urban poverty. Walsh mobilizes a distinctly Catholic understanding of the origins of poverty. In contrast to the Protestant social reform approaches of the day, which insisted that the poor lacked moral fortitude and that this caused poverty, Catholic approaches refused to blame the poor themselves and often looked to larger political or social forces.

In addition to his father's likely influence on his approach to adapting Kildare's memoir, Walsh was also influenced by his early training with D. W. Griffith at the Biograph Studio. He began his film career as an actor and appeared in several of Griffith's short films, including *The Musketeers of Pig Alley*, and as John Wilkes Booth in Griffith's epic, *The Birth of a Nation*. Walsh learned the craft of filmmaking by working as an assistant director on *Birth* and directing one- and two-reel films at Biograph, sometimes as many as three a week. While Walsh was not the kind of director who pursued social problem films as the mainstay of his career, exposure to Griffith's interest in the genre must have had an influence on his approach to some of the films Fox assigned him. Walsh recalled later in his life that the studio had given another director the choice of two films, one of which was *Regeneration*. The director chose the other film, which Walsh characterized as "the wrong script." He felt that his strong directorial work on *Regeneration* represented a turning point in his career as the film's success made him "the fair-haired boy with old man Fox."[9]

Although Walsh and Kildare had their Irish heritage in common and both were native New Yorkers, their life experiences differed in significant ways. Kildare was orphaned at a young age and then ran away from the abusive neighbors who took him in, living on his own on the streets from the age of seven. In describing his life as a "kid of the tenement," Kildare emphasized the impact of poverty on the "unfortunate moral condition" of the residents of the Bowery neighborhood of Manhattan in which he grew up and other areas like it. Kildare wrote of the lack of affection he experienced as a child and the poverty of expression of the adults around him. He was especially critical of the hypermasculinity of his male role models. "There, not yet mentioning the other detrimental defects of environment," Kildare reflected, "the child grows up, and then, . . . in the manhood days this foundation, faulty and vicious, breaks and crumbles to pieces and leaves naught but a being condemned by society and law, and seemingly by God."[10]

The force of Kildare's memoir lies in the story of his transformation from an illiterate gang leader to a professional writer under the tutelage of Marie Deering, a schoolteacher with whom he eventually fell in love. Although Marie died shortly before they were to be married, Kildare wrote of his experiences with her as inaugurating a profound spiritual transformation, although one not set in a specific religious context. "To me, it is all a miracle," he concluded. "Before it I did not even grope about in the darkness searching for light. I was satisfied. Now I know at least that there is a soul, a mind within me, and that they were given for a purpose."[11] Kildare eventually came to be known as the "Kipling of the Bowery" and went on to publish essays in newspapers and magazines and, in addition to the memoir, wrote a number of other books about life in lower Manhattan. It is easy to see why the memoir, with Kildare's strong, engaging writing and a powerful story of transformation, appealed to studio head William Fox, who bought the rights to the story.

Violence, poverty, and death characterize the urban environment in which young Owen Conway (John McCann), the film's central character, grows up. As in Kildare's memoir, *Regeneration* makes a strong argument for understanding this environment as central to his moral development. As the film opens, ten-year-old Owen watches from the window of his tenement-house apartment as his mother's body is taken away for burial. The orphaned Owen is taken in by the couple across the hall, both of whom are physically abusive to him, and he eventually leaves them for the streets. As an adult, Owen will become the leader of a local gang, but the audience knows from the first introduction of the young adult character that he is not inherently brutal, but has been shaped to behave as such by his environment. There is, for example, a disjuncture between the intertitles that describe the teenaged Owen (H. McCoy), who is working as a longshoreman, and the actions on-screen. The titles tell viewers, "And then years pass and Owen still lives in a world where might is right—and where the prizes of existence go to the man who has the most daring in defying the law, and the quickest fist in defending his own right." What transpires in the scene, however, is Owen's quick and vigorous defense of a weaker teenager who is being picked on by other boys. In fact, the audience never sees him defying the law or asserting his own will. The film presents Owen only as acting in defense of others. Although the titles inform viewers that criminals prosper in the Bowery world in which Owen finds himself, the film provides no evidence that this is what leads him to succeed in the gang. We never see Owen representing what the film's intertitles describe as "the virtues the gangsters admire most." His defense of the weaker boy represents a turning point for him. Even as Owen's fighting skills bring him recognition and move him into gang life, the film makes clear that the men around Owen have misread his motivation for fighting by focusing on his courage rather than on his vigorous defense of the weak. Indeed, Walsh continually emphasizes the purity of Owen's character, suggesting that environment rather than race, ethnicity, class, or religion led him to crime. When, for example, Walsh presents the adult Owen (Rockliffe Fellowes) at the height of his power as the leader of the gang, he never shows him doing more than smoking, drinking, and gambling. In one striking instance, Walsh uses a dissolve to flash back from the adult Owen drinking a frothy beer to Owen as a child licking an ice cream cone and then back to the adult man. The overlay of the two images underscores the impression that Owen's enjoyment of the beer is as innocent as the pleasure a poor, lonely child might take in eating sweets. The cinematic effect of the dissolve reinforces the film's argument that it is "the only environment he knows" that shapes Owen in ways that are contrary to the fundamental core of his character. The primary drama of the film's narrative throughout the first half derives from the cultivation in the audience of the desire to see Owen recover his true character.

The film is structured, as is Kildare's memoir, for audiences to accept Marie Deering (Anna Q. Nilsson) as the agent of Owen's transformation. A socialite turned settlement house worker, Marie encourages Owen to participate in various activities organized for the neighborhood so that he will not end up like the local alcoholics. Eventually, she becomes his romantic interest. While the film's focus is clearly on the effects of poverty on character development and on presenting Owen as an example of someone who rises above his circumstances, it also makes an argument, through Marie, against the idleness of the rich. Whereas in the original memoir, Marie was a simple schoolteacher, in *Regeneration* she is a rich young woman "whose butterfly existence has hidden, even from herself, the knowledge of her nobler qualities," as the intertitles tell viewers. The audience's first view of Marie is of her lolling in bed in the afternoon, and she moves on shortly thereafter to a lavish dinner in her family's home with District Attorney Ames (Carl Harbaugh). Walsh's use of parallel editing to make arguments through contrast is quite powerful throughout the film. This scene is exemplary as he moves back and forth between Owen and his gang at Grogan's, and Marie and her family at dinner. Just as Owen's environment has directed him into a criminal life, the film insists that Marie's environment has cut her off from the world and left her with no desire to be useful or productive. Her introduction to working-class life and to gangsters at Grogan's club, coupled with hearing a soapbox speaker's impassioned call for attention to urban poverty, brings "an awakening to the duty she owes her fellow men." She joins the speaker in his work at a settlement house in the Bowery, where she finds satisfaction in her efforts. Much of the film is structured around the first encounters between Marie and Owen and the moments at which Marie finds herself in danger and in need of rescue, all leading to the development of a romantic relationship between the two. In keeping with the general Catholic approach to aiding the poor, *Regeneration* promotes the value of living a productive life of service. The film holds the wealthy to be as accountable as the poor for their actions and places moral value on acts rather than on social status, religion, or ethnicity.

While Marie becomes an important motivator for Owen to reform his life, the opportunity to recapitulate a central moment in his past and rescue a baby from an abusive father is what truly sets Owen's transformation in motion. In this sequence, Walsh uses a set that appears quite similar to the one he used for the film's opening scene of the apartment in which Owen and his mother lived, thus underscoring the sense that Owen is, in essence, rescuing himself and recapitulating his past "correctly." The sequence begins with an intertitle noting that the domestic problems of the Flahertys constitute a recurring issue for the settlement house workers. Mrs. Flaherty appeals to Marie to help retrieve her baby from the apartment where Mr. Flaherty is drunk and angry. When the skinny and weak male settlement worker fails to get the baby, Marie turns to Owen, who readily agrees. In short order, Owen rescues the baby and returns him to his mother. Walsh stops briefly on a close-up shot of Owen holding the baby, his enjoyment of the infant apparent. Owen enters the settlement, hands the child over to Marie, and takes a moment to look around. He notices the words "God is love," written in large letters on the blackboard amid calculations from a math lesson, looks briefly to the male settlement worker and then to his friend, and then leaves before Marie can thank him for his good deed.

2.1. Owen (Rockliffe Fellowes) returns the Flahertys' baby to Marie (Anna Q. Nilsson) and enters the settlement house for the first time.

Neither Catholicism nor Protestantism is implicated in explicit ways in this sequence. However, the film does link Catholicism with poverty and hopelessness, and Protestantism with intellectual growth and progress. Owen regards the proposition written on the blackboard that "God is love" as if he had never heard or imagined such a thing before. This is a world in which the Catholic church is profoundly absent in projects to aid the poor, and the settlement house, an implicitly Protestant institution, is a powerful presence. Catholicism, the presumptive religion of families like the Conways and Flahertys, has failed to make itself present in the urban landscape while the generic religion (Protestantism) of the settlement house reaches out into the streets and even into the homes of the residents of the neighborhood. The film's visual and narrative emphasis on the settlement house as the institution that structures neighborhood life is noteworthy. Over the course of the film the audience becomes familiar with key elements of the neighborhood's physical and social geography as the camera takes us to scenes in the saloon, Chicory Hall (the gang's clubhouse), the docks, tenement buildings, and the settlement house. In the film the Catholic church has no literal physical presence until quite late in the narrative, and there is no sense that the neighborhood might be constituted as a parish. It is Marie who keeps watch over the neighborhood from the window of the settlement.

This emphasis on the presence of the settlement and the absence of the church is contrary to the reality of the late nineteenth-century New York in which Kildare grew up and the early twentieth-century city in which Walsh filmed *Regeneration*. By 1890 there were 70 Catholic parishes in New York City, and by 1920 there were 114. The Fourth Ward, where Kildare lived as a child, featured at least 3 parishes, one of which supported services for homeless boys. Even more remarkable is the absence from the world of the film of the work of Catholic sisters, who were central to providing aid to the poor and to children in particular throughout the late nineteenth and early twentieth centuries. The presence of a Protestant social reform figure like Marie in the neighborhood would have been possible, but she would have had much company from nuns involved in charity work. Even while Walsh's film makes manifest a Catholic sensibility that resists blaming the poor for their situations, *Regeneration* positions the settlement house and its Protestant grounding as more effective than the Catholic church in providing opportunities for the urban poor.

Particularly striking in terms of Walsh's aesthetic approach to demonstrating Owen's slow but steady progress away from the gang and into the new life enabled by the settlement house is his use of the tracking shot. In the scene in which Owen enters the settlement for the first time, the camera tracks back as he enters and continues moving even after he stands still. The film cuts away quickly to Mrs. Flaherty. The next time Owen enters the settlement house, the audience is convinced that he means to commit himself to change, and Walsh repeats the tracking shot. Owen enters in precisely the same way, but Walsh extends it, underscoring with the camera's widening angle the sense that a new world has opened up for Owen. As the film has made clear in emphasizing the importance of nurture and environment over nature in its early presentation of Owen's life, the seeds of the new world already exist within its main character. At the same time, the film seems to argue that the cultivation of the seeds cannot take place in the urban streets of the (absent) Catholic church, but only in the domestic space of the (Protestant) settlement house.

While the majority of the film figures Catholicism and Protestantism in subtle and implicit ways, there is a significant sequence in which Walsh represents Catholicism explicitly and critically. Although the settlement house, the saloon, and the gang's clubhouse dominate the social and moral geography of the neighborhood and the Catholic parish is largely absent, it is not the case that Owen has *no* connection to or interaction with the church. Toward the end of the film, Skinny (who took over the gang after Owen left, played by William Sheer) runs into the settlement house. There he appeals to Owen to hide him because he has stabbed a police officer. Owen knows that he will lose Marie if she finds out that he is still involved with the gang, but he feels an obligation to the man who had saved him from arrest when the two were in the gang together. Marie is indeed devastated when she finds out what Owen has done. Trying to work through his moral quandary, Owen goes to see the parish priest. His brief interactions with the priest are intercut with other scenes as part of a longer sequence, most notably scenes of Marie looking for Owen at Chicory Hall and being assaulted by Skinny, requiring Owen's rescue once again. All told, the shots of Owen in the church last for less than one minute but taken together they prove critical for understanding Walsh's critique of the institutional Catholic church and its place in urban social welfare work.

It is significant that Walsh begins the scene on the steps of the church. Owen and his loyal friend, the young man he had defended as a teenager, arrive at the church and find a dark-haired woman sitting on the steps. A look of despair on her face, she cradles a baby. Owen looks down at them as he climbs the steps, and Walsh lingers on the urban Madonna and child briefly in a medium-close shot. Even the holy family itself has been exiled from the church, this image seems to say. The presence of the woman and her child, who represent the hopelessness of life in the Bowery, move Owen finally to renounce his connection to the gang and recommit to the project of the settlement house. He pulls a pencil and paper from

2.2. An urban Madonna and child sits on the steps of the church when Owen goes to consult the priest. Signaling the hopelessness of life in the Bowery, Owen finally renounces his connection to the gang and recommits to the project of the settlement house.

his pocket and leans against the church door to write a note, which Walsh allows the audience to see. Owen writes to Skinny to say that he will help him no more and that he should consider Owen's debt paid.

Although Owen decides to continue into the church to speak with the priest, Walsh has made clear in this very brief scene his sense of the institution's neglect of the neighborhood's people and the unlikelihood that Owen will find resources inside to address his situation meaningfully. Particularly striking here is Walsh's location of Owen's literacy outside the doors of the church. In a gesture to the image of reformer Martin Luther posting his 95 Theses on the door of Castle Church in Germany, the film displays Owen's literacy as a central element of the transformation inaugurated at the settlement house and unavailable to him in the world inside the Catholic church. In this respect *Regeneration* participates in the anti-Catholic discourse that envisions Catholicism as discouraging reading, a limitation that then makes members particularly subject to the control of the hierarchy over things secular as well as religious. In such a view, literacy, provided by a Bible-centered Protestantism, frees the masses from clerical control.

Owen's priest, however, does not appear to be a particularly negative force. He is friendly, but useless. Once inside the church, Owen finds a welcoming, sympathetic ear in the priest, and nothing more. After listening to him, the priest responds, "Go back, my boy, and keep up the good work. We are proud of you." In *Regeneration*, Owen's "progress" has been made possible by the settlement house to which the priest encourages him to return and not by the church. The film's priest does not function as a tyrannical conduit of papal control, as anti-Catholic forces would typically imagine, but he can offer Owen nothing of use. More important, the priest in effect denies the religious superiority of Catholicism by affirming Owen's choice to seek opportunity in the broader (Protestant) world.

Despite the film's argument that the implied Protestantism of the settlement house offers literacy, order, and love, Walsh never completely forsakes the underlying Catholic sensibility he brought to the project from his own background. By the film's concluding sequences Walsh has produced a Catholic-Protestant hybrid that softens the critique of the institutional church. The completion of Owen's regeneration entails the embrace of the Bible-centered world view of Protestantism. At the same time, however, Owen experiences two transformative moments of miraculous intervention that invoke a Catholic understanding of religious power and convince him to renounce violence.

The first of these interventions comes when, while lying on her deathbed (the victim of a bullet from Skinny's gun, which was intended for Owen), Marie raises her hand and gestures. Next to her in the frame a tablet mysteriously appears that reads, "Vengeance is mine saith the Lord. Romans 12:19." As with most of the film's representations of religion, the appearance of the biblical verse is not sectarian. The fact that Owen can now read the Bible extends the earlier emphasis on the Protestant settlement house as providing him with access to literacy and the Bible in ways that Catholicism did not. The film's final intertitle—"It was she, my Mamie Rose [Marie], who taught me that within me was a mind and a God-given heart. She made of my life a changed thing and never can it be the same again."—underscores intellectual and moral development as central elements of the character's transformation. Moreover, Marie's function as a conduit for God's work in Owen highlights Walsh's interest in the activities of middle-class, educated, settlement house women in urban reform. At the same time, Marie's ability to make God's will manifest in the appearance of the tablet—an event that demonstrates the fluidity of the barrier between this world and the next—is distinctly Catholic.

In the second instance of miraculous intervention, near the film's end, it is Marie herself who penetrates the boundary between this world and the next. Despite the admonition provided by the tablet and the biblical verse against taking

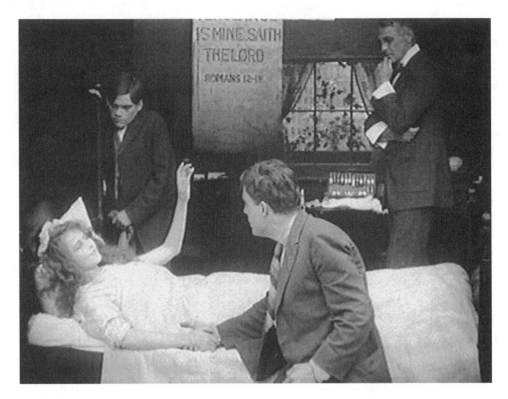

2.3. A miraculous intervention while Marie (Anna Q. Nilsson) lies on her deathbed prevents Owen (Rockliffe Fellowes) from taking revenge.

revenge, Owen is overcome by Marie's death and seeks out Skinny to enact retribution. An apparition of Marie, her lips moving—in prayer or counsel is not clear—finally convinces Owen not to kill Skinny. Here Walsh invokes the Catholic belief in miraculous appearances of the Virgin Mary, such as those in Lourdes and Fatima, in which Mary often provides believers with a divine message. In taking this approach not only does Walsh produce a hybrid of Catholic and Protestant religious sensibilities, he makes exciting use of the unique qualities of film to represent the power of the miraculous in Catholic belief. Walsh's turn to the miraculous at the film's conclusion leaves audiences with clear and strong traces of Catholicism even as Owen moves ever more fully into a Protestant world.

The Power of Representation

Regeneration stands as a creative attempt on the part of a filmmaker of Irish Catholic descent to understand the life story of another Irish Catholic urbanite. Kildare's uplifting story of redemption, despite his own tragic end, had profound appeal in the first decades of the twentieth century. Walsh's interpretation of Kildare's life navigated the course between Catholic and Protestant approaches to urban reform, even as it placed ultimate significance on Protestant values. His moderate approach led to the production of a nuanced religiopolitical text in conversation with Protestant and Catholic social reform work of the period and with social problem films that attempted to dramatize social needs. Audiences, perhaps Catholic viewers in particular, appreciated its art and its subtlety and saw hope in the potential that opened up for Owen by the film's end. The success of *Regeneration* portended the possibility of silent movies serving as a useful arena of discussion and encounter between Catholics and Protestants in America.

By the end of the silent film era, events in the broader American context, including increased anti-immigrant sentiment that resulted in restrictive immigration legislation, made the social and political climate for film representations more complicated. Even as the future immigration of Catholics and Jews from Southern and Eastern Europe was curtailed with this legislation, by virtue of numbers and organization Catholics were in an unprecedented position of political power in many urban areas. By 1928 it was even possible for an Irish American Catholic, Al Smith, to be nominated as the Democratic candidate for the presidency. This increased power and visibility enabled American Catholics to become outspoken in their opposition to what they understood to be demeaning representations of their religion and ethnic heritage. The case of the 1927 MGM silent comedy *The Callahans and the Murphys* demonstrates the social power and consequences of film representations of religion and ethnicity. The heated response to the film provides some indication of how the climate had changed from twelve years earlier when *Regeneration* was released.

The Callahans and the Murphys traces the interactions between two Irish American families in a New York City tenement and explores the difficult and yet close relationship between Mrs. Callahan and Mrs. Murphy. Neither the early screenings nor the initial reviews by critics prepared the producers for the prolonged and intense protests that the film would generate among Irish Americans and Catholic clergy in cities across the country. At various theaters in the New York metropolitan area, angry spectators threw rotten fruit and vegetables, light bulbs, and rocks at the screen. At Loew's Theater on 42nd Street protestors used "malodorous chemicals."[12] The end of August saw numerous arrests in the New York area in connection with such dramatic responses to the film but discontent was not limited to New York. Protests erupted in cities and towns across the country (and even in Australia) as the movie opened in additional theaters.

The grievances focused alternately on discomfort with images of Roman Catholicism in the film and on objections to representations of the Irish American
characters. "My mother never acted like that," one man reportedly yelled at a New
York screening in response to Mrs. Callahan and Mrs. Murphy getting drunk at a
St. Patrick's Day picnic. The protests—some organized by Irish American and
Catholic groups and some apparently spontaneously erupting—were so vigorous in
some locations that theater owners refused to exhibit the film.[13] As Irish American
organizations began to question the film's content, the studio responded by releasing details of the process of the film's development to the public, emphasizing
both the participation of Irish American actors and consultation with Irish
American groups. MGM officials had pinned special hopes of box-office success
on the film because it featured its first female comedy team, composed of the well-
known actresses Marie Dressler (as Mrs. Callahan) and Polly Moran (as Mrs.
Murphy). Like *Regeneration*, *The Callahans and the Murphys* was based on an earlier
text, in this case a novel. Despite MGM's public relations maneuvering, the Irish
American press continued to condemn the film and protests erupted at screenings
in New York as some in attendance rose from their seats, calling for audience
members to walk out. Eventually, MGM withdrew it from circulation.

It is clear that much was at stake for many of the parties involved in the dispute
over *The Callahans and the Murphys*. Its exhibition in theaters brought to the surface in
powerful ways the tensions among film, religion, and ethnicity in America. For their
part, the film studios were struggling with the constraints of existing censorship
mechanisms at the state level and were attempting to resist the growing movement
by reformers (mostly Protestant and Catholic) who saw the movies and their makers
(mostly Jews) as a danger to American morals. Such an argument was made explicit
in the case of some, but certainly not all, responses to *The Callahans and the Murphys* in
particular. One newspaper account insisted, "The Jews control the film industry and
they are using their power to demoralize this Christian country. What they are doing
to-day against the Irish they will do to-morrow against every other element in the
American population with the exception of the 'chosen people' who must not be
ridiculed in the movies or criticized in the press."[14] These reformers promoted
federal oversight of the industry as the preferable solution to the problem while the
studios looked for less restrictive means, such as self-regulation. In response to
mounting calls for censorship, the Motion Picture Producers and Distributors of
America adopted in 1927 the "Don'ts and Be Carefuls." A set of guidelines for
handling particular topics, including religion, race, and national origin, the list was a
precursor to the Production Code that served as the basis for industry self-regulation
from 1930 through the 1960s.

The Catholic church found MGM's production and release of *The Callahans and the Murphys* to be particularly disturbing. Although explicit representations of Catholicism were apparently few in the film, it is particularly striking that for audiences, representations of Irish characters necessarily invoked Catholicism. It made no difference that Catholic beliefs and practices were presented in implied and deflected ways. As the National Catholic Welfare Conference declared in 1927 of *The Callahans and the Murphys*, "In its introduction of Catholic 'atmosphere'—the name of St. Patrick, the Crucifix, the Sign of the Cross—it is a hideous defamation of Catholic beliefs and practices."[15] Undoubtedly, the heightened response to *The Callahans and the Murphys* stemmed from the power of the conjunction of images of religion and ethnicity. The film linked images of Irish Americans as rowdy urbanites with a portrayal of Catholicism as an unsuitable religion for Americans.

Not only were the film's Irish characters loutish, as critics of the movie insisted, but the film also implied that they were not racially white and, so, not worthy of a place at the top of America's racial hierarchy. One Irish American newspaper insisted that Marie Dressler had "successfully impersonated a gorilla" and another charged that "they had been given the manners of 'Fiji Islanders.'"[16] In seeking a higher place on the racial hierarchy, Irish Americans attempted to construct and maintain an identity as white Americans even as images of themselves as barbarous and fundamentally foreign were readily available for popular consumption as entertainment. While these challenges and concerns were not as explicit in *Regeneration* as in the later *The Callahans and the Murphys*, Fox's *Regeneration* nevertheless engages the history of representations of Irish Americans and redirects it in important ways.

The controversy over *The Callahans and the Murphys* stimulated the increasing involvement in film censorship by the Catholic hierarchy and the leaders of some Catholic lay organizations. This involvement resulted in participation in the formulation of the Production Code in 1930 and the formation of the Catholic Legion of Decency in 1934. In the wake of this pressure, American Catholics became important arbiters of the moral standards that dominated the production of movies in America until the 1960s. Irish Americans were not the only constituency of early film spectators who reacted with vigor when they felt themselves portrayed negatively on the screen, nor were Catholics the only religious leaders calling for the imposition of moral standards on the industry. Nevertheless, the organization and authority of Irish Americans in contesting what they took to be unfair and politically and socially damaging representations of themselves as ethnic Americans and as Catholics provided useful models for other ethnic, racial, and religious groups in their own responses to films.

Because of the loss of so many silent films, it is difficult to draw definitive conclusions about the part that Walsh's *Regeneration* or MGM's *The Callahans and the Murphys* played in setting the terms for representations of Catholics in early film. *Regeneration* survives as an early entrant in a representational history that culminated late in the silent period with episodes of conflict and contestation like that over the exhibition of *The Callahans and the Murphys*. As a powerful exploration of early twentieth-century urban poverty, *Regeneration* stands as a creative contribution to the genre of the social problem film. The film is, in part, an insider's critique of the Catholic church's failure to eradicate poverty among Irish American New Yorkers. It is also an avenue for Raoul Walsh to promote the position that the poor will find opportunity by embracing the Protestant values that underlie seemingly secular social reform work. *Regeneration* does not reject Catholicism outright, however. Walsh's inclusion of miraculous interventions as central to Owen's transformation opens up the possibility for viewers to imagine an identity in which Protestant and Catholic sensibilities can coexist and perhaps even reinforce one another. The reappearance of *Regeneration* so many years after viewers first encountered it in movie theaters provides us with an unexpected opportunity to examine a unique cinematic exploration of early twentieth-century urban ethnic Catholicism.

NOTES

1. *Chicago Daily Tribune*, 9 January 1904. See also *Washington Post*, 12 October 1903.
2. Owen Frawley Kildare and Walter Hackett, *The Regeneration*, produced by Liebler and Company and staged by Arnold Daly at Wallack's Theatre. For reviews of the play, see *Chicago Daily Tribune*, 9 March 1908; *New York Times*, 2 September 1908. According to the *New York Times* (25 November 1908), Kildare's wife, Leita Russell Bogardis Kildare, attributed his institutionalization in November 1908 to his dismay at the representation of his memoir on-stage. She told the press:

   > Mr. Kildare is ill because of the failure of "The Regeneration," which was offered early in the present season at Wallack's Theatre. It was not played as Mr. Kildare wrote it. He saw it only once and was so furious with Arnold Daly [who played the lead role] for the changes in it that he wanted to fight him. It was all he could do to keep from attacking the actor. He became morose, morbid, and frequently talked of suicide. Finally he was attacked by the nervous collapse from which he is now suffering.

   Kildare was eventually placed at the Manhattan State Hospital on Ward's Island, where he died in 1911. See *Chicago Daily Tribune*, 7 February 1911. On *Fool's Highway*, see *Los Angeles Times*, 28 April and 18 May 1924.

3. Owen Frawley Kildare, *My Mamie Rose: The Story of My Regeneration* (New York: Baker and Taylor, 1903), 14.

4. A Report of the Librarian of Congress, *Film Preservation 1993: A Study of the Current State of American Film Preservation*, vol. 1 (June 1993), located at http://www.loc.gov/film/study.html. Cellulose nitrate was used in professional film until the early 1950s when the studios switched to "safety" triacetate film stock. On the history of nitrate films, see Roger Smither, ed., *This Film Is Dangerous: A Celebration of Nitrate Film* (London: FIAF, 2002).

5. *Atlanta Constitution*, 19 and 20 September 1915. The quote is from a 1976 interview of Raoul Walsh by Peter Bogdanovich, *Who the Devil Made It?* (New York: Knopf, 1997), 160.

6. Plot summaries are drawn from the *American Film Institute Catalog* (http://afi.chadwyck.com).

7. "The Smalleys Have a Message to the World," *Universal Weekly* (1915), quoted in Jennifer Parchesky, "Lois Weber's *The Blot*: Rewriting Melodrama, Reproducing the Middle Class," *Cinema Journal* 39 (Fall 1999): 26.

8. Raoul Walsh, *Each Man in His Time: The Life Story of a Director* (New York: Farrar, Straus and Giroux, 1974), 61.

9. Bogdanovich, *Who the Devil Made It?* 153.

10. Kildare, *My Mamie Rose*, 20–21.

11. Ibid., 287. After his death, friends from Kildare's Bowery childhood insisted that his real name was Tom Carroll and that he had been born in Maryland. These friends also claimed that he was connected to the renowned Irish Catholic Carroll family of Carrollton, Maryland. *New York Times*, 12 February 1911.

12. *New York Times*, 26 August 1927.

13. Ibid. The film was banned in Bayonne, New Jersey, and exhibitors in San Antonio, Cincinnati, Syracuse, Jersey City, Washington, D.C., and Bridgeport pulled the film. On Bayonne, see *New York Times*, 7 September 1927. On other cities, see *New York Times*, 30 August 1927, and Francis R. Walsh, "'The Callahans and the Murphys' (MGM, 1927): A Case Study of Irish-American and Catholic Church Censorship," *Historical Journal of Film, Radio, and Television* 10, no. 1 (1990): 39.

14. *Gaelic American*, 20 August 1927.

15. "An Affront to Catholics," press release, National Catholic Welfare Conference News Service, 25 July 1927, quoted in Jeffrey A. Smith, "Hollywood Theology: The Commodification of Religion in Twentieth-Century Films," *Religion and American Culture* 11 (Summer 2001): 195.

16. As quoted in Frank Walsh, *Sin and Censorship: The Catholic Church and the Motion Picture Industry* (New Haven, CT: Yale University Press, 1996), 41.

FURTHER READING

Baylor, Ronald H., and Timothy J. Meagher, eds. *The New York Irish*. Baltimore, MD: Johns Hopkins University Press, 1996.

Bernardi, Daniel. *The Birth of Whiteness: Race and the Emergence of U.S. Cinema*. New Brunswick, NJ: Rutgers University Press, 1996.

Brown, Dorothy M., and Elizabeth McKeown. *The Poor Belong to Us: Catholic Charities and American Welfare*. Cambridge, MA: Harvard University Press, 1997.

Brownlow, Kevin. *Behind the Mask of Innocence: Sex, Violence, Prejudice, Crime: Films of Social Conscience in the Silent Era*. New York: Knopf, 1990.

Davis, Allen F. *Spearheads for Reform: The Social Settlements and the Progressive Movement, 1890–1914*. New York: Oxford University Press, 1967.

Fitzgerald, Maureen. *Habits of Compassion: Irish Catholic Nuns and the Origins of the Welfare System, 1830–1920*. Urbana: University of Illinois Press, 2006.

Ross, Steven J. *Working-Class Hollywood: Silent Film and the Shaping of Class in America*. Princeton, NJ: Princeton University Press, 1998.

Slide, Anthony. *Lois Weber: The Director Who Lost Her Way in History*. Westport, CT: Greenwood, 1996.

Sloan, Kay. *The Loud Silents: Origins of the Social Problem Film*. Urbana: University of Illinois Press, 1988.

Walsh, Raoul. *Each Man in His Time: The Life Story of a Director*. New York: Farrar, Straus and Giroux, 1974.

3

Boys to Men

Angels with Dirty Faces (1938)

Thomas J. Ferraro

On 18 February 2006, a Catholic church–sponsored, parochial school–affiliated community center opened in Durham, North Carolina. Durham is a small post-industrial city where once cigarettes were made but no more. The church lies on the edge of a tough neighborhood, cut off by a highway from the old downtown, not two blocks from a violence-plagued convenience store known as "The Murder Mart." Honoring the mother of its principal donor, Duke University basketball coach, Mike Krzyzewski, the complex is called the Emily Krzyzewski Family Life Center. There are classrooms and computer clusters, but the downtown buzz surrounds the basketball court, which is regulation size and very well outfitted, including an actual NCAA championship floor (from the 2001 Final Four). Dedicated to what social workers now call "early age intervention," the idea is to give latchkey kids, especially the boys, somewhere to go after school and to de-glamorize the life of the streets, especially the gangs.

This would seem to be an old American story: the boys' (and now girls') club offered as an after-school center in service of working and broken families, reaching out to downtown neighborhoods that are plagued by rogue gangs driven by too much testosterone, by not enough father figures or stay-at-home (grand)mothers, and by the glamour of seemingly easy money. In Durham, it is the distanced offspring of European Catholic ethnics who have taken the lead in building and staffing the community center, while it is a combination of the distanced offspring of slavery (African Americans) and the most recent surplus labor—Latinos, East Asians—whom the Catholic workers fear, rightly, to be in trouble. Such demographics would surprise no one. But once upon a time in the late 1930s when the notion of parish-sponsored basketball rescue first came into being, almost all of the protagonists were Irish—the priest from the old neighborhood (ever so Irish), the hoodlum stealing hearts and headlines, also from the old neighborhood (more stage Irish), and the young roughnecks loose in the old neighborhood, suffering the competing influences of padre and padrone (more or less Irish, too).

Angels with Dirty Faces (1938) places an Irish American working-class ethos of masculine camaraderie, charisma, and courage at the center of just such a generically pitched battle between the Catholic church and the criminal underground. The battle between the social-work church and the parasitic streets is, of course, romanticized, even sentimentalized. Here we have a passel of juveniles at risk without a mother or a daughter, a sister or a Sister (scarcely even a girlfriend) anywhere in sight. Men without women is a marked departure from movie formulas, and it doesn't stop there: director Michael Curtiz's intriguing, often beautifully noirish portrayal of the male underclass encodes more than corner-boy bonding, intimacy in the streets. It discovers and enacts an alternative spirituality, an unofficial Catholicism of the streets. *Angels with Dirty Faces* brings to the fore, in imperfect but still illuminating ways, the incarnate, indeed sacramental, interplay between the quality of life for boys and men in the naked city together and the state—or rather, the fate—of their immortal souls.

A Formula Film?

At first glance, *Angels with Dirty Faces* looks like the generic 1930s gangster picture—as flatfooted in its psychosocial insight (boys just wanna have fun) as in its black-and-white morality (break the allure of the mobsters or there will be hell to pay). A loner priest, Father Jerry Connolly (the sweet-faced Irishman Pat O'Brien), and a near-loner gangster, Rocky Sullivan (the stone-faced but impish-eyed James Cagney, already synonymous with Irish American gangsterdom), battle for the hearts and minds of a group of male teenagers (played by the Warner Brothers studio acting troop, the Dead End Kids) who fancy themselves a gang. No parochial schools are on the scene yet, at least not in the movies—that's up to

Bing Crosby and the well-publicized construction boom after the Second World War. Instead, the centerpiece of Father Jerry Connolly's uplift scheme is a makeshift basketball court, converted from an abandoned storefront that Father Jerry hopes to turn into a legitimate gym. To add to the well-worn plot devices, it turns out that Father Jerry and gangster Rocky were boyhood friends: Rocky was set onto his life of crime only because, when the two of them as boys tried stealing fountain pens from a train yard, Rocky got caught and sent to reform school while Jerry got away clean. In movie shorthand, this means that the social environment, not genetics, makes criminals. The boys can therefore be rescued, if only their environment or their relationship to certain parts of their environment can be shifted. It goes without saying that decency and respectability are God's way.

Certainly, the movie critics and journalists who first saw the movie thought of it as very much a formula film: tautly made, with some nice touches, but basically just another gangster flick with high entertainment value and the requisite crime-ultimately-doesn't-pay moral. "It's a crackling cops-and-robbers melodrama" that nonetheless "runs true to type," commented Frank S. Nugent in the *New York Times*. "A fine job of cinematic technique," the reviewer in *Time* magazine confirmed. "Rowland Brown's story and Michael Curtiz' direction bring nothing new to racketeer melodrama, but the brisk rattle of Cagney's conversation and his associates' machine guns has a pleasantly nostalgic quality." The only issue up for debate was whether the plot and character conventions were too familiar to bear. "That 'Dead End' kid story," *Variety* concluded, "has been told too many times." The more populist the venue—judged by liberties of colloquial diction and syntax—the greater the support: "We offer it as our well considered opinion," *Film Daily* reported, "that this story has never been topped in its theme-field for downright excitement, close-knit driving punch, glamour of gangsterism contrasted with the finer things in life building to a great emotional climax with the humanities triumphing." Or my favorite: "[Warner Brothers] have provided showmen with a surpassing demonstration of their unquestioned ability in the field of cinematic criminology."[1]

Moviegoers voted with their feet, making *Angels with Dirty Faces* one of the most financially successful films of 1938. The motion picture industry offered qualified praise, nominating Cagney, director Curtiz, and storywriter Brown for Oscars, which they did not win. I suspect Hollywood was particularly nervous about what it sensed in Cagney's edgy screen appeal, giving its Oscar to that safer Irish American, Spencer Tracy, for his portrayal of another, strictly avuncular, social-work priest, in *Boys' Town*. Interestingly, the New York Film Critics and the National Board of Review, representing the more intellectual or at least elite end of the professional movie community, seconded the sensation-struck masses, each naming James Cagney as the best actor of 1938.

Given the generic accolades, it is not surprising how little was said about the portrayal of Catholics in the movie. There was absolutely nothing in the secular press, beyond acknowledging Pat O'Brien's character as a crusading priest. All *Commonweal* (the most important of the Catholic magazines) had to say was a complaint about the spinelessness of the Catholics (read: O'Brien) on-screen (would real Catholics really be that attracted to gangsters?). Otherwise even *Commonweal* thought the film was par for the course: "Michael Curtiz's direction of *Angels with Dirty Faces*, although emphasizing no new note, is good for its photo-montage, its carefully depicted slum scenes and built-up suspense."[2]

Although one of the two main characters is a priest, the institutions, people, and rites of official Catholicism are scarcely present in the film at large. We enter the sanctuary and sacristy of Father Jerry's church one time only, shadowing Rocky's return to the old neighborhood. We listen to the boys' choir practice, but we witness no mass, no communion, no confession. The large families as well as the unusual number of single women (including nuns) and of devout men (again, thanks to the Irish) who historically filled the pews and coffers are entirely absent. Many of the policemen and random officials in the film are played by Irish American actors with movie-Irish accents, but the church's ties to civic authority go unremarked and uninvestigated. This is a notable absence since by the time of the Great Depression, when this movie opens, in a northeastern city of the type being invoked, the political influence of the Catholic church would have been considerable.

A literary critic might be tempted to say that the institutional church is "personified" by the one priest, Jerry Connolly. The fact is, however, that organized religion is *reduced*, unrealistically, to this single, unguardedly earnest man. Father Jerry, cast as a relic of the days before ward politics, has somehow corraled an ethnically motley crew of small boys into a choir (the only sign of communal devotional life we see). Father Connolly otherwise occupies himself with his pet project: trying to counter the temptations to vice—petty thievery, especially—of the older boys. The boys don't really frighten us. They are more a menace to themselves than they are to society, which turns out to be more corrupt than they. It is hard to decide through most of the film whether it is their immortal souls we should be worrying about (underneath the grime, they are angels after all) or simply their prospects for less messy lives (involving cleaner faces, better circumstances, and fewer jail terms).

In the final scene of the film, the boys follow Jerry Connolly (J.C., get it?) up the stairs from their basement hideout to the bright striated light up and beyond.

3.1. A newspaper's headline reveals to the Dead End Kids that Rocky died "yellow."

The daylight of regular lives comes streaming down the back wall of the stairs, which until then has been lit like a dungeon. The camera provides viewers with the Holy Ghost of salvation, the halo of Connolly's achievement. The newspapers have testified that their hero, Rocky Sullivan, died "yellow," a coward. Asked to confirm the reports, Father Jerry, who was there, does so. The kids are being lifted up into the light, and it would appear that social-work Catholicism, as pure as the white of the black-and-white film stock, has won the day. Rocky the killer has gotten his just desserts. Saint Jerry of the Neighborhood has won the day. And the boys, freed from their delusions, can now grow up straight. Well, how easy, for a genre film, is that?

As it turns out, not very.

Twenty-three years earlier, in Raoul Walsh's *Regeneration* (1915), we saw how an Irish American hoodlum, the dashing leader of the neighborhood gang, is saved morally and spiritually by a Protestant settlement house worker. They fall in love, but the settlement house worker dies tragically, having been sexually attacked and inadvertently killed by the former buddy of the ex-hoodlum, now leader of the gang. Our hero contemplates revenge, only to be visited by an apparition of Marie, his beloved—the Protestant Virgin in film incarnate—urging him to forgive their betrayer while reminding him that "God is love." Two decades before *Angels with Dirty Faces*, then, the Catholic faith was seen as ineffectual, indeed uninvolved, in the war against crime and poverty, despite its long-standing tradition of urban uplift. In 1915 the energy of redemption in the American city was still associated almost exclusively with the activism of chaste white womanhood, with the sociological extension of Protestant domesticity, and with the emasculating discipline of sentimental romance. The streets and cellar dens of gangdom were understood to be strictly evil: greed and violence were unmitigated, buddyhood routinely betrayed both directly and indirectly, and white women sacrificed to the cause of saving men. You might think, then, that *Angels with Dirty Faces* was much the same reform movie but with the gangster factor intensified. In the update, the role of the Protestant settlement house worker is split between an Irish Catholic priest (out to save his friend the adult hoodlum as well as a crew of teenagers) and a working-class Irish girl (a reformed moll who falls in love with Rocky and wants to save him too). But the real energy of redemption lies elsewhere, in the most unofficial and unsuspected of places.

It is common sense or at least a long-term American habit of mind to presume a simple split between the sacred and the secular—good versus bad, church versus street, decency versus greed. The generic structure of *Angels with Dirty Faces* is so premised. We have the ethos of Jerry versus the ethos of Rocky. The contrast is there, however, only to get the story going so that the film can explore the reciprocal shapings, interpenetrations, and dialectical movement between the two worlds. Even as the institution of the Catholic church is too much distilled into the personhood of Jerry, so there is an unexpected, competing excess of radiance about Rocky. His is a radiance that partakes of greed and glamour and guns but isn't a matter only of earthly belongings and earthy behavior. It is a radiance that has more than a little of the supernatural in it than we're accustomed to seeing, in ways we're not at all accustomed to thinking about. I want to suggest that Rocky represents or, better, embodies not so much the opposite of divine energy as an alternate incarnation of it. The mystique of Irish American urban masculinity unites passion and compassion, competition and loyalty, protection and violence in one figure—that of James Cagney, who turns out to be the real "J.C." superstar. If *Angels with Dirty Faces* is to be understood as Catholic in force, not just clerical in theme, then we have to recognize this: the all-American, yet especially Catholic, social imperative to raise boys to men (represented by Father Connolly) is inextricable from the power with which it seems otherwise to be competing (incarnated by Jimmy Cagney). That power is adult male charisma, in this case Irishly developed, which casts a spell—at once loving and violent—not only over boys but also over women and, most especially, over men.

Cagney and Street Catholicism

It's difficult to imagine *Angels with Dirty Faces* without its introductory framing scenes, though they were in fact filmed last.[3] Over the credits, Max Steiner's music kick-starts the movie. With a hard-boiled melodramatic feel, it tells us that this is a serious business. Warren Harding has just been nominated president, making it 1920. Newspapers—media exposure, manipulation—increasingly matter in the country. The camera pans around a series of three- and four-story tenements lining city streets, with women on almost every fire escape, beating rugs and hanging laundry. The streets are paved, but McConaghy's grocery store, horse-drawn carts, peddlers, and an organ grinder remind us that this is an earlier era of the poorer, tougher part of town. We've seen the scene many times before in the movies but also, before them, in the illustrated magazines. We are in the old neighborhood. Set modes of pictorialization—the central avenue is called Dock Street—put us in an unnamed, presumably northeastern, port city. It looks familiar, and it is. We're seeing Warner Brothers' famous city set, built in 1930 for its early gangster pictures. The same set was used and reused as a faux Gotham all the way from *The Public Enemy* (1931) to *Batman Returns* (1992). And yet, for all its recognizable conventions, this tenement corner feels pungently real, viscerally there, in part because of Sol Polito's brilliant cinematography, especially the low-key lighting and engaged camera movement. But it also feels real because being on stage in everyday life is what the naked city is all about.

The camera pans up from the street to one of the landings on a fire escape, where there are two boys, bored, movie-hopeful but penniless. Each is roughly clad, yet behatted, one of them jauntily so. The jaunty one, called "Rocky" in the very first exchange, takes a cigarette out of the other boy's mouth—phallic intimacy, comfortably untroubled as we shall see. Three girls are espied and the taunting commences. Young Rocky has the courage to take it to the next level, coming down the stairs and pulling the cap of the girl in the middle, who already has him in mind. She protests, along with the others, but this is what they've wanted.

The second scene is set in the railroad yards, which quietly evoke the industrial sublime. Bulls (members of the railroad security staff) eerily stalk the top of the freight cars. A telegraph pole bifurcates the alley-like pathway between the freight trains. All of this is filmed with the uncanniness of the great urban photographers (like Lewis Hines) and illustrators (like Joseph Stella) of the early twentieth century. The urban environment of *Angels* is at once stylized and compelling, stagy yet blood-touching, so much so that I want to name it, in the manner of today's graphic novelists, "Dock City." So be it: Sol Polito's Dock City is a provocation to but also a fit setting for the thick-skinned, tough-minded, but ultimately other-directed radiance that is at the film's center: the cinemagraphic mysticism of film noir capturing and conjuring the mystique of urban masculinity.

Rocky talks the other boy, Jerry, into pilfering from one of the freight cars, breaking open a crate marked Everright Pens, Hartford, Ct. The joke of the film is that Jerry becomes a priest rather than a gangster only because he could run faster than Rocky—a joke repeated by many a critic, then and now.[4] In fact, Jerry is a goody two-shoes from the first: "We don't need those pens," he warns. More important, Rocky gets caught only because Jerry trips over the train tracks with the coppers in hot pursuit, just at the instant a train roars into view, bearing down upon him. In the cheesiest moment of melodrama in the film (which is tolerable only because it happens so fast and we scarcely know who is who yet), Rocky stops short and runs back to get Jerry. Picking him off the tracks, Rocky gives Jerry the crucial push that saves his life and, as it turns out, also keeps him out of reform school.

Rocky's toughness is inextricable from his devotion to Jerry, indeed, from his protection and even nurturing of him. When the young Rocky awaits trial, we learn—for the first time—how smooth a talker he is, and how the rhetoric of gutter realism allows him to screen his intentions. Rocky is a tough guy with a steady loyalty, a devotedness, and a beguiling way. He is a boy who not only keeps his friend out of jail but who establishes the terms that allow his friend to rationalize being out of jail: sacrifice is on the table from day one. The stronger male acts on behalf of the weaker one. The Irish male street code *says* each man only for himself—"don't be a sucker"—but that's a screen. In young Rocky's canny rhetoric, it's a decoy for something else, for taking care of his buddy. In the visitor room of the city jail, still young and not yet toughened, Rocky is upfront about it. "It's only business" is Italian Mafia-speak for "I'm taking this personally." "Don't be a sucker" is Irish hoodlum-speak for "let me take the fall; I want to be the sucker." The explicit, official Catholicism preached in the film is aligned with social decency, right behavior, and the sacrifice of one's own needs. But in the imaginative structure of the film, there is a related yet subtler ethos, perhaps even a Christian ethos. This "street Catholicism" is more complex and perhaps more powerful than social-work earnestness.[5] An alternative yet increasingly allied form of right behavior resides in masculine commitment, street and media skills (including smoothness of tongue), and protective indirection.

The ultimate significance of girl taunting, its relation to the friendship of boys, and the guy-rescuing-guy plot are uncertain in these opening scenes. What is certain, however, is that one of the boys is the more righteous and resigned, the other the more adventuresome and needy. "It ain't like stealing coal to keep warm," Jerry moralizes. "What we don't take we ain't got," Rocky rebuts. The former has certain masculine skills (he vaults the fence into the hideout with ease) for all his gentleness and stumbling, while the latter has clear signs of a generous heart and protective soul. The audience guesses, if only from the credits, that the sweet-faced boy, the official ethicist, is going to grow up to be the character played by Pat O'Brien. And the audience has no doubt that the tougher minded of the two, the street ethicist, is going to grow up to be the character played by James Cagney.

I don't think we can underestimate the importance of Cagney to the meaning of the film. By 1938 James Cagney was an icon of the crime epic, arguably *the* icon of crime epics, so much so that the actor had to fight, repeatedly, to avoid being typecast. Viewers knew "Jimmy Cagney" as a tough guy with varying degrees of impetuosity and sweetness, generosity and rage. They had seen him on both sides of the law, from the quintessentially tragic beloved-son-gone-wrong in *The Public Enemy* (1931) to the gutter kid–turned–federal avenger in *"G" Men* (1935). Audiences had been treated throughout to his Irishness, sometimes subtly but often not. Cagney's Irishness was dramatized not only through urban immigrant comedy (Cagney played with Frank McHugh and, yes, Pat O'Brien in a film called *The Irish in Us* [1935]) but also through the hoodlum persona itself. His roles were in marked contrast to the ethnic malleability of, say, Edward G. Robinson or Paul Muni. Of his breakout performance in *The Public Enemy*, one film scholar comments, "Cagney does not merely inhabit or present this figure; in the precise dictionary sense, he creates it. With his body [and, I would argue, his voice] he causes it to exist in a photographed image on a movie screen—he brings it into being."[6]

The reason that director Michael Curtiz held up filming the opening scenes is that the studio could not find an actor to play the young Rocky Sullivan who could yield a credible version of Cagney's palpable effect. The actor they finally found was an unknown by the name of Frankie Burke, who is simply brilliant. Reviewer after reviewer celebrated his acting at the time. Burke produces neither the forced mimicry which betrays Andy Garcia in *The Godfather, Part III* (1990) as he tries to invoke James Caan's Sonny Corleone, nor the quiet evocativeness of Robert De Niro playing the young Vito Corleone in *The Godfather, Part II* (1974). Instead he has the mannerisms, the bodily movement, and the diction down pat, so much so that imitation and actuality converge. The original audience for *Angels* would have recognized instantly that the teenager on the screen was Cagney's boyhood self. Early in the film, then, the icon of Cagney is fully invoked, reanimated, made present. In the first three scenes what is made real is his complex charisma: his easy way with other guys and an aggressive magnetism with girls, his physical grace under pressure that serves male loyalty and accepts risk, his ability to talk a blue streak. Rocky's verbal strength, dexterous and proactive, stands in sharp contrast to the self-protective "empty volubility" that novelist Mary Gordon characterizes as classically Irish.[7] His talk is more than just defense, more even than charm, will, negotiation. Rocky's talk is protective and sacrificial, a movie Irishness of blessed strength. If their boyhoods are any indication, Rocky is going to be a tough act for Jerry to compete with, in more ways than one.

A series of terrifically evocative scenes work "with the precision and speed of the Twentieth Century Limited"—cinematic photomontage at its best—to take us from the boys' past (1920) into the time present of the film (circa 1935).[8] In quick succession Rocky moves from a work farm called the Warrington Reform School to three years at the state reformatory (assault and battery) to being fingerprinted and entered into the record for the state "pen" (where we see a forbidding line march, underscoring the bleakness of captivity). Then a headline announces that Sullivan has beaten "a bootlegging rap" (we see him fiercely bossing his smuggling crew down on the docks). The sordid history continues: Rocky emerging from the darkness with a gun, which he fires, followed by another headline saying he has beaten a manslaughter charge. Then comes a beguiling set of double exposures featuring roulette wheels and glamorous women and champagne glasses and leggy dance lines, their sensuous spell violently interrupted by a car bomb and another headline spinning by. This time, it announces that Rocky has been captured as "Terror Sweeps the City." Always already corrupt and inhumane, the American city serves up the brilliant appeal of its underside: a Catholic space which is decadent but of course incandescent, a sensual heaven on earth worth buying, it would seem, even with stolen money, worth seeking, perhaps, even at the expense of body and soul.

The closing scene of the montage, taking place in a prison visitors' hall, is an explicit replay of Rocky's visitor room sitdown with Jerry. This time Rocky agrees not to rat out his lawyer, James Frazier (Humphrey Bogart), but it is obvious even in this quick vignette that they are not really buddies, only partners in crime, and that there are strings attached in such an arrangement. Rocky will take the fall alone only on condition that in the interim Frazier goes to work for both of them and saves every penny of the stolen loot, an even $100,000, for Rocky to reclaim upon release. The montage of past-into-present ends with Rocky making a threat—wisely, but the audience registers the determination better than Frazier does, as we shall see. "Look. I know you're a smart lawyer, very smart, but don't get smart with me." Rocky, once a selfless friend, now a desperate deal maker, has been backed into a corner by the system. What, then, is to be done?

Curiously, it is not Jerry whom we first identify inside the church but Rocky, who has come looking for Jerry upon his release from jail. With his characteristic shrug of the shoulders, Rocky walks the central aisle in subtle pace to the choir music, looking about with an aura of quiet familiarity. He is wearing a suit, formal but understated, hence respectful, just right for a layman in a sanctuary of the 1930s. Catching sight of a nun (the only female devout in the film) at prayer on a side kneeler, he acknowledges her presence—properly, to himself. Rocky the felon, who has just done hard time in the state penitentiary, is surprisingly at home before altar and saint, kneeler and confessional. Our perception of his comfort level is mostly a function of what he does. But it is a function, too, of how the movement is staged, how he is framed ("held within" the church, as Christ is said to hold the individual sinner), and how lighting indicates character. Looking up to the choir, Rocky recognizes the tune that the boys are singing and mouths the words to himself in Latin. His face is lit from above, suggesting a rough-hewn renewal of cherubic boyish attitude, as if divine light were at that moment shining upon him.

This scene is a movie equivalent of a "heads up." Pay attention now. Presumed to have a strict Catholic upbringing, the Irish gangster is forced to come to terms with both God and the institution of the church. Rocky is no longer a practicing Catholic, but the idioms and attitudes of Christian devotion lie within him still. The questions then are: how? and to what effect?

Men and Boys

From the start of the film, what we are mainly watching is a fraught game of love and volition between two old and, as it turns out, very special friends. The good-natured but unworldly and righteous priest with a hidden core of resilience plays with and against the hardened, willful, utterly engaging gangster. His appeal is a function of a self-ironic eye and a secretly protective heart. Both men are quietly conflicted about the relation of the seemingly secular ethos of masculine self-assertion, aggrandizement, and reputation to the seemingly emasculating virtues of

Christian nurturing and sacrifice. For the audience of 1930s America, these were feminine values. One man has a coterie of boys under the sway of his hyper-masculine image and, increasingly through the movie, his confirming presence. The other is working to sway them away from that image, but he himself does not have quite the presence to succeed on his own. The priest is as mesmerized by the gangster as we are, all the while being worried about that charismatic one's soul and the relationship that endures between them.

There is only a brief moment of awkwardness when Rocky enters the sacristy, giving Jerry his signature greeting—"whaddaya hear? whaddaya say?"—for the first time in fifteen years. Soon he is seated on a desk talking intimately with Jerry, who has been following his criminal exploits in the newspapers. Jerry is annoyed that Rocky has never written to him. The reunion scene ends with them crooning to-gether an old popular song, as they reminisce about having once slipped its sheet music into the choir's music books. Physical gestures could not be more informative here. It is Rocky who cues up Jerry, and Jerry who keeps his eyes locked on Rocky the whole time. Rocky shifts from a modest downward or inward gaze to meeting Jerry's look directly, only then to bow his head, practically touching Jerry's forehead. Jerry's wit is surprisingly nuanced. When Jerry tells Rocky he has cost him a lot of prayer, the word "cost" is sentimental and ironic, chastising and self-deprecating, all at the same time. It's a good pastoral touch and something more. Rocky is smooth but not super smooth, which makes him only more appealing, not less. When Jerry un-comfortably pauses, unsure how to label Rocky's occupation, Rocky fills in the blank, volunteering, "[you mean] hoodlums like me." Speaking openly and emanating good will, Rocky helps to restore the comfort level between them. But a generous forth-rightness alone can't make their differences disappear. When Rocky makes quips such as "You've got the kids shilling for the parish?" or "I've been on a kind of re-treat myself," the two of them laugh, at that moment very much together. But the issues—Jerry's struggle for charity, Rocky's debt to society—remain.

The question of the right kind of masculinity is not simply an obsession of our own gender-adventurous, gender-anxious, sexually obsessed historical moment. Father Jerry Connolly is staged, from the beginning, as a particular kind of softie, with a warm and sentimental, domestic heart. The first time we see him as an adult, he is conducting the boys' choir, his face lifted heavenward, his eyes glazed over with tenderness, looking as cherubic as his young charges. Though tall, he is round of face, fleshy, "a good-looking priest" in Rocky's compliment. The collar feminizes him, as does the sanctimonious habit of address. Quickly we learn that Jerry's mother wanted him to be a priest, and after some time he gave himself over to her wishes.

The conceit of the maternal wish is a heavy form of movie shorthand. In the popular culture of the day, it is mothers who are reputed to ask their sons to serve God as directly as possible, sacrificing their sexuality, their social influence, and their reputations as "real men" to the increasingly marginal enterprise of the holy priesthood. In *Angels*, it is one son in particular—Jerry Connolly—who believes in his mother and takes to heart her vision for him. In *Angels*, the priest produces no progeny, protects no family. What he does is social work, a form of celibate "mothering," less paternal than maternal as even the tools of redemption that are the special masculine preserve of the priesthood—the sacraments—are of little use. Having made the requisite sacrifice, then—desexed, domesticated, and dedicated to the welfare of others—Jerry Connolly is the Virgin Mary figure in Roman-collar drag, *except* that the circle of his determined attention and beneficence turns out to be thick—oh so thick—with boys.

The scenes in which friendship, intimacy, or love are discussed—the reunion scene and especially the scene in which Jerry and Laury (Ann Sheridan), Rocky's girlfriend, compare notes—make no bones about the guys' affection. "We both love him, Father." "Yes, Laury, we both love him; I've loved him since we were kids six years old." Still, it is possible to argue that these days we look too hard for homoerotic subtexts, that we attach too much of a sexual dimension to the love between men. I suspect if you viewed these scenes out of context, however, especially the gleam in Father Jerry's eye, you'd begin to wonder. There is something deeply tolerant in Rocky, who time and again is unthreatened by this male attention, perhaps due to his inner security. So too, Rocky's romantic interest, the widowed and reformed moll Laury Ferguson, is not a true distraction. She is nothing close to the defining female presence anticipated by *Angels*' opening scene or familiar to viewers from the Cagney crime oeuvre. Sweet-faced, somewhat dowdy, and ultimately ineffectual, Sheridan is miles away from the full-bodied double trouble of both women in *The Public Enemy* (pre-censorship bombshell Jean Harlow versus pre-censorship bombshell Joan Blondell). She is even further from the decisive action of the women in *"G" Men* (when the boss's sister is kidnapped, the moll intervenes). With Laury a comparative afterthought, then, the larger context in which the Rocky-Laury-Jerry triangle is situated, with no other women anywhere in sight, suggests an open secret, among the filmmakers at least.

The Dead End Kids are from the start pranksters—a coterie of young teens without parents or kin whose need for discipline is apparent in their pranks (they "steal" the baby carriage of an Italian couple with the baby in it, for about five yards). Homeless, they have shaped for themselves an alternative domesticity that seems waiting—begging—for Rocky's appearance. The scene in the hideout echoes the Fagin of *Oliver Twist* and his boys, because the first thing they do is pickpocket. They have names reminiscent of the Seven Dwarfs (the Disney film came out only the year before), and they are introduced just like them, too—though there are only six. In *Dead End* (1937), the film that introduced the troupe of "kids," there *are* mothers, sisters, daughters, and teenage girls, as there are in Cagney's *The Public Enemy* and *The Irish in Us*. But here there are only guys.

Indeed, the first thing they do after Rocky's arrival is reconvene for lunch in Rocky's room: domesticity is all male. When Rocky is present, Jerry's only choice is to take a place at the table, and only upon Rocky's bidding. It is chaotic and earthy—manners not necessary, and of course the beans have their inevitable effect. Respecting Jerry's desires, Rocky insists that the boys now go to play basketball, against a team of regular, more experienced boys. Midway in the game, stepping onto the court to serve as referee, replacing Jerry, Rocky disciplines the gang of boys by turning their roughhousing—bear cubs at play, really—back upon them. The channeling of violence is compounded: the Irish Catholic male hoodlum has taken over a mother's role of civilizing ruffians, whom he half-inspires, half-forces to channel their youthful roughness into constructive play. Rocky harnesses the physicality that is constitutive of his masculine glamour to the "right raising" of the male young. It is muscular uplift—big brotherly, involving a jocular style—that deepens their appreciation of him. At the same time, it sidelines Jerry, who stands in Laury's corner watching in gratitude and rekindled admiration.

It is crucial to the sexual dynamics of the scene that Laury is already there, on the sidelines, watching. Determined to be good, Laury is nonetheless drawn to the combination of violence and discipline. She enjoys both the rough, potentially dangerous energy of the boys and the disciplining of that energy by Rocky's own rough hand. Later in the film, Laury begs Jerry not to go "after" their friend. But in truth she is less a competitor to the rekindled buddydom of Jerry and Rocky than she is a coconspirator. Laury bears witness to male-male love in all its permutations (paternal, avuncular, brotherly, filial). She bears witness to the centrality of controlled ferocity. And she bears witness to the kinds of sacrifice—individual self-discipline, sporting teamwork, good cop/bad cop role playing—that sharpen the competitive edge. In this utopian moment on the basketball court, hypermasculinity meets with the girl's approval. "No matter whether he is right or wrong, we both love him," she attests.

In the following segment, while the boys take what my mother calls "sponge baths" at a public facility, Laury is, reasonably enough, nowhere in sight since this is male-only space. But as it turns out, she's still there, just outside the door, ready with the needed towels, in effect waiting on the guys while also waiting, pre-

3.2. Father Jerry (Pat O'Brien) and Rocky (James Cagney) together in friendship, while Laury (Ann Sheridan) can only watch.

sumably, for Rocky's particular attention. And while nearly universal gender proprieties leave the scene to her imagination, we in the audience, including the women and girls among us, receive a locker-room treat, to the fullest extent possible given the era. We watch the boys bathe their upper torsos at a long, two-sided (affording us views fore and aft) communal sink, in a cliché of gay visual representation. Of course it is Rocky who presides, insisting that each of the boys cough up the requisite nickel. At the end of the scene, Jerry pulls what looks to be a deflated basketball from the back of ringleader Bim's (Leo Gorcey) trousers. (Rocky has them so taken with basketball now that they want to practice on their own, thus the pilfering of the ball.) Even in 1938, what is the film doing putting Father Jerry's hands down the boy's pants?

Loyalty in Jeopardy

To point toward the physical if not sexual—erotic, sensual—dimensions of this male world is not, however, to underestimate its sentimental commitments. From the beginning, the issue between Jerry and Rocky is loyalty: Rocky saves Jerry twice, first at the train, then by talking him out of turning himself in. The issue with Frazier, the crooked lawyer, is one of loyalty, too. When Rocky agrees to take the fall for both of them, he warns Frazier that they have made a deal. After prison, when Rocky is forced to blackmail Frazier and the crooked politician/racket boss Mac Keefer (George Bancroft) in order to retrieve his part of the loot, for Rocky it's a matter less of greed than of honor among thieves. In the reunion scene, after Jerry says that Rocky has been costing him a lot of prayer (meaning, he has been watching over him even when they've been out of touch), Rocky confesses that he saw Jerry—who apparently played fullback for, say, Fordham or Notre Dame— make some locally famous game-winning run (meaning, with pride, I've been watching you too, old friend).

Jerry was once a football player, Rocky his secret cheerleader? So, underneath his priestly frock, Jerry is tougher than the citified boy scout (nay, den mother) he appears to be. Self-reliant and proactive, Rocky is nonetheless more worshipful—more loving of Jerry *and* more God-struck—than he admits, even to himself. The sex roles are not as straightforward as they first may seem.

Hollywood films are driven by what contemporary studio executives call "jeopardy": what is placed in danger. At risk throughout *Angels* is the bond between Jerry and Rocky. In the crucial plot turn, midway through the film, Jerry discovers that his uplift program, which looked so promising after Rocky's help, is actually in trouble, in part because Rocky has been handing out easy money but also simply because he is who he is: the gangster as urban folk hero, endlessly glorified by the press and in street talk. The recent bright promise of the gym, it appears, is about to go up in poolroom smoke. Coming to the realization that the glorified gangster reflects the corruption of society at large, Jerry vows to fight the system as a whole, above all the illicit connection between the mobsters and city hall. That means "going after" Rocky, of course, despite their friendship. Not only is Rocky in his way, as Jerry attests, but, in Jerry's opinion, Rocky is beyond salvation, at least beyond earthly salvaging: "I would give my life for him, if I thought it would do any good. But it won't."

The ensuing crusade against organized crime triggers the events that send Rocky to the electric chair. Predictably enough in gangster films of the thirties, it's the little guy who has clawed his way to the top of the underworld who dies at the end, defeated and inglorious. But the kicker is how and why. If love between men is the acid test for God's work on earth (as *Angels with Dirty Faces* wants us to believe), then it is of sacred significance that Rocky the Lion-Hearted (who is the secret true believer) won't let his special loyalty to his old friend, Jerry, go. As it turns out, Rocky does what he does, garnering the death penalty, because of his love for Jerry. As it also turns out, Rocky dies the way he does because of his love for Jerry. In that otherwise tragic death miraculously lies multiple redemptions, including even, perhaps, Rocky's own.

At key instances, director Curtiz arranges the actors into striking tableaux: the boys huddled around Rocky in the cellar hideout, the detectives and uniformed cops huddled around Rocky in the police station, Rocky addressing Laury from the side while she watches the game and we look head on. The blocking of movement, in sync with the camera motion and shift of focus, is never better than in the great confrontation scene: Jerry returns Rocky's anonymous $10,000 donation to the gym fund and announces his resolve to expose the corruption in which Rocky is knee deep. Halfway through their confrontation, Rocky (to the right of the screen) turns his back on Jerry (to our left), signifying his renewed alienation from the too-innocent world view that Jerry is articulating. Rocky crosses the room to sit down at the desk pressed tightly against the wall, his impish smile returning. Jerry follows, preaching honesty as the best policy, while admitting—under Rocky's interrogation—that it doesn't always come out that way. Rocky then walks in front of Jerry, and their positions on-screen before us are suddenly switched. Jerry's face becomes sharpened just in time for him, standing tall now, to announce his anti-corruption campaign. Placed for once on the right side of the screen, he uncustomarily shows us the "tougher" side of his face. The two are close, almost in each other's faces, but they remain respectful. The height differentiation is muted, and they are slightly backlit. Neither of them is treated to that angelic lighting from on high.

"There's a lot of people going to be stepped on," Jerry insists. "And if you happen to get in the way, I'll be sorry, but you'll be stepped on just as hard." Even before Jerry finishes, Rocky is smiling once again: "All right, Jerry, go to it." Paternalistically, Rocky warns him that the quest for an indictment might go for naught. He wants Jerry not to worry about hurting him but also wants Jerry prepared psychologically in case he doesn't succeed. "But yes, go to it, kid. And well if I'm in the way, just keep on stepping just as hard." Rocky and Jerry shake on it, man to man, but their hands are below the bottom of the screen, as the camera holds their two solid upper torsos and their two pairs of pledging eyes in its own strong gaze. Only then does Jerry ask "a favor" of Rocky: to back away from the boys.

It is difficult to read every nuance of Rocky's response. Rocky takes Jerry's announcement of his crusade with amused, even supportive grace. But he finds the request to leave the boys alone a harder pill to swallow. What Jerry is asking him to abandon are the interpersonal dynamics—the worshipful, emulative attention—of his own glamour. Yet swallow it, he does. In the end it seems he is more than a little proud of his priestly friend. There is a wicked tolerance and affection in his eyes: even Jerry is turning into a fighter. And Rocky now has the opportunity to take on a new role, that of a winged protector. With Jerry's unwitting help, Rocky is putting himself in the position—literally but also morally (since he is a sometime killer)—to make the ultimate sacrifice. In going after one another, they are to become closer, in fact and in spirit.

All along we've been indulged in our taste for violence, the genre violence of the gangster flick. The one recurring observation of real value in the contemporary reviews is how Curtiz and company managed to get gambling, girls, and guns—also corrupt cops and corrupt government officials—past the movie censors. In fact, the Warner Brothers studio executives, watching the rushes and leaning on Curtiz, were in constant negotiation with Joseph Breen over each and every turn of plot. While the film was eventually released in the United States, its distribution was prohibited in many countries, including Jamaica, Denmark, France, Poland, Francophone Switzerland, China, and the most Catholic province in North America, Quebec.[9] It did not screen in Montreal, Paris, or Geneva. So, how did *Angels* get away with it in puritanical America?

It would appear to be a simple accommodation: the rescue plot allows vice to be indulged because in the end vice does not win. And yet, bit by bit, violence of one sort or another is legitimated along the way. This lets us have our blood-thirst along with a little righteousness. Early on we watch Rocky trick Keefer's gangsters into shooting down one of their own men, in the phone booth in the drugstore. The turnabout may be fair play, but Rocky's sweet reversal is fairly brutal when you think about it (couldn't you have escaped any other way, ingenious Rocky?). It is not, however, nearly as brutal as it was supposed to be. In the original script the victim gunned down in the phone booth was supposed to be an innocent bystander—and not just any innocent bystander, but a pregnant woman.[10] The censors would not condone the murder of a pregnant woman even to signify deep immorality. Thanks to censorship, Rocky is saved from being a true beast. He is never the killer, even inadvertently, of innocent women and children, only of dubious men. The neat substitution of an anonymous, expendable bad guy for a mother-to-be preserves for us the better part of Rocky's aura.

Toward the end, when Rocky spontaneously shoots Frazier and then guns Keefer down, initiating the final crescendo of violence, the ethical justifications could not be finer. Rocky has just learned that Frazier and Keefer plan not only to betray him once again but to murder Father Jerry. And yet if guilt be known from the longer perspective, it is Rocky who has cornered himself into this fatal mess. He long ago failed Jerry, whose campaign against urban corruption was provoked not only by Rocky's lawlessness but by his undesirable hold over the boys. The moral self-cornering of Rocky is reflected in his capture. Taking flight into an empty building, Rocky is immediately surrounded by the police with spotlights, tear gas, and the proto-SWAT gear of the 1930s. In the final moment of the shootout, after Rocky has used Jerry as a screen to get out of the standoff alive, Rocky's face is lit eerily from below. The cornered gangster looks like a clown at a shrill pitch of sardonic glee—like Jack Nicholson's portrayal of the Joker in *Batman* (1989). It looks like, for a moment, the devil has won.

Redemption

Of course, it is not just gangster films that work the intersections of love and sacrifice, pain and witness. Christianity does, too, and on a much larger scale, a scale large enough, I argue, to absorb sociological angst and penal brutality into its myth-making shadow. The semi-justifiable murders of Frazier and Keefer escalate through Rocky's murderous last stand and then to one more death, Rocky's own. On a first viewing, we may well anticipate the deeper Christian question: is anyone saved by such a death, even Rocky? But little do we realize this first time through how Christ-like the answer is going to be: "all souls" are saved. Or rather, all the souls we have come to care about in the imagined world of the film.

The careful twists of the film put Rocky into the proper position—cornered killer turned avenging angel turned cornered killer—for a glorious redemption. Like a mass, the climax of the film is its penultimate moment. It is not when Father Jerry commands the boys to rise out of their cellar hideout, but the previous sequence, which takes us from Rocky's jail cell down the corridor to the public execution room to his death, that first terrifies, then stuns, and ultimately exhilarates the audience, bringing it to its feet. Even contemporary reviewers recognized the progression as the best part of the movie—"one of the most spine-tingling sequences of the year," "a punch...that few pictures have equalled for downright drama."[11]

Rocky, the focus of most of our affections and many of our hopes, goes to the electric chair. He marches, a dead man walking, accompanied by Father Jerry (whose last rites he has refused), a vicious guard, and the guardians of the state. Center right, we see the electrical box, in clear view, then the chair and the electrocutioner, in mysterious, forbidding silhouette. Jerry prays silently. The press

3.3. Father Jerry (Pat O'Brien) beatifically joins in the formal march to the electric chair.
Courtesy of the Academy of Motion Picture Arts and Sciences

looks on in morbid anticipation. Rocky presents the square-shouldered, firm-jawed defiance that has defined his public personality throughout the film. But as he climbs onto the death platform, silhouetted still, he suddenly cries out: "I don't want to die! I don't want to die!" Shadowed against the back wall, Rocky twists and struggles against the guards, piercing the room with primal squawks of outrage and fear. Then the camera moves in for a direct shot of his hands making their last grasps at a radiator nearby. "Please don't do this. Please don't kill me, please!" What an actor is Rocky, if acting this be, and acting probably it is. Jerry disconcertingly looks upward, radiant with gratitude. Then, with brilliant understatement, the switch is thrown, the lights flicker out, and with them Rocky's life.

The scene sends shivers down our spines. Even on a first viewing, the audience knows it has just witnessed something very special: this is not gangster business as usual. It is a peculiar yet powerful shadow form of the Christian passion in which Rocky, who has gunned down his enemies in vengeful but beneficent passion, is justly punished, wondrously absolved, and fantastically martyred, all at the same time.

Dying yellow was in fact Jerry's idea: Rocky refuses last rites but agrees at the last moment to one final chat with Jerry, who asks him to forgo his proud stoicism and act like a coward. Rocky shakes his head "no" but goes ahead and does it extravagantly, shrieking to high heaven with a terrible beauty. The act secures to varying degrees three facets of palpable redemption: the emotional consummation of Rocky's boyhood friendship with Jerry (assured on multiple accounts), Rocky's positive influence on the Dead End Kids, and Rocky's own soul, which lies outside the scope of realist representation but has a happy probability about it. The question of Rocky's intent puts agency at issue. Ultimately it ought, I think, to be seen as graced volition. Rocky freely chooses because he is enabled and affirmed—"blessed"—by the workings of the Holy Spirit. There is no question that the act is meant to be understood as fulfilling divine will, and that it does so by means of both earthly love (Jerry for Rocky, Rocky for Jerry, Jerry and Rocky for the boys) and all-too-human death (murderers murdered, avengers avenged, martyrdom secured)—all for our pleasure and illumination.

In *Angels with Dirty Faces*, Michael Curtiz transforms masculine sacrifice into salvific masculinity by means of violence experienced and witnessed. The theatrical display of the state-tortured male body enacts an intergenerational redemptive wish, an intragenerational male-male love, and a personal salvation. It harnesses the ironclad secret of a priest's otherwise too-righteous social agenda to the closeted goodness of an alternative form of saving action, to a form of street Catholicism. The body is redeemed—not literally, at least not as we can see it in the film, but in terms of the earthly desires and commitments that have made it tick. The male-male intimacy, physicality, and communion are especially sanctified. And that redemption is not for the squeamish. Violence as both lived reality (inward pain, externally generated and visibly registered) and ritual theater (the crowd, the newspapers, and then, ultimately, *us*—watching) is integral to the spiritual force. Violence is the vehicle of salvation. The apparent sacrifice of masculinity becomes a real salvific masculinity—really redemptive, because, at the last, it is an even stronger version of an Irishman's dangerous charisma.

The newspaper headlines pronounce just punishment; it's in sync with the official Catholic judgment of record. But the open secret of Rocky's sacrifice suggests a true redeeming force of street Catholicism that operates underground and unofficially, close to the bone of real male experience, emotion, and action. And from that perspective, Rocky might be said in the end to redeem Jerry's social-work vision, a vision that stands in for official Catholicism itself. The sinner saves all, even the social efficacy of the Catholic church.

Rocky may be saved, he may even be a savior, but his story is no conversion narrative. With the sudden, shocking clarity of 20/20 movie hindsight, we now see that Rocky has been primed for this act, in his own ways has even courted this act all along. But what is at stake in *Angels with Dirty Faces*, finally, is not the personal achievement of transcendence, the Emersonian heritage of Protestant disembodiment that lays the responsibility for salvation on the mental state of the individual, radically alone. Rather, it is the collective realization of Catholic immanence, that dream of incarnate grace that comes through friendship and gangs and couplings.

In one of the truly insightful comments at the time of the movie's release, an anonymous reviewer for *Time* magazine noted that the movie doesn't really stop at the very final scene, with the boys climbing to light and freedom, but continues via the viewers, who are "in" on what has really happened.[12] Not the gang but the audience becomes the witnessing, hence saving, community. Mrs. Richard M. White, chair of the Los Angeles District of the California Federation of Women's Clubs, wrote a letter of complaint to censor Joseph Breen on that very point. She understood the implicit message of collectivity, arguing that "in the eyes of the five or ten MILLION REAL boys and girls who may see this, the gangster is a glorious hero, even in his death."[13]

Yes, Rocky is a hero. Of what does his glory consist? It's impossible to know how the young of 1938 actually responded. In the twenty-first century, *Jarhead* (2006) uncovers how the dead-end kids of patriotic, post-9/11 America used the antiwar films of the Vietnam era as a pre-battle psyche-up for Desert Storm soldiering. All we can be sure of is this: the Rocky whom I experience, the Rocky the film asks us to experience, dies in the embrace of the courageous, altogether Christian hope that others might live better—perhaps even saved—lives.

NOTES

1. Frank S. Nugent, "The Film Runs True to Type," *New York Times*, 27 November 1938; "The New Pictures," *Time*, 5 December 1938, 29; "Angels with Dirty Faces," *Variety*, 26 October 1938; "Angels with Dirty Faces," *Film Daily*, 24 October 1938; "Angels with Dirty Faces: Study in Criminology," *Motion Picture Herald*, 29 October 1938. Other reviewers weighed the issue of too much "familiarity" but judged there were enough "new trappings" to yield "one of the most picturesque and dramatic of this year's crime studies"; see Edwin Schallert, " 'Angels with Dirty Faces': Superior in Melodrama," *Los Angeles Times*, 25 November 1938, and Frank S. Nugent, " 'Angels with Dirty Faces': Racy Guttersnipe Drama," *New York Times*, 26 November 1938.

2. Philip T. Hartung, "Return of the Waltz, Gangster and Submarine," *Commonweal*, November 1938, 133.

3. Dana Polan, "Commentary," *Angels with Dirty Faces* (DVD, Warner Home Video, 2005), ch. 1.

4. For example, see "The New Pictures," *Time*; Hartung, "Return of the Waltz, Gangster and Submarine"; Ray Zone, "Wrap Shot," *American Cinematographer* 83 (August 2002): 104.

5. Although he does not develop the concept, Christopher Shannon observes the same phenomenon. He writes that "Catholicism in *Angels with Dirty Faces* roots the grace of God in the city streets themselves." See "Public Enemies, Local Heroes: The Irish-American Gangster Film in Classic Hollywood Cinema," *New Hibernia Review* 8 (2005): 61.

6. Robert Sklar, *City Boys: Cagney, Bogart, Garfield* (Princeton, NJ: Princeton University Press, 1992), 33.

7. Mary Gordon, "'I Can't Stand Your Books': A Writer Goes Home," in her *Good Boys and Dead Girls and Other Essays* (New York: Viking, 1991), 202.

8. J. M. Jerauld, "Angels with Dirty Faces," *Motion Picture Daily*, 24 October 1938.

9. *American Film Institute Catalog*, s.v. "Angels with Dirty Faces."

10. Polan, "Commentary," ch. 12.

11. Nugent, "The Film Runs True to Type"; "Angels with Dirty Faces," *Film Daily*.

12. "The New Pictures," *Time*, 29.

13. Mrs. Richard M. White to Joseph Breen, n.d., *Angels in America*, MPAA Breen Office Files, Margaret Herrick Library, Academy of Motion Picture Arts and Sciences, Beverly Hills, CA.

FURTHER READING

Abbott, Megan E. *The Street Was Mine: White Masculinity in Hardboiled Fiction and Film Noir*. New York: Palgrave Macmillan, 2002.

Grieveson, Lee, Esther Sonnet, and Peter Stanfield, eds. *Mob Culture: Hidden Histories of the American Gangster Film*. New Brunswick, NJ: Rutgers University Press, 2005.

Kirkham, Pat, and Janet Thumim, eds. *You Tarzan: Masculinity, Movies, and Men*. New York: St. Martin's, 1993.

Lang, Robert. *Masculine Interests: Homoerotics in Hollywood Film*. New York: Columbia University Press, 2002.

Lehman, Peter, ed. *Masculinity: Bodies, Movies, Culture*. New York: Routledge, 2001.

McCabe, John. *Cagney*. New York: Knopf, 1997.

Munby, Jonathan. *Public Enemies, Public Heroes: Screening the Gangster from Little Caesar to Touch of Evil*. Chicago, IL: University of Chicago Press, 1999.

Rafter, Nicole. *Shots in the Mirror: Crime Films and Society*. New York: Oxford University Press, 2000.

Robertson, James C. *The Casablanca Man: The Cinema of Michael Curtiz*. New York: Routledge, 1993.

Sklar, Robert. *City Boys: Cagney, Bogart, Garfield*. Princeton, NJ: Princeton University Press, 1992.

4

JEWS AND CATHOLICS CONVERGE

The Song of Bernadette (1943)

Paula M. Kane

As often is the case in motion pictures, the backstory to a production can be as interesting and illuminating as the film itself. This is true of *The Song of Bernadette*, a sincere religious epic about a nineteenth-century French peasant girl who had a series of visions of the Virgin Mary and struggled during her lifetime to convince others of their reality. In *The Song of Bernadette* a fortuitous combination of Jews and Catholics produced what is still regarded as a genuinely affecting motion picture about Bernadette Soubirous. The film became immensely popular soon after its release two days after Christmas at the height of World War II. Its promotional poster was illustrated by none other than Norman Rockwell. Nominated for twelve Academy Awards, it won four, including best director (Henry King)—with Jennifer Jones beating out Ingrid Bergman and Greer Garson for best actress.

An equally significant part of the story is the history of the novel behind the screenplay, and the religious identity of its author and his family. *The Song of Bernadette* was based on a 1942 novel by Franz Werfel, a Jewish writer who fled Nazi Czechoslovakia with his wife. As reviewers were fond of pointing out, the book resulted from a vow that Werfel made during his escape to tell the story of the Lourdes miracle, an action that certainly appealed to Catholics, who knew all about making vows. For centuries, Catholics have promised Jesus, Mary, and the saints to perform special acts in return for answers to their prayers. Werfel's interest in Marian visions stemmed from the fact that while fleeing from the Nazis he had been sheltered by Catholics in Lourdes, the home of Bernadette and the famous pilgrimage site on the border between France and Spain. Within three months of his arrival in New York, Werfel wrote *The Song of Bernadette* in longhand to fulfill his vow "that I would evermore and everywhere in all I wrote magnify the divine mystery and the holiness of man." As a reviewer for *Catholic World* observed, "Franz Werfel has himself become a sequel to the very tale he told." The reviewer estimated that by 1944 readership for the best-selling novel numbered over one million with purchased copies of the book documented at over 500,000.[1] By the time the movie appeared, it was commonplace to cite both Werfel's escape and his writing of the novel as further evidence of Bernadette's miracles.

Werfel's wife, Alma, was a devout Catholic and the widow of the famous composer Gustav Mahler, who was born a Jew but baptized a Catholic in 1897. Alma became so immersed in the film project that she attended the recording sessions for the film's remarkable musical score by Alfred Newman. Newman, a secular Jew praised for his lush orchestrations, researched Catholic choral, convent, and liturgical music in order to produce sounds to complement Werfel's descriptions of French Catholic culture. A contributor to the accuracy of the novel's religious details was Father Cyrill Fischer, an early critic of Hitler who fled Europe and befriended Werfel in Santa Barbara, California, where he provided him with copious notes and information about Catholic rituals. The authenticity of Werfel's novel was hailed uniformly by the Catholic and secular press as a triumph of reverence for faith and an expression of love for humanity.

When translated to the screen, the commercial success of *The Song of Bernadette* was due to its successful integration of the preoccupations of secular, nonobservant Jews with those of religious, practicing Catholics during an era of heavy-handed censorship of Hollywood films. The combination provided war-weary Americans with a way to make sense out of their sacrifices and sufferings by allowing them to see themselves as Bernadette—embattled but eventually triumphant. *The Song of Bernadette* also illustrates how the ethical concerns and cultural position of Hollywood's Jews could be articulated through the religious images of Catholics, another minority American religion. There is no evidence that secular Jews and practicing Catholics intentionally sought to make a movie that spoke to a common set of values. Rather, what we have are a series of individual associations, where Jews and Catholics worked together on a religious film that reflected the concerns of a nation at war. Each individual had his or her own reasons for participating in *The Song of Bernadette*. It was the Hollywood studio system that brought them together, requiring them to subsume their own individual artistic impulses under larger industry needs. The result is a backstory that illustrates how very different personalities came together to make a film about faith that would appeal to a multireligious audience.

The Film and Its Visual Impact

Catholic director Henry King picked the unknown actress Jennifer Jones (née Phyllis Isley) to play the visionary. Early in his career King had shown himself a fan of themes of the struggle between divine and earthly delights. In 1932 he had directed Lillian Gish in *The White Sister*, based on the 1909 novel by Marion Crawford about an Italian heiress who believes her fiancé has died in World War I combat and decides to enter the convent, only to have him return. A decade after this film, King was happy to consider the real-life tale of a French saint. Phyllis Isley, a product of Catholic convent schooling from Tulsa, Oklahoma, was twenty-four years old when she was asked to play the fourteen-year-old Bernadette. Although Isley was then Mrs. Robert Walker with two children, this information was deliberately kept from the public by the studios in order to construct her innocent and radiant image. Jones's portrayal of the visionary is heartfelt but not saccharine, and her adolescent faith provides a contrast to the eroticized screen females of the Hollywood studio system that was then promoting Joan Crawford, Marlene Dietrich, and Mae West.

During the filming of *Bernadette*, Jones became the protégée of David Selznick, the independent producer who had brought *Gone with the Wind* (1939) to the screen. Selznick was captivated by the newcomer both professionally and personally. On the first day of filming, he gave her a leather-bound first edition of the novel signed by its author. A nonobservant Jew, Selznick would later divorce his wife, Irene (the daughter of Jewish producer Louis B. Mayer), and, after her divorce from Walker, marry Jones in 1949. The collapse in 1945 of the Cinderella marriage of Robert and Phyllis Walker (Jennifer Jones) was shocking. Robert, also an actor, suffered a series of nervous breakdowns following the end of his marriage, was arrested for drunkenness on several occasions, and relied upon sedative drugs administered by his physician to periodically calm him. He died in 1951 from respiratory failure at the age of 33.[2]

Jennifer Jones played a French peasant girl who in 1858 believed she had received visions of the Virgin Mary. In addition to the visions, a spring appeared and people who washed in it or drank from its water felt they were miraculously healed. From the late nineteenth century, American Catholics began importing and using water from the shrine at Lourdes. The story of Bernadette's visions at the grotto had gained enough popularity by the 1940s that devotion to Our Lady of Lourdes registered as a favorite Catholic practice in the United States. Distribution of the water underscored the belief in miraculous healing and affirmed Catholics' desire for connections to the maternal kindness of the Virgin Mary. Catholics even gave Protestants vials of the water with the hopes that miraculous cures would prompt their eventual conversion. Ever since the Victorian era, some Protestants had shown an almost erotic desire for the physicality of Catholic devotion. By using Lourdes water, Protestants indulged in the practices and symbols of Catholicism, a material faith denied them since the Reformation. The Virgin Mary in particular held fascination for many of those who had traveled to Europe. The dynamic of attraction to and repulsion from Catholicism has long defined the identity of Anglo-Protestants in the United States. A film about Bernadette and the events at Lourdes served as a twentieth-century vehicle to explore the power of Mary and of miracles.

4.1. An overriding theme of the film is the power of simple faith to change even the stoniest of hearts. Here the imperial prosecutor (Vincent Price) challenges the sincerity of Bernadette (Jennifer Jones). *Courtesy of the Academy of Motion Picture Arts and Sciences*

A written "Foreword" appeared on-screen before the movie action began, setting the motion picture's tone: "To those who believe, no explanation is necessary. To those who do not believe, no explanation is possible." David Selznick wrote to his trusted friend Ben Hecht (who chose the epigraph from the novel) commenting, that was "the only good foreword to a picture I ever saw outside of those you have written for me." Selznick's letter to Hecht indicates that he had given considerable thought to how an audience should be addressed: appeals to the heart, to the invisible dimensions of life, were best because they neither negated nor ridiculed the viewer. A reviewer for *Catholic World* slyly hinted that divine intervention permitted the Foreword to appear verbatim: "The motion picture producers, generally ruthless in tampering with fact to make it fit popular demand, apparently were awed into letting *The Song of Bernadette* stand as it was. Some unseen influence may well have been at work."[3]

The quotation dissolves to the film's opening scene of the rainy rooftops of Lourdes, panning to the interior of a home where two sisters are asleep in bed. We soon see that the entire Soubirous family sleeps in the same one-room dwelling built into the town wall, which some have identified as the jail; the impoverished parents arise before dawn so the husband can seek work. Later, the daughters head out to collect firewood, traversing the bridges, paths, and squares of Lourdes. Set designer Thomas Little rendered Lourdes as a credible French village, with poorer and richer citizens, old stone walls, a church, a café, and the town hall. (The art and interior direction received one of the film's four Academy Awards.) Alfred Newman collected hymns and themes from the nineteenth century that he crafted into its Oscar-winning music. The actors speak in English but trill as they pronounce "Berrrrnadette."

The movie's European locale and Old World atmosphere of peasant faith and miraculous springs made it a far cry from the urban ethnic neighborhoods that were already defining American Catholic existence in film. *The Song of Bernadette* is unique among Catholic-themed movies because it points back toward a medieval (or at least Victorian) Catholicism. This was a world of the cult of saints and belief in the power of faith to redeem, not a world of urban parishes populated by quarrelsome and anxious immigrants trying to become Americans. Still, the conversations heard in the village streets and discussed in the cafés made sense to a modernizing people: how should one judge the validity of claims about the supernatural? How can one persuade people of the truth of personal experience? How does one stand up against the powerful systems of family, government, and science that negate religion?

While waiting at one side of the river for her two sisters, Bernadette has her first vision of "a beautiful lady" near a cave known as Massabielle. Mr. Soubirous

4.2. The art and interior direction received one of the film's four Academy Awards for creating both a realistic French village and a believable apparition. *Courtesy of the Academy of Motion Picture Arts and Sciences*

thinks his daughter is merely showing off. At her next vision, however, the lady speaks and asks Bernadette to return to the same place for the next fifteen days. Soon neighbors and town officials are involved, each expressing their opinions at length. The imperial prosecutor, Vital Dutour (Vincent Price), is an archpositivist convinced that "The entire reputation of the town is at stake!" (Could he be referring to Los Angeles as well as Lourdes?) A doctor finds in Bernadette no evidence of hysteria or catalepsy, mental illness or fraud. The senior church official in the region, the Dean of Lourdes (Charles Bickford), finds no religious significance in the alleged apparitions. Throughout, as Bernadette is questioned by an array of doubting doctors, police, scientists, and churchmen, the sincerity of her responses is undeniable.

A blind stonecutter experiences the first miracle when his sight is restored by the spring water discovered by Bernadette. The crowds accompanying her to the apparition sites grow. In the lady's final revelation of herself as the "Immaculate Conception," the seer has to be told by a priest what this means. The town's civil bureaucrats become concerned about crowd control and invoke a 1789 law to close the grotto and its "miraculous" spring. It is then reopened by order of the emperor when his child's aristocratic governess is among those arrested for visiting the grotto. Bernadette meets with nothing but skepticism throughout her life, which sees no improvement with her increased notoriety. Her modest goal is to become a lady's maid, but this is not to be as she is put into a convent and receives the habit of the Sisters of Charity of Nevers. At the convent she meets up with a former adversary who is now her novice mistress, Sister Marie Therese Vauzous (Gladys Cooper). The nun manages to heap the heaviest convent chores upon the seer and interprets even Bernadette's foot injury as part of an egotistical desire for attention. In spite of her difficult life, Bernadette expresses nothing but happiness about her condition. Of course all of the cynics are converted at the end, when Bernadette's death from painful tuberculosis of the bone is shown in a prolonged bedside scene where the saint is graced with a final vision of the lady.

The comments of the real nuns and priests who were present on the set are credited with helping to create religious characters who act as ordinary humans with feelings and flaws. Director Henry King consistently opted to show how

4.3. Bernadette's (Jennifer Jones) modest goal is to become a lady's maid, but this is not to be as she is put into the convent and receives from the bishop the habit of the Sisters of Charity of Nevers. *Courtesy of the Academy of Motion Picture Arts and Sciences*

Lourdes transformed the lives of believers (and unbelievers) rather than glamorizing the visions as a source of instant comfort, health, or prosperity. He does not ignore the opportunism of town officials who imagined that the visions would promote local tourism. (They were prescient, since four million pilgrims still visit the town each year.) King also further developed Werfel's representation of the arrogance of the nuns and priests who came into contact with Bernadette, particularly the novice mistress who insists that Bernadette could not possibly have seen Our Lady because she has not known suffering. The cult of suffering, associated with the heyday of devotional Catholicism contemporaneous with the film, is integral to the film's sense of Bernadette's life. Thus her torturous death at the end of the movie is presented as the enviable chance to be reunited with Mary in heaven. An overriding theme of the film is the power of simple faith to change even the stoniest of hearts: the dean of Lourdes, the stern novice mistress, and even the prosecutor for Emperor Napoleon III finally become convinced by the girl's sincerity and lack of duplicity.

Judging from reviews, American audiences loved *The Song of Bernadette*. In its opening week, *Variety* commented, "Despite the deeply religious tone of the dramatic narrative, the theme has been handled with utmost taste and reverence.... But to every person who sees 'Bernadette,' there is warmth, inspiration and pause for reflection regardless of creed or non-belief." Reviewers did not see a film about a French Catholic saint but rather a universal story of spiritual conviction. "No matter what your faith," said the *World Telegram*, "no matter whether you like the novel, no matter whether you like movies at all, *Bernadette* will give you solidly enduring pleasure." The reviewer for the *Hollywood Reporter* fully understood the reverberation of the film with the home front of World War II. He concluded that "the inspired message it brings to a war-torn world is impelling and impressive by virtue of an inner essence to which audiences instinctively respond." Catholics were overjoyed by their presentation on the silver screen. The editor of the Los Angeles Catholic newspaper was so deeply moved that he wrote to the producer, William Perlberg: "So long as I live I shall not forget the artistry of Jennifer Jones, of the director, Mr. King, and of the cameramen in that magnificent scene wherein Bernadette's face, transfigured by the vision, suddenly loses its expression of enthrallment as the Lady bids farewell. Such a scene is art of a high degree."[4]

Criticism was slight: a woman who attended an opening night benefit with a group of Catholic ladies reported for the *Catholic World* that a few found the picture "over-long," while others found it "over-sad," especially the gloomy convent scenes. Some wanted Bernadette to have been encouraged to marry, prompting one reviewer to respond, "they forget that earthly joys must seem ephemeral to those who have glimpsed all eternity." Well-regarded film critic James Agee delivered the sharpest criticism. While recalling the Catholic resonances of his childhood and admitting being moved by the film, he cynically called it "a tamed and pretty image, highly varnished, sensitively lighted," fixed behind a glass window that was at once a shrine and a box office. His jaundiced view of *Bernadette* in the pages of the *Nation* is consistent with his general critique of the stifling power of American middle-class "genteelism" as a "fungus which by now all but chokes the life out of any hope from Hollywood." In a second article about *The Song of Bernadette*, Agee expressed concern that the film's admirable cinematic perfection is being dedicated to such "worthless effects" as the naïve ecstasy of a young girl. His view has not prevailed. More than six decades later, modern audiences may deem Bernadette too oblivious to the normal worldly concerns of those around her, but Web sites devoted to reviewing older films as they are converted to DVD formats still consistently award *Bernadette* their highest ratings.[5]

Censoring Catholics

The village of Lourdes on-screen appeared in a certain way because Catholic censors had much invested in their own representation to an American public. *The Song of Bernadette* brought together Jews and Catholics, who each imposed their own stamp on the film. To fulfill his vow, novelist Franz Werfel wrote pious reflections about a saint, thus cultivating ties to Catholics, who were happy to promote his novel to Hollywood's largely Jewish-controlled movie industry. Catholic censors, concerned to insinuate themselves into the heart of Jewish Hollywood, would eventually become themselves industry insiders by shaping production standards in ways that benefited the studios and punished independents and foreign rivals to the American movie industry. Jews would benefit from their efforts through box-office profits and in terms of increased cultural capital. By delivering high-minded and even sacred topics on-screen as antidotes to the charges of vulgarity that were launched against them by Catholics and Protestants, Jews joined Catholics as new participants in the American cultural and moral mainstream.

The Song of Bernadette was made in Hollywood during the era of the Production Code for motion pictures, which remained in effect until 1966. The Production Code was widely hailed by its supporters as protecting national morality and blasted by film critics and filmmakers as attempts to straitjacket aesthetic freedom and to meddle in the mechanisms of a private industry. The contents of this code, coauthored by Daniel Lord, a Jesuit priest from St. Louis, and Martin Quigley, a Catholic publisher of a film trade journal based in Chicago, defined censorship norms for movies for over thirty-five years.[6] These men and many like them believed that the movies worked in two ways upon the public: immoral films fostered immoral actions, whereas uplifting films inspired good deeds. Bad language, "unnatural" sexuality, the mixing of the races, making fun of religion—these were immoral acts to be eliminated. Righteousness was to be promoted. After Joan of Arc became a saint in 1922, she was memorialized in more than thirty films. Bernadette, canonized in 1933, could potentially edify and inspire an equal if not larger audience. While enforcing the code frustrated Hollywood moviemakers and infuriated progressive Americans, studios tried to uphold the standards presented to them and to adopt self-regulation. Rebellion did occur but it was the exception rather than the rule.

It may seem odd to consider here the effects of censorship upon a film depicting a Catholic saint, but all movies, even religious ones, came under the scrutiny of the code. Before *The Song of Bernadette*'s production began in 1943, the script was reviewed like any other. The film did not appear to represent any of the difficulties of the sex comedies or criminal dramas which drew frequent demerits on the censors' checklists, but it did bear the notable burden of purporting to represent supernatural episodes in the recent history of a living religious tradition. A Catholic visionary had to be represented with respect and authenticity. Also, *The Song of Bernadette* was being made during a world war defined by heightened social anxiety over the "godless" Nazi threat, suspicion of Hollywood Jews, and the decline of world markets for Hollywood films. Care had to be taken that no parties would be offended by the film.

William Hays and Joseph Breen were the major enforcers of the Production Code. William Harrison Hays, a Hoosier Presbyterian from Indiana, had run the Republican party's campaign to elect Warren Harding as president in 1920. Hollywood studio heads appointed Hays as president of the Motion Picture Producers and Distributors of America (MPPDA) and charged him with making sure that the films that were made were worthy and met the standards of the Production Code. From 1922 to 1945 he spoke for the motion picture industry from his office in New York City. The "Hays Office" became synonymous with studio self-regulation, which enabled the studios to avoid government interference with movie production. Hays's credentials as an upright Protestant American helped to deflect criticism of Hollywood movies.

In 1934 Joseph Breen, a salty Irish Catholic originally from Philadelphia, became Hays's West Coast assistant. It would be Breen, and not Hays, who would read and comment on every movie script produced in Hollywood. Joseph Breen genuinely liked movies and was known to help doctor an ailing script to health, yet like many Irish American Catholics he had Victorian taste in aesthetics. Books, drama, and the movies should not portray the real, scruffy world of life but rather should aim to uplift and to cultivate high sentiments. He took the arts and entertainments very seriously, assuming that if they represented evil, violence, or vulgarity then people would be socialized into acting in an antisocial manner. Breen had no sense that a film could be "just a movie" or "mere entertainment." Nor did he feel that serious issues should be explored in a realistic manner to raise questions and engage thought instead of directly presenting answers. Among the many epithets he acquired in his day was the "Hitler of Hollywood," although a more recent scholar has described him more generously as "the agent of ambivalence" since he was not the unswerving mouthpiece of his boss, Will Hays, Wall Street bankers, or the Legion of Decency. Breen's high moral standards, however, did not keep him from sharing the sentiments of many Christians of the 1920s and 1930s. He too believed that Jews were an unsavory and money-grubbing people and not to be trusted. In 1932 Breen wrote to Martin Quigley, "The fact is that these damn Jews are a dirty, filthy lot." Breen's anti-Semitism was not only a personal prejudice; it reflected a calculated strategy of playing Jewish movie studio executives and Catholic bishops against each other in order to consolidate his own influence over Hollywood. Like many Catholic intellectuals of the period, Breen felt that he was defending what we might call "Western civilization." He understood his values not to be specifically Catholic and thus only appropriate for one community of people but rather he believed that his worldview encompassed all morally upright Americans. For twenty years, until his retirement in 1954, Breen carefully read scripts and laid out his objections, thus crafting movies in his aesthetic and moral image.[7]

When he arrived in Hollywood, Breen immediately attacked the representations of prostitution, narcotics, sex, and rough language that were the mainstays of many films. He honed in on an easy target, the actress Mae West, supervising with an eagle eye the production of her third film, *Belle of the Nineties* (1934). In it, such one-liners as "It pays to be good—but it don't pay much" did not amuse the guardians of the Code. Four and a half pages of deletions were demanded, and the Hays Office insisted that the scriptwriter establish "compensating moral values" to atone for its overall degrading tone.[8] By the time that *The Song of Bernadette* was in production almost ten years later, movie censorship was well established. Even a movie about a saint, especially a movie about a saint, would feel the hand of Joseph Breen.

The sections of the Production Code dealing with religion stated merely, "No film or episode may throw *ridicule* on any religious faith. *Ministers of religion* in their characters as ministers of religion should not be used as comic characters or as villains. *Ceremonies* of any definite religion should be carefully and respectfully handled."[9] Henry King and his film crew made every effort to observe these three norms, as studio production notes attest. Any lines in the script that seemed critical of the Catholic Church and its representatives were recommended for deletion, the village priest's contempt for Bernadette was toned down, and advice on the correct performance of religious rituals was sought from Catholic sisters living in the Brentwood neighborhood of Los Angeles.

Things seemed to be going well at the outset of *The Song of Bernadette*: Overall, Joseph Breen approved of the script: "We are pleased to advise you that, in our judgment, this material seems to conform to the provisions of the Production Code, and contains little, if anything, that might be questionable from the standpoint of political censorship." Breen then went on to identify those pages of the script where expressions uttered by characters, such as "Mother of God" or "God above" or "What in God's name?" or "Why for the love of Christ?" should be removed. He also requested that the director "eliminate from the scene in which [Mr.] Soubirous gets drunk all reference to his being a member of the Holy Family. We are certain that this will give serious offense to a great number of people. It might well be that you could eliminate the entire scene." Thus, *The Song of Bernadette*'s potentially objectionable aspects concerned blasphemy, not crime or sexuality. Breen therefore asked the producers to remove from the script references to God when used for swearing. With its customary precision, the Production Code forbade: "Pointed profanity (this includes the words, God, Lord, Jesus, Christ—unless used reverently—Hell, S.O.B., damn, Gawd), or every other profane or vulgar expression however used."[10] The reproduction of the reality of peasant *patois* was no excuse for having to listen to bad language.

Other objections by Breen were merely appeals for accuracy in the use of the Catholic Church's religious titles, such as replacing the word "Ecclesiasticals" by "Ecclesiastics." As with the phrases above, Breen edited content to avoid blasphemy and to avoid giving the impression that Catholics treated sinfulness lightly or that Hollywood was ridiculing their piety. For example, "We suggest the rewriting of the Bishop's speech at the bottom of the page: 'A saint who flirts with boys and takes a husband and bears children would be too much of an amusing innovation.'" Breen's attention to detail was impressive. "Again," he wrote, "on Page 127 you ought to check with a priest concerning the technique of the action set forth in Scene 281. It is our impression that a priest would not be wearing a surplice, and he would not be administering the Sacrament of Extreme Unction to a baby. It might be well, also, to have your technical adviser check the various prayers which are set forth throughout the entire story." Breen recommended to Henry King that he "secure the services of a very competent Catholic priest, who will serve as a technical adviser on this picture. We think it is enormously important that you have a very competent priest read the script thoroughly in order to check much of the dialogue and action."[11] As a result both priests and nuns were regularly present on the set for consultation. Father John J. Devlin, the executive secretary of the Legion of Decency in Los Angeles, was the chosen cleric who oversaw many Hollywood movies.

The Lourdes apparitions of 1858 were believed to uphold and confirm the 1850 pronouncement by Pope Pius IX of the dogma of Mary's Immaculate Conception. Consequently it is not surprising that Breen asked for a check of the "speeches by the Dean, setting forth the doctrine of the Immaculate Conception," along with "various scenes wherein the Chaplain, at the death of Bernadette, recites certain excerpts from the Song of Songs, and also the statement of the Pope, set forth on Page 229." Otherwise, there was little fuss about a relatively arcane "mystery" of the Catholic faith except to emphasize Bernadette's refusal to retract it. Clearly, religion per se was not a target of Hollywood censors. Of the 157 films made between November 1939 and November 1943 that received a "B" rating from the Legion (a rather imprecise category of films which all viewers were to avoid on the grounds that they violated some moral standards), only one was cited for disrespect for religion.[12]

American Catholics eagerly supported wholesome alternatives in Hollywood and guaranteed audiences for them. Father Emmett Regan, director of Cathedral Book Club in Chicago, wrote to Joseph Breen with such a plan for *The Song of Bernadette*:

> The preview would be held at the Esquire Theatre, which I am sure I can get for the day. There would be three performances—one at 2:00 for the nuns; one at 4:00 for the Priests and Brothers, and the Big One at 8:30 p.m. with all the Church dignitaries attending. Of course, the Mayor etc. would be there. I have some of the cream of Chicago society [who] would act as the committee. In short we would give it the biggest possible blow.... Catholics predominate in Chicago, and I know it would take. If it were the great success it should be, other towns could follow suit.

America's bishops had already concluded ten years earlier that "many apparently have lost all sense of discrimination between right and wrong," and so Father Regan's plan answered this moral vacuum. *The Song of Bernadette* would permit Americans to see the right. Regan sought to bring the captains of industry and politics together with princes of the Church to enjoy a good motion picture.[13] The

Church's paternalist strategy of trying to mediate between high culture and the masses had a long history, albeit one whose time was soon to run out.

Book clubs and special screenings were positive ways of exerting pressure on Hollywood, but Catholic pressure was also expressed negatively. In 1933 Catholic bishops and lay leaders established the idea of a "Legion of Decency" that would enlist Catholics only to attend wholesome motion pictures and to condemn all others. To join, individuals stood up and recited a pledge: "I unite with all who protest against them [vile movies] as a grave menace to you [Christ], to home life, to country and religion. I condemn absolutely those salacious motion pictures which, with other degrading agencies, are corrupting public morals and promoting sex mania in our land." The text of the pledge remained unchanged until 1957. The Legion of Decency's pledges were administered through parishes and schools but no accurate total is available because not every Catholic organization sent its figures to the diocese. One report by the American bishops suggested a total of more than five million pledgers as early as 1934. Another estimate from June of that year claimed that an astounding eleven million Catholics had signed pledges.[14]

Eventually the Legion of Decency, with headquarters in New York City, came to rate individual films. Studios would try to send their reviewers films before they were released to the public in order to learn what the Legion found to be objectionable. The Legion of Decency claimed no power to censor film content but in effect did just that by rating every film for its moral value and publishing "black lists" of objectionable and condemned films and "white lists" of acceptable films. More than a moral watchdog, the Legion of Decency forced filmmakers "to change dialogue, cut scenes, and add prologues and/or epilogues (which often changed the meaning of the film) in order to avoid Legion condemnation." By wielding its threat of condemnation, "the Legion effectively censored films."[15] Pope Pius XI exhorted other nations to follow suit and establish organizations like the Legion of Decency. In 1936 his encyclical *Vigilanti cura* ("With Vigilant Care") acknowledged the American bishops' efforts to "safeguard the recreation of the people," and the pope attributed the improvement of motion pictures to their attentiveness.

Although there were other Christians and Jews who supported the Legion of Decency, Protestants were divided about Catholic censorship efforts. Particularly after *Vigilanti cura*, when the American hierarchy doubled its efforts to mobilize Catholics against objectionable movies, Protestants began to fear popish domination in addition to the film industry's immorality. As we have seen, Protestants historically were wary of Catholics, who were thought to blindly follow their pope. Striking a typically sour tone, a minister attacked the Legion in the *Protestant Digest*, noting that "the minority control of the most vital amusement sources of the nation is one of the most astounding things in the history of the United States."[16] Nevertheless, films like *Bernadette* appealed to many Protestants precisely because they defended common values—piety and godliness—as the mainstays of civilized people against the barbarism of fascism.

Were Catholics asserting too much in assuming that their values alone should determine what films could be made and seen? Did Hollywood's Jews regard the Legion of Decency as a nuisance or a violation of the First Amendment? Not necessarily. Studio heads rarely challenged the administration of the code and insisted their writers submit their scripts and integrate Breen's suggestions. The film studios acted in conservative fashion because they did not want to jeopardize profits. During the golden era of Hollywood, studios not only made films, they also distributed them and owned the theaters in which they were shown. The threat of a boycott or even diminished theater attendance could have serious financial repercussions. Therefore, studios welcomed the centralized form of censorship represented by the Production Code, which was preferable to piecemeal or localized efforts that would have created an uncertain climate for a film's reception. By having their own industry oversee the moral quality of films, studios also avoided having the federal government regulate the movies as was done in England. When audience members objected to something on the screen, studios could simply point to the eagle eye of Joseph Breen. David Selznick was one of the few producers who disliked the censorship system generated by the Production Code enough to confront it with the release of *Duel in the Sun* (1946). However, Selznick was an independent producer who never had the support of the other studio heads to challenge the power of the Legion of Decency. In short, "the industry deserted him."[17]

While there is no question that Jewish artists and intellectuals chafed at the standards of decency promoted by Joseph Breen and Catholic organizations, there also is evidence of grassroots Jewish support for the Legion of Decency pledge. In Denver, the Council of Jewish Women and the Sisterhood of Temple Emmanuel signed up a thousand pledgers.[18] Middle-class Jewish women mobilized to pressure Hollywood for proper movies in the same ways that Catholics did. By supporting Catholic efforts to promote ennobling films, such Jews were joining forces with fellow religious outsiders in America to claim citizenship and to assert that they too belonged to mainstream society. Protestants were not the only religious Americans who upheld values that restricted sexual expression, promoted an idealized community over the real city, and valued disciplined personal behavior. As minority groups were being destroyed in Europe by Nazis and fascists, in the United States they strongly claimed that they were the true upholders of American morality—as could be demonstrated in the life of a French saint.

Making and Unmaking Saints

Hollywood could not predict how long St. Bernadette would be a popular saint among Catholics, hence it was savvy business practice to cash in on her fame on film at the same time that Werfel's novel was topping the bestseller list. This meant that, for director Henry King, avoiding scandal was crucial in the casting of its central character, the young visionary, Bernadette. This role, Bishop Cantwell of Los Angeles opined, should be given only to "one whom no breath of scandal has ever touched." This "unknown girl" must be free of connections to any film character associated with marriage comedies, divorces, "sarongs, bathing suits, etc."[19] When the part was given to a relatively unknown actress, one of the striking behind-the-scenes stories became how "Jennifer Jones" was created in order to establish her purity and spiritual devotion, as though she herself were a saint.

As we have seen, David O. Selznick was the Jewish power behind the making of a Catholic saint. Selznick claimed that when he first read *The Song of Bernadette* he suggested Phyllis Isley Walker for the part. He then suggested the name change, began an affair with the new star, married her in 1949, and went on to manage her screen career. Even so, Selznick also was not above trying to lowball her signing salary with MGM, describing Phyllis as "a girl who has done nothing, or next to nothing, and we think of starting her at $200.... I think we are losing all sense of proportion.... We have been thrown way out of line by such exorbitant figures as we paid to Vivien Leigh and Ingrid Bergman at the time we signed them. Let's get down to earth." A workaholic who let no detail slip his notice, Selznick terrorized staff and stars alike with long detailed memos and personal confrontations. Selznick told his advertising and publicity director what to say about Jones in screen magazines, including the anecdote that he himself had insisted she stay in New York for nearly two years to receive dramatic coaching prior to launching her Hollywood career.[20]

In the 1940s a Hollywood star's off-screen life corresponded to her on-screen image. Selznick fashioned a public façade of perfection by his obsession with the details of Jones's costuming, lighting, and public appearances. To a certain degree this fantasy aspect of Hollywood paralleled the Catholic Church's reigning Thomist aesthetics of "the good, the true and the beautiful," which likewise idealized reality. Representation equaled reality. In the same way that the life story of a saint is pared of its unorthodox details to fashion the official hagiography, Phyllis Isley was crafted into Jennifer Jones and then into St. Bernadette. Her name was changed; the fact that she had made films before *The Song of Bernadette* was suppressed; her marriage and children were off-limits to reporters. Once the family was revealed, however, Jones was portrayed as living a Cinderella existence. Her separation from her first husband, Robert Walker, during *Bernadette* was concealed. Off-screen, Jones was to be blameless. On-screen, as the nonsexual, convent-enclosed, mystical Bernadette, she fulfilled the expressed demand from Church authorities, the Legion of Decency, and the Production Code administration for more respectable female characters in film.

David Selznick, however, had no interest in cultivating Jones as a motion picture mystic. Selznick realized that playing a Catholic visionary would limit Jones's career options and perhaps undermine his role in influencing her professional development and her personal attachment to him. He did not want her to be typecast as Ingrid Bergman was after playing a nun in *The Bells of St. Mary's* (1945). Consequently, he cast Jennifer Jones in a steamy role in *Duel in the Sun*, a saga of Texas ranchers and railroads in the 1880s. Apparently Selznick found the film so arousing that he stood near the set, moaning aloud at Jennifer's scenes. Hollywood insiders dubbed the film "lust in the dust." The Legion of Decency accused Selznick of coarsening the "dignity and loveliness of . . . Saint Bernadette" into "a wholly immoral subject of the flesh." They demanded thirty-two cuts be made in the film to prevent it from being rated "condemned." Selznick was so outraged by the requirements to alter his film that he requested a Gallup poll on movie ratings, which discovered that only 5 percent of moviegoers would refuse to see a film with a "C" rating. But most of the changes were eventually made, and when the film opened in the Catholic strongholds of Boston, Chicago, and Philadelphia it did a booming business with its less-problematic "B" rating. Jennifer Jones's portrayal of a sensual half-breed Indian woman in *Duel in the Sun* helped to reconstruct her as a screen fury, but her saintly image was also maintained. Her subsequent divorce and marriage to Selznick, her miscarriage, and a suicide attempt in 1967 were kept from the public view. Selznick's intuitions about the era's audiences had merit. In 1950 when Ingrid Bergman (*Joan of Arc*, 1948) left her husband for the Italian director Roberto Rossellini, she caused a scandal that sent her popularity plummeting. By the mid-1950s the couple was in financial ruin. Audiences took seriously their nuns and saints during this golden age of movies by conflating representation and reality.[21]

Techniques of the Miraculous

Making Bernadette seem real on-screen was no easy task. Through the masterful use of the special effects of the day, Bernadette became a luminous yet real saint who participated in what looked like real miracles. The film not only provided a powerful notion of how saints (especially female ones) acted, it showed audiences how the holy actually *looked*. Getting audiences to believe in the miracles of *The Song of Bernadette* was the result of powerful performances by its cast and the work of technicians behind the cameras. Special lighting techniques for the film were the brainchild of Arthur Miller, a colorful and strong-willed artist. As cinematographer for Twentieth Century Fox, the studio that produced *The Song of Bernadette*, Miller had directed the photography for *Brigham Young* (1940), *Tobacco Road* (1941), and *How Green Was My Valley* (1941). The same year he did *Bernadette* he filmed *The Ox-Bow Incident* (1943), and in 1950 he would work again with King on *The Gunfighter*. "I very much enjoyed making *The Song of Bernadette*," Miller reported. He "always got on" well with its director, Henry King, but Miller scoffed at what he termed King's "mysticism." Miller, unlike movie audiences and the film's director, did not confuse Hollywood dream making with the "real" supernatural. He ridiculed King's gullibility in mistaking his technical achievements for "something spiritual," which "had crept into the picture from heaven!"[22] Nonetheless, King's sure-footed and respectful touch in *The Song of Bernadette* was essential for the movie's ability to represent the spiritual without becoming sappy or laughable.

Arthur Miller preferred high-contrast lighting with crisp, sharp, and solid images rather than the soft-focus style of some of his contemporaries. Even in *The Song of Bernadette*, where gauzy images of the Virgin Mary appear in several scenes, Miller left his mark. He photographed the stony niche that would surround the Virgin (Linda Darnell) before special effects director Fred Sersen inserted Mary's figure. The hard, physical presence of the cave contrasted with the glow surrounding Bernadette, a glow that grew stronger and stronger. To generate Bernadette's aura of holiness, Miller employed a theater lighting technique that he had mastered working with the child movie star Shirley Temple. He created Shirley's "aureole of golden hair" by using the radiant effect of an electric lamp with a 250-watt bulb behind a metal reflector. With a rheostat attached to the lamp, Miller turned the light up and down from a position several feet above her eyes to place the other actors in low light and illumine the star in "high key." The result was a glowing blonde halo on the child "that made her whole damn image world famous." Miller used the same technique for Jones as the saintly Bernadette, explaining how the actors' gaze helped his strategy: "I'd have the actors look down a little in that one, too, while Jennifer would look up." On the screen, the actress glows with what looks like a heavenly light.

Miller skillfully mustered the elements of darkness as well as light to accentuate sanctity. Both the cave-like Soubirous home set into the village wall and the

JEWS AND CATHOLICS CONVERGE

interior of the grotto prior to the Virgin's visit are devoid of illumination. Near the close of the film in the first shot of the shrine after it has become a major pilgrimage site, light breaks the grotto's darkness. As the camera slowly pans the cave's interior, now lit by the long candles of hundreds of pilgrims, it reveals the many crutches from healed visitors left to hang from the walls and ceiling of the shrine. The scene gradually shifts focus from the reverent crowd singing hymns and reciting the litany of the saints, to the figure of the imperial prosecutor, shown in close-up gazing upon the vision site from behind the bars now guarding the Virgin's statue. His spiritual conversion, one of Bernadette's spiritual triumphs, is enhanced by the cinematography of the twinkling of the points of candlelight behind him. In contrast with more recent films about miracles and saints, such as *Household Saints* (1996) and *The Third Miracle* (1999), whose supernaturalism remains ambiguous, *The Song of Bernadette* is unequivocal.

Crucible of War

The Song of Bernadette was a supernatural wartime film, albeit an apolitical one. As Americans on the home front managed to make do with less of everything during wartime rationing, they felt pride in making themselves useful to the all-encompassing effort of defeating the Nazis. Hollywood responded in various ways, from producing all-out propaganda films such as the *Why We Fight* series (1943) to more subtle representations of common national goals, such as the need for Jews and Catholics to bond together over their faith in faith. Rather than referencing the war even indirectly (although a discreet notice to "buy war bonds at this theater" appears on-screen before the final credits), *Bernadette* achieves its effect by detailing how Bernadette spiritually transforms her eventual champion, the Dean of Lourdes, and her convent mistress. Bernadette, a much-abused peasant girl, gains the power to change minds through her purity and integrity. Unlike the feisty and ubiquitous neighborhood priests of other Catholic movies, she carries no reference to Catholicism challenging Protestant authority in America's urban centers. Rather, as a woman, she reflects beloved attributes of the cult of domesticity in both her piety and her submission to spiritual authorities. Bernadette listens to the higher authority of God and the voice of her "lady," and she never gives up trusting in what she knows is right.

Bernadette embodied an important way of imagining the victory of the Allied forces over the Nazis. Even the embattled prevail over the powerful as long as they stick to what they know to be true. Bernadette's unjust persecution by nearly all of those around her was also a subtle way of suggesting that, like the saintly girl, the Jews of Hollywood were victims, not victimizers. While Hollywood's moviemakers refused to use their movies to send messages about the destruction of European Jewry or even to reflect on Jewish life in America, it was possible on-screen to send a message that Jews were not the money-grubbing and base demons of Joe Breen's imagination. They too were moral and upright seekers after the good, the true, and the beautiful. Even the ego of David Selznick could be hidden beneath the constructed beauty and innocence of Jennifer Jones.

For Catholic audiences, the visual and aural evidence of Lourdes as the home of a real saint and of real miracles made *The Song of Bernadette* into "a living song." Bernadette insists, against the wills of her family, the French state, and the institutional church that her religious experience is true. *The Song of Bernadette* shows that God, through Mary, really does intervene in history to remind humans of the power of faith. At a time when the nation was asked to come together, overlook their differences, and support a generic religious "faith," *The Song of Bernadette* reminded Catholics that they still had a very specific history and devotional lives. They could embrace that difference *and* be true Americans at the same time. Franz Werfel, the genius behind Bernadette's song, was the source of such a project since he was judged a trustworthy Jew because he was nearly Catholic. The Catholic community embraced this refugee/novelist for his ability to represent them with sensitivity and affection. In return, Catholics admired and publicized his novel and the film to the fullest extent possible. In his review of *The Song of Bernadette* James Agee noted the film's artfulness and sincerity. Although from his perspective this a wasted effort, the combination assured box-office gold.[23] Saintliness aside, that was the perennial miracle sought by Hollywood. It seems that with *The Song of Bernadette*, everyone's prayers were heard.

NOTES

1. Franz Werfel, *The Song of Bernadette*, trans. Ludwig Lewisohn (1942; reprint, New York: St. Martin's, 1989); Raoul E. Desvernine, "*The Song of Bernadette*: A Literary Mystery," *Catholic World* 159 (1944): 248. Prior to the novel's publication, Werfel had sent the manuscript to Archbishop Francis Rummel of New Orleans for comments and had received helpful advice from other priests as well. See UCLA Library Special Collections, Franz Werfel Papers.

2. David Selznick to Franz Werfel, 24 February 1943, cited in *Memo from David O. Selznick*, ed. Rudy Behlmer (New York: Viking, 1972), 317. On Robert Walker,

see his obituary, *New York Times*, 30 August 1951, reprinted in Jeffrey L. Carrier, *Jennifer Jones: A Bio-Bibliography* (Westport, CT: Greenwood, 1990), 125.

3. David Selznick to Ben Hecht, 24 November 1948, quoted in Behlmer, *Memo from David O. Selznick*, 376; and Desvernine, "A Literary Mystery," 248.

4. Rev. Thomas J. McCarthy to William Perlberg, 15 October 1943, Werfel-Mahler Papers, Annenberg Rare Book & Manuscript Library, University of Pennsylvania.

5. *Variety*, 22 December 1943; *World Telegram*, 27 January 1944; *Hollywood Reporter*, 22 December 1944; Euphemia Van Rensselaer Wyatt, "The Song of Bernadette," *Catholic World* 158 (March 1944): 584; James Agee, *Nation*, 29 January 1944 and 20 January 1945, cited in *Agee on Film* (New York: Modern Library, 2000), 56, 124–25.

6. The fullest account of the adoption of the Production Code is Stephen Vaughn, "Morality and Entertainment: The Origins of the Motion Picture Production Code," *Journal of American History* 77 (June 1990): 39–65.

7. Leonard J. Leff and Jerold L. Simmons, *The Dame in the Kimono: Hollywood, Censorship, and the Production Code* (Lexington: University Press of Kentucky, 2001), cite Breen's reputation as the "Hitler of Hollywood" on page 60, and Leonard Leff gives him the kinder appraisal in "The Breening of America," *Pacific MLA* 106 (1991): 443. The letter from Breen to Quigley dates from May 1932 and is also cited in *The Dame in the Kimono* (47).

8. Leff and Simmons, *The Dame in the Kimono*, 48.

9. Motion Picture Production Code of 1930, Section VII, "Religion."

10. Joseph Breen to Jason Joy, 29 January 1943, Production Code Administration Files for *Song of Bernadette*, Margaret Herrick Library, Academy of Motion Picture Arts and Sciences, Beverly Hills, CA (hereafter cited as PCA). I thank Colleen McDannell for securing this reference and subsequent citations from the Herrick Library. Motion Picture Production Code of 1930, section V, "Profanity."

11. Joseph Breen to Jason Joy, 11 March 1943, PCA. All quotations in this paragraph are from this letter.

12. Paul Facey, S.J., "The Legion of Decency: A Sociological Analysis of the Emergence and Development of a Social Pressure Group" (Ph.D. diss., Fordham University, 1945), reprinted in the *Dissertations on Film* series (New York: Arno, 1974), 98.

13. Rev. Emmett Regan to Joseph Breen, 11 January 1944, PCA.

14. Report of Bishop John T. McNicholas at 1934 meeting to create the Legion of Decency, cited in *Ecclesiastical Review* 91 (August 1934): 113. The five million figure comes from Facey, "Legion of Decency," 57; and the eleven million estimate from Olga J. Martin, *Hollywood's Movie Commandments: A Handbook for Motion Picture Writers and Reviewers* (New York: Wilson, 1973), 33.

15. Gregory D. Black, *The Catholic Crusade against the Movies, 1940–1975* (Cambridge: Cambridge University Press, 1997), 240.

16. "Breen—Super-Censor," *Protestant Digest* (June–July 1940), quoted in "Report to the Episcopal Committee on Motion Pictures, 1940" (made annually by the executive secretary of the National Legion of Decency), cited in Facey, "Legion of Decency," 206.

17. Black, *Catholic Crusade against the Movies*, 243.

18. "Facey, "Legion of Decency," 60, citing the Episcopal Committee report.

19. Bishop Cantwell's sentiments were cited by Florence Rounds to Joseph Breen, 16 August 1942, PCA.

20. On Jones's pay, see Selznick to D. T. O'Shea and Katharine Brown, 24 July 1941, cited in Behlmer, *Memo from David O. Selznick*, 301; on her need for coaching, see Selznick to Don King, 30 May 1944, in ibid., 331ff.

21. This discussion of *Duel in the Sun* is drawn from Black, *Catholic Crusade against the Movies*, 45–55 (quote on 50). On the Ingrid Bergman divorce scandal, see her many biographies and fan Web sites.

22. The discussion of Miller's cinematography is drawn from an interview published in Charles Higham, *Hollywood Cameramen: Sources of Light* (Bloomington: Indiana University Press, 1970), 142– 43, 149.

23. James Agee, *Nation*, 20 January 1945, cited in *Agee on Film*, 124–25.

FURTHER READING

Black, Gregory. *The Catholic Crusade against the Movies, 1940–1975*. Cambridge: Cambridge University Press, 1997.

Buhle, Paul. *From the Lower East Side to Hollywood: Jews in American Popular Culture*. London: Verso, 2004.

Carrier, Jeffrey L. *Jennifer Jones: A Bio-Bibliography*. Westport, CT: Greenwood, 1990.

Gabler, Neal. *An Empire of Their Own: How the Jews Invented Hollywood*. New York: Anchor, 1989.

Harris, Ruth. *Lourdes: Body and Spirit in a Secular Age*. New York: Viking, 1999.

Kaufman, Suzanne K. *Consuming Visions: Mass Culture and the Lourdes Shrine*. Ithaca, NY: Cornell University Press, 2005.

Leff, Leonard J., and Jerold L. Simmons. *The Dame in the Kimono: Hollywood, Censorship, and the Production Code*. Lexington: University Press of Kentucky, 2001.

McDannell, Colleen. "Lourdes Water and American Catholicism." In *Material Christianity: Religion and Popular Culture in America*, ed. McDannell. New Haven, CT: Yale University Press, 1995.

O'Toole, James M. *Habits of Devotion: Catholic Religious Practice in Twentieth-century America*. Ithaca, NY: Cornell University Press, 2004.

Rogin, Michael. *Blackface, White Noise: Jewish Immigrants in the Hollywood Melting Pot.* Berkeley: University of California Press, 1996.

Schatz, Thomas. *Boom and Bust: American Cinema in the 1940s.* Berkeley: University of California Press, 1999.

Skinner, James M. *The Cross and the Cinema: The Legion of Decency and the National Catholic Office for Motion Pictures, 1933–1970.* Westport, CT: Praeger, 1993.

Solomon, Aubrey. *Twentieth Century Fox: A Corporate and Financial History.* Metuchen, NJ: Scarecrow, 1988.

Thomson, David. *Showman: The Life of David O. Selznick.* New York: Knopf, 1992.

Walsh, Frank. *Sin and Censorship: The Catholic Church and the Motion Picture Industry.* New Haven, CT: Yale University Press, 1996.

5

America's Favorite Priest

Going My Way (1944)

Anthony Burke Smith

During the summer of 1944, the movie *Going My Way* introduced American film audiences to a new role for Bing Crosby. The popular movie star, singer, and radio host was cast as Father Chuck O'Malley, a young Catholic priest who rescues a working-class parish from financial ruin. Picking up where *The Song of Bernadette* left off, the movie dominated the box office in 1944 and earned seven Academy Awards, including best picture and best actor for Crosby's performance as the smooth, modern priest. *Life* magazine marveled that his performance "is one of the few satisfying interpretations of the priesthood to emerge from Hollywood." The *Christian Herald* called it "one of the finest pictures of the year." The Jesuit magazine *America* gushed, "[T]his is the freshest, most original material that has recently been brought to life on celluloid."[1] An upbeat story about Catholic clerics had become the sensation of wartime America. The character of Father Chuck O'Malley was so well loved that "Father Chuck" characters have become a staple in popular Catholicism.

But the movie's impact did not stop there. While Father O'Malley was forced to leave his parish by the end of *Going My Way*, the film's version of the priest has repeatedly turned up in movies ever since. A year after Crosby strolled out of St. Dominic's, he returned as Father O'Malley in a sequel, *The Bells of St. Mary's* (1945).

There he did gentle and barely concealed romantic battle with a strong-willed Sister Mary Benedict, played by Ingrid Bergman. The acclaimed *On the Waterfront* (1954) transformed Crosby's affable parish priest into a hard-hitting champion of social justice, Father Barry (Karl Malden), who works on the Jersey docks. Later in the decade, *Say One for Me* (1959) resuscitated the cleric/king of the 1944 box office by casting Bing Crosby as another Catholic priest, Father Conroy, serving a parish of Broadway performers. The effort, however, only resulted in clarifying how tired the *Going My Way* formula had become.

An attempt to update the formula came with Otto Preminger's *The Cardinal* (1963). Based on a 1950 novel, the movie pushed the priestly persona in new directions as it situated the story of a young parish priest in Cold War America. The film pays homage to *Going My Way* by having its young priest, Stephen Fermoyle (Tom Tryon), start out in an urban parish. Like Father Chuck, he butts heads with an older Irish superior. Yet this priest enjoys wider vistas and has much grander ambitions. Gone is the familiar neighborhood. Father Fermoyle prays and plays politics in the choicest spots of the Catholic world, including Vienna and Rome. By the end, the movie has Fermoyle (now a cardinal) mouthing the platitudes of American civil religion. As he is given the red hat that symbolizes his new power as a cardinal, a prince of the church, he proclaims that "all men alike are the children of God, endowed by their creator with the unalienable right to life, liberty, and the pursuit of happiness. That is America's creed; that is the gospel of the Church." The new cardinal is sounding the same sentiments as John F. Kennedy, the recently assassinated Catholic president. By the 1960s, the Catholic ethnic neighborhood—which Hollywood used as a microcosm of the nation in general—was being eclipsed. In its place were the images of an international Catholicism that more closely paralleled the growing American global empire.

As demonstrated by the numerous incarnations of Father O'Malley in movies, *Going My Way* marked a key moment in the cultural history of Catholics in America. Crosby's performance as a cleric hip to the ways of the world set a new standard for the representation of Catholicism in the popular imagination. Audiences encountered a powerful new image that overturned long-standing stereotypes of Catholic authority. Father O'Malley, more than any depiction of the celibate Catholic cleric up until then, created a new icon in the nation's religious vernacular—the priest as American hero. Idealized and even fantastic, *Going My Way* offers a powerful benchmark to help us understand Catholicism's place within American culture, and it has influenced the representation of Catholics ever since.

The movie revolves around two priests, the young Americanized Father O'Malley and the elderly Irish pastor of St. Dominic's, Father Fitzgibbon (Barry

5.1. Sent by the bishop to quietly take charge of parochial affairs and set the parish straight, Father O'Malley (Bing Crosby) faces the resistance of the stodgy Father Fitzgibbon (Barry Fitzgerald), who is suspicious of O'Malley's youthful attitudes. Here, Father O'Malley signals to the older generation who's really in charge of American Catholicism.

Fitzgerald). The older priest takes pride in the church he has built over forty-five years into an influential institution in its New York working-class neighborhood. His achievement, however, is threatened by mounting debts and the threat of foreclosure on the parish mortgage by Knickerbocker Savings and Loan. Sent by the bishop to quietly take charge of parochial affairs and set the parish straight, Father O'Malley faces the resistance of the stodgy Fitzgibbon, who is suspicious of O'Malley's youthful attitudes. Despite the older priest's skepticism, Father Chuck quickly starts revitalizing the parish community. He guides the local gang of street kids, led by Tony Scaponi (Stanley Clements), out of trouble by taking them to ball games and movies and forming them into a choir group. He lends a hand to a young, single woman who is new to the city and keeps her from falling astray. He runs into an old girlfriend who is now a star with the Metropolitan Opera, and she enables him to turn one of his songs into a contract with a recording company, which pays off the debt on St. Dominic's. All the while Father Chuck and Father Fitzgibbon increasingly overcome their personal differences. Even a fire that destroys the parish church is not able to ruin the two priests' growing friendship. At the end of the film, when O'Malley leaves to rescue another parish, St. Dominic's has already begun to rise from the ashes, and Father Chuck's easygoing modern style of priesthood has triumphed, winning over even the curmudgeonly Fitzgibbon.

West Coast Catholics

The relaxed playfulness that informs *Going My Way*'s portrait of Catholicism struck a decidedly different note from the rigid and contentious image usually associated with urban Catholics in America. This may have been due to three of the film's main creators and their West Coast Catholicism where the cultural power of the church was not as great as in the Northeast. Bing Crosby grew up in a mixed Irish Catholic–Yankee household in Spokane, Washington. His mother was a strict Catholic, while his father converted to the faith in order to marry her. Crosby attended the local public schools for his primary education. As a teenager he served as an altar boy in his parish and transferred to the Jesuit-run Gonzaga High for secondary schooling. He attended college at Gonzaga but left before graduating in order to pursue a musical career, joining a group of kids from the public high school to form a band.[2]

Going My Way's director, Leo McCarey—who also wrote the story and produced the film—was another West Coast Catholic of mixed ethnic background. His father, Thomas Jefferson McCarey, was an Irish American and a famed boxing promoter in early twentieth-century Los Angeles. His mother, Leona, was French. McCarey attended both Catholic and public schools in Los Angeles and earned a law degree from the University of Southern California. One of his aunts was a nun at the Immaculate Heart Convent in Hollywood, and McCarey claimed she was an important influence on his life. A third Catholic involved in *Going My Way* was the songwriter Johnny Burke, who penned some of the film's top hits, including "Swinging on a Star." Burke, like Crosby and McCarey, was born on the West Coast. Originally from northern California, he attended the University of Wisconsin before making it big as a songsmith.[3]

The backgrounds of Crosby, McCarey, and Burke all suggest Catholic experiences distant from the ethnic tribalism of the Northeast and Midwest. It is significant that the film that epitomizes urban Catholicism in America was made by men with little attachment to the fabled Catholic enclaves of Boston and New York, Chicago and St. Louis. *Going My Way* privileges a fluid, almost boundaryless Catholicism thoroughly at ease in modern America. Freed from the restraints,

memories, and practices of ethnic traditions that might trouble Catholic participation in modern America, the film valorizes the informality of California living.
Catholics who in later years railed against *Going My Way* for its distortions of
Catholic life have missed the fact that the filmmakers were never rooted in
"ghetto" Catholicism to begin with. Rather, the film embodies a West Coast vision
of big city Catholicism. *Going My Way* reimagines and remakes the dense, complex,
and fractious world of the urban parish into an easygoing, supportive, and savvy
community. Although the film is set in a New York metropolis filled with tenement apartments, McCarey leads us to imagine a future of endless golf greens,
sweetly sung jazz, and fulfilled dreams. McCarey uses the Catholic parish and its
priests to imagine a postwar future in the tolerant and modern suburbs. There,
leisure and self-realization triumph over the hard work and traditions of the past.

Safe Spaces

At the center of *Going My Way*'s construction of a new-style Catholicism is its
rendering of space. The film attends quite consciously to the spaces of Catholicism
and its urban context in order to blur the borders between Catholic particularity
and modern, popular Americanism. In so doing, the movie addresses the long-
standing fear in American culture of Catholicism as a religion of dark and dangerous places. Stretching back to the antebellum era when nativists attacked
convents in Boston and bestsellers chronicled the depravity of priests, depictions
of space have long functioned to signify Catholicism as an alien and threatening religion. In *The Awful Disclosures of Maria Monk* (1836), for instance, a young
woman is held captive in a convent where she is forced to perform degraded
and ungodly acts. The enclosed and protected sacred spaces of the Catholic
tradition—convents, monasteries, cathedrals, shrines—were construed by Protestants to be spaces of entrapment, bondage, and superstition. In those semi-
secret places, many nineteenth-century Americans imagined a powerful and corrupt Roman church reigning against the purifying influence of reason and
individual freedom. By giving special attention to the physical and social world of
the Catholic urban parish, *Going My Way*'s story of the two priests of St. Dominic's
directly challenges this image of Catholicism as dangerous or mysterious. Visual
depictions of space in the movie encourage the construction of the Catholic priest
as an American urban hero by transforming the Catholic place of danger and
incomprehension into the place of the ordinary and the prosaic. Further, as Father
O'Malley travels through the city, Catholicism becomes woven into the forces of

contemporary culture. Like Father Chuck, Catholicism is imagined as effortlessly crossing numerous cultural boundaries and bridging many distinct spheres of American life.

Early in the movie, Father O'Malley makes his first appearance in a long scene on the crowded tenement streets of a poor, working-class neighborhood. He is looking for St. Dominic's, his new parish church. The scene opens with a low-angle shot of a woman, Mrs. Quimp (Anita Sharp-Bolster), washing her apartment window. Off-camera we hear someone politely introducing himself and asking directions. That voice, of course, is Crosby's. The film audience, therefore, *hears* America's favorite crooner before it actually sees Father O'Malley. The next shot, a high-angle one that looks down on the priest in Roman collar and straw boater hat, isolates O'Malley on the street. Bing Crosby is dramatically presented in this shot, casting a shadow against a building, looking up, neatly appointed in a crisp clerical suit. Yet the straw boater stands out against his black suit, signifying O'Malley's character as a different kind of priest. Sitting jauntily atop the priest's head, the boater suggests a sense of ease and relaxation that undermines the traditional association of clergy with the rigidities of doctrine and the powers of ecclesiastical office. The film's initial construction of the priest emerges in the play between orthodox religion signified by the Roman collar and black suit and the leisurely insouciance of the boater. The boater's casualness exploits the audience's understanding of the persona of Bing Crosby, who was loved in the 1940s as a singer with an easygoing, relaxed manner. From the beginning, McCarey exploits the audience's prior familiarity with Bing Crosby in order to facilitate the creation of a particular kind of Catholicism. Crosby makes the space a known space.

The scene unfolds as O'Malley takes the place of a youngster in a game of stickball on the busy city street. This playfulness ends with the baseball flying through an apartment window. The irate window owner confronts O'Malley, demanding he take responsibility for the damage. The placement of the disgruntled owner on the second floor looking down at O'Malley as he chastises the priest reiterates Quimp and her cold response from her second-floor window to the priest's request for directions. As the confrontation escalates, the camera follows O'Malley up the stoop to the man's second-floor balcony. The priest's saunter creates a smooth and confident bodily performance paralleling what the boater signified in the earlier establishing shot of O'Malley. This figure of Catholic authority confronts a hostile environment with good humor and ease. His voice, dress, and walk all function to disarm the edgy neighbors. The scene ends with O'Malley being sprayed with water from a cleaning truck. Any sense that all priests are distant and authoritarian characters is dissolved in the slapstick. Father

5.2. Father Chuck O'Malley (Bing Crosby) uses the front steps as an informal place to discuss business with Ted Haines, Jr. (James Brown) while Mrs. Quimp, one of his parishioners (Anita Sharp-Bolster), listens in. The priest's straw boater sits jauntily atop his head, suggesting a sense of ease and relaxation that undermines the traditional association of clergy with the rigidities of doctrine and the powers of ecclesiastical office. *Courtesy of the Academy of Motion Picture Arts and Sciences*

Chuck's role in the neighborhood will be that of a regular guy. His character reflects the feel of the space around him: casual, direct, physical, and busy—a distinctly American space.

Father Chuck is surrounded throughout the movie by spaces that have lost their traditional confining character. An enclosed rectory garden is situated between the rectory and the church. Far from signifying entrapment, the garden functions as an oasis of nature and light that contrasts with the busyness of the city streets. A gently gurgling fountain that Fitzgibbon shows O'Malley assumes a prominent position in the camera shots of the garden. A statue of the Virgin Mary and another of St. Anthony linger in the background but neither draw attention. Here again the focus is on the "non-Catholic" character of Catholic space.

The depiction of place to signify the world of the priests is further developed by the rectory itself. Its interior design exudes the values of cleanliness, propriety, and solidity thus suggesting not Gothic isolation but Victorian middle-class respectability. Early in the film a dinner scene with O'Malley and Fitzgibbon shows the two priests enjoying the trappings of traditional bourgeois living. A Tiffany-style lamp hangs from the ceiling over a white-tableclothed dining table set with crystal glassware and china. Oak doors, wainscoting, and wallpaper color the background. As O'Malley gets up to answer the door and the camera follows the young priest, we glimpse other rooms that feature well-upholstered furniture and vases of fresh-cut flowers. The dinner sequence is immediately followed by a shot that epitomizes the movie's framing of its priests as paragons of respectability: O'Malley seated at a piano playing a traditional tune in the rectory parlor. Even the lace curtains on the windows behind Father Chuck convey gentility. Farther in the background lies the garden, deepening the image of lightness and order. McCarey and set decorator Stephen Seymour have given us grandma's parlor, which is supremely respectable but also warm and comfortable. McCarey opens the domestic world of priests to us, and we see it filled with delicious food and tasteful appointments. This Catholic space turns out not to be secret and alien but rather familiar and desirable.

Father O'Malley as a modern priest knows more than the genteel world within the rectory walls. When a young woman, Carol James (Jean Heather), is brought to the priest for help in navigating the big city, O'Malley can speak with authority about the desires of youth. While this scene is in many ways an excuse to get Crosby singing, it also develops O'Malley's character as a man of the world. It is the priest who coaches the aspiring singer in how to sing a modern love song. Indeed, O'Malley even croons the tune to Carol. Though celibate, Father Chuck has experienced the world of romance and sexual attraction as we later learn that he has had a girlfriend, Genny Linden (Risë Stevens). Now a famous opera star, Genevieve not only helps to save the church, she functions in the movie to ground the young priest in "normal" heterosexuality.

Underscoring Father Chuck's sexual worldliness is Fitzgibbon's very different response to the young woman: he tells her to go home. "Being a wife and mother is a good enough start for you, like your mother," the older priest scolds. O'Malley, however, encourages Fitzgibbon to "open up our hearts, Father" and persuades the pastor to give Carol some money to help her stay off the street corners. This is, of course, not old-fashioned church charity but rather a loan just so she can get by. Father Chuck realizes that women have dreams of lives beyond their parents' homes and need to be treated like adults, not children.

The film's presentation of Catholic spaces as sites of normal human life extends to its inclusion of the church basement. Once the underground site of

5.3. Gone is any sense that Catholics are hiding something as the basement of St. Dominic's now serves as a place of song and male camaraderie. In this shot of the filming of a scene, note the lighting equipment. *Courtesy of the Academy of Motion Picture Arts and Sciences*

Catholic political and sexual perversion in the anti-Catholic imagination, the basement of St. Dominic's serves as the place where O'Malley gives his first singing lesson to a group of neighborhood street kids, led by the skeptical Tony Scaponi. A wide, long-distance shot incorporating the low ceiling and sheets draped over furniture makes the basement appear as a large and airy storage room rather than the labyrinth of hidden chambers and dark passageways of nativist literature. When O'Malley appears clad in his St. Louis Browns jacket and baseball cap, he breaks down the kids' skepticism by appealing to their sense of fun ("I like fun as much as anybody") and leads them in the singing of "Three Blind Mice." He wins them over to his idea of forming a choir through his humor and his self-deprecating manner. With Father Chuck at the helm, the basement becomes a rehearsal hall, audition room, and stage with the boys the aspiring showmen. Highlighting the basement space as a stage for secular purposes is the crosscut to a shot of Fitzgibbon upstairs in the church kneeling before a side altar. He tries to pray, but the voices of the boys singing "Three Blind Mice" disrupt his meditations. A return to the basement shows O'Malley leading the boys in voice lessons.

In the background are a wheelbarrow, wooden boxes, and hay, which make the church basement (once imagined as a place of bondage) no more threatening than a well-used barn.

Father Chuck takes command not only of the interior basement spaces but also of the public urban world. He negotiates city places with ease, familiarity, and enjoyment. McCarey has the young priest taking the neighborhood kids to the movies, assisting an ornery and destitute parishioner, and playing a round of golf with Father Fitzgibbon and another young curate. We watch as he watches his old girlfriend perform as Carmen at the Metropolitan Opera House. Finally, we notice O'Malley playing his music with the parish kids at the Metropolitan in the hope of winning a record contract whose earnings will save the parish. By situating Father O'Malley in diverse places where the Roman-collared priest is welcomed by those he meets, Leo McCarey imagines a Catholic presence at the center of contemporary American culture. O'Malley functions as a Catholic link between working-class neighborhoods and elite cultural institutions such as the Metropolitan Opera. The multitalented priest has a jazz background, writes the whimsical song that wins the music contract, and trains the boys' choir in sacred music. Whether assisting a poor parishioner about to be thrown out of her apartment or playing a round of golf, O'Malley passes as both a socially conscious priest and a modern consumerist male. Calling on Bing Crosby's off-screen love of sports, McCarey creates a character comfortable with the many forms of American popular culture.

This all amounts to a continuous enactment of border crossings. The ease with which O'Malley crosses from the world of the parish into the wider city is contrasted with the difficulty that Father Fitzgibbon has in leaving the rectory. When the Irishman does move beyond the rectory, church, and garden, he finds himself lost. Yet this is not so much Fitzgibbon's personal failure as a sign of an older, ethnic Catholicism unable to negotiate modern mass-culture America. For both Leo McCarey and many postwar Catholics, quaint Old World priests needed to be replaced by American priests who were engaged with the modern world. *Going My Way* renarrates Catholicism as a story of acculturation in which ethnic parochialism gives way to mid-twentieth-century American cosmopolitanism.

A True Picture

That *Going My Way*'s light, easygoing story of priestly affairs touched deep cultural currents in 1940s America is apparent from the intense response the film generated. The movie had its premiere on 3 May 1944 at New York's Paramount Theater and enjoyed a record-breaking run of ten weeks. Movie houses around the country reported intense audience appeal, and it became the box-office champion of the year, towering over its competition particularly during the summer months of its initial release. Critics were generally quite pleased with the film. Manny Farber in the *New Republic* wrote that "though *Going My Way* is continually jazzed up with obvious entertainments and too-fortuitous circumstances, there are a number of fine things done with the circumstances, the most commendable being the natural, informal way that the people are allowed to go about." *Newsweek* described the movie as "a warm, delightful comedy of a kind that is universal in its appeal and close to tops as entertainment." The *Christian Herald* movie reviewer, A. O. Dillenbeck, asserted that the film "transcends all bounds of sect or creed in its human, wholesome handling of the politics and problems common to any Church of God." James Agee in *Time,* however, complained, "Strictly speaking this hardly has a right to pose as a religious film. There is no real contest with evil or with suffering and the good itself loses half its force." Apparently *Time*'s critic felt that the highly Americanized O'Malley lacked the proper gravitas necessary for authentic religion. And yet almost in spite of himself, Agee found himself admiring the film as a "beautiful piece of entertainment."[4]

In contrast to Agee, Catholics and Catholic reviewers applauded the film's religion. In September 1944 Sister Mary Madeleva, poet and president of St. Mary's College in Notre Dame, Indiana, wrote to McCarey, "It is hard to speak temperately of your picture. It so completely satisfies all the things for which I have hoped from the screen." With a doctorate in English from the University of California, Berkeley, and heading the only Catholic institution of higher education that granted advanced degrees in theology to women, Sister Mary Madeleva was no naïve moviegoer. She not only enjoyed the film but realized its potential. "*Going My Way* is synonymous with the Catholic way and can become," the nun reflected, "if it is not already in essence, the American way. You have been rarely intuitive in understanding and expressing this." Philip Hartung in *Commonweal* described *Going My Way* as "steeped in practical Catholicism." *Extension* magazine wrote that "so many of the clerical characters who trod the silver screen are priestly sticks—too solemn, too pompous or too superior to bear any resemblance to Father Tim whom we've known and loved all our lives." But about the priests of *Going My Way*, the magazine continued, "They're *real: they're the priests we've known all our lives.*" It concluded its review by asserting, "*Going My Way* isn't just a funny picture! Underneath its frothy surface, it has managed to give a true picture of the Church and her priests. They're human—yes! They have their foibles and faults—but they're great guys."[5]

We do not have a representative selection of what average moviegoers thought about the film as only letters from a few of the disgruntled have been preserved. In 1946, a Mrs. James Dant of Birmingham, Michigan, wrote to Eric Johnston, the president of the Motion Picture Producers' Association, of her displeasure with Hollywood's current fare. "How much longer do we have to tolerate Catholic pictures?" she wondered. "As much as we like to hear Bing Crosby, I, and many others have resolved *not* to see any more of his pictures—until he adopts a different theme. After all America is still a Protestant country, and the majority prefer non-sectarian stories."[6] While we might now be surprised at her assertion, we can understand why she might be threatened by a film that portrayed Catholic leaders as so amiable, talented, efficient, and lovable. If America had such persuasive non-Protestants, then exactly what kind of country was it?

Mrs. Dant was not wrong in perceiving a flurry of Catholic movies. *Going My Way*'s success among American filmgoers built upon a veritable pile of Catholic films coming out of Hollywood. These films included some of the most successful and acclaimed movies of the late 1930s and early 1940s, such as *Boys Town* (1938), *Angels with Dirty Faces* (1938), *The Fighting 69th* (1940), and *Knute Rockne, All American* (1940). The powerful Catholic watchdog group of Hollywood, the Legion of Decency, had made the movie studios sensitive to Catholic concerns, which resulted in a surfeit of movies with friendly images of the church. These earlier films also manifested a larger pattern of cultural change in Depression-era America when class-based and ethnic concerns informed popular films. By the time of *Going My Way*, Hollywood had long established what might be called the conventional Catholic priest: urban, rooted in ethnic neighborhoods, and associated with—even signifying—working-class Americans.[7]

The Legion of Decency was only part of a wide-ranging move among Catholics to insert their perspectives into American culture and politics. Social reform efforts during the Depression led by activist priests such as John A. Ryan, Charles Coughlin, and Charles Owen Rice expressed the belief that an energized Catholicism could solve America's problems during a period of social uncertainty and turmoil. Catholic leadership also forged a national Catholicism beyond local and ethnic traditions by making use of the "common man" rhetoric and imagery popular in the Depression era. The National Eucharistic Congress in Cleveland in 1935, the Catholic Youth Organization, and the *Catholic Hour* show on NBC radio all directed their attention toward lay Catholics. In addition to Catholic organizations depicting their clergy as ordinary Americans and their laity as involved in their church, literature stressed the everyday lives of Catholics. In 1943 Sister Mariella Gable edited a collection of stories called *They Are People: Modern Short*

Stories of Nuns, Monks, and Priests. In her introduction, Sister Mariella applauded the recognition by contemporary fiction writers that nuns, monks, and priests "teach rapid addition to children in parochial schools, drink the proverbially bad coffee brewed in monastery kitchens and are occasionally jealous of each other." Leo McCarey bought in 1945 the rights to one of the *They Are People* stories, "Fighting for Sister Joe" by Richard Coleman, and included it in *The Bells of St. Mary's*, the sequel to *Going My Way*.[8] This discourse of the ordinary which appeared throughout Catholic culture in the 1940s helped to create the warm reception of *Going My Way* by America's Catholics.

War Weary

If the 1940s saw a confident popular Catholicism asserting itself widely in American culture, the decade also witnessed profound social changes that equally shaped the context for *Going My Way*'s reception. World War II deeply affected the home front in many ways. Enormous social, economic, and ideological pressures had converged to mobilize the American people for war. The result was a more highly ordered, organized society. The war effort demanded that men, women, and families put on hold their plans for their future. Men went off to fight. Families struggled with rationing and shortages of essential goods such as heating fuels and gasoline. Work schedules became tied directly to war-production drives, and a limited housing stock contributed to the restrictions that characterized everyday life for many Americans during the war.

In addition to the disruption of four years of war were the rapidly changing series of events of 1944 itself when *Going My Way* was released. The D-Day invasion, Allied successes throughout Northern Europe, hopes for an early end to the war, renewed economic prosperity, discussions about industrial demobilization, and plans for a United Nations organization—all dominated headlines. In addition 1944 was a presidential election year with the two political parties holding their summer conventions. Notably, at the Democratic convention in Chicago, Franklin D. Roosevelt would replace the liberal Henry Wallace with Harry Truman, a defeat for the progressive wing of the New Deal. Together these events manifested the array of social, political, economic, and global changes confronting Americans during the mid-1940s.

Thus it is not completely surprising that a movie about a reassuring moral authority figure such as Father O'Malley, who saves his community from social ruin, would find a positive reception among war-weary audiences. O'Malley's wide-ranging successes throughout his city—from church basement to golf course to rectory to opera house—embodied a confident and practical modern leader who could allay people's fears at a time of intense social change. The ease with which the young, highly Americanized priest rescued St. Dominic's provided a soothing story of social revitalization during a wartime era when many Americans faced a future pregnant with both anxiety and possibility.

Religion was not insignificant in allaying those fears. Father Chuck—a celebrated Roman Catholic—demonstrated how outsiders were essential to America's best future. Catholics were not foreign aliens bent on destroying democracy but facilitators of the American dream. The war in Europe precipitated a renewed attraction to American values and ideals. *Americans All* was both the name of a late 1930s radio program sponsored by the government to encourage an appreciation of pluralism in American life as well as the message of American ideology during the 1940s. Unlike in World War I, government propaganda welcomed and retold the contributions of ethnic and religious minorities, placing them firmly within the American democratic tradition. This definition of a culturally pluralist Americanism was not simply a product of government propaganda. Many ethnic, working-class people developed their own commitment to a vision of a culturally diverse America. The war years witnessed the highest rate of naturalization among immigrants for any five-year period since the Census Bureau began recording such statistics.[9] Ethnic communities proudly sent their boys to war and participated in home-front causes. An understanding of a pluralist American identity was being driven by the desires of ethnic minorities as well as by government propaganda.

American and Catholic

During the 1940s, Hollywood acknowledged ethnic and cultural difference in America but only to subordinate it to the needs of national unity. As with government propaganda, diversity could only exist if it contributed to the greater good, to America's war effort. *Air Force* (1943), directed by the noted Howard Hawks, is particularly instructive in foregrounding the cultural differences of Americans. The movie tells the story of the flight crew of a B-17 bomber (dubbed the *Mary Ann*) just before and after the bombing of Pearl Harbor. The captain, Quincannon (nicknamed "Irish"; played by John Ridgely), leads a team of men that includes Weinberg (George Tobias) from New York City, Peterson (Ward Wood) from Minnesota, and a salty veteran called Whitey (Harry Carey). The bomber also takes aboard fighter pilot "Tex" Rader (James Brown) and Callahan

(Edward Brophy), a Marine from New Jersey. The most difficult character of the crew is the Polish American Joe Winocki, played by John Garfield. At the start of the film, Winocki makes clear his determination to get out of the army as soon as possible. Other members of the crew fear that Winocki's jaded, cynical attitude will undermine morale, particularly for the younger members of the bomber team. Ultimately after Winocki sees the damage inflicted by the Japanese on Pearl Harbor, he abandons his skepticism toward authority and embraces his job as a gunner on the bomber. Ethnicity in *Air Force* functions to signify the collective diversity of Americans united in the effort to wage war. The bomber plane, an explicit sign of state power and an ever-looming presence in James Wong Howe's moody cinematography, provides both the visual context and narrative rationale for the newly energized community of committed war fighters.[10]

Going My Way's rendering of Catholic difference as a sign of modern American vitality tapped into this shifting definition of national community. The film neither erases Catholicism nor attends to its complex social realities. It transforms the Catholic priest into the embodiment of popular America. O'Malley represents the modern Irish American Catholic, who has roots in older ethnic communities but who now embraces mainstream America. Father Chuck is recognizable enough with his love of sports and popular music to be American but different enough as a Catholic priest to suggest the flourishing of distinctive subcultures. Such cultures have not died out but continue to shape the experiences of many Americans. Indeed, in O'Malley the signs of Catholicism serve the important task of identifying him with the alternative traditions of the urban, ethnic world that make his Americanism seem all the more inclusive and appealing.

An America in deep transition, therefore, provided the social and cultural context for *Going My Way*'s unprecedented success at theaters. That success suggests that the film translated a powerful Catholic cultural presence in the United States into a sign of a changing America. *Going My Way*'s depiction of O'Malley, more adept at playing golf than at explaining why he became a priest, offers a highly Americanized Catholicism. Yet if *Going My Way* tracks the larger transformation of ethnic cultural difference in Hollywood and by extension American culture in the 1940s, it does so on its own terms. Above all, the movie grants a privileged place to the parish community within Catholic life. While Catholic priests appeared in films like *San Francisco* (1936) and *Boys Town* (1938), they were largely disconnected from the prosaic realities of Catholic parish life. While Father Jerry is placed within a parish in *Angels with Dirty Faces*, he is overshadowed by other, more charismatic figures, such as Rocky the gangster. In these earlier films, the priest was lifted out of his customary parish context and inserted into other more dramatic locations—the San Francisco earthquake of 1906, the violent streets of Dock City. *Going My Way*, however, brings the American cinematic priest back into the parish. Indeed, crucial for this film's lasting impact is its sustained gaze on the Catholic parish. This presentation of the parish is no repetition of actual Catholicism but a new creation, an imagining of the Catholic parish priest as a sign of modern American cultural vitality. For Catholics Leo McCarey and Bing Crosby, enjoying the gentle climes of California, the parish can be nothing other than the backdrop for a tolerant, progressive, sports-loving Catholicism.

By representing the Catholic parish at the center of cultural vitality, Hollywood shifted the articulation of pluralism away from the state and toward religion. Once the war was over, the melting-pot platoon movies of the 1940s like *Air Force* would hold less appeal. The future would not be a world at war but the tolerant, modern city and suburb. That difference enabled an alternative rendering of American cultural pluralism, one that foregrounded the historic reality that ethnic, religious, and racial outsiders were central agents in the creation of modern popular culture. Catholics, McCarey seems to be saying, are at home in the city because they invented it.

If we compare *Going My Way* to another popular religious film of the era, *One Foot in Heaven* (1941), we can see how Protestantism loses out to Catholicism as the religion of modern America. *One Foot in Heaven* chronicles the life of a Methodist minister, William Spence (Fredric March), from his conversion experience at the turn of the century through his old age in the Depression era. A number of prominent Protestant clergy, including Norman Vincent Peale and Daniel Poling, assisted in the production of the film, suggesting that Protestant leaders were playing catch-up to the Catholic Legion of Decency's widely known influence in Hollywood. *One Foot in Heaven* depicts the stresses that ministerial life has on Spence's wife and children, showing the constant moves that characterize the career of a minister and the awkward negotiations that ministers conduct with difficult and powerful members of their congregations. The film takes place in the early years of the twentieth century and in rural, small-town settings, thus giving the movie an intensely retrospective view of religion in America. When Spence becomes pastor of a large church in Denver, the urban landscape is remarkably absent until the very final scenes. Even then, the cityscape appears more like a small town than a major metropolis.

In contrast to *Going My Way*, *One Foot in Heaven*'s preoccupations with an earlier historical era and its village setting suggest a hesitation to depict religion as a modern urban phenomenon. Indeed, the *Motion Picture Herald* dubbed the film "Grassroots and Nostalgia" and opined, "Here is a warm, appealing, human drama woven of the stuff that will carry city audiences back to the grass roots of rural America and give solid, small town citizens a nostalgic excursion to a slower paced way of life when the America that lies between the mountains was untroubled by the strains of modern life." Further, *Variety* speculated that the film's treatment of a Protestant clergyman "may with proper exploitation attract great numbers of folk who seldom go to picture theaters."[11] Hollywood's portrayal of Protestantism rooted that faith in an ideal rural past that while comforting was disconnected from the realities of modern America. By the 1940s, the majority of Americans no longer lived on farms and even those who lived in small towns looked to the big city for their entertainment. Radio, movies, popular music, and magazines were all produced far from the farm. Movie depictions of Protestant ministers never permitted them to be integrated into the city or to be shown as masters of modern living. They remained like Father Fitzgibbon, preservers of the old order in the countryside.

Unlike *One Foot in Heaven*, *Going My Way* embraces the changing social landscape of twentieth-century America, especially the growth of the city and the rise of the suburbs. Its appeal derives from its wholehearted effort to make Catholic outsiders an integral and knowledgeable part of modern America. Crosby and McCarey fashioned a movie that turned out to be perfectly timed to capture larger social and cultural changes in 1940s America. Its upbeat rendering of Catholic life wrapped the uncertainties of the nation's wartime domestic front in reassurance and hope. A story of two generations of clerics gave film audiences a way of imagining the Catholic priest as a friendly and supportive companion in their own midcentury march to a new America of religious pluralism, affluence, and leisure.

Legacies

Father Chuck O'Malley cast a long shadow on popular depictions of Catholicism in the postwar era. However, as we will see in later chapters, *Going My Way*'s happy Catholics eventually became strikingly out of date. In spite of this, the movie's powerful imprint on popular consciousness has continued. In the fall of 1997, Father O'Malley was back in the media news as a controversial television show, *Nothing Sacred*, premiered. Television critics and cultural commentators were entranced by how different the show's story of a young priest, Ray Reyneaux (Kevin Anderson), was from Crosby's Chuck O'Malley. An article in the Long Island newspaper *Newsday* gushed, "And make no mistake about it. Father Ray is no Bing Crosby or Barry Fitzgerald, and that is one of the great positives of this weekly drama."[12] The show would ultimately succumb to poor ratings, network bungling, and the cultural wars of the decade. Yet in retrospect what is striking about *Nothing Sacred* was precisely how closely it followed *Going My Way*. Again we saw American Catholic life through the lens of a young priest in an urban parish. Like "Father Chuck," the name "Father Ray" was merely a secularized nickname for the very Catholic and ethnic-sounding Francis Xavier Reyneaux. Even the hip Father Reyneaux's love of jazz suggested the influence of Crosby/O'Malley buried beneath the show's effort to overcome the power of the potent father from the 1940s.

The greatest crisis to affect the Catholic church in America, the pedophile priest scandal that dominated the press and traumatized Catholics beginning in 2002, also drew *Going My Way* into its vortex. Indeed, the crisis struck at the very relationships that the movie celebrated—the priest as trusted religious authority in the lives of young people. The scandal undermined the image of the priest as a modern, well-adjusted guide (especially for troubled boys) that *Going My Way* helped to create. It would be inevitable, then, that *Going My Way* would serve as a common reference point for media discussions about the scandal. As Maureen Dowd, a columnist for the *New York Times* and a Catholic, speculated, "The last happy, hetero, celibate parish was run by Barry Fitzgerald and Bing Crosby. (Or was it?)" So great was the reassessment among Catholics about their understanding of priests and parish life that Kenneth Woodward, *Newsweek*'s religion reporter, felt compelled to remind readers that the Church had actually produced decent, moral, and trustworthy priests. Woodward, as many others had before him, called on the popular imagery of Catholicism that was so closely entwined with Hollywood: "Bing Crosby Had It Right," he titled his essay.[13] Woodward wrote of priests he had known in his youth who, like Father O'Malley, had created a boys' choir, turned church basements into places for social activities, and loved sports. For Woodward and many Catholics, there was and still is a "*Going My Way* world." Practically sixty years after its release, *Going My Way* remained a touchstone for Catholic experience in America.

NOTES

1. Movie of the Week, *Life*, 1 May 1944, 69; A. O. Dillenbeck, "Going My Way," *Christian Herald*, August 1944, 47; Mary Sheridan, "Films," *America*, 18 March 1944, 669.

2. On Crosby, see Gary Giddins, *Bing Crosby: A Pocketful of Dreams: The Early Years, 1903–1940* (Boston: Little, Brown, 2001), 53–75, 92–100.

3. On McCarey, see "Comedy and a Touch of Cuckoo," *Extension* 39 (November 1944): 5, 34; William H. Mooring, "What McCarey Forgot to Tell," in ibid., 5; Jerry Cotter, "Hollywood's Other Leo," *Sign*, December 1944, 236–37. On Burke, see Giddins, *Bing Crosby*, 422, 581.

4. On the film's success at theaters, see *Motion Picture Herald*, 21 October, 11 November, and 18 November 1944. For reviews, see Manny Farber, "Fathers and Song," *New Republic*, 8 May 1944, 629; "Young Father Crosby," *Newsweek*, 15 May 1944, 78; *Christian Herald*, August 1944, 47; *Time*, 1 May 1944, 90.

5. M. Madeleva to Leo McCarey, 1 September 1944, File: M Correspondence, Box 10, Leo McCarey Collection, American Film Institute; Philip T. Hartung, "Your Way Is My Way," *Commonweal*, 28 April 1944, 41; "Comics in Cassocks!!" *Extension*, August 1944, 10 (italics in original).

6. Mrs. James Dant to Eric Johnston, n.d., Religion file, Box 2, MPAA Breen Office Files, Special Collections, Margaret Herrick Library, Academy of Motion Picture Arts and Sciences, Beverly Hills, CA.

7. On the Catholic films of the late 1930s and 1940s, see Charles Morris, *American Catholic: The Saints and Sinners Who Built America's Most Powerful Church* (New York: Vintage, 1997), 196–209.

8. Sister Mariella Gable, *They Are People: Modern Short Stories of Nuns, Monks, and Priests* (New York: Sheed and Ward, 1943), xiii. The acquisition of the story is discussed in William Dozier to Joe Dolan, 15 January 1945, Leo McCarey Correspondence, 1956, Box 5, Leo McCarey Collection, American Film Institute, Los Angeles, CA.

9. Gary Gerstle, "The Working Class Goes to War," in *The War in American Culture: Society and Consciousness during World War II*, ed. Lewis A. Erenberg and Susan E. Hirsch (Chicago, IL: University of Chicago Press, 1996), 115.

10. On *Air Force*, see Lary May, *The Big Tomorrow: Hollywood and the Politics of the American Way* (Chicago: University of Chicago Press, 2000), 151.

11. *Motion Picture Herald*, 4 October 1941; *Variety*, 30 September 1941.

12. Dick Ryan, "This TV Show Must Be Taken on Faith," *Newsday*, 8 October 1997.

13. Maureen Dowd, "Father Knows Worst," *New York Times*, 20 March 2002; Kenneth Woodward, "Bing Crosby Had It Right," *Newsweek*, 4 March 2002, 53. I thank Mel Piehl for bringing Woodward's article to my attention.

FURTHER READING

Doherty, Thomas. *Projections of War: Hollywood, American Culture and World War II*. New York: Columbia University Press, 1999.

Duis, Perry R. "No Time for Privacy: World War II and Chicago's Families." In *The War in American Culture: Society and Consciousness during World War II*, ed. Lewis A. Erenberg and Susan E. Hirsch. Chicago, IL: University of Chicago Press, 1996.

Franchot, Jenny. *Roads to Rome: The Antebellum Protestant Encounter with Catholicism*. Berkeley: University of California Press, 1994.

Friedrich, Otto. *City of Nets: A Portrait of Hollywood in the 1940s*. New York: Harper and Row, 1986.

Gehring, Wes D. *Leo McCarey: From Marx to McCarthy*. New York: Scarecrow, 2005.

Giddins, Gary. *Bing Crosby: A Pocketful of Dreams: The Early Years, 1903–1940*. Boston: Little, Brown, 2001.

Gleason, Philip. *Speaking of Diversity: Language and Ethnicity in Twentieth-Century America*. Baltimore, MD: Johns Hopkins University Press, 1992.

Heineman, Kenneth J. *A Catholic New Deal: Religion and Reform in Depression Pittsburgh*. University Park: Pennsylvania State University Press, 1999.

May, Lary. *The Big Tomorrow: Hollywood and the Politics of the American Way*. Chicago, IL: University of Chicago Press, 2000.

Morris, Charles. *American Catholic: The Saints and Sinners Who Built America's Most Powerful Church*. New York: Vintage, 1997.

O'Brien, David J. *American Catholics and Social Reform: The New Deal Years*. New York: Oxford University Press, 1968.

Schatz, Thomas. *Boom and Bust: American Cinema in the 1940s*. Berkeley: University of California Press, 1999.

6

GOD AND GUNS

Seven Cities of Gold (1955)

Theresa Sanders

In 1954 two events took place that would affect American public life for decades to come. In May of that year, the U.S. Supreme Court handed down a decision in the *Brown v. Board of Education* case that effectively ended the legal basis for racial segregation. A few months later and half a world away, the Viet Minh took possession of North Vietnam. These two issues, race relations and communism, form the context for interpreting the 1955 movie *Seven Cities of Gold*. The film tells the story of the real-life eighteenth-century Catholic missionary Junípero Serra, who, accompanied by soldiers from Spain, helped to colonize present-day California.

In dealing with race, the film affirms that the Indians whom Serra and his fellow Spaniards encountered were truly human and thus were truly children of God. At the same time, it gives guidelines about the proper way for different races to interact. One subplot in the movie involves a romance between a Spanish soldier and a native woman who wishes to marry him. The relationship ends in misery and death. *Seven Cities of Gold* thus makes the implicit argument that there is a clear (and perhaps divinely ordained) boundary between racial groups. This was a message that would have been particularly relevant as the United States began to desegregate its schools.

With regard to politics, the movie takes for granted that the European colonization of the New World was not only beneficial but was also the will of God. However, it also sets up a sharp contrast between the "godless" approach of the Spanish soldiers and the Christian actions of Serra, who brings civilization and enlightenment to the benighted Indians. It thus offers a critique of the spread of non-Christian philosophies (which in 1955 meant communism), on the one hand, and it provides a model for Christian missionary efforts, on the other.

Hollywood in the 1950s

The plot of *Seven Cities of Gold* is fairly simple. In Mexico City, the Spanish captain Gaspar de Portolá (Anthony Quinn) is commissioned to head north to California. His job is not only to counteract recent incursions into the area by other European nations, but also to find the seven cities of gold that, at least according to legend, exist north of San Diego. To Portolá's dismay, he must take along the Catholic priest Junípero Serra (Michael Rennie), a Franciscan missionary who wants nothing more than to bring the gospel to the Indians. After some argument the expedition begins, but soon the Spaniards find themselves threatened by hostile-looking natives. Without regard for his own safety, Serra convinces the soldiers to hold their fire as he befriends the Indians by offering them beads. The group then proceeds to San Diego.

Upon their arrival, however, they discover that the Spanish settlement there has been decimated by hunger and sickness. To make matters worse, hostilities erupt as Diegueño Indians attack the fort. During the battle, the native chief Matuwir (Jeffrey Hunter) is injured, and Serra nurses him back to health. This gains the priest some favor with the tribe, and Serra is allowed to visit the nearby Indian village. There he amazes the locals with various trinkets; particularly popular is a pair of scissors, something the Indians have not seen before. Meanwhile, Portolá heads north to find the cities of gold, though he returns shortly thereafter, crushed to have discovered that the cities do not exist.

Things go well for Serra in San Diego as he preaches the gospel, provides European-style clothing to the Indians, and persuades the Indian boys to have their hair cut. Nonetheless, Portolá decides that the expedition must return to Mexico since their food and water are running low and since their supply ship has apparently been lost at sea. Serra convinces the captain to delay leaving, and Portolá agrees to give the priest time to make a novena (a special set of prayers offered for nine consecutive days) for the safe arrival of the cargo.

6.1. Captain Gaspar de Portolá (Anthony Quinn) and Franciscan missionary priest Junípero Serra (Michael Rennie) have the same determined gaze, but their desires are radically different. Father Serra wants nothing more than to bring the gospel to the Indians while Captain Portolá wants to secure the imperial conquest of Spain and find the legendary seven cities of gold that allegedly exist north of San Diego.

Soon after, a crisis erupts when Matuwir's sister, a young maiden named Ula (Rita Moreno), declares her love for the roguish Spanish soldier José Mendoza (Richard Egan). When Ula makes it clear that she wishes to accompany Mendoza back to Mexico, she discovers that her devotion is unrequited. Mendoza refuses to take her with him, telling her that she would not be welcomed by his people. In despair, Ula begins to run from the soldier, and when she loses her footing, she tumbles over the edge of a cliff and falls to her death. Angry at what they perceive as a murder, the Diegueños prepare to attack the Spanish settlement once more. After some tense hours and some serious soul searching, Mendoza decides to sacrifice himself rather than risk the safety of the whole group. The soldier kneels and asks for Serra's blessing, and then he walks through the gates of the fort to his certain death. Serra recovers his body soon after; Mendoza's heart has been cut out. (As one reviewer noted, this part of the plot appears to have been borrowed from a film released by the same studio five years earlier, *Two Flags West*.) Despite this tragedy, the movie ends on an optimistic note. Just as Serra's novena ends, the

6.2. Like myriad other movies of that era, *Seven Cities of Gold* could not countenance the prospect of marriage between people of different races. A young Indian maiden named Ula (Rita Moreno) has fallen in love with the roguish Spanish soldier José Mendoza (Richard Egan). While the film exploits both of their shapely figures, the sexual attraction ends in the brutal deaths of both of them.

Spanish supply ship arrives and brings with it not only goods for the soldiers but also church bells for the next mission.

In its review of *Seven Cities of Gold*, the weekly Jesuit magazine *America* called the movie "an unusual phenomenon—a pious Western."[1] Perhaps the film's mixing of two genres was unusual, but the genres themselves were not. Religious dramas and cowboy movies were two of Hollywood's staples in the 1950s. In 1951 the biblical saga *David and Bathsheba*, starring Gregory Peck and Susan Hayward, grossed $6 million and earned five Oscar nominations. That same year, *Quo Vadis* received eight Oscar nominations and won two Golden Globe awards. These religious dramas were followed in 1953 by the racy *Salome*, which featured Rita Hayworth in the title role (tagline: "Your eyes will see the glory"). Twentieth Century Fox's blockbuster hit *The Robe* (1953) set box-office records on its opening day. Starring Richard Burton and Jean Simmons, it earned two Oscars as well as the Golden Globe award for best drama. The following year, the same studio released a sequel to *The Robe* entitled *Demetrius and the Gladiators*. Indeed, religious movies had become so prevalent that in July 1954, *Newsweek* magazine observed that a dozen Bible pics were scheduled for shooting in the following year, including *The Big Fisherman* (released in 1959, starring Howard Keel as Simon Peter), *The Ten Commandments* (1956), and *Ben Hur* (1959). The news magazine noted that, in addition, Twentieth Century Fox had just bought the rights to produce *The Greatest Story Ever Told* (1965), a movie about the life of Jesus.[2] Another life of Jesus, *King of Kings*, would be released in 1961, starring blue-eyed Jeffrey Hunter in the title role.

At the same time, Hollywood was grinding out westerns by the dozen. Many of these were forgettable potboilers, but some have achieved iconic status. For example, in 1950, James Stewart starred in *Broken Arrow*, a drama about the conflict between white settlers and the Apache leader Cochise. The film was nominated for three Oscars and won the Golden Globe award for "best film promoting international understanding." In 1956 it spawned a television series of the same name. Other notable 1950s westerns include *High Noon* (1952), *Shane* (1953), *The Man from Laramie* (1955), *The Searchers* (1956), *The Big Country* (1958), *Río Bravo* (1959), and three Lone Ranger films (1952, 1956, 1958). Robert Webb, who directed *Seven Cities of Gold*, also directed three other westerns during this decade: *White Feather* in 1955, *The Proud Ones* in 1956, and *The Way to the Gold* in 1957. (Webb and his wife, Barbara McLean, coproduced *Seven Cities of Gold*. McLean had previously done the editing for several religious films, including *The Song of Bernadette* [1943], *David and Bathsheba*, and *The Robe*.) And, of course, it was in 1955 that the legendary television series *Gunsmoke* began its twenty-year run.

If genre were any predictor of success, then, *Seven Cities of Gold* should have been a hit. However, the opposite proved to be true. The film opened in New York on 7 October 1955 to decidedly mixed reviews. True, some Catholic publications offered praise. *Commonweal* applauded the "splendid performance" of Michael Rennie and commended the film for its "calm tone of restraint and understatement throughout." The monthly Catholic magazine *The Sign* commented, "Father Serra's tremendous Faith, unconquerable spirit, and great zeal are strikingly depicted" and concluded that the movie was "an inspirational feature, and therein lies its greatest value." *America* magazine was more tepid: "The film is far from great, but its action, its color and CinemaScope scenery, and especially its essentially religious motivation, do recommend it for the *family*."[3]

The secular critics tended to be more critical, although some were mildly complimentary. *Variety* called the film "a satisfactory entry for top-of-the-bill bookings in the general program market," and it commended the "notably good performances" of Rennie and Quinn. *Time* magazine also approved of Quinn, who "wears the conquering swagger of Castile like one to that overbearing manner born." However, the magazine was actually more interested in having fun at the movie's expense by comparing the Indians who lived in Serra's day to the current residents of California (i.e., Hollywood): "They swam in the afternoon and painted themselves luridly before going out in the evening. When they disliked someone, they cut out his heart and sent the rest of him back to his family."[4]

The other reviewers were scathingly negative. The *New York Times* opined that "the plot is lurid in some of its major details, especially in the episodes of contact between the Spaniards and the aborigines. We have seldom seen such acrobatic Indians as the painted and feathered demons who pop up here to harass and battle the Spaniards, until Father Serra passes a few small 'miracles.'" The review panned the movie's romantic subplot as "an embarrassingly pat and foolish thing" and concluded that the scene in which Richard Egan offers himself as a sacrifice "is a display of theatrical heroics that takes this week's cornmeal cake." The *New Yorker* was equally brutal. It noted, "Father Serra is a great one for ribbons and gauds," but "alas, he doesn't work the miracle of elevating this CinemaScopic saga above the level of religious baby talk." Criticizing Michael Rennie's performance, the review concluded, "He looks gaunt and fanatical, which makes his somewhat arch attempts to convert the Indians a little hard to credit. It's rather like watching Savonarola try to get into the spirit of Disneyland."[5]

Significantly, the Legion of Decency gave *Seven Cities of Gold* an "A-1" rating, deeming it "morally unobjectionable for general patronage." It is difficult to say whether or not the movie's producers would have welcomed this designation.

Though a stamp of approval from the Legion might have eased the minds of some Catholic moviegoers, it might also have turned away audiences looking for racier fare. A few years earlier, the Supreme Court had considered the case of *Burstyn v. Wilson* and had ruled by a vote of 9–0 that movies were protected by the First Amendment and thus not subject to censorship. This decision opened the door for films such as Otto Preminger's *The Moon Is Blue* (1953), which was condemned by the Legion of Decency for dialogue that included the words "virgin," "seduce," and "mistress." When the Motion Picture Production Code refused to approve the movie, Preminger released it anyway, and it became a box-office success. The public did not mind a bit of titillation. Perhaps one of the posters advertising the Australian release of *Seven Cities of Gold* hoped to appeal to just such viewers. It included drawings of a bare-chested Quinn brandishing a sword, a painted Indian baring his teeth in battle, and the Indian maiden Ula passionately kissing her Spanish lover. Superimposed on the romantic pair was the warning "Not Suitable for Children."

As it happens, 1955 saw considerable controversy over the question of moral purity in motion pictures. In May of that year, the executive secretary of the Legion of Decency charged that movie producers, "as a matter of deliberate policy, have been contracting for a considerable amount of literary material which is gravely offensive to the moral law." A week later, Cardinal James Francis McIntyre, archbishop of Los Angeles (and thus of Hollywood), made a special statement urging pastors to warn the youth of their congregations about the dangers of attending objectionable films. Shortly thereafter, Pope Pius XII addressed representatives of the Italian movie industry, exhorting filmmakers to recognize their grave responsibility to create movies that upheld the dignity of human beings. The pope acknowledged that "everyone knows that there is no difficulty at all in producing seductive films, by making them accomplices of the lower instincts and passions which overthrow man, luring him from the precepts of his sane thinking and better will." However, he called the producers to a higher standard, asserting, "To bring into existence the ideal film is a privilege of artists gifted beyond the ordinary; certainly, it is an exalted goal toward which, fundamentally, your ability and your vocation summon you." Apparently spurred on by the pope's words, in the following November, the American Catholic bishops announced plans to revitalize a campaign for morality in films.[6]

And yet in all this furor over the dangers of moviegoing, *Seven Cities of Gold* seems not to have made much of an impression on audiences in 1955. The critics were right; the movie is simply not very good. Even today, it is not widely distributed. As of this writing, used copies are available on VHS, but the movie has not yet appeared in DVD format. Despite its lack of popularity, however, *Seven*

Cities offers a significant window into the concerns of American audiences in the mid-1950s. Its treatment of race relations shows how the culture was dealing with the imminent prospect of desegregation, and its portrayal of missionaries offers clues about how Christian America thought of itself in relation to the rise of communism.

Race and Religion

By 1954, when the Supreme Court ruled that separate educational facilities for whites and blacks were inherently unequal, some Catholic institutions had already begun to desegregate. As soon as he had become archbishop of New York in 1939, Francis Spellman had ordered the Catholic schools in his jurisdiction to admit qualified African Americans. In the South, Archbishop Joseph Rummel began to integrate the churches of New Orleans as early as 1949, though an official plan to end segregation in the New Orleans Catholic schools did not get under way until 1962. Many Catholics of European descent, however, resisted these efforts to integrate African Americans into their schools and parishes. In 1942, when the federal government attempted to build a housing project for blacks near a Polish Catholic parish in Detroit, three local priests spoke vociferously against the plan and succeeded in blocking it. A similar protest in Buffalo prevented the construction of defense housing for African Americans within certain Catholic parishes. Even if the people in question were fellow Catholics, white parishioners often did not welcome them. In Chicago three African American women who attended mass at an all-white parish were jeered at and assaulted as they left the church. Likewise, a poll at a Catholic high school in Philadelphia found that while 92 percent of the students considered "baptized Negroes" to be members of the body of Christ, 94 percent of them favored restricting African Americans to certain parts of the city.[7]

Even some of the most ardent Catholic spokesmen for the rights of minorities hesitated when it came to that historically thorniest of issues, racial intermarriage. John LaFarge was a Jesuit priest who wrote extensively about the duty of the Catholic church to welcome and minister to African Americans. He published several books on the topic, including *Interracial Justice: A Study of the Catholic Doctrine of Race Relations* (1937) and *No Postponement: U.S. Moral Leadership and the Problem of Racial Minorities* (1950). And yet when it came to intermarriage, the priest hesitated. In a work published in 1943, he acknowledged that, as he put it, "No scientific proof appears to be available as to the deleterious effects from a *purely biological standpoint*, of the union between different races of mankind." He further conceded that "the Catholic Church does not impose any impediment...upon racial intermarriages, in spite of the Church's great care to preserve in its utmost purity the integrity of the marriage bond." (The church even today does impose impediments to marriage in certain circumstances if, for example, the partners are underage, closely related, or already married to other people.) And yet, at the same time, LaFarge argued that "there are *grave reasons* against any general practice of intermarriage between the members of different racial groups. These reasons, where clearly verified, amount to a moral prohibition of such a practice."[8] The primary factors that LaFarge cited were laws against such unions in certain states, the tensions that an interracial marriage would produce within the family, and the difficulty of raising mixed-race children.

With regard to laws against interracial marriage, it is worth observing that such prohibitions had been in force in various parts of the United States from the country's inception. Nearly all states have had laws against "miscegenation" at one time or another, and it was only in the middle of the twentieth century that these were definitively overturned. Some laws prohibited white Americans and African Americans from marrying each other, while others broadened their scope to include Native Americans, Malays, and Hindus. Of course, the notion of "race" is not a scientific one. Research suggests that all human beings share a common ancestry and that racial categories have no basis in biology. And yet both racial categorizing and racism persist as powerful social factors.

Regarding the tensions that interracial marriage might cause, LaFarge wrote, "A white partner might be willing to face the consequences of discrimination, but would naturally hesitate at the prospect of his children being disadvantaged."[9] (That black partners might have similar misgivings does not seem to have occurred to LaFarge.) Racial difference was so powerful, he felt, that it could prevent the happiness of an interracial couple. Thus, even the most progressive Catholic thinkers shrank from the thought of widespread racial mixing. All peoples, they argued, were to be granted basic human rights, all were to be treated with courtesy and respect, and all were to be welcomed into the church. But when it came to marriage, that was a different matter.

This attitude is mirrored perfectly in the movie *Seven Cities of Gold*. On the one hand, the movie is a stirring indictment of racial hatred. When Portolá's expedition is about to embark, the captain asks Father Serra to bless the troops. Serra's speech, though, is not quite what Portolá expects. The priest excoriates the soldiers in words that would have had a certain resonance in 1955, at the dawn of the civil rights movement:

A long time ago we came to Mexico. We took a group of simple Indians, Indians
of childlike love. We turned them into a race of slaves. Their skin was darker
than ours and because of that they were beneath us. And so we told ourselves that it
was just. So a handful of soldiers like yourselves stripped them of their gold, their
love, and their freedom. Now in the dawn of a wonderful mission, you're starting
out in the same way. You plan to walk across their fields—to take their gold and
leave them nothing. You plan to pillage and plunder and loot and lust, and all
because their tongue is strange and their skin is colored. In the name of Saint Joseph
and all the saints who surround the throne of God, I say, "How dare you!"

Throughout the movie, Serra speaks several times about the need to treat the
Indians with respect. He calls the Diegueños his brothers, and he tells them that
they and the Spanish are all children of the same God.

And yet, like myriad other movies of that era, *Seven Cities of Gold* could not
countenance the prospect of marriage between people of different races. The subplot
of the film in which the Indian maiden Ula falls in love with the Spanish soldier
Mendoza simply could not, in 1955, have ended with the two living happily ever after.
Hollywood romances between a white person and a Native American invariably
ended in tragedy. In *Broken Arrow* (1950), for instance, the Indian woman played by
Debra Paget is killed, leaving behind a brokenhearted Jimmy Stewart. In *Across the
Wide Missouri* (1951), Clark Gable's Indian wife is killed off, and in *Colorado Territory*
(1949), Joel McCrea marries a woman of part-Indian heritage and ends up being
killed. Interracial shenanigans were not to be countenanced.

The romantic plot in *Seven Cities of Gold* is especially significant given that the
novel on which the movie is based tells a far different tale. In Isabelle Gibson
Ziegler's *The Nine Days of Father Serra* (1951), the Spanish soldier named Viamonte
(Mendoza) is a cruel man who preys on the weak. Because of his blond hair,
Viamonte is taken for a god by the natives, and he abuses the deference they show
to him. One day Viamonte goes out walking in the hills, and he runs across a young
Indian woman who is mentally disabled and who, as a result, is considered sacred
in the village. He leads her into a cave, saying, "Come with the white god. Come
and see where the white god lives." The girl goes willingly, but when Viamonte
undresses her and throws himself upon her, she begins to scream. Viamonte strikes
her in the face, but the girl manages to escape. She runs away toward the sea, and
Viamonte chases her until she is lost in the waves. One of the Indian men dashes
into the water after her, but he is unable to save her from drowning.

It is clear in the novel that Viamonte has no remorse for what he has done.
When he is confronted by Serra, he remarks that he is bored by the whole episode.

In anger, Serra replies, "A girl too weak and full of trust to defend herself is raped and slain, but Miguel Viamonte is bored. A man breaks two of God's commandments and he is bored. He yawns. He does not trouble himself to conceal his yawn."[10] The brutish Viamonte does not offer himself up in self-sacrifice, as does the Mendoza of the movie. He remains unrepentant.

In this respect, the novel perhaps presents a more accurate depiction of the Spanish incursion into California than does the movie. Historians note that during the years when the real-life Serra was establishing missions along the coast, the sexual abuse and rape of Indian women by soldiers was a serious problem. In one instance, Spaniards used lassos to capture women like cattle, and, after rounding them up, they raped them. Serra also received reports of soldiers molesting Indian boys and men. The army was reluctant to punish the perpetrators of such crimes for two reasons. First, honoring natives' demands for justice could make Spain appear weak. Second, incarcerating criminals could leave military posts understaffed. In 1955, Hollywood was not prepared to confront such ugly facts and censorship would not allow realistic representations of colonial conquest. Instead, it turned the novel's rape of a disabled girl by a vicious soldier into a love affair between a handsome (but commitment-phobic) hero and a beautiful (but naïve) Indian maiden

Beads for Peace

As we have seen, if Catholics in the 1950s did not relish the thought of interracial marriage, many of them did vigorously support civil rights for African Americans. Significantly, one of the reasons they did so was as a defense against communism. Catholic leaders sensitive to America's racial problems were well aware that those who defended African Americans against racists were frequently members of communist and socialist groups. John LaFarge, for example, called interracial justice "a direct answer to Marxist theory and to world-communist propaganda." Likewise, Robert Kennedy told a Catholic Interracial Council meeting in 1955 that any effort to reach "colonial peoples" would depend on America first attending to its own racial strife.[11] With its message of universal comradeship and economic parity, communism appealed to populations on the bottom rungs of society. The best antidote to this, in the eyes of some Catholic thinkers, was for the church to beat the communists to the punch by working to overcome racial discrimination and by welcoming African Americans into its ranks.

The fight against communism had become something of an obsession in American Catholic circles. In 1937 Pope Pius XI issued an encyclical in which he charged that communism "strips man of his liberty, robs human personality of all its dignity, and removes all the moral restraints that check the eruptions of blind impulse." While acknowledging that "unusual misery has resulted from the unequal distribution of the goods of this world," the pope nonetheless condemned the communist movement, offering the salvation wrought by Jesus Christ in its place. To Catholics who found themselves tempted by the godless philosophy, especially those in Europe, the pope wrote, "We earnestly exhort them to hear the voice of their loving Father. We pray the Lord to enlighten them that they may abandon the slippery path which will precipitate one and all to ruin and catastrophe, and that they recognize that Jesus Christ, Our Lord, is their only Savior: 'For there is no other name under heaven given to man, whereby we must be saved.'"[12] But communist philosophies and governments continued to spread from Russia and China both south and west, and Catholics became increasingly preoccupied with countering the Red Threat. In 1949 Mao Zedong formally declared China to be a communist republic, and a year later the Korean War began. In 1954 Ho Chi Minh took control of North Vietnam, and a few years later Americans entered what is now called the Vietnam War.

Catholic magazines and journals from this period reflect the increasing sense that communism was a threat to the church. For example, the *China Missionary Bulletin* in March 1950 featured only one short article on communism and devoted only one page to a section entitled "Gleaning Communist Policy in China." By 1953 the journal (retitled *Mission Bulletin*) was devoting eight or ten pages of each issue to "Reporting Communist Policy" and "Jottings from the Communist Press." An issue from 1955 offered an editorial on "Red China Prisoners," a feature entitled "Chinese Priests, Brothers and Sisters Known to Be Still in Communist Jails," and an article on forced labor in Red China. In these essays, a clear contrast was set up between the communist expansion and the spread of the gospel of Christ.

Of course, it might be said that the gospel and communist economic theory actually have much in common. The early Christians, says the New Testament, "had all things in common; they would sell their possessions and goods and distribute the proceeds to all, as any had need" (Acts 2:44). That sounds remarkably like the communist dictum, "From each according to his ability, to each according to his need." As a Franciscan friar committed to a communal lifestyle, Serra might well have found the communist philosophy more in tune with Christianity than modern capitalism.

However, for Americans of the 1950s, communism meant not an economic theory based on the principle of "share and share alike," but rather an oppressive form of government that had no concern for individual rights, that promoted atheism, and that sponsored worldwide revolutions. Thus, ironically, in *Seven Cities of Gold*, Serra actually represents the freedom of American capitalism, and the soldiers represent godless communist tyranny. The soldiers are interested only in exploitation; their imperial desire is to steal land and to rob the people who live on it.

The movie's opening scene sets the tone. As the film begins, Gaspar de Portolá's carriage races along the road toward Mexico City, paying no heed to the people in its path. An old woman is unable to escape the thundering hoof beats of the horses, and she is killed. Serra, who is traveling the same road on foot, stops to perform a blessing over the dead woman and to preside at her funeral. Thus the contrast is established; in his beautiful clothes and expensive carriage, Portolá is every inch the military commander whose time is too valuable to spend attending to peasants. Serra, on the other hand, chooses to walk to Mexico City rather than to ride, since his Franciscan order is dedicated to poverty. A few scenes later, the contrast between the two is again emphasized. As the expedition prepares to set out, Serra asks one of the muleteers to carry in his bag a small statue of the Virgin Mary. The man agrees, but just then Portolá appears and declares that every inch of cargo space must be dedicated to military supplies. Military expansion does not need religion. Serra protests to no avail, and he ends up carrying the "little Virgin" himself.

Serra's insistence on bringing along a statue of the Virgin Mary is not merely an indication of how "real" missionaries converted native peoples. The expansion of Serra's religious empire is closely associated in the film with the presentation of positive, helpful goods to the residents of California. The exchange of "primitive" dress for the clothing of civilization is presented as a contribution to the well-being of the Indians. It is Serra who will offer the natives beads to win their affection and thus secure the explorers a peaceful journey through the wilderness. While the Franciscan offers wealth, in the form of alluring private property, the Spanish (like the communists) take what they want through force and violence. Though his journey entails considerable hardship (Serra walks with a limp due to an unexplained injury), the priest prefers the simplicity of his coarse brown robe and his own two feet rather than the finery of Portolá.

Serra's democratic spirit easily combines with his understanding of what will "calm the savage." The importance of such "beads" to the real world of democratic capitalism would later be dramatically acted out in the famous "kitchen debates" of Soviet premier Nikita Khrushchev and Vice President Richard Nixon. During Nixon's 1959 visit to Moscow, the two argued in a U.S.-built model kitchen about who made the best color television sets and whether or not variety in

6.3. Father Junípero Serra (Michael Rennie) offers the natives beads to win their affection and thus secure the explorers a peaceful journey through the wilderness. While the Franciscan offers wealth, in the form of alluring private property, the soldiers will take what they want through force and violence. *Courtesy of the Academy of Motion Picture Arts and Sciences*

washing-machine types was important to a country's citizens. Americans were asking the world to choose between consumerism and communism, between democracy and authoritarianism. In the Cold War 1950s, Catholicism was represented in the movies as bringing the positive gifts of capitalism to a world supposedly eager for American wealth.

Go Forth and Baptize

As the Red Threat grew, Catholics countered communism by spreading their own gospel, at times risking their lives in the process. In 1951, Pope Pius XII issued the encyclical "On Promotion of Catholic Missions" to encourage evangelists to live out their vocations with steadfast courage. The pontiff urged missionaries to stand against the deceptions propagated by worldly revolutionaries and to guard the "simple and untutored" from pernicious errors that might put their salvation in jeopardy.[13] Those to whom the pope's call were directed were the twentieth century's answer to Junípero Serra. Their dedication to spreading the Christian faith was celebrated in films such as *The Keys of the Kingdom* (1944), *The Seventh Sin* (1957), *The Awakening* (1958), *The Nun's Story* (1959), *The Devil at 4 O'clock* (1961), and *Satan Never Sleeps* (1962).

The years following the end of World War II saw an explosion of missionary efforts by American Catholics. The United States had itself been considered missionary territory up until 1908, and until the end of World War I (1918) there had been few American efforts to send missionaries to other countries. The years between the wars brought some growth in missionary activity, but it was only after the Second World War that such efforts really took off. When that conflict ended in 1945, there were an estimated 2,693 American Catholic missionaries in foreign lands. By 1954 the number had jumped to 4,755, a more than 75 percent increase.[14] In the 1950s, American Catholics were sending their priests and nuns, as well as their dimes and nickels, to teach, give medical assistance to, and, of course, baptize people around the world.

During this era, schoolchildren were encouraged to support Catholic missions by sending money and supplies to missionaries in order to convert non-Christian youth. For example, in 1953 the Academy of Mary in Wichita Falls, Texas, included these items in its annual report: they sent "three shipments of religious articles to the missions; had a candy sale; gave two baskets to poor families; bought two pagan babies."[15] The campaign to "buy" pagan babies (that is, to donate money toward the baptism of non-Christian children) was quite popular in American Catholic schools and lasted into the 1960s. Gina Cascone (b. 1955) remembers that she bought her first pagan baby at the age of six and that by the time she was in fifth grade, she had accumulated eight babies at $5 apiece: "No one was very clear about exactly what I was getting for those five bucks. I was buying a pagan baby. I really didn't know what 'pagan' was or why it made babies marketable.... For five dollars, I got no proof that a baby even existed. To me, this was a gyp." And yet, despite her reservations, Cascone still sent her money to those foreign lands: "I had visions of an infant who, by accident of birth, could expect nothing more than hell on earth, and not even a chance at heaven. It didn't seem fair. And if five dollars from me could change that agony to ecstasy, I was more than happy to give it."[16]

Not all Catholic missionaries saw their job as giving babies an otherwise-impossible shot at heaven. A 1955 article in the quarterly review *Worldmission* argued that missionaries should avoid giving the impression that one had to be Catholic in order to be saved. The article, "The Problem of the Salvation of the

Heathen," argued that "every pagan receives sufficient grace from God to save his soul." It continued, "A heathen, therefore, even the remotest from Christian belief, can become a child of God without being a member of the Church, i.e., of the Mystical Body of Christ. He can acquire the state of grace without external baptism or sacraments." The author recognized the difficulty that this might pose for missionaries: why should one evangelize if people could be saved apart from Christianity? The answer, he affirmed, was that evangelization is God's will: "The sole purpose of all grace and enlightenment is . . . to direct men toward the harbor of salvation, which is the Catholic Church to which exclusively Christ entrusted all grace and truth."[17]

Clearly, when it comes to the value of religious dedication, *Seven Cities of Gold* sides with Serra. Three scenes confirm the power of the priest's faith. The first occurs on the journey to San Diego, when Serra and Mendoza are accidentally separated from the rest of the caravan. The two men soon find themselves surrounded by hostile Indians, and Mendoza scares the natives off by firing his gun. Lost in the California desert, the priest and the soldier struggle through a fierce dust storm until suddenly they spy a light in the darkness. Following its beam, they come upon a house in which live a bearded old man wearing a robe, his beautiful young wife (dressed in blue), and their baby. The couple silently offer their guests food and water, and they smile as the Spaniards fall asleep at the table. When Serra and Mendoza awake, they find themselves back in the desert. Mendoza interprets the event as a dream, but Serra knows better. He knows that they were saved by the holy family of Jesus and that they will soon be rescued. As soon as words to this effect leave his mouth they are proven true; a search party shows up, and priest and soldier happily rejoin the rest of the expedition.

The second instance of divine approval of Serra's mission takes place once the party reaches San Diego. The Spaniards who preceded Serra's group have been decimated, largely due to a drought. As soon as Serra hangs his small church bells in the trees, however, rain begins to fall, and Serra falls to his knees in gratitude.

Finally, the film ends with a confirmation that the mission of Father Serra is a godly one. When Captain Portolá decides to head back to Mexico City, Serra convinces him to wait for nine more days. Portolá believes that their supply ship must have been lost at sea, but Serra counters that the ship is carrying bells for the next mission he hopes to found, and he has never known a ship carrying church bells to go down. In the end, Serra is proven right. Just as the Spanish are preparing to depart, the ship is sighted, and the mission is saved. Once again, God wins over the godlessness of the soldiers. Only if colonization is done with faith, implies the movie, will it succeed.

Film versus History

Before closing this analysis of *Seven Cities of Gold*, let me give some consideration to the relation between the history of the Spanish missions and how that history has been represented in film. *Seven Cities* claims that the story it presents is accurate. At the very beginning of the movie, an authoritative-sounding male voice tells viewers that what we are about to see is a faithful account of Serra, his companions, and the Indians whom they encountered: "The only change we have made is to set their words in English." And yet in recent years, considerable controversy has arisen over how best to tell Serra's story. Should the priest be praised as an inspiration to Christians everywhere or condemned as a colonialist oppressor?

One of the factors that precipitated this controversy was Pope John Paul II's decision in 1988 to declare Serra "Blessed." The beatification ceremony moved the Franciscan one step closer to canonization, to being officially declared a saint in the Catholic church. This action was protested by some Native Americans who charged that Serra and his fellow missionaries contributed to the large-scale destruction of native populations. For example, Rupert Costo, a Cahuilla Indian, and his wife, Jeannette, of Cherokee descent, have charged the missionaries with genocide. George Tinker, a Lutheran minister and a member of the Osage nation, has compared the missions to concentration camps.[18]

Historian James A. Sandos, on the other hand, takes a more moderate view. He agrees that the Spanish efforts at evangelization did devastate California's Indian tribes. In 1770, he notes, roughly 65,000 Native Americans lived in the mission zone of the Spanish. Sixty years later, only 17,000 remained, a loss of 74 percent. Within the bounds of the missions themselves, more Indians died than were born, and so constant recruitment was the only way to keep the settlements populated. However, Sandos argues that the epidemics of hunger and disease that came in the wake of colonial expansion were unintentional and thus not comparable to the willed destruction of populations in the twentieth century. He observes that by 1820, Franciscans themselves were realizing the deleterious effects of mission life on Indians, and they were questioning the methods by which the settlements were run.[19] Though the missions did succeed in baptizing large numbers of people (roughly 80,000 in seventy years), they brought disease and starvation in their wake.

As for Serra himself, he was a product of his times and had a paternalistic attitude toward the natives whom he had come to convert. At one point in his journal, he recorded that several of the company's Indian guides had deserted: "We had no notion why. And so, little by little, we find ourselves deprived of the services of these men, who are more useful than people realize, for only a person who is right on the spot can form a proper idea of how hard they have to work—on poor food and no salary."[20] The fact that Serra could not fathom that native guides might resent working in such poor conditions shows a blindness that surely impaired his ability to serve them.

As the spiritual leader of the newly founded communities, Serra asserted that his Franciscans alone had the power to punish the Indian people, demanding:

> [N]o chastisement or ill-treatment should be inflicted on any of them whether by Officer or by any soldier, without the Missionary Father's passing upon it. This has been the time-honored practice of this kingdom ever since the conquest; and it is quite in conformity with the law of nature concerning the education of the children, and an essential condition for the rightful training of the poor neophytes.[21]

If Serra acted as a father to the Indians, however, his paternal care could be harsh. History tells us that his punishments included whipping with a barbed lash, mutilation, branding, use of stocks, and execution.

None of this is even hinted at in *Seven Cities of Gold*. The Indians in this film are, for the most part, portrayed as simpletons who could only benefit from the kind tutelage offered by Father Serra. In this respect, the scene in which Serra and another priest cut one Indian boy's hair (to the child's delight) and dress another in European clothing is particularly lamentable. Historically, many Native Americans and aboriginal Canadians deeply resented being forced to change their hair and clothing and to attend schools run by whites. In the eyes of many, this amounted to cultural genocide, as those who continued to honor native religious practices or to speak native languages were often punished severely.

It is tempting to think that the image of Native Americans as bestial or, at best, as childlike recipients of the white man's largesse, was the only one available to Hollywood at the time. However, this is not the case. Consider, for example, the 1947 movie *Captain from Castile*, which was released by Twentieth Century Fox, the same studio that produced *Seven Cities of Gold*. This earlier film stars Tyrone Power as a sixteenth-century soldier who accompanies the Spanish conquistador Hernando Cortés to Mexico. Here, however, the Indians whom the Europeans meet are portrayed with dignity. For one thing, for the most part they speak in their own language, communicating with the soldiers through a translator. Moreover, when an ambassador from the Aztec emperor Montezuma arrives with gifts for Cortés, he is accompanied by an entourage every bit as magnificent as that of a European monarch.

Perhaps most significantly, the Aztecs are portrayed as having their own religious beliefs and practices—unlike the Indians in *Seven Cities of Gold*, who seem to have none at all. *Captain from Castile* includes some remarkable dialogue between an Aztec warrior named Coatl (played by Canadian Mohawk actor Jay Silverheels, most famous for his role as Tonto in the Lone Ranger series) and Tyrone Power's character, Captain Pedro de Vargas. Coatl had first met Pedro in Spain, where along with other Aztecs he had been enslaved by a Spanish nobleman. With Pedro's help Coatl had escaped and returned to Mexico, and it is there that the two meet again. Though Coatl recognizes his debt to Pedro, he vows to fight the Spanish invasion.

> *Coatl:* This is my country, Señor. These my people, my gods. We not come tell you to stop loving your gods. We not come make you slaves. Why you do this, Señor?
>
> *Pedro:* Well, I'm afraid I haven't any answer for that. [Pauses, looks up toward the sky] It isn't right for men to worship idols. There's only one true God.
>
> *Coatl:* Maybe your God and my God same God. Maybe we just call him by different names.
>
> *Pedro:* Perhaps.

This is the only moment in which the movie allows itself to question the morality of the Spanish invasion of Aztec lands, however. By the film's end, all doubt is wiped away as Cortés and his men march toward their battle with Montezuma. As they head out, the priest accompanying the conquistadors gives a speech that prefigures the one given by Serra in *Seven Cities of Gold*. He proclaims, "I charge you, put this greed out of your hearts. Open your eyes to what lies before you. Go forward not as conquerors but as men of God. . . . And, in God's own time, [the New World] will blossom forth under the cross of Christianity, a haven for the weak and a refuge for the strong, with all the good of the old world and none of its ills." The unmitigated optimism, which so contrasts with the historical record, can make this movie—and others of colonial conquest—difficult to watch.

In the same way, history challenges the rosy outlook of *Seven Cities of Gold*. As that film draws to a close, we see Father Serra ringing his new church bells and crying, "A clear voice—and loud. One my Indians will love. I can hear them coming. I can hear them coming!" As viewers, we are asked to share in Serra's eagerness, but it is difficult to ignore contemporary knowledge of what will happen to those Indians who do heed the call of the bells.

None of these considerations would have been on the minds of viewers when *Seven Cities* was released in 1955. In May of that year, Poland, East Germany, Czechoslovakia, Hungary, Romania, Bulgaria, and Albania—nations that had been historically Christian, if not Catholic—signed the Warsaw Pact with the USSR. That agreement stipulated that the signatories would defend each other if one or more of the members were attacked, while respecting each other's internal affairs and national sovereignty, but many Western nations interpreted the gesture as a triumph of world communism. Indeed, a year later, in 1956, and again in 1968, Soviet tanks rolled into Hungary and later Czechoslovakia, crushing their attempts to withdraw from the pact. As contemporary Christians found their message threatened by the gospel of communism, the filmic example of Serra's dedication in the face of adversity seemed reassuring. At the same time, American Catholics were dealing with growing unrest in their own country over racial discrimination and the push for civil rights. Serra's message of tolerance, and at the same time the movie's refusal to sanction interracial marriage, might have been perceived by many white Catholics as a comforting reaffirmation of the status quo. While *Seven Cities of Gold* may hold little intrigue for the contemporary filmgoer, it does provide us with a rich portrait of the religious world of Cold War America.

NOTES

1. Moira Walsh, "Films," *America*, 15 October 1955, 83.

2. "Biblical Boom," *Newsweek*, 5 July 1954, 79.

3. Philip T. Hartung, "No Color Line," *Commonweal*, 14 October 1955, 41; Jerry Cotter, "Reviews in Brief," *The Sign*, November 1955, 28; Walsh, "Films," *America*, 83 (italics in the original).

4. "Brog.," *Variety*, 14 September 1955; *Time*, 31 October 1955, 55–56.

5. Bosley Crowther, "Story of Spaniards in West at Roxy," *New York Times*, 8 October 1955; John McCarten, "The Current Cinema," *New Yorker*, 15 October 1955, 183.

6. "Production Code of Movies Scored," *New York Times*, 13 May 1955; Thomas M. Pryor, "Cardinal Scores Laxity in Movies," *New York Times*, 20 May 1955; Pope Pius XII, "Exhortations of His Holiness, Pius XII to the Representatives of the Cinema World," 21 June 1955, par. II.1.d; "Catholics Assail 'Indecent' Films," *New York Times*, 23 November 1955.

7. John T. McGreevy, *Parish Boundaries: The Catholic Encounter with Race in the Twentieth-Century Urban North* (Chicago, IL: University of Chicago Press, 1996), 74, 76, 98, 107.

8. John LaFarge, *The Race Question and the Negro: A Study of the Catholic Doctrine on Interracial Justice* (New York: Longmans, Green, 1943), 194–96 (italics in the original).

9. LaFarge, *The Race Question*, 197.

10. Isabelle Gibson Ziegler, *The Nine Days of Father Serra* (New York: Longmans, Green, 1951), 152–53, 163.

11. John LaFarge, National Catholic Conference for Interracial Justice, Keynote Address, delivered 25 August 1958, cited by McGreevy, *Parish Boundaries*, 106. Kennedy's speech is also cited by McGreevy, 106.

12. Pope Pius XI, "Divini Redemptoris," 19 March 1937, pars. 10, 8, 80.

13. Pope Pius XII, "Evangelii Praecones," 2 June 1951, par. 49.

14. Franciscan Clerics of Holy Name College, *The National Catholic Almanac: 1947* (Paterson, NJ: St. Anthony's Guild, 1947), 353; *The 1956 National Catholic Almanac* (Paterson, NJ: St. Anthony's Guild, 1956), 460.

15. *Junior Sodalist* 6 (April 1953), cited by Paula M. Kane, "Marian Devotion since 1940," in *Habits of Devotion: Catholic Religious Practice in Twentieth-Century America*, ed. James M. O'Toole (Ithaca, NY: Cornell University Press, 2004), 100.

16. Gina Cascone, *Pagan Babies and Other Catholic Memories* (New York: Washington Square, 2003), 53, 56.

17. John de Reeper, "The Problem of the Salvation of the Heathen," *Worldmission* 6, no. 3 (Fall 1955): 363, 369.

18. George E. Tinker, *Missionary Conquest: The Gospel and Native American Cultural Genocide* (Minneapolis, MN: Fortress, 1993), 42.

19. James A. Sandos, *Converting California: Indians and Franciscans in the Missions* (New Haven, CT: Yale University Press, 2004), 180, 105–6, 177.

20. Junípero Serra, *Writings of Junípero Serra*, 4 vols., ed. Antonine Tibesar (Washington, DC: Academy of American Franciscan History, 1955), 1:103.

21. Ibid., 1:307.

FURTHER READING

Corkin, Stanley. *Cowboys as Cold Warriors: The Western and U.S. History*. Philadelphia: Temple University Press, 2004.

Friar, Ralph E., and Natasha A. Friar. *The Only Good Indian . . . the Hollywood Gospel*. New York: Drama Book Specialists, 1972.

Kashner, Sam, and Jennifer MacNair. *The Bad and the Beautiful: Hollywood in the Fifties*. New York: Norton, 2002.

Lightfoot, Kent G. *Indians, Missionaries, and Merchants: The Legacy of Colonial Encounters on the California Frontiers*. Berkeley: University of California Press, 2005.

McGreevy, John T. *Parish Boundaries: The Catholic Encounter with Race in the Twentieth-Century Urban North*. Chicago, IL: University of Chicago Press, 1996.

Rollins, Peter C., and John E. O'Connor, eds. *Hollywood's West: The American Frontier in Film, Television, and History*. Lexington: University Press of Kentucky, 2005.

Sandos, James A. *Converting California: Indians and Franciscans in the Missions*. New Haven, CT: Yale University Press, 2004.

Shapiro, Michael J. *Cinematic Political Thought: Narrating Race, Nation, and Gender*. New York: New York University Press, 1999.

Whitfield, Stephen J. *The Culture of the Cold War*. Baltimore, MD: Johns Hopkins University Press, 1991.

7

LIFE ON THE FRONTIER

Lilies of the Field (1963)

Jeffrey Marlett

Location, location, location: the three most important things in real estate. In the movies, the location where a film's narrative is set also plays a critical role in the message it conveys and its ability to capture the attention of the audience. Set in the wild Arizona desert, *Lilies of the Field* introduces an odd assortment of characters who seem out of place in the Western frontier. Nuns in full "penguin" habits have moved to the edge of civilization to escape East German communism. There they learn to sing catchy black gospel tunes from a black man wandering freely from place to place. The local Mexican population of this frontier outpost, although thoroughly Catholic, needs an outsider's help—a black Baptist outsider no less—to construct a Catholic church. Everybody in the movie thinks the sisters are crazy to build the church, but they help out nevertheless. *Lilies of the Field* reasserts the American frontier myth: go somewhere remote and remake yourself. And it does so with an unlikely combination of characters: nuns and a black man.

In the early 1960s, Catholics were poised for such a new endeavor. The previous decade had ended with American Catholics flush with success. Catholics' support of American nationalism, particularly obvious in their enthusiasm for anticommunism, had secured their place in the political system. The GI Bill helped Catholic colleges to fill with students. Young people crowded into semi-naries and convents as calls to the vocation of the religious life burgeoned. Suburbs across the nation teemed with the newly affluent Catholic middle class. Several Catholic figures dominated popular culture: the Cramdens of *The Honeymooners* and Monsignor Fulton Sheen of *Life Is Worth Living* on television, Frank Sinatra in music, and Joe DiMaggio of the Yankees and the Notre Dame football team in sports. After a century or more in urban ghettos, suddenly Catholics were everywhere.

The success of *Lilies of the Field* grew out of the Catholicism of the two Johns—Pope John XXIII and President John F. Kennedy. These men symbol-ized the vibrant and fresh new beginnings being made by the Catholic church and the nation. Kennedy's presidential victory in 1960, albeit by a razor-thin margin, crowned a postwar Catholic ascendancy. The era of the New Frontier had begun, and the Kennedy White House soon earned the nickname "Camelot" for its embodiment of the American dream. Further, the Vatican itself seemed to be catching up. In 1958 the new pope, John XXIII, had announced a major church council to be held in Rome. Pope John called for *aggiornomento*—updating—in a confident, not ashamed, manner. Beginning in the fall of 1962, the bishops and heads of religious orders who gathered for the Second Vatican Council would discuss how to reconfigure Catholicism's age-old teachings. What would change? Would Latin be retired as the language of the sacraments? Would priests be allowed to marry? Would the international church uphold the separation of church and state as practiced in the United States? *Lilies of the Field* appeared in this world of new beginnings and new situations. Rather than looking backward to the cold war era of anticommunist Catholic militancy, it looks forward to an imagined era of religious, racial, and gender equality.

Lilies of the Field captures this moment of unfiltered optimism in American history by using the frontier as a place where an ideal harmony can be created by the strangest of characters. It rearticulates, in a Catholic idiom, the long-standing American belief that in a new environment old hostilities give way to new part-nerships. Out in the Arizona desert, *Lilies of the Field* carves out a space where ecumenical spiritual growth, new institutional identity, and liturgical experi-mentation can freely occur. At the same time the movie's main characters—five white nuns and a black man—explore racial cultures without cynicism or gloomy resignation. *Lilies* also addresses the sexual frontier, as women and men struggle to build a church and a community. An unlikely coterie of Protestants and Catholics in the Arizona desert works out the tensions of religion, race, and gender with the enthusiasm and exuberance of the early 1960s.

The Place of the Possible

As we saw in chapter 6, Spanish Catholics explored the Southwest in the seven-teenth and eighteenth centuries and set up towns in what are now California, New Mexico, and Arizona. However, in the world of the movies, "American Catholic" typically means a resident of the urban Northeast. Although historically Catholics have lived throughout the nation, they clustered in East Coast cities. The old neighborhood became an imaginary space modeled on life in the highly populated Catholic enclaves of New York and Boston. This old neighborhood is a crowded city of Irish and Italian Catholics who are organized by families and parishes. Working in factories or on the docks, joining gangs or convents, the movie Catholics of *Angels with Dirty Faces* or *Going My Way* control the city's streets. Even the more romantic village of *The Song of Bernadette* has an urban feel with its cafés and dense living spaces. Arizona, though explored by Spanish Catholics a century before Boston's founding, would be an exotic and strange place to act out a Catholic drama.

On the other hand, for many Americans the desert setting made more sense as a place for enacting a transformation. Starting with the New England Puritans, Protestants claimed the "wilderness"—a desert, a forest, or the mountains—to find and remake themselves. This solitude offered the key for beginning anew. With nobody else around, one could reinvent oneself—or even an entire community. New England's dense forests and long winters only reinforced the Puritans' conviction that they really were the "city on a hill" described in the Gospel of Matthew. The expansive American wilderness came to be seen as a second, or perhaps new, Eden. The Mormon prophet Joseph Smith went so far as to claim discovery of the location of the original Eden in northwestern Missouri. The Mormons then helped to create the westward flow of the nation when they began migrating to Utah, the promised land of the New World. In the nineteenth century Thoreau viewed his solitary life at Walden Pond as an escape from the artificial life in nearby Boston. This included taxes and the moral tedium of Boston's Puritan establishment.

Retreating to the wild places was not an American invention. In the Bible, Moses and the Hebrews struggle forty years in the desert before reaching Canaan. Elijah escapes Ahab and Jezebel by living in the desert, surviving on food brought by birds. Prior to his temptation by Satan, Jesus spends forty days in the desert. Christian monasticism emerged in wild places; the monks sought isolated, hostile terrain as sites for spiritual combat with earthly temptations. Only later did monks begin building communities amid settled areas. American Christians still found the frontier inviting them to go deeper—within the continent as well as themselves. In the 1850s, when Catholic settlers moved out of Dubuque, Iowa, their wagons bore signs that read "Moving where nobody else lives."

Therefore, it is not surprising that Catholics also saw the "emptiness" of the Western frontier as a place where they could remake themselves. Out there in the wild and woolly West—without the clergy that dominated life back east or the fixed structures of parish life—a new type of Catholicism could be constructed. The movie's only priest, the rather sweaty Father Murphy (Dan Frazer), has seen the rat race of career advancement for what it is and has chosen the road less traveled. His appearances in the film are highly circumscribed, limited largely to distributing holy communion. In the relative absence of a well-defined clergy, the movie fills the desert with those assumed to be marginal to American life (African Americans), to Catholic life (semi-cloistered women religious), and to the ethnic communities of the era (Mexican Americans). It is here, in this frontier spun out of the imagination of novelist William E. Barrett and director Ralph Nelson, that American constitutional freedoms emerge unencumbered from the old city neighborhoods. The nuns build a chapel (thus embodying freedom of religion) and a black man makes this possible without fear of coercion or racism (hence the exercise of "life, liberty, and the pursuit of happiness"). *Lilies of the Field* moves the stage of Catholic life in America out of the city—crowded with expectations and complications—and into a world waiting to be made.

God Will Provide

Lilies of the Field tells the story of Homer Smith (Sidney Poitier), a young black man recently discharged from the army. Driving through the desert Southwest, he stops at a small farm for water. Once there he realizes that only five nuns inhabit the place. Not only are they Catholic sisters, all five speak with thick German accents.[1] Their stern Mother Superior Maria (Lilia Skala) understands Homer's arrival as a prayer answered. Homer wrestles with the choice of staying to build the chapel or leaving to continue his whimsical tour of the West. He and the mother superior routinely trade verbal barbs; he stays, he goes, he comes back. Eventually the "shapel" is built but Homer leaves before the first mass can be said. As Homer's station wagon disappears, the nuns' voices follow, carrying the song he has taught them: "Amen, Amen..."

Screenwriter James Poe adapted *Lilies of the Field* from a short 1962 novel by William E. Barrett. Not surprisingly, Barrett's life and outlook pervade his literary production and thus shape the novel as well as the eventual film. Born in New York in 1900, at sixteen Barrett moved with his family to Denver, Colorado. He later returned to New York to attend Manhattan College but promptly returned to Denver and pursued his two interests: writing and aircraft. Barrett, who was drawn to the unusual, began his career writing pulp fiction for magazines like *Dime Detective Novel*. His first book, *Woman on Horseback* (1938), was a fictional account of Paraguay's nineteenth-century despot, Francisco López. By the time *The Lilies of the Field* was published, Barrett had achieved a modicum of fame with his novels *The Left Hand of God* (1950) and *The Empty Shrine* (1958). Published by major commercial presses, their Catholic characters and themes did not stop them from being marketed to the general public. *The Left Hand of God* (1950), about a downed American pilot in China hiding as a Catholic priest, was made into a movie in 1955 staring Humphrey Bogart, Gene Tierney, and Lee J. Cobb. Later, *The Wine and the Music* (1968) became the motion picture *Pieces of Dreams* (1970), which told a priestly love story.

Despite being born in New York, Barrett saw Catholicism through optimistic, Western frontier eyes. His stories take place far away from the main corridors of American Catholic influence and exude hopefulness rather than a fascination with expressions of power. Barrett's popularity as a novelist was closely linked to his Catholic faith, and his attitude toward representing religion differed widely from that of more well-regarded Catholic authors such as Graham Greene. Although Barrett appreciated the realistic styles of Ernest Hemingway and Sinclair Lewis, he wrote books that were uplifting and had sympathetic characters. In his writings Barrett represented human growth and transformation. For him, men and women were basically good, and his novels were fables to illustrate his commitment to seeing the positive in life. He found novelists like James Joyce and William Faulkner, who explored the dark side of human nature, to be unreadable and unedifying. Barrett disliked postwar literary trends that depicted Catholic priests as troubled, compromised men. In a 1961 interview with the Catholic weekly *Ave Maria*, Barrett chided Greene for depicting "Catholic principles by showing the horror of sin rather than the positiveness of virtue."[2]

Barrett was typical of many Catholics of the 1950s who saw in their faith and in Christianity in general an openness to the modern world. American Catholics now stood ready to engage the world, not deny or condemn it. Barrett's realistic but ultimately positive faith represented the conviction that not only should something be done to improve the nation but that Catholics now possessed the wherewithal to do it. This enthusiasm and earnest good will was matched in the international arena by Pope John XXIII and the Second Vatican Council. While not a Catholic, *Lilies* director Ralph Nelson correctly surmised that Barrett's book would connect with the national ebullience surrounding the Kennedy White House and the curiosity about the Vatican Council.

Barrett's perspective on Christianity resonated strongly with many of those who read *Lilies of the Field*. A California literary agent, Fred Engel, enjoyed the book so much that he pitched it to movie studios hoping they would buy the rights to film it. Although he had worked with Mel Brooks and so had an "in" in Hollywood, neither studios nor independent producers were interested in the upbeat tale. Finally, Engel turned to a relatively unknown director who had been working in television. "I was kind of at the bottom of the list," Ralph Nelson admitted. Nelson had just finished *Requiem for a Heavyweight* (1962), in which he had directed Cassius Clay (not yet renamed Muhammad Ali) in a boxing drama. Nelson also became enchanted with *The Lilies of the Field* and agreed to work with Engel to get it made into a movie. One producer predicted failure: "Your lead is a Negro," he observed, "and your leading lady is a mother superior. Poison. Change it to Steve McQueen and this novice who never takes her final vows, see?" United Artists eventually agreed to fund the film up to $250,000, but Nelson had to mortgage his own house to ensure the project. With the money secured, the entire project took only two weeks to shoot in the desert near Tucson.

The key to the success of *Lilies of the Field* was Fred Engel's choice of lead actor. Engel had approached Sidney Poitier, who had been nominated for an Academy Award for his role in the controversial *The Defiant Ones* (1958) and who had cultivated a successful Broadway career performing in *A Raisin in the Sun*. His performance as an inner-city teacher in *Blackboard Jungle* (1955) had shown his ability to combine humor with hard-headed edginess. Already the veteran of eighteen films, Poitier had managed to steer away from the demeaning roles offered to black men. Poitier became enthusiastic about the *Lilies of the Field* script and agreed to accept a low $50,000 salary and 10 percent of the film's gross. The wage was only 20 percent of what he typically earned. In spite of securing the talents of Poitier, shopping the movie to Hollywood studios for funding was profoundly frustrating. In 1980 Poitier reflected that "the ludicrous, punitively low budget grudgingly allocated to the project by United Artists left no margin for even the slightest error." Poitier performed his own stunts for the film and used real construction materials and ladders. But the gamble paid off. Poitier's portrayal of Homer Smith heightened the character's flustered warmth and genuine goodness. The film was a success; even before it won its Oscar (Poitier as best actor) it was predicted to gross $2.5 million.[3]

Nelson and Poitier both worked hard to ensure that success. In the summer of 1963, Nelson entered the film in the Berlin Film Festival. Poitier meanwhile visited many large European cities—London, Rome, Paris, Copenhagen—to promote the film. In like fashion, he embarked on a rare American publicity tour. He organized a benefit screening of *Lilies* for the nation's leading black civil rights organizations. A biographer of Poitier has noted that Nelson, seeking to garner the best possible response from black Americans, connected the film specifically to the nation's civil rights movement through a nonmilitant racial posture. *Lilies of the Field* allowed all sorts of Americans to appreciate Poitier as a black man "without assaulting racial sensibilities."[4] One after another, rave reviews poured in. The *New York Times* glowingly reported "Sure, it's *Going My Way* with a Negro (and without the songs) in mood and moral. But we can do with a nice chunk of sweetness and optimism in a movie, for a change."[5]

There was no mistaking the movie's success. The humor, optimism, and convictions expressed by the film's characters was real. Americans, always looking for happy endings but even more so in postwar America, were ready to watch how a set of unusual people could eventually "just get along." The writing, directing, and acting of *Lilies of the Field* captured the attention of critics and the Motion Picture Academy. The film was mentioned in the *New York Times*'s "Top Films of 1963" along with *To Kill a Mockingbird* and Fellini's *8½*.[6] It received five Academy Award nominations, with Sidney Poitier winning an Oscar for his portrayal of Homer Smith, beating out Paul Newman in his performance in *Hud* and Rex Harrison in *Cleopatra*. Almost forty years would pass before another black man would win for best actor, Denzel Washington in *Training Day* (2001). In 1965 NBC considered making the movie into a television series, and five years later it was transformed into a Broadway musical, *Look to the Lilies*. Billy Dee Williams played Homer Smith in a 1979 made-for-television movie, *Christmas Lilies of the Field*, directed by the same Ralph Nelson who did the original.

Catholics and movies about Catholics had previously won Oscars, but the Catholic press simply adored *Lilies of the Field*. Moira Walsh, a movie reviewer for *America*, claimed that Catholics could scarcely demand "moral" movie content if they did not go to see it. *Commonweal* noted the movie's sentimentalism but concluded that the "delightfully engrossing film" radiated a "warm spirit and good will" that would "convey a lesson in integration of race and creed far more valuable than many elaborate religious spectacles." Nine months after *Lilies*' release and Poitier's Oscar, *Ave Maria*'s reviewer, Edward Fischer, had to admit that he had been wrong. When *Lilies of the Field* first appeared, Fischer had dismissed it as "a double dose of propaganda, religious and racial." In light of the film's success Fischer relented and watched it again. He then concluded that *Lilies* "assures us that the human spirit does have strength after all. That is an assurance we need after seeing so many pictures that are saturated with the attitude that nobody and nothing is no damn good."[7] *Lilies of the Field* did more than make Catholics look good; it made them look relevant and progressive. For decades many American Catholics were "militant Catholics" whose staunch anticommunism produced men like Senator Joseph McCarthy. But in the early 1960s all that was changing. A new day had dawned—for the church and the nation—and it was time to get to work.

The Land Was Big

The Arizona desert provides the background for *Lilies of the Field*, an "empty space" where Homer and the sisters seek new lives. Recently discharged from the army, Homer has a beat-up station wagon and nowhere to go. The sisters have fled East Germany's atheist, communist regime. Smith needs a job, and the sisters need help. Things look a little grim. In the desert, though, a black man might live free of the segregation and racism he would experience elsewhere in the nation. A small group of German Catholic nuns might find a physical and spiritual space to build a church of their own. Both the movie's dialogue and its black-and-white cinematography reinforce the openness that a big land bestows on those who live there. In his novel William Barrett explains that Homer recognizes that "the land was big" and thus full of possibilities.[8]

While the Arizona landscape is presented as big enough to fulfill the dreams of two sets of marginal people, the filmmakers themselves made a virtue out of the restrictions on their budget. The restraint and focus of *Lilies of the Field* contrasts sharply with more expansive films of the era. The early 1960s witnessed the emergence of epic movie blockbusters such as *El Cid* (1961) and *Khartoum* (1966). The year that *Lilies* was made with its meager budget, *Cleopatra* was finally finished, turning out to be the most expensive movie in film history—costing over $44 million. The grandiose scale of these productions reflected America's sense of its own greatness at a time when it was being subjected to serious domestic trials. John Ford and Henry Hathaway's *How the West Was Won* (1962), boasted twenty-four stars and spanned theater screens in Cinerama. It presents a very different picture of the West from the simple austerity of *Lilies of the Field*. Director Ralph Nelson created the frontier not from the vast expanses of the landscape, as Ford did, but out of the expansive human characters who meet in a place where they can be both their distinctive selves and yet come together to accomplish mutual goals.

William Barrett understood the ideal frontier as a place where ecumenical exchange could take place. The film works as a statement of the possibility that on the frontier the best of each Christian denomination can be expressed and shared. The movie uses dietary differences to broach the sensitive subject of Catholic-Protestant dialogue. Several times Homer Smith compares the sisters' diet to his male, black, Baptist expectations of what to eat. "That must be a Catholic breakfast," Homer mutters the first morning when a sister places in front of him a single scrambled egg and a half-filled glass of milk. Several mornings of the same fare explain Homer's desire to "fill his Baptist stomach" on Sunday instead of attending mass. The connection between food and religion indicates a much larger conflict between European Catholics and southern Protestants. While we think of Italian Catholics as enjoying their pasta and Polish Catholics their sausage, the meager food ways of convents are also a part of Catholic tradition. Nuns eat a different diet as a sign of their obedience as well as a spiritual exercise. Even for lay Catholics, meatless Fridays and fasting during Lent were taken as commonplace during the early 1960s. Fed up with his Catholic hosts' meager rations, Homer shops in a local store for more substantial fare. He returns with several kinds of meat, including pigs' feet. The sisters shriek with glee when Homer unpacks the last of the groceries: a string of cellophane-wrapped lollipops. Mother Maria scowls. Homer's effusive food gift might erode her authority over the sisters, yet she recognizes his graciousness and giving spirit. The film makes it clear that the sisters respect his approach and are charmed by his concern for their well-being. We are to feel it is in this mutual exchange—they receive the lollipops and he their smiles—that basic human understanding is achieved. Barrett and Nelson stress that it is through the small, intimate details of living together that people discover their mutual humanity.

Throughout the film, the commonalties of Christian traditions—rather than their differences—are stressed. In the "dueling Bibles" scene, it is clear that both the Catholic mother superior and the Baptist ex-soldier can claim the scriptures. To overcome his protests that God did not send him to build their "shapel," Mother Maria grabs an enormous Bible and selects her proof text: "The simple will be endowed with shrewdness and the young with knowledge and prudence" (Proverbs 1:4). Armed with his pocket New Testament, Homer shoots back with Luke 10:7: "Stay in that one house, sharing their food and drink; for the worker earns his pay." Homer emphasizes the last phrase for his own benefit and smiles triumphantly. Mother Maria responds with Matthew 6:28–29 and thus provides the film's name: "Consider the lilies of the field; they do not work, they do not spin; and yet, I tell you, even Solomon in all his splendor was not attired like one of these." Whatever good happens comes solely from God's grace. Homer looks flummoxed. A Catholic nun has just beaten a Baptist at the quintessential

Protestant game of Bible quoting. It is not only Protestants who rely on the Bible to set standards of behavior. For William Barrett, Catholicism is also grounded in biblical truth and the sisters understand well the sacred text. Though the protagonists differ in their interpretations, the scene underlines the fullness of revelation and the malleability of the written word. It also points to the increasing importance that scriptural study and biblical scholarship had begun to play in Catholicism. The scene ends with each individual gaining a greater respect for the religious expertise of the other.

Relaxing one evening with his guitar, Homer hears the nuns singing Latin hymns. Offering to share some of his songs, he teaches the nuns "a real tent-

7.1. In the "dueling Bibles" scene, it is clear that both Mother Superior Maria (Lilia Skala) and Baptist ex-soldier Homer Smith (Sidney Poitier) claim the scriptures. *Courtesy of the Academy of Motion Picture Arts and Sciences*

meeting song." Homer chooses the tune "Amen," and the sisters quickly recognize the word and join in. "Amen" uses a call-and-response technique, but the sisters sound more like they are performing a Gregorian chant than black gospel music. The sisters understand the patterns because they learned antiphonal singing for Vespers and mass. Homer, however, corrects their pronunciation: "Nicht 'Ah-men,'" Homer explains. "AY-men!" At this point Mother Maria clearly (but silently) disapproves. Both Homer and the sisters praise God through song, but Homer teaches the nuns a new way of articulating the well-known Christian response of "Amen." Homer's song details the life of Jesus from the Bethlehem manger to crucifixion and resurrection, ending triumphantly "But He rose on Easter morning!" to which the nuns respond with an angelic "Amen, Amen, Amen." By the end of the song even Mother Maria has joined the chorus. The sisters already know the meaning of "Amen," but now they are experiencing it through the idiom of the new land. The scene functions not only to illustrate how the German sisters are becoming Americanized (at least theoretically) but, perhaps more important, it underlines the continuation of Christian forms of music. Homer and the sisters can relate to one another because they have Christianity—although experienced through different idioms—in common.

On the Arizona frontier, the Baptist builds a Catholic chapel. He complains, he jokes, he goes away, he comes back. But he does not convert. Neither William Barrett nor Ralph Nelson intimate that his encounter with Catholics will lead to Homer's religious rebirth. Homer may get over some of his distracted aimlessness, but the movie is not about major transformations. The frontier in *Lilies of the Field* does not function as a crucible that tests and then remakes, rather it works to allow individuals and groups to open up to their God-given personalities. The frontier gives them room to be who they are. The sisters also help to build the chapel, and they engage their handsome and clever new friend. But they also do not convert. They do not fall in love with him; they continue to lead their semi-cloistered lives. Neither Barrett nor Nelson tell us what they will do on the frontier. Will they teach? Will they run a hospital? Or will they pray and live off donations? All they remain is what they are: sisters on the frontier.

On a larger scale, Barrett and Nelson move toward a compromise of Protestant and Catholic modes of Christianity. The film's emphasis on simplicity resonates with Protestantism's twin emphases on "only faith" (*sola fide*) as the single source of spiritual authority and "only the Bible" (*sola Scriptura*) as the source of God's revelation. While the nuns and the itinerant priest represent the Catholic church's visible leadership structure, the film erases any sense of an extensive hierarchy. The priest and nuns look more like members of the quintessential frontier churches of

Protestant Baptists, Methodists, and Disciples of Christ. Part of the movie's humor relies on Homer's astonishment that, twenty years after the Second World War, he has stumbled across Catholic nuns in the desert. Despite centuries of Catholic settlements in the West, Homer—like the audience—is surprised to see sisters outside of the city. Here again is the mixture of traditions, the hope that the rigid boundaries that keep people in their places can be dissolved.

The very physicality of the Catholic "church" is also remade in the film— transforming it into something more Protestant. *Lilies of the Field*'s visual humor includes playful scenes about what constitutes a chapel. Homer cannot believe that the supposedly inflexible Catholic church, symbolized by the inflexible nun bossing him around, has commandeered a trailer as a substitute worship space. Here we see James Poe's screenplay and Ralph Nelson's directing departing from the original novel. The novel depicts the sisters walking to mass in a nearby dilapidated town with an equally decrepit church. In the film, Father Murphy operates out of a trailer chapel: a camping trailer equipped with an altar, stations of the cross, a generator for loudspeakers, and living facilities. Not a Hollywood contrivance, Catholic priests and laypeople actually used such trailer chapels to conduct Catholic revivals in rural America from the 1930s through the mid-1960s. *Lilies of the Field* illustrates how Catholics sought to reclaim their presence on the frontier but without the weighty institutional frameworks of the East Coast. They still have the essentials of the rituals—the priest's vestments, the bread and wine, the altar boys' robes—but the triumphant attitude has been left behind. Religious commitment brings service to the desert, not institutional posturing. Even if the interior of the newly built "shapel" looks like familiar Catholic space, the bareness of its location and the simplicity of its form reminds the audience that even a permanent Catholic church must look different in the desert.

The ecumenical spirit that Barrett, Nelson, and Poe express in *Lilies of the Field* is perhaps best delineated in comparison with another film about Catholics that opened in 1963: Otto Preminger's *The Cardinal.* Based on a popular 1950 novel by Henry Morton Robinson, *The Cardinal* traces the burgeoning career of a young Boston priest, Stephen Fermoyle (Tom Tryon). Filmed in sweeping full color, *The Cardinal* resembles the epic films of the early 1960s that indulged in visual and political expansionism. En route to becoming a prince of the church—a red-hatted cardinal—Fermoyle encounters racist southern vigilantes, German Nazis, his own pride, and a possible romantic interest. Fermoyle successfully negotiates these temptations, and he does so with no compromises, no thoughtful reflections, no prolonged debating. Jews who have eyes for Catholic girls must convert. Young women who have difficult pregnancies and need abortions must die. Those with

7.2. Father Murphy (Dan Frazer) says mass at a trailer chapel, which is a camping trailer equipped with an altar, stations of the cross, a generator and loudspeakers, and living facilities. *Courtesy of the Academy of Motion Picture Arts and Sciences*

secular questions must accept things solely on blind faith. Fermoyle's superior, Monsignor Monaghan, insists that such faith is precisely the only safe path to truth. *The Cardinal* wallows in the world of 1950s militant Catholicism but by the early sixties this drama, triumphalism, and assuredness was evaporating. Robinson's novel had been quite popular, but the movie never quite captured public attention. It won none of its six Academy Award nominations.

The Cardinal seems bloated and inauthentic compared to the trimmed-down *Lilies of the Field*. Fermoyle's rural Protestant antagonists are mere caricatures and even the Catholic stronghold of the urban Northeast appears wooden and superstitious. When a statue of the Virgin Mary miraculously bleeds, the parish's Italian immigrants crowd the church in search of more miracles, much to the Irish monsignor's chagrin. Fermoyle calms the crowd, and then later discovers the "real" cause: a leaking, rusty pipe above the statue. However, he refuses to break the hard news to his parishioners, allowing his followers to believe something he knows is not true with the tepid explanation, "God caused the pipe to leak." The flashy, uncompromising, power-driven world of *The Cardinal* may have reflected the realpolitik of the early 1960s, but it did not engage the dreams of Americans.

Audiences gravitated to *Lilies of the Field* precisely because it offered a different vision of the world—one that was honest, authentic, straightforward, humorous, and giving. On the frontier, the old neighborhood's suffocating determinism could be shed while its communal spirit could be cultivated. Both Homer and Mother Maria struggle with their individual wants and desires, but it is only when they come together as a team that the chapel can be built. Standing before the newly finished altar, Mother Maria tells Homer that God "answered my prayer through you." *Lilies of the Field* imagines a way that people who have little in common on the surface can reach beyond their differences and join together into a productive, mutually supportive community.

The Frontier of Race

"Schmidt!" The word wakes Homer every morning and precedes every new demand from Mother Maria. Since she is the mother superior, she expects obedience. Homer marvels at the readiness with which the other four nuns meet Mother Maria's orders. Following their lead, he takes to addressing her as "Mother," too. In heated arguments, he reduces her title to the more familiar "Mama." Still, he quickly grows tired of her bossiness. After all, he just left the army and, being black, he'd rather not listen to yet another white person issuing demands. "I ain't no nun. I ain't no one you can boss around!" he retorts after one of Mother Maria's more intrusive requests. Later he calls her "an old warmonger" and "a regular Hitler" under his breath. Homer realizes that, despite all his wandering through the desert, he is no further from the racial divisions traumatizing the rest of America. "Oh Mama coming early to feed the slaves," he mutters sleepily one morning as Mother Maria approaches with his breakfast. When the nun once again describes another job instead of payment for work, Homer insists: "You pay me! You wanna take advantage of a poor little country boy!" The movie's racial awareness culminates when, flabbergasted by the mother superior's incessant demands, Homer shouts, "Go get yourself another boy!"

It is no surprise that critics and audiences alike understood *Lilies of the Field* as a race film. *Ebony* magazine proclaimed, "For warmth, good humor and dialogue, the film is a standout." The publication conceded that "the film can hardly be considered a message picture" since only two scenes involved racial prejudice, but this was not a problem since *Lilies* "largely overlooks the issue of color, which may really be a message in itself." "When our nation's strained interracial tensions have reached the snapping point," another reviewer summarized, Homer appeared at an auspicious time.[9] The year 1963 saw the apogee of the civil rights movement. Slightly more than a month before *Lilies of the Field* opened on the first of October, over 250,000 people gathered in Washington to protest racial injustice. A diverse group of organizations supported the March on Washington for Jobs and Freedom with the National Association for the Advancement of Colored People, the national Urban League, the Congress of Racial Equality, the Student Nonviolent Coordinating Committee, and the Southern Christian Leadership Conference organizing African Americans across the country to come to the nation's capital. The National Catholic Conference for Interracial Justice, the National Council of Churches, and the United Auto Workers also participated in the march. After the national anthem was sung by Marian Anderson, Patrick O'Boyle, the Catholic cardinal of Washington, D.C., delivered the opening invocation. Calls for economic and social justice were made by many, but Martin Luther King, Jr.'s "I Have a Dream" speech made at the foot of the Lincoln Memorial is what we now remember from that monumental day.

The march was a peaceful exercise in freedom of speech, but the year was also marked by violence. On June 12, Medgar Evers, an activist for voting rights in Mississippi, was shot in his home's driveway; he was carrying T-shirts saying "Jim Crow Must Go." Two weeks before *Lilies of the Field* opened, four young girls were killed when a bomb blew up a black Baptist church in Birmingham, Alabama. Many African Americans were demanding their rights as citizens, and every day images of racial disharmony flashed across the nation's televisions screens. Could black and white Americans ever live together? How might their interactions be reimagined such that their conversations would not end with violence?

Lilies of the Field plays out race relations in ways that gave hope to both black and white audiences. Consistently, humor between Homer and the nuns defuses what would ordinarily escalate into tense confrontations. An English-language lesson becomes a place of cultural exchange. Previously the sisters had learned English by using ridiculously outdated phonograph records. Chuckling at their attempts to repeat "we need a butler to take our luggage," Homer turns off the record player and has them repeat his words instead. First he teaches them "I stand up," but then quickly—with a broad smile—has them repeat "I stands up!" After that he uses his own skin color to differentiate between black and white, correcting their use of *schwarz* and *weiss*. It is important to note that this scene came primarily from Poitier and Nelson. Barrett's original novel includes Homer teaching the nuns English but without such specifics or provocative humor.[10] While from our more jaded perspective in the twenty-first century, this scene might look patronizing, we must recognize the power it exuded at the time. Only the hippest white Americans acknowledged in the early 1960s the contributions that African Americans made to music, language, and the arts. This period was also a time when easy conversations between whites and blacks were rare. The public language of 1963 was more often whites taunting black protestors rather than learning how to "talk black." Homer gives part of himself through his recognizably black dialect, and the nuns move closer to becoming citizens by learning how to speak as Americans.

In the 1950s and 1960s almost all Americans understood "race" in opposing binary categories of "black" and "white." Music offered one opportunity to

7.3. While from our twenty-first-century perspective, Homer Smith's (Sidney Poitier) effort to teach "black English" might look patronizing, we must recognize the power it exuded at the time. The public language of 1963 was more often whites taunting black protestors rather than white nuns moving closer to becoming American through embracing African American culture. *Courtesy of the Academy of Motion Picture Arts and Sciences*

overcome such division. Americans were already familiar with black singers such as Harry Belafonte (one of Poitier's best friends), Mahalia Jackson, and Little Richard. Just before *Lilies* was released, the March on Washington had filled the nation's capital with people—and music. Black opera star Marian Anderson sang the national anthem, and white folk singer Bob Dylan sang "Only a Pawn in Their Game." Whites joined blacks in the black church tradition of call and response as the speakers' messages were punctuated by loud, rhythmic shouts of affirmation. Television often broadcast black and white civil rights protesters linking arm in arm as they sang "We Shall Overcome." Since *Lilies of the Field* opened only a month after the march, the exchanges between Homer and the nuns through the English lesson and the song "Amen" appeared to emulate that summer's ideals. Language and music had become a middle ground where blacks and whites could share their cultures.

Black choreographer and musician Jester Hairston arranged the "Amen" piece and sang the male lead for the movie. Sidney Poitier then lip-synced (badly, according to some reviewers) the lyrics. Hairston was a sought-after choral director who had organized Hollywood's first integrated choir. A talented composer, he arranged and published more than 3,000 black spirituals.[11] Hairston walked the thin line between preserving the dignity and protest of the spirituals while making them safe for both white and black consumption. A summer of protest music had created a background of racial tension for writing black music, and Hairston needed to ease that tension without diluting the music or its racial roots. Just as *Lilies* alludes to a future color-blind America, its music affirms a simple (not simplistic) celebration of Jesus' death and resurrection. On the imagined frontier, it is perfectly possible for a black man to teach nuns a thing or two about Christianity. Underneath, they are all human beings and ultimately share the same faith.

Today, scholars no longer view race in America as a binary opposition between black and white. To do so ignores the significant ways in which Latinos (and other groups) have triangulated considerations of race in American life. In 1963, however, Mexican Americans maintained a shadowy existence in the world of the movies. Apart from the café owner, Juan (Stanley Adams), the desert Mexicans of *Lilies of the Field* are an anonymous, faithful, diligent group. Mother Maria glides past them, often quite haughtily. At first Homer gets testy when they try to help him build the chapel. On the other hand, the Mexicans embody some of the film's highest ideals. Their Catholicism is simple, deep, and quite capable of surviving without having a priest living in their midst. They work hard and give their free time to help Homer (who accepts their assistance once he realizes that, despite his dreams, he cannot finish the project without them). Mother Maria wants the chapel built for them. In Barrett's novel she and the sisters name their new church St. Benedict the Moor (a popular black-skinned saint) to honor Homer, but their vocation is to serve those who already inhabit the desert. Two years later, in 1965, American immigration policy would change significantly, producing noticeably higher rates of immigration from Mexico, Central and South America, and Asia. Cesar Chavez would organize a boycott of California's grape farms and bring the despicable conditions under which Mexican migrants labored to public attention. *Lilies of the Field*, however, represents race like many Americans still think of it—as a drama in black and white. It would not be until films like *The Mission* (1986) or *Santitos* (1999) that audiences would begin to experience Catholicism from a different direction.

Gender Frontier

Homer's line "I ain't a nun. I ain't no one you can boss around" does not allude only to the African American pursuit of justice. The words resonate quite clearly as a stereotype of Catholic nuns. They gave orders and Catholic laypeople obeyed. *Lilies of the Field* conveys the mixture of reverence and dread, fear and fascination, that circled around America's sisters. One Sunday when Homer accompanies Mother Maria toward the trailer chapel, the Mexican American locals quickly move out of their way. The reverential treatment startles Homer, but Mother Maria tells him coolly: "Smile at the people but don't say anything." Mother Maria knows that her presence is a gift. The Catholic church might be led by celibate men, but celibate women enabled the institution to realize its service mission and to run effectively. This was especially true in the United States, where sisters taught in the schools, staffed the hospitals, and established charitable organizations around the country. Women religious built and shaped everyday American Catholic life. Becoming a sister often offered young Catholic women the only opportunity to escape the marriage-and-children expectations they all faced. Granted, the celibacy vow posed an obstacle for many, but in exchange for marriage with Jesus, sisters gained spiritual authority, education, professional training, and meaningful work outside of the nuclear family.

Catholic sisters had long been visible in the country and so it is not surprising they entered the movies. Nuns figured in silent movies, and Ingrid Bergman won the hearts of Americans with her portrayal of Sister Mary Benedict in *The Bells of St. Mary's* (1945), the sequel to *Going My Way*. In *Heaven Knows, Mr. Allison* (1957) the familiar trope of sacred meeting profane is acted out during World War II when a missionary sister is left on an island with a Marine. As with *The Bells of St. Mary's* and *Lilies of the Field*, the movie contains not a whiff of romance. In *The Nun's Story* (1959), Audrey Hepburn plays a Belgian sister who tries to pursue her dream of becoming a medical missionary. The 1960s continued this flourishing of nun movies with *The Sound of Music* (1965), *The Trouble with Angels* (1966), *Where Angels Go, Trouble Follows* (1968), and Elvis Presley's last movie, *Change of Habit* (1969). These movies depict nuns as real women and not neutered misfits, even after the restrictions of the Production Code were exchanged for a film rating system. During the 1950s and 1960s, Hollywood neither ridiculed nor relegated to a background issue a woman's decision to join a community of sisters. The nuns' humanity shines through, not despite, their white and black habits.

The success of *Lilies of the Field* in presenting the frontier as a place where stereotypical gender roles could be moderated is due to the chemistry created between Sidney Poitier and Lilia Skala. Skala's portrayal of the unflinching mother superior relied on her firsthand experiences with totalitarianism. Born in 1896, Skala became a career actress in her native Vienna prior to the Nazi takeover of Austria. She and her Jewish husband subsequently moved their two sons to England and then in 1939 to the United States. Within two years Skala had reestablished her acting career, using her German-accented English to her advantage. Prior to *Lilies of the Field* she starred in several television soap operas and Broadway productions. She portrayed Mrs. Frank when *The Diary of Anne Frank* toured the country in the 1950s. Even so, she was working in a Long Island factory when she heard Nelson was filming *Lilies*. Without having read Barrett's novel, she asked Nelson about the possibility of casting one nun with a foreign accent. She was understandably pleased when she learned the full story.

William Barrett based his story of Mother Maria on a community of real nuns who had settled near his Denver home. In the mid-1930s, Nazi persecution had convinced the nuns of Eichstätt Abbey, one of the oldest Benedictine convents in Bavaria, to send some of their sisters to the United States. Three arrived in Boulder, Colorado, where they were able to buy 150 acres of land and a dilapidated church. The women quickly set about repairing the farm's buildings, including turning the old church into a tool shed. Five more nuns from Germany arrived and each nun performed specific farming duties—milking cows, herding cattle, maintaining equipment, haying, and driving the farm tractor. They named their abbey St. Walburga and neighbors quickly became accustomed to the nuns' daily work schedule punctuated by ringing chapel bells. Although the community moved to a more remote Colorado location in 1997, for decades they offered those

7.4. The success of *Lilies of the Field* was due in large part to the chemistry created between Sidney Poitier and Lilia Skala. Skala's portrayal of the unflinching mother superior relied on her firsthand experiences with totalitarianism and her ability to present a Catholic nun as a moderator of stereotypical gender roles. *Courtesy of the Academy of Motion Picture Arts and Sciences*

living near Denver and Boulder a glimpse of the monastic life of work and prayer.[12]

Lilia Skala captures in her portrayal of Mother Maria the human complexity of a woman dedicated to God and her sisters. Far from marching around with a perpetual scowl, the mother superior more than once loses her tough façade. Often she signals her approval with a silent, disarming twinkle in her eye and a barely detectable smile. Homer's language lessons spark her curiosity and by the end of "Amen" she is singing along with the younger nuns. Not leaving the construction of her convent entirely up to God, she sends wealthy Catholics and civic groups letters asking for donations. Predictably, she receives one rejection letter after another. When the last one arrives, she slams it on the table and cries, "I put my trust in men instead of God, and they failed me!" At the movie's end, she finally acknowledges Homer's efforts with a simple but utterly heartfelt "thank you."

Skala's representation of Mother Maria's imperfections emphasizes her humanity and thus makes her a far more believable nun than others portrayed in film. The youthful beauty of movie nuns Ingrid Bergman, Audrey Hepburn, and Deborah Kerr accentuate their cinematic appeal but also set them off as perfect, mild, and otherworldly. Hepburn's Sister Luke serves as a nurse in the Belgian Congo, but her habit remains sparkling white. On the other hand, the well-into-middle-age Mother Maria wears a bonnet and apron when toiling out in the sun, just as the Boulder Benedictines probably did. She dresses to work on the frontier, not to look pretty against an exotic background. Further, there is no question that Mother Maria and her sisters would have built that chapel by themselves if Homer had not stopped by. Mother Maria and her charges work hard and get dirty, and they are also committed to their faith. In *The Nun's Story*, Sister Luke endlessly struggles with her vocation, and the real Catholic sisters who saw the film complained bitterly about the movie's mendacity. For all of her reflection and self-assessment, Sister Luke is not nearly as free as the indomitable Mother Maria. *Lilies of the Field* offers through all its optimism and simple piety a far more realistic view of Catholic nuns. Mother Maria's pride and dignity match Homer's. She demands much from the younger sisters, but they genuinely respect the mother superior.

Living as nuns had offered Catholic women an alternate family structure since the earliest Christian communities, but in 1963 women were reading about other ways to structure their lives. That year witnessed the publication of Betty Friedan's landmark, *The Feminine Mystique*. Friedan argued that the dis-ease, the "problem that has no name," that many educated women felt with their lives was due to their isolation in the suburbs with their children and husbands. Women needed more meaning in their lives and that meaning could be generated through professional careers. *The Feminine Mystique* helped to mobilize middle-class white women to understand the growing need for a feminist movement. This active, enthusiastic embrace of education, mobility, and individual freedom also appeared in Helen Gurley Brown's *Sex and the Single Girl* (1962). As with Friedan's analysis, *Sex and the Single Girl* challenged the ability of domesticity to satisfy women, and it urged its readers to become educated, find a career, and prepare themselves for the day when men would "leave them like dishes in a sink." In the independence and determination of Mother Maria is a model of female behavior that echoes the independence of Friedan and Brown but still is fully clothed in acceptable religious norms for women. The authority and competence of a Mother Maria, which many Catholics had experienced in their schools, hospitals, and social services, was now being suggested as a goal for women who would not be bound by churchly traditions and celibacy. As with other media nuns, the sisters of *Lilies of the Field* stood at the "crossroads between the best of the past and the best of the future."[13]

Mother Maria also is used in the film to demonstrate the age-old problem that besets both religious communities and the nation in general: leadership. Whom to follow? Do we follow the inspired prophet (Mother Maria) whose grasp of practical realities might be lacking, or the hard-headed realist (Homer Smith) who probably overlooks the spiritual magnitude of what the community might do? This question appears late in *Lilies* when an argument erupts between Homer and Mother Maria over who directs the Mexican workers. (The active agency of the workers themselves goes utterly unnoticed.) With the chapel half-completed, Mother Maria starts an impromptu homily about the chapel's importance. Building the chapel will bring everybody together spiritually as well as physically. At the same time Homer—standing at the other end of the chapel space—begins showing the workers what he really wants done. Confusion ensues as the workers are torn between their ageless reverence for the nun and their more immediate appreciation of Homer's wall-building skills. Soon Mother Maria is shouting to be heard ("and everybody vill vork together!") but the workers turn to follow Homer.

Homer's pragmatic directions win the battle but Mother Maria's astute theological argument wins the war. She successfully paraphrases St. Paul's notion of the "mystical body of Christ": through the contributions of all assembled, God's presence is made real in their midst. On the frontier, all must use whatever talents they have to build a community. They must not be satisfied with traditional notions of what is appropriate behavior for women, or for blacks, or for Mexicans. This elemental joy comes from both the filmmakers and the optimism of the early 1960s, but it also bubbles up from the deepest wells of Christianity. St. Paul's letters to the Corinthians and Romans speak of the "mystical body of Christ." God gives each member of the body specific duties to perform. Together these constitute Christ's living body until his return.

American Catholics had rediscovered this radical assertion of Christian equality earlier, in the 1930s, but it took the combination of Kennedy, Vatican II, and the new frontiers of the 1960s to cement this conviction in the American Catholic mind. Mother Maria essentially affirms it when she shows Homer the chapel's completed interior. Everybody gave as they could to help build the chapel, and now all may enjoy its presence. The Catholic notion of sacramental grace, that God takes material objects and imbues them with supernatural love, could scarcely be clearer. God is in that place. Homer, the nuns, and the area's Mexican residents have made that possible. Mother Maria warmly tells Homer that at the first mass tomorrow morning he'll sit in the front row with her. That night, though, Homer slips away into the desert. With the work done, he need not stick around for a mass. His legacy remains, though, as a joyous "Amen, Amen, Amen, Amen!" is sung repeatedly as *Lilies of the Field* ends.

The Problem of the Good

In filmmaking—as in other cultural representations—it is always difficult to portray the good. How can one show a hopeful, positive Christianity that is realistic without succumbing to clichés and sugary sentiments? Is it possible to make an optimistic movie that seeks to provide alternative ways of imagining a future without making it utterly captive to the mood of its historical time such that it becomes laughable when that mood changes? While reviewing a DVD boxed set of Sidney Poitier films, a journalist suggested that viewers first watch several of the excessively violent and sexual "blaxploitation" films of the 1970s and "then atone for your sins with a little Poitier. Two Hail Marys and one *Lilies of the Field* and you're good as new."[14] The goodness of *Lilies of the Field* seemingly has had little relevance to film history or race relations because of its naïve association of faith with reworking the social order. From the vantage point of 2004, *Lilies* was an overly innocent film with little to say to contemporary viewers. Indeed, if we consider two performances by black men that the Academy of Motion Picture Arts and Sciences has awarded Oscars, the differences between then and now could not be more stark. In 1964 Sidney Poitier won an Oscar for best actor for his portrayal of Homer Smith, while in 2002 Denzel Washington won the same Oscar for playing a degenerate, corrupt policeman, Alonzo Harris, who was hated equally by his white apprentice cop and by black gang members. It is difficult to revisit *Lilies of the Field* in the new millennium and to try to understand the optimism of the Kennedy years.

That optimism, reflected in *Lilies of the Field*, was profoundly shaken scarcely two months after the film entered the theaters. On 22 November 1963 John

F. Kennedy was shot and killed in Dallas, Texas. Pope John XXIII had died that June but his passing was expected. Already past seventy when elected pope, he was viewed as an interim pontiff who was not supposed to rock the boat much. John Kennedy, though, was vigorously, glamorously young. His wife and children were equally beautiful and vibrant. His assassination served notice that time was short for the hope celebrated in his presidency, Vatican II, and *Lilies of the Field*. Suddenly the bright horizons seemed quite gloomy. The Vietnam War intensified as did protests against it in the United States. The outcry over Paul VI's 1968 encyclical *Humanae vitae*, which reaffirmed the Catholic church's prohibition on artificial birth control, indicated to many that the good feelings of Vatican II were fading. Race issues became increasingly militant. In spite of fantastic box-office success—in early 1969 he was recognized as one of the world's highest-paid actors[15]—Poitier found himself estranged from the black American community he sought to empower. Within a decade black critics lambasted his characters, especially Homer Smith, as innocuous black cartoons produced for white America. With Martin Luther King, Jr., assassinated (1968), Poitier's dignified characters suddenly seemed not only irrelevant but insulting. In 2000 Poitier still carried the scars: "In essence I was being taken to task for playing exemplary human beings."[16]

While it is easy to fall into the pit of despair over the fragility of dreams and hopes—spoken with a Catholic accent or not—we must not underestimate the power of movies and movie stars to motivate individuals to choose the good. In spite of all the criticism Poitier endured, he remains an iconic figure in both film and American history. Black entertainers as diverse as Bill Cosby and Spike Lee cite Poitier's legacy as inspiration for their own work. As his biographer aptly declared: "For a generation he shouldered a burden, created sympathy for black equality, delivered liberal films within a conservative system. He became the screen symbol of a morally righteous political movement." It is difficult to underestimate the importance of Poitier for African Americans going to the movies in the 1960s. By watching "that tall, beautiful, suave and elegant Black man" accept the Oscar in 1964, Oprah Winfrey "realized that anything in the world was possible." Moved to tears of joy, that ten-year-old girl found inspiration in the film and the man. With a net worth in 2006 of $1.4 billion and a highly influential media empire, Oprah Winfrey reflects the positive attitude and inviting "you can do it too" message that flows out of *Lilies of the Field*. Like Homer Smith, she is loved for her robust humor, soulful tenderness, empathy, and plain speaking. She also is one of America's foremost philanthropists, donating almost $52 million to charitable causes in the year 2005 alone.[17] In an America continually beset by racial, gender, sexual preference, and age divisions, Oprah engages a diverse audience that ranges from baby boomer white homemakers, to gay African American men, to college students.

At the same time, Ignatius Press, an unabashedly conservative publisher of traditional Catholic materials, includes *Lilies of the Field* in its DVD/VHS catalog. Amid movies about St. Joan of Arc, Mother Angelica, and Charles de Foucauld—all models of Catholic self-denial and unbending faith—*Lilies* stands as an inspiring, uplifting story. For the Catholics who look to the era before the Second Vatican Council for both comfort and a justification for their devotions and theology, *Lilies of the Field* reflects Catholicism at its high point in the country. It is the enduring legacy of the film that it can speak to the hopes of Oprah Winfrey and to the editors at Ignatius Press. For a diverse group of Americans, *Lilies of the Field* continues to reassert the frontier myth of cultural remaking as it works against the hyperindividualism of modern society. In America, sometimes, the "new" frontier actually introduces something ancient and primordial. *Lilies of the Field* testifies to the irreducible goodness of God's last and best creation: humanity.

NOTES

Several people facilitated the research and writing of this chapter. Maria de la Camara, St. Rose's dean of arts and humanities, and David Szczerbacki, the college's provost and vice president for academic affairs, generously awarded a St. Rose scholar's grant. My St. Rose colleagues provided valuable insight and guidance: Steve Black, Ben Clansy, Kim Middleton, and Peter Osterhoudt. Several students chipped in, too: Ashley Bowman, Emily Bruce, Matt Marlow, Ashley Melsert, and Theresa Zanni. Will Gravely contributed research at the University of Denver on William Barrett. My thanks go to all.

1. There is a technical difference between a "nun" and a "sister." A *nun* refers to a woman religious who is cloistered, who stays out of the public world and commits herself to a life of prayer. A *sister* is a woman religious who, while taking vows of poverty, chastity, and obedience, also is committed to acting out her religious convictions in the world. Sisters work as teachers, missionaries, and medical workers and perform other duties useful in public life. It is unclear in *Lilies of the Field* if these are nuns or sisters, and so I have used the terms interchangeably—as they often are used in popular parlance.

2. Robert T. Reilly, "William E. Barrett: Profile of a Conversation," *Ave Maria*, 25 November 1961, 6.

3. On the funding, see Murray Schumach, "Hollywood Trick; or, How to Turn Cheap 'Lilies' into Gold," *New York Times*, 9 February 1964; on production difficulties,

see Ralph Nelson, "Considering 'Lilies of the Field'," *New York Times*, 29 September 1963; on Nelson's contribution, see his obituary: "Ralph Nelson," *Chicago Sun-Times*, 24 December 1987; also see Sidney Poitier, *This Life* (New York: Knopf, 1981), 249.

4. Aram Goudsouzian, *Sidney Poitier: Man, Actor, Icon* (Chapel Hill: University of North Carolina Press, 2004), 214.

5. Bosley Crowther, "Screen: A Disarming Modern Parable," *New York Times*, 2 October 1963, 45.

6. Bosley Crowther, "Top Films of 1963," *New York Times*, 29 December 1963.

7. Moira Walsh, "Lilies of the Field," *America*, 12 October 1963, 439–40; Philip T. Hartung, "See How They Spin," *Commonweal*, 11 October 1963, 78–79; Edward Fischer, "Well, I Was Wrong—Again," *Ave Maria*, 27 June 1964, 9.

8. William E. Barrett, *The Lilies of the Field* (1962; reprint, New York: Warner, 1982), 59.

9. "Lilies of the Field," *Ebony*, October 1963, 55–58, quotations from 55 and 58; Arthur Knight, "SR Goes to the Movies: Lily White, Simon Pure," *Saturday Review*, 7 September 1963, 32.

10. Barrett, *The Lilies of the Field*, 25f.

11. Obituary: "Jester Hairston," *Bergen County* (NJ) *Record*, 27 January 2000.

12. On the Boulder community, see Thomas Noel, *Colorado Catholicism* (Boulder: University Press of Colorado, 1989); and on the nuns' current activities, see "Abbey Offers Peace, Prayer, Community, and Vocation," Catholic News Service (25 May 2006), available at http://www.catholic.org/hf/faith/story.php?id=19970.

13. Rebecca Sullivan, *Visual Habits: Nuns, Feminism, and American Postwar Popular Culture* (Toronto: University of Toronto Press, 2005), 74.

14. Marke Andrews, "Two Very Different Views of Black America Out on DVD," *Vancouver Sun*, 23 January 2004.

15. Goudsouzian, *Sidney Poitier*, 293.

16. Sidney Poitier, *The Measure of a Man* (San Francisco, CA: HarperSanFrancisco, 2000), 118; and "50 Years of Blacks in Entertainment," *Jet*, 26 November 2001, 43–64.

17. Goudsouzian, *Sidney Poitier*, 377; "Hallelujah! The First Winning Duo, Halle & Denzel," *Afro-American Red Star*, 5 April 2002; "Gifts and Grants, 2005," *Chronicle of Philanthropy*, available at http://philanthropy.com/stats/donors/2006/detail.php?ID_Gift=1135.

FURTHER READING

Albanese, Catherine. *Nature Religion in America: From the Algonkian Indians to the New Age.* Chicago, IL: University of Chicago Press, 1991.

Cripps, Thomas R. "The Death of Rastus: Negroes in Films since 1945," *Phylon* 28 (1967): 267–75.

Deloria, Philip. "Polarized Tribes: Colorado, Wyoming, and Montana." In *Religion and Public Life in the Mountain West: Sacred Landscapes in Transition*, ed. Jan Shipps and Mark Silk. Walnut Creek, CA: Alta Mira, 2004.

Diawara, Manthia. *Black American Cinema*. New York: Routledge, 1993.

Fisher, James. "Alternative Sources of Catholic Intellectual Vitality," *U. S. Catholic Historian* 13 (1995): 81–91.

Hoberman, J. *The Dream Life: Movies, Media and the Mythology of the Sixties*. New York: New Press, 2003.

Janosik, Mary Ann. "Madonnas in Our Midst: Representations of Women Religious in Hollywood Film," *U.S. Catholic Historian* 15 (1997): 75–98.

Kogan, Herman. *Toms, Coons, Mulattoes, Mammies, & Bucks*. New York: Continuum International, 2001.

Levy, Emanuel. *And the Winner Is . . . The History and Politics of the Oscar Awards*. New York: Ungar, 1987.

Marlett, Jeffrey. *Saving the Heartland: Catholic Missionaries in Rural America, 1920–1960*. DeKalb: Northern Illinois University Press, 2002.

Massa, Mark S. *Catholics and American Culture: Fulton Sheen, Dorothy Day, and the Notre Dame Football Team*. New York: Crossroad, 1999.

Poitier, Sidney. *This Life*. New York: Knopf, 1981.

Slotkin, Richard. *Gunfighter Nation: The Myth of the Frontier in Twentieth-Century America*. New York: Harper Perennial, 1992.

Sullivan, Rebecca. *Visual Habits: Nuns, Feminism, and American Postwar Popular Culture*. Toronto: University of Toronto Press, 2005.

Weisenfeld, Judith. *Hollywood Be Thy Name: African American Religion in American Film, 1929 1949*. Berkeley. University of California Press, 2007.

8

Praying for Stones
Like This

The Godfather *Trilogy* (1972, 1974, 1990)

Carlo Rotella

When I told Boston College's dean of arts and sciences that I was writing about *The Godfather*, he nodded knowingly and said, "Best scene of all time: when Moe Greene..." and he pointed at his own bespectacled eye. There was no need to say more. The dean is not alone in his high opinion of the scene in which Moe Greene gets it in the eye. If you were to ask American men—Catholic and non-Catholic, of Italian and non-Italian descent (the dean, shockingly, was Irish)—to name the greatest movie scenes of all time, I bet the baptism scene from *The Godfather* would finish at or near the top of the list. It's the "Stairway to Heaven" of American cinema. Like the classic-rock warhorse of nearly identical vintage, the baptism scene enjoys its elevated status because its admirers regard it not only as enjoyable but also as important. More than merely demonstrating artistic virtuosity or entertaining its fans, *The Godfather* offers those fans a fantasy of a usable past, embracing both the imagined 1940s and 1950s in which the movie's action takes place and the early 1970s moment in which it was made, which says something significant about who they think they are or wish they could be.

In the baptism scene, the movie's narrative and stylistic climax, Moe Greene (Alex Rocco) does indeed get it in the eye, the bullet memorably passing through the lens of his glasses when he looks up from a massage table. Other victims are gunned down on the steps of a courthouse, in bed, on an elevator, and through the glass panel of a revolving door. This braided series of murders is elaborately intercut with and grounded by a richly staged church baptism in which the priest intones, anoints, and otherwise goes about remitting the child's burden of original sin as he ushers him across the threshold of the spiritual life. Somber organ music plays throughout, and Michael Corleone (Al Pacino), the baby's godfather, who is responsible for the whirlwind of score-settling murders that will consolidate his rise to power, speaks for the baby as he deadpans the responses to the priest's liturgical cross-examination. Having renounced Satan, all his works, and all his pomps on the baby's behalf, Michael later finishes up his busy day at the office by supervising the garroting of the baby's father, Carlo Rizzi (Gianni Russo), his own brother-in-law, who had betrayed the Corleones to their now-dead enemies.

The Godfather: Part II (1974) picks up the story of Michael's rise to power—and concomitant loss of almost everything else that matters to him—right after the action of *The Godfather*. This narrative thread alternates with a second one, which precedes the action of *The Godfather*, in which Michael's father, Vito (Robert De Niro), comes to America in 1901 as a nine-year-old orphan, forges a life for himself in New York's immigrant ghetto, and embarks on a career as an upwardly

8.1. Michael Corleone (Al Pacino) and his wife, Kay (Diane Keaton), as godparents in *The Godfather*. *Courtesy of the Academy of Motion Picture Arts and Sciences*

mobile gangster. *Godfather II* also extends and deepens *The Godfather*'s signifying juxtaposition of Catholic ritual with lethal criminality. In Sicily, gangsters murder Vito's older brother during their father's funeral service. In New York, the young Vito stalks Fanucci (Gastone Moschin), a local crime boss, at a street festa in honor of a saint, cornering his prey and gunning him down as a priest gives the blessing. On a boat out on Lake Tahoe, one of Michael's hit men ends the second movie's climactic montage of murders by shooting Michael's brother Fredo (John Cazale) just after Fredo says a Hail Mary. Michael watches Fredo's murder from a distance, just as he watched his brother-in-law Carlo strangled in *The Godfather*.

Even when a Catholic ritual or image is not directly juxtaposed with murder, the family's dark business shadows it. The second movie's first big set piece is a party on the occasion of Michael's son's first communion, just as the first movie begins with a wedding reception. In both scenes, the don manages his criminal empire from his shadowed study while the rest of the family and their guests celebrate in the sunshine. The movies' decor offers similarly resonant juxtapositions. For instance, we can see a cheap reproduction of a painting of the Madonna and child tacked askew to the wall of the young Vito's storefront office in Little Italy. Madonna and child seem to watch over Vito's shoulder as he intimidates a

8.2. The young Vito Corleone (Robert De Niro) does business in his office in Little Italy in *Godfather II*. *Courtesy of the Academy of Motion Picture Arts and Sciences*

8.3. Mobsters kissing Michael Corleone's (Al Pacino) hand, as if he were a bishop, in *The Godfather*. *Courtesy of the Academy of Motion Picture Arts and Sciences*

slumlord on behalf of a neighbor. The same kind of juxtaposition inheres in the repeated stage business of supplicants kissing the godfather's hand as if he were a bishop. Seeking a favor, worldly advantage, or a reprieve from fate, they beg for his blessing or his intercession on their behalf as if he could speak into the ear of God. (In a scene cut from *The Godfather* but included as an extra in the boxed set of the whole trilogy on DVD, a dying man actually does beg Vito to use his influence to keep him out of hell.)

From wedding to baptism in *The Godfather*, from first communion to a final prayer at the hour of death in *Godfather II*, organized religion and organized crime reveal themselves as two faces of a single, blood-stained coin. What do we do, interpretively, with this pervasive signifying pattern?

Iconography

One standard way to read the *Godfather* movies' Catholic imagery has been as an element of their critique of the damage, hypocrisy, and bad faith that inevitably accompany the assimilation of immigrants. The movies melodramatically retell a familiar story in which the immigrant must hurt his own people and compromise himself in the name of making it in America. By the end of *Godfather II*, Michael has made it by all standard American measures—he owns a big detached house, he has a lot of money, his kids can have any material thing they want—but at the cost of divesting himself of any vital connection to other people, including his own family. Catholicism provides an instrument with which to examine the shocks and injuries of the Corleones' entry into the American mainstream.

In its simplest version, this standard reading emphasizing the critique of assimilation treats the movies' Catholic imagery as an implicit moral rebuke to individual characters and, more generally, to American capitalism's systemic tendency to turn people against their deepest beliefs and commitments. Since America reveals itself to be just like Mafia-ruled Sicily, only awash in money and with a veneer of democracy and the rule of law, making it in America entails even more profound criminality and sinfulness than does life in Sicily—and a great deal more hypocrisy, too. Vito may end up rich and powerful, able to buy judges and politicians, but he remains at heart a simple peasant-turned-bandit, a bootstrap striver who came to America with nothing but a strong will and an eye for others' weaknesses. His son Michael, by contrast, meets his future wife at Dartmouth, inherits the family business, operates legal gambling casinos, manipulates and outmaneuvers the Senate, influences U.S. foreign policy, and can promise his wife that the Corleones' business operations will soon be completely "legitimate." The haziness of the line separating Michael's criminality from the exercise of legitimate political and economic power tends to diffuse the moral rebuke from the individual to the social order through which he rises. That Michael attains far greater wealth and influence than his father ever did, and while doing far more terrible things than his father ever did, provides one measure of the Corleones' drive into the mainstream. If family, for instance, matters more than anything else in these movies, consider the relative sins of father and son: Vito murders with his own hands the Sicilian crime lord who killed his father, mother, and brother, while Michael orders the killings of his own brother and his own sister's husband (and, once he succeeds to the throne, never sullies his own hands with the labor of violence). The *Godfather* movies provide a viewer with the equipment to recognize and condemn both men's offenses, and especially Michael's, by employing a variety of cinematic techniques to contrast those offenses with moralizing images of Catholic ritual and iconography. The editing creates striking juxtapositions of piety and murder, variations in lighting contrast dark criminality to brightly lit celebrations with religious overtones, and resonant mismatches of sound and action layer church music and the echoes of prayer over murder.

That, as I said, is a basic version of the standard reading, which, while it may have the virtue of force and clarity, does not do justice to the complexity of the texts. For one thing, while the movies may be read as condemning Michael and Vito, they devote far more energy to presenting these characters as exemplary citizens of their world. A more advanced version of the standard reading, then, would focus less on elementary moral critique than on how competing moral claims ironically contradict and undermine each other. "Family," for instance, means unconditional commitment to one's children and parents and siblings, but "family" is also one of the Mafia's basic organizational units: Vito and Michael Corleone successively head one of the five families that rule organized crime in New York City. Each definition of family troubles the other, as evidenced by their violent interpenetration. Michael has his brother Fredo killed for betraying the interests of the Corleone crime family. Michael's wife, Kay (Diane Keaton), takes a similarly hardboiled approach to domestic life when she has an abortion—in effect, she orders a hit on her own unborn son. She wants to do something for which Michael can never forgive her, thus freeing herself of his oppressive love and protection. In these Vietnam War era movies, Michael and Kay destroy their own family in order to save it. The double-edged thematic notion of "being strong for the family" pares away the easy assumption of innocence from domestic life and the easy assumption of moral alienness from the Mafia family's criminal activities. The interpenetration of the two kinds of family reveals both as aspects of one ironic whole.

Apply that same logic to the explicitly Catholic imagery that pervades the movies, and one's reading of that imagery changes. Now, the church and its iconography do not simply give one a means to sit in judgment of the characters; rather, Catholicism enters into a two-way signifying transaction with their sins and does not escape untainted. Catholicism may seem to offer a vantage point from which to recognize the strength of gangsters as moral weakness, but organized crime also unmasks organized religion. Catholicism is revealed as another racket, another set of opportunities to gain advantage by lying to yourself and to others, another hand-kissing hierarchy of absolute power imported from the Old World and adapted to a supposedly democratic America supposedly governed by the rule of law.

How might we read the baptism scene now? The baptism itself no longer rests comfortably above the intercut murders as the moral high ground from which to judge them and to judge Michael. The murders, with their prefatory images of solitary hit men readying their clothes and weapons in a visual parody of priests preparing for mass, now reveal the baptism as just one of several rituals that miraculously transmute Michael's sins into virtues. For instance, the bland inauthenticity of his responses to the priest's questions—or the strong possibility that he's not lying at all and really knows himself to be a good Catholic who has to do what he must to take care of his own—anticipates his similar ritual blandness in *Godfather II* when he lies to and otherwise confounds a Senate committee investigating organized crime in America. During his testimony, Michael reminds the committee of his patriotic service to his country during World War II and of his good citizenship since then. And he's not really wrong to do so. The hidden influence exerted over the committee by both Michael and his archrival, the Jewish gangster Hyman Roth (Lee Strasberg), shows us that the Senate is fully implicated in the business of the Corleone family, Las Vegas casinos, the exploitation of Cuba by the mob, and other criminal enterprises inextricably tied to legitimate enterprise. Michael may well be the exemplary citizen of the movie's America. One way to read the repeated pronouncement by Francis Ford Coppola, the director, that "Michael is America" would be to recognize the peculiarly Catholic horror of Michael's discovery that in attaining this elect status he has become a parody of a Protestant. Cut off from a defining community, he becomes an isolated soul adrift in the sea of separate swimmers, unconnected to anyone or anything except his fate.

Or reconsider the image of the Madonna and child looking over the young Vito's shoulder while he dispenses his hard-handed substitute for justice in his storefront office in Little Italy. Otherworldly and gentle, patently unfit for the rough and tumble of life in the immigrant ghettos of early twentieth-century New York, the figures in the painting are not simply there to afford us a means to judge this profoundly sympathetic character—who comes to America alone after being brutally orphaned—and find him wanting. His story is also, in turn, an implicit rebuke to such naïve notions as God's love, mother love, and especially Christian morality. Vito's mother is a good woman who loves her family and no doubt enjoys the love of God. But when she finally comes face to face with Don Ciccio (Giuseppe Sillato), the Sicilian crime boss who killed her husband and older son, she pulls a very big knife on him—a gangster move—to buy Vito time to run to safety. Once Vito establishes a foothold in America, working hard to get ahead and to provide for his wife and young children, he knows what to do when Fanucci and other gangsters, who also own the local police, demand their cut of his business. Vito makes his gangster move before his enemy anticipates it, which makes the murder of Fanucci at the festa seem cold-blooded, but Vito's just thinking a couple of moves ahead, like a good chess player or businessman.

Given the world imagined by these movies, to deny the appropriateness or astuteness of Vito's conduct is to deny the roundness of the earth. If they're going to get you, you get them first. Turning the other cheek, forgiveness, or any other weak, sentimental response would amount to asking for it. Vito's pragmatic realism mounts an authoritative counterargument to any critique of his actions we might be tempted to read into the feebly affronted gaze of the Madonna and child on his office wall.

History

But the foregoing readings of the marriage of Catholicism to murder, whether basic or advanced, may well make a mistake in locating any significant religious meaning at all in the movies' use of prayer, mass, the saints, and other distinctly Catholic imagery. I think it is possible to read Catholicism in these movies as not a content but a form. Coppola uses religious imagery as a convenient visual and aural vocabulary with which to imagine what it means to be Italian American, in particular, and to imagine immigrant ethnic identity in general. Religion can be a crucial part of ethnic identity, of course, but matters of faith and ultimacy can become relatively trivial when the soul that matters is not one's eternal soul but rather the authority of one's claim to be an ethnic soul brother or sister. In an ethnic reading, the properly religious content drains almost entirely out of the *Godfather* movies' Catholic imagery, leaving it to function mostly as an ethnic marker, like food and music. Like eating cannoli or singing Sicilian songs, attending church or praying to God become ways for characters to show us where old-school tough guys get the wherewithal to do what an Italian American man's gotta do. Here, then, we turn from reading the religious iconography of Catholicism in the *Godfather* movies to considering their imaginative engagement with the social and cultural history of American Catholics—a considerably different matter requiring us to back up and come at the movies again from a different angle.

When *The Godfather* debuted in theaters, Francis Ford Coppola was surprised to find that audiences cheered during the baptism scene, responding to Michael's gangster apotheosis as stirring heroism rather than tragic-ironic antiheroism.[1] In my own experience of discussing the movie with all sorts of people, I often hear something on the order of "My God, what a lonely, two-faced monster Michael turned out to be." But I also hear appreciations of his strength, perhaps best expressed by a Dominican woman named Doris who said, "Jesus, Michael's got stones like this," accompanying her statement with a gesture of spreading wide the hands to approximate *coglioni* so grotesquely huge as to make bipedal locomotion nearly impossible. Faith didn't give Michael stones like this. Rather, his Catholicism merely helps to suggest where and how he, and his father before him, did get his resolve and inner strength—that is, from being Italian American, from the flow of tradition assumed to pass to the immigrant ethnic from the old country through the old neighborhood.

Rocky Balboa, the hero of *Rocky* (1976), draws from the same source to acquire the wherewithal to hold his own in the ring with the great Apollo Creed (Carl Weathers). On his way to fight Creed for the title, Rocky (Sylvester Stallone) yells up to his parish priest for a hurried blessing from a window of the rectory. That scene, like those of Rocky's training runs through the streets of the old immigrant ethnic urban villages of South Philly, wants to confirm for us our hero's unimpeachable credentials as an Italian American. He's a regular guy from the old neighborhood who can go the distance with any "colored" champion you've got. In *Rocky* that's about all Catholicism is good for.

So let's reconsider the *Godfather* movies' scenes of Catholicism and murder as arguments for the potency of white ethnic gangsters—and, more generally, white ethnic men, or white ethnicity itself. The scenes significantly trace such potency to the gangsters' ethnic heritage, with Catholicism providing a convenient reservoir of imagery appropriate to that task. As such they exemplify a larger cinematic habit of the 1970s, one also evident in scenes like that of Rocky receiving the prefight blessing in South Philly or of *The French Connection* (1971) cops—Popeye Doyle (Gene Hackman) and Cloudy Russo (Roy Scheider)—chasing down and beating up a hapless drug dealer in the wasteland fronting All Saints Church in Brooklyn.

During the 1970s, there was a flowering in American popular culture and especially in the crime genres of white ethnic American tough guys: characters of Italian, Irish, Polish, Greek, Jewish, and other European, non-WASP descent. Think of the Corleones as part of a cohort that includes all of the mobster heroes in all of the gangster movies that sought to exploit the success of *The Godfather*, plus all of the mobster villains who serve as fall guys in blaxploitation movies, private eye narratives (Jim Rockford of *The Rockford Files* referred to the mouth breathers he outwitted as "cloves of garlic"), and other genres. The cohort also includes the equally iconic cops in *The French Connection* and all of the movies and television series that came after: *The Super Cops* (1974; featuring mavericks named Greenberg and Hantz, played by Ron Leibman and David Selby) and *The Seven-Ups* (1973; featuring an elite squad led by a cop named Manucci, played by Roy Scheider), Theo Kojak (Telly Savalas), Tony Baretta (Robert Blake), Wojciehowicz (Max

Gail) and Fish (Abe Vigoda) on *Barney Miller*, and their many blood brothers on TV and in the movies. Throw in Martin Scorsese's Italian American hardcases in *Mean Streets* (1973) and *Raging Bull* (1980) and, of course, not only Rocky Balboa but many other characters played by Sylvester Stallone, Robert De Niro, Al Pacino, John Travolta, Dustin Hoffman, Christopher Walken, Harvey Keitel, Tony Franciosa, Tony Lo Bianco, and other actors whose careers boomed in the 1970s.

This cohort of white ethnic protagonists and antagonists proliferated in popular culture in a moment when the potency of the once-new and now-old ethnics was widely understood to be under attack. The pressure came not only from without, in the form of the assertion of the black and Hispanic inner city and the counterculture, but perhaps more crucially from within. White ethnics' own prosperity, suburbanization, and assimilation (the generational trajectory of the Corleones) seemed to be carrying them away from an imagined ethnic authenticity. Scenes with Catholic resonance like those in the *Godfather* movies use religious imagery as shorthand for "culture" writ large, tracing white ethnic characters' efficacy to the old neighborhood and the old country, insisting on their continued access to ethnic belonging and a deep well of tradition from which to draw purpose and meaning.

One useful historical frame for the *Godfather* movies, then, is the ethnic revival of the 1970s, a widespread reawakening of interest in the ethnic heritage of European immigrants. "Family," in this context, means one's imagined blood connection to a cultural tradition and thus to the identity that proceeds from it. A great many people pursued such connections by turning to ethnic identity and heritage as a political and not just a cultural force, by tracing family trees, by participating in ethnic festivals, and by retelling both familial and national origin stories to emphasize the experience of immigrants. None of these aspects of the general movement was particular to Catholics, but a great many Catholics were caught up in it, and it produced fresh ways to think about some of the most important processes and events in the social history of Catholics in America. We can see the ethnic revival as at once a major phase *in* the cultural history of American Catholics and a major phase of attention *to* their history.

The ethnic revival was not just a matter of individuals' reawakened interest in their heritage; it also revised the formulation of nationhood itself. Matthew Jacobson, who in the book *Roots Too* makes the first attempt at a comprehensive history of the ethnic revival, argues that the movement asserted and made canonical "an alternative myth of origins for the nation, whose touchstone is Ellis Island rather than Plymouth Rock, and whose inception is roughly in the 1890s rather than in the 1600s."[2] This myth decenters the Pilgrims' voyage on the *Mayflower* as well as the slaves' Middle Passage in favor of the immigrants' passage in steerage, culminating in the stock spectacle, lovingly rendered in *Godfather II*, of European peasants massing on the deck of a crowded ship to gaze up at the Statue of Liberty as they arrive in the Port of New York. Puritanism, the founding fathers, the American Revolution, the frontier, slavery, and the Civil War become prehistory. True American history now consists of arrival, upward class mobility, and assimilation. Its central drama is the pluralist encounter of immigrants with each other and with the WASPs and African Americans who were "already here" (and therefore function as this narrative's Native Americans, so to speak). The Ellis Island–centered account imagines a "hyphen nation" that coheres around shared commitments to immigrant roots (various though they may be), ideals of political and economic freedom, and unifying struggles against defining outside threats like fascism and communism.

A multitude of converging factors gave rise to the ethnic revival but two stand out. First and most important, the black civil rights movement of the 1960s provided both a challenge and a model, a way of conceiving and acting on group rights that inspired others, including the women's movement, the gay rights movement, and a variety of ethnically based assertions of identity. Jacobson argues that the civil rights movement offered a "new language for an identity that was not simply 'American'" while at the same time heightening whites' uncomfortable consciousness of their own skin privilege. But "Ellis Island whiteness" allowed white ethnics to contest the view that all white people are equally complicit in America's history of racial injustice. They could argue, "Hey, my ancestors didn't own any slaves. They were poor, they were oppressed, they arrived with nothing but the clothes on their backs and a good work ethic, and they didn't even get here until after Lincoln freed the slaves," or "They fought the Civil War because the WASPs needed somebody to do their dirty work." Tired, also, of trying to subsume themselves to a melting-pot ideal dominated by Anglo-Saxon cultural habits, white ethnics abandoned the idea of eliminating the hyphen and instead took to celebrating it as a major determinant of their cultural identities and thus, following the premises of identity politics, of their social and political beings. "Italianness, Jewishness, Greekness, and Irishness," Jacobson writes, "had become badges of pride, not shame."[3]

Second, a kind of tribal antimodernism, expressed via an ethnic fundamentalist rhetoric of blood and honor, which mobster movies offer in heaping portions, lent ideological strength to the lionizing of ethnic heritage. Many people, especially those recently arrived in the suburban middle class whose family lore sustained increasingly nostalgic memories of the urban village, took refuge in ethnicity as a shelter from the great forces shaping their lives: mass culture, bureaucracy, commercialism, consumerism, and so on. The more that immigrants and their descendants achieved full belonging in American life, the more these forces operated upon them and inspired nostalgia for a nearly lost tradition of ethnic authenticity, the sacred ground of which was the opposite of the suburb—the old neighborhood.

The urban village, a cozier name for the immigrant ghetto or slum, becomes the old neighborhood when you leave it, and by the 1970s the urban village was a memory, a fantasy, or a nearly lost cause for most white ethnics. "Urban village" refers to the typical neighborhood orders fashioned by Italians and other immigrants and their descendants in the high-industrial period between the Civil War and the mid-twentieth century. Suburbanization, deindustrialization, ethnic assimilation, upward social mobility, redevelopment, and the arrival of successors broke up and transformed the immigrant ethnic urban villages of America's cities during the mid- and late twentieth century. As white ethnics looked back on it, the urban village became a nostalgic artifact, a romantic ruin of its former self: the old neighborhood, which is to the suburb as the old country is to the old neighborhood—near but far, within reach but irrecoverable.

The parish church, like the saloon or the boxing gym or the icehouse, often performs the function of compressing the story and meaning of the urban village in visual shorthand. Rocky's parish church, like the gym or the dive bar he frequents, functions as a marker of his authenticity as the Italian Stallion. Churches do the same work in the *Godfather* movies—not only in the old neighborhood (as in the scene in which Vito stalks and kills Fanucci) but also in the old country. For instance, in *Godfather II* there's a narratively extraneous but thematically important portrait shot of Vito, his wife, and their American kids in front of a church during their visit to Corleone, his hometown in Sicily. It comes right after the scene in which Vito stabs Don Ciccio, avenging the murder of his father and mother and brother, and right before the scene in which the family waves from a train pulling out of Corleone's station, the first leg of their return trip to America. The interpolated family portrait in front of the church seems to ratify Vito's act: he did what tradition demanded, what the ideal *paisan* authentically in touch with his roots had to do to be strong for the family. At the very end of the movie, Michael flashes back to that departure by train, recalling a childhood moment of wholeness in his father's arms that is also a moment of leave taking, a moment of plenitude (in every sense: familial, ethnic, and in terms of gangsters' honor) that contains within it the seeds of his future hollowness and isolation. By the end of *Godfather II*, Michael has both gained and lost the content of ethnic identity that the church is made to signify. From his heritage he gains the potency to be strong for the family, but by exercising that strength in the American context he loses the family itself.

The Corleones' trajectory provides a thumbnail of the larger signifying landscape within which churches become credentials of ethnic authenticity. Vito comes from the corrupt, picturesque Old World and settles in New York City's Little Italy, a crowded place of festas, gumption, and aspiration. His success takes him to what the Corleones call "the mall," their suburban family compound on Long Island. Michael's further success takes him to an even more isolated mansion on Lake Tahoe. As the connection to Little Italy and to Sicily, to old neighborhood and old country, grows more tenuous, Michael must perform or order ever more egregious acts of violence to recharge himself with authentic Italian American manhood—or to prove that he still has any to call upon. That's what he's doing in church in the baptism scene: reconnecting to his heritage as a source of strength. In that sense, Michael models a set of anxieties *about* and claims *to* authenticity that make him an iconic figure of the latter decades of the twentieth century—when Italian Americans and other white ethnic Catholics could look back from an assumed suburban middle-class vantage point and reach the nervous-making conclusion that they had finally arrived as entirely legitimate Americans.

The history of Catholicism in the mid-twentieth century helped to identify the urban parish church as a crucial site where what had been lost in this process of assimilation might be symbolically reclaimed. The liberalizing reforms proceeding from the Second Vatican Council tended to recast as premodern or superstitious many of the older devotions associated with parish churches—processions, novenas, and other special rituals outside of regular mass, which had often been brought over from one old country or another. Some of these devotions were declared obsolete, others merely marginalized or trivialized. As the rituals acquired an atavistic tang, becoming throwbacks to another time, they became available to stand for an old neighborhood golden age when Italians were Italians, Catholics were Catholics, and immigrant white ethnics fairly oozed the confidence that comes of unquestioned authenticity. By the 1970s, a scene of a street festa, like a baptismal mass in Latin, carried roughly the same payload of heroic atavism as touring cars with running boards, snap-brim fedoras, and the unreconstructed gangster ethic of vengeance and honor that endeared both Vito and Michael Corleone to audiences.

During the ethnic revival, the culture industries—the movies, television, publishing, the news media, the academy—undertook to map anew the landscape of ethnic assimilation and to narrate anew the heritage-centered rendition of American history. The *Godfather* movies may well be this project's most authoritative product, the masterpieces that most influentially exploited its artistic possibilities. The timing of their appearance amplified their influence, too. The bestselling novel by Mario Puzo on which the movies are based was published in 1969, when the ethnic revival was still building up its initial momentum in the shadow of the civil rights movement. The even more wildly successful first two *Godfather* movies (which set box-office records, won Oscars, established phrases like "an offer you can't refuse" in common parlance, and otherwise took the culture by storm) were released in 1972 and 1974. By then the ethnic revival had burst into flower, but it had not yet reached full maturity. Further iterations of immigrant and ethnic narrative were able to look to the *Godfather* mythos as a model or foil, further canonizing it.

My reading has come far from baptism or the image of Madonna and child in framing the historical moment in which Puzo's novel and then the *Godfather* movies took American culture by storm. But the appeal of the baptism scene only achieves its full resonance of ethnic assertion and anxiety in the context of its moments: the fraught 1950s moment of accelerating postwar prosperity it depicts and the early 1970s moment in which it was made, when the departure from the urban village could be imagined as nearly complete. Now, by way of conclusion, let's look at how the two approaches—iconographic and historical—might flow together in an analysis of the *Godfather* cycle's exhaustion and renewal.

After the End

I mark the ethnic revival's crossover point, the stage at which the movement developed to a full maturity that rapidly gave way to baroque excess and rote repetition, as roughly the bicentennial year of 1976. That's the year of *Rocky*, which, in the course of imagining a heavyweight title fight as a moral victory by a doppelgänger of Rocky Marciano over a doppelgänger of Muhammad Ali, definitively moves the *ur*-ground of nationhood several blocks south from the site of the Liberty Bell in Center City to the rowhouse terrain of South Philly. Continuing the pas de deux between the civil rights movement and the ethnic revival, Alex Haley's *Roots* was also published in 1976, and in 1977 the television adaptation of *Roots* became a major cultural event. It produced a veritable forest of family trees and the final canonization of ethnic or racial heritage as the basis of nationhood—and as cliché. The wholesale appropriation of the *Roots* template by white ethnics, coming on the heels of the bicentennial moment of *Rocky*, completed the crossover. In the late 1970s the ethnic revival began to run out of fresh things to say, increasingly repeating the same old ideas as it receded from cultural center stage. To watch *Rocky II, III, IV, V*, and, now, *VI*, in which the Italian Stallion's Italianness undergoes progressive demotion from principal theme to minor subtext, is to watch the ethnic revival become both conventional and trivial, deeply established in the culture but also artistically moribund.[4]

It makes sense to separate *The Godfather: Part III* (1990, the same year as *Rocky V*) from the earlier installments of the *Godfather* cycle. Had it been made in the late 1970s, featuring Sylvester Stallone and John Travolta or other emergent stars of the time, it might have flowed together with *I* and *II* as a proof text of the ethnic revival. But it came almost twenty years later and instead serves as proof of the exhaustion of both the *Godfather* cycle and the ethnic revival. I am tempted to cite *Godfather III* as negative evidence of the greatness of the 1970s as a period in American filmmaking. The decline of American cinema from the high point of the high 1970s might help to explain how so many of the same people who worked on the first two movies could make one so unmusical, forced, and stiff in its pace, plot, acting, and dialogue, so contrived and weak in its thematic purpose, so pretty to look at but so gaseous, self-important, and vapid. But that's an argument for another day. Suffice to say that there does not exist a critic—in the academy, in a barroom, anywhere—so gifted or deluded as to be able to argue convincingly that *Godfather III* deserves to keep company, artistically, with its older siblings. It's the Fredo of the litter.

Godfather III is also, and perhaps not coincidentally, far more ostentatiously Catholic than the first two movies, at least in the most literal-minded sense. It begins with Michael receiving a special papal honor at St. Patrick's Cathedral in New York City as part of an elaborate plan to launder not only the Corleone fortune but possibly his own soul so as to truly, finally, become entirely legitimate. A thinly fictionalized rendition of the Vatican Bank scandal of the early 1980s supplies the complication that threatens his scheme and drives the plot. This movie does not pussyfoot around with the mere ironic juxtaposition of Catholicism and murder. Not only does the shady cardinal who heads the Vatican Bank get whacked, but the *pope himself* gets whacked, for God's sake, shortly after he hears Michael's eventful confession. And both murders take place in the Vatican, for good measure, with assassins dressed in clerical robes. If there's a point about assimilation, American capitalism, the Catholic church, or anything else hiding somewhere in this business, it is either too obvious or too obscure to make an impression in its own right; the baptism scene in *The Godfather* has already covered the territory with infinitely greater subtlety and artistry.

Like the opera in *Godfather III* (another offense to hold against this movie is its abuse of Mascagni's masterpiece, *Cavalleria Rusticana*), the function of all of the

8.4. Assassins in clerical robes in *Godfather III*.

over-the-top Catholic material seems to amount to little more than insistently re-peating, "Did we mention that we're Italian American?" For years, Francis Ford Coppola has offered Catholicism as proof of ethnic authenticity, his own and that of his characters. Discussing *The Godfather*'s baptism scene, for instance, he said, "I decided to include some Catholic rituals in the movie, which are part of my Catholic heritage. Hence the baptism. I am familiar with every detail of such ceremonies, and I had never seen a film that captured the essence of what it was like to be an Italian American."[5] Following to its pathological extreme this logic of equating "Catholic rituals" with "the essence of what it was like to be an Italian American," *Godfather III*, which seems to know it's a terrible movie, frantically swaddles its clanking action in Catholicism (and opera, and a gnocchi-making love scene that anticipates the boomlet of ethnic soul-food romances such as *Like Water for Chocolate* [1992]) in the apparent hope that these trappings of authenticity will protect it from the brickbats sure to be launched by disappointed admirers of *I* and *II*.

We might take *Godfather III* as an example of a story told too late, after its moment has passed. The movie suffers for not having had the context of the ethnic revival around it to give it added meaning and to inspire its makers to their best efforts. But we should remember that the ethnic revival did not fizzle out; rather, it began to end when its basic premises took hold as received wisdom in American culture. The movement lost its impetus as it succeeded, not because it failed.

The ethnic revival, intent on hustling its premises toward canonical status, was not particularly self-conscious about its own workings. But *Godfather III*, coming well after the revival lost its momentum, does show signs of greater self-consciousness. After all, its romantic gnocchi makers are cousins, an icky variation on the self-regarding search for ethnic soul. Or take the character of Joey Zasa (Joe Mantegna), a mobster who opposes Michael. Zasa establishes some ironic distance from the movie's scramble to achieve ethnic authenticity via Catholicism and opera by making laughably earnest speeches about the contributions of Italian Americans, including a standard Sons of Italy riff on Marconi inventing the telephone before Edison did. Zasa is based on two historical figures. One is Joseph Colombo, a minor martyr of the ethnic revival, a wiseguy who took up and waved the flag of ethnic pride until he was gunned down at an Italian Unity Day event in Columbus Circle. Zasa meets a similar fate at a street festa (natch), just after making another of his speeches about ethnic pride. The other inspiration for Zasa, who extends membership in his crime family to blacks and Hispanics, is Joey Gallo, a mobster known for the same practice. The black shooter who killed Colombo was part of Gallo's crew. Fusing the two adversaries in one fictional character, played by the winkingly affected Mantegna, constitutes a post–ethnic revival joke, one of the few signs of life in a movie that has little left to say about the Corleones.

8.5. Immigrant piety and cold hard cash at a street festa in *Godfather II*.

The presence of Catholicism in *Godfather III* is also shaped by the movie's awareness of coming after its moment, when there's little point any more in offering narratives that perform the proper work of epic by imagining the formation of a new order. *Godfather III* tries to find a thrill in the corruption and murder of high-ranking clerics and in the size of the dollar figures—$500 million, $600 million—that Michael and the head of the Vatican Bank throw around in their negotiations. But in doing so it concedes openly that baroqueness and self-consciousness may be all it has to offer. And nobody in it prays for stones like this because everybody, having imbibed a thousand Mafia stories in the two decades since the advent of *The Godfather*, already knows where Hollywood mobsters get theirs.

The petering out into success of the ethnic revival does not mean that the Mafia narrative has nothing left to say, nor does it mean that Catholicism cannot be a source of fresh meaning in such narratives. One case in point is the television series *The Sopranos* (1999–2007), which finds new life in the exhausted *Godfather* cycle's ironic juxtaposition of the two kinds of family and in Tony Soprano's (James Gandolfini) obsession with being an authentic Italian American. The show makes a foundational running joke out of Tony's post-ethnic pining for the days when the old neighborhood produced unself-conscious wiseguys who knew who they were, and out of his failure to get back into the womb of ethnic authenticity no matter how hard he tries. He faints dead away at the sight of capicolla (a type of cold cut) in the refrigerator of his suburban McMansion because it raises a long-suppressed memory from the old neighborhood of his father mutilating the family butcher. It's telling that Tony's capacity for decisive violence, the potency required to be strong for the family, proceeds not from his Italian Americanness but from his problem *with* Italian Americanness. Psychotherapy largely displaces religious ritual and language in the representation of Tony's inner life, the principal content of which is not his Catholicism but his psychological "issues around" (as the therapeutic world likes to say) being Italian and Catholic and a gangster. In the same way that Michael Corleone turns into a parody of a Protestant, Tony has become a parody of another stock type: he's a hulking, violent, spaghetti-bending variant of the spindly Jewish neurotic codified by Woody Allen.

Catholicism forms a principal resource, instead, for Tony's wife, Carmela (Edie Falco), whose full thematic participation as a three-dimensional female character distinguishes *The Sopranos* from the *Godfather* movies. Even though her parish priest is just another hand kisser mooching around for a free meal, Carmela's faith sometimes offers her a vantage point from which to judge her husband's failings and even helps her to break with him. But, of course, the flesh is weak and the break doesn't last. She kicks him out of the house, but he talks and buys his way back in, and she returns to her compromised life as a respectable upper middle-class suburban Catholic wife and mother subsidized by organized crime. Still, if anyone in the world of *The Sopranos* derives any potency from being Catholic, it's Carmela, one of the many plays on the *Godfather* formula that give shape and life to *The Sopranos*—and to gangster narrative in general.

In the *Godfather* movies and their generic successors one can read Catholicism, like food or music, as little more than a convenient form with which to talk about ethnic identity and heritage; or one can accord to Catholicism the status of a content in its own right. There are those who would see pursuing both approaches at once as a typically Catholic thing to do. Francis Ford Coppola has said, for instance, that it seems "very Catholic" to him "to do one thing yet believe another."[6] Maybe it's a distinctively Catholic habit to tell stories in which the "officially" Catholic material isn't really about religious belief at all—and in which, if those who insist on discerning a sacramental imagination or analogical aesthetic in such texts are right, the material that isn't "officially" Catholic (the cannoli, the tarantellas, the old neighborhood, the suburban houses, the murders) is all about religion. If so, the *Godfather* movies couldn't get any more Catholic. More than simply using Catholic imagery to make meaning, they are deeply about and informed by the social and cultural history of American Catholics. Considering their fame, influence, and lasting resonance, it's not going too far to say that they are a major event in that history.

NOTES

1. Lee Lourdeaux, *Italian and Irish Filmmakers in America: Ford, Capra, Coppola, and Scorsese* (Philadelphia: Temple University Press, 1990), 188.

2. Matthew Frye Jacobson, *Roots Too: White Ethnic Revival in Post–Civil Rights America* (Cambridge, MA: Harvard University Press, 2006), 76. Even where I do not quote Jacobson's pathbreaking book directly, my account of the ethnic revival owes much to his. To acknowledge the large debt is not to say that I always agree with him. I think his argument focuses so single-mindedly on white ethnics' defense of racial privilege against blacks that it misses most of what's interesting about the movies and novels of the ethnic revival—as works of art, or even just as ideology.

3. Jacobson, *Roots Too*, 2.

4. I have considered the changing meaning of the *Rocky* movies at greater length in "The Stepping Stone: Larry Holmes, Gerry Cooney, and Rocky," in *In the Game: Race and Sports in the Twentieth Century*, ed. Amy Bass (New York: Palgrave,

2005), 237–62. I seem to have stones on the brain when it comes to this subject; in my defense, so does American culture.

5. Gene D. Phillips, *Godfather: The Intimate Francis Ford Coppola* (Lexington: University Press of Kentucky, 2004), 105.

6. Lourdeaux, *Italian and Irish Filmmakers*, 188.

FURTHER READING

Ferraro, Thomas. *Feeling Italian: The Art of Ethnicity in America.* New York: New York University Press, 2005.

Gardaphe, Fred L. *From Wiseguys to Wise Men: The Gangster and Italian American Masculinities.* New York: Routledge, 2006.

Gilbey, Ryan. *It Don't Worry Me: The Revolutionary American Films of the Seventies.* New York: Faber & Faber, 2001.

Jacobson, Matthew Frye. *Roots Too: White Ethnic Revival in Post–Civil Rights America.* Cambridge, MA: Harvard University Press, 2006.

Lourdeaux, Lee. *Italian and Irish Filmmakers in America: Ford, Capra, Coppola, and Scorsese.* Philadelphia: Temple University Press, 1990.

Messenger, Chris. *The Godfather and American Culture: How the Corleones Became "Our Gang."* Albany: State University of New York Press, 2002.

Orsi, Robert Anthony. *The Madonna of 115th Street: Faith and Community in Italian Harlem, 1880–1950.* New Haven, CT: Yale University Press, 1985.

Shadoian, Jack. *Dreams & Dead Ends: The American Gangster Film.* New York: Oxford University Press, 2003.

Slocum, David J. *Violence and American Cinema.* New York: Routledge, 2000.

9

Catholic Horror

The Exorcist (1973)

Colleen McDannell

The opening of *The Exorcist* establishes a theme that is emblematic of the film as a whole. I am not referring to the scene where Father Merrin discovers the clay head of the demon or the shot of a snarling pack of dogs fighting as the sun sets in a blood-colored sky. Rather than a sight, the theme grows from a sound. Before any action begins on the screen, a series of words that most viewers do not understand are sung. As the title *The Exorcist* appears in red etched against a black background, we listen to a man chant *Allāhu Akbar, Allāhu Akbar*. The text fades out and the screen goes black, but the chanting continues, *Allāhu Akbar, Allāhu Akbar*. Then, we hear twice the phrase *Ashhadu an lā ilāha illā Allāh* as a white circle appears and slowly transforms into an yellow sun. Still the chanting continues, but now the screen shows a desert landscape with ancient ruins shimmering under a hot sun. *Ashhadu anna Muhammadan rasūl Allāhu*. And again we hear *Ashhadu anna Muhammadan rasūl Allāhu*. As the camera focuses on the ruins, we see men digging with pickaxes. The noise of their movement now joins the chanting. The laborers wear headscarves and robes. A flock of sheep driven by shepherds moves in front of the excavation and, in the opposite direction, a herd of camels lumber by. As the words "Northern Iraq" appear over the dig, the last verse is chanted: *Hayya 'alā al-salāt*.

When *The Exorcist* opened in 1973, most of the audience did not know they were listening to the Muslim "call to prayer" (*adhān*). Why did *The Exorcist* open with a muezzin (*mu'adhdhin*) chanting: "God is most great, God is most great. I testify that there is no god but God. I testify that Muhammad is the Messenger of God. Hurry to prayer"? This opening underscores the creative tension that provided much of the energy behind *The Exorcist*. On the one hand, writer and producer William Peter Blatty wanted to make a movie that explored serious religious and existential issues. Having recently experienced the death of his mother, he was plagued by questions about life after death. Having had eight years of education in Jesuit schools, he had a set of answers to those questions. Beginning *The Exorcist* with the statement about God and a call to the faithful to pray—but in Arabic—enabled Blatty to assert his faith without anyone *really* knowing that he did it. This was a powerful but secret assertion about the glory of God.

On the other hand, director William Friedkin, an agnostic Jew, delighted in making realistic films that pushed the boundaries of acceptability. Friedkin included the chanting in order to establish an exotic and slightly mysterious mood that aurally reinforced the Middle Eastern character of the opening scenes. Horror movies are highly dependent on sound to establish mood and to drive action. Evil (we will come to learn) is associated with an ancient land, the very cradle of civilization. Friedkin was also making a not-so-subtle jab at the Arabs, who at the time were battling with Israelis over control of the holy land.[1] What more evocative and exciting place to dig up a statue of a demon than in the place of Western desire—for God and for oil.

The opening sounds of the movie contain the ambiguities of *The Exorcist*. The collaboration between Blatty and Friedkin resulted in a complicated film that communicates in many different ways. Friedkin established a standard for horror, terrifying generations of viewers. The film was so powerful that when it opened, people ran screaming from the theaters. At the same time, the film left audiences wondering about almost everything. How did the demon get from Iraq to Washington, D.C.? Why did it enter an innocuous girl? What really killed Father Karras? Where did the devil go after it left Regan MacNeil? Embedded within this movie about demon possession, however, is the statement "God is most great." Just as the unfamiliar language of Arabic masks for American audiences a religious assertion, the special effects and notorious character of *The Exorcist* distracts viewers from the wider spiritual message set out by its producer/writer. William Peter Blatty sought to bring to the screen his real theological concerns and answers. It is this creative tension between Friedkin and Blatty—between good horror and good story—that gives *The Exorcist* its energy and endurance. *The Exorcist* then is not merely a horror film; it is a *Catholic* horror film. And, more specifically, it is a *Jesuit* horror film.

Real Horror

The Exorcist tells the story of twelve-year-old Regan MacNeil (Linda Blair) whose mother, actress Chris MacNeil (Ellen Burstyn), has come to Georgetown University in order to make a movie about student unrest. Paralleling this narrative is the story of Father Damien "Dimmy" Karras (Jason Miller), a young and handsome priest who is a psychiatrist for the Jesuit order. Karras's Greek mother (Vasiliki Maliaros) becomes sick and eventually dies, and her death exacerbates the priest's questioning of his faith. While living in an upscale house near the campus, Regan begins to act in a bizarre manner. She eventually becomes violent, obscene, and untreatable by modern medicine. As a last resort her panic-stricken mother asks Father Karras to do an exorcism, to drive out the demons (or the devil) from her possessed daughter. While asking permission to perform the ritual, Karras is told he must do it under the leadership of a more skilled exorcist, Father Lankester Merrin (Max von Sydow). Merrin was shown in the opening scenes recovering a demonic-looking archaeological artifact. In the end, the devil is driven out and Regan returns to normal, but both priests die.

From the moment the film came out, its author and producer, William Peter Blatty, was not happy. It seemed that many who saw the film thought that in the end evil had won. The devil had left Regan and Father Karras had been flung down seventy-plus steps, barely receiving absolution for his sins before dying. Didn't the devil kill him? Regan returns to normal, but her mother shows only slight interest in the priest who comes to say goodbye. Indeed, she gives back a silver medal, the one physical reminder she has of the man who gave his life to save her little girl. "Father Dyer," she laconically remarks, "I thought you'd like to keep this." Father Dyer (William O'Malley) then walks away in sadness, and the movie ends with a few bars of suspenseful music from a piece called *Tubular Bells*.

In later interviews, Friedkin defended his choice of this ambiguous ending. For him there was nothing wrong with each viewer arriving at his or her own conclusion about what had happened. Not so for Blatty. Six months after the film debuted, Blatty published both his original screenplay and his explanation of what he had hoped to accomplish in the film. In particular, one critical conversation between Fathers Merrin and Karras, as they rested after their first unsuccessful exorcism, had been eliminated. For Blatty, this scene had provided "an explicit

9.1. Jason Miller, William Peter Blatty, and Ellen Burstyn discuss a scene from *The Exorcist.*
Courtesy of the Academy of Motion Picture Arts and Sciences

articulation of the theme that gave the film clarity and a definite moral weight: clarity because it focused the story on Karras and his problem of faith; and moral weight because it put the obscene and repellent elements of the film into the context of evil's primary attack on mankind: namely, the inducement of despair."[2] Friedkin disagreed. For him (at least according to Blatty), the scene disrupted the movie's dramatic movement by stopping the film's action and was basically a "theological commercial."

Blatty was a victim of the old dictum: "be careful what you ask for." Warner Brothers executives had wanted Blatty to hire a known director like Stanley Kubrick of *2001: A Space Odyssey* (1968). Blatty wanted to make a "real" version of an exorcism he had read about while a student at Georgetown. He was impressed with the realistic films of director William Friedkin. In 1972 Friedkin had walked away with an Oscar for directing *The French Connection* (1971) in which he elevated realism to a new height. The movie contained unplanned car crashes as well as subway conductors and police officers playing themselves. Friedkin did not mind placing either his actors or the public in harm's way if it increased the authenticity of the movie. Hyperrealism was just being introduced in mainstream cinema, with films like *The Pawnbroker* (1965) and Robert Altman's *M*A*S*H** (1970). Until *The*

Exorcist, however, science fiction and horror had not been accorded the respect of the documentary.

In *The Exorcist*, William Friedkin consistently breached the line between representation and reality in order to produce horror. For Friedkin, it was not good enough to *act* realistically. Friedkin wanted the actors to *experience* the reality they represented. Just as writer/producer William Peter Blatty wanted a "real" film, Friedkin wanted to make one. Friedkin and his crew prowled the set, firing guns to put the actors on edge. He had special rigging constructed that sharply pulled Chris MacNeil away from her possessed daughter. Linda Blair was also thrashed about by a complex rigging and the screams of the pair heard in the film often were their actual reactions to the pain caused by these contraptions. Burstyn reported that she was jerked so hard as to permanently damage her back. When William O'Malley, the Jesuit priest who played Father Dyer, was having a difficult time expressing his shock and sorrow at seeing the brutal death of his friend Father Karras, Friedkin slapped him in the face and the camera rolled. Blair underwent hours of makeup and prosthetic applications for each day of filming. In order to illustrate how the demon sucked out the warmth from the environment, frozen breath was needed so the set was chilled, sometimes to ten degrees below zero, and the actors and crew really shivered. Unintentional disasters also contributed to the movie's horror. One weekend, the New York interior set burned down, delaying filming for six weeks. As the production schedule stretched out—extending from a planned three months to a full eight months—everyone was getting very nervous and stressed. Eventually one of the actor/Jesuits, Father Thomas Bermingham, blessed the set and said a few reassuring words to the cast and crew.

The result of Friedkin's directing was not merely intense performances but a cinematic record of "real" horror. Even before the movie opened, controversies over how it was being made had become a daily part of the media rumor mill. Such rumors were useful in 1973, when movies opened at only a few theaters in a handful of large cities. To be successful, a horror film had to maintain audience curiosity since it might be months before the movie arrived at one's local theater. Films were allowed to stay longer in the theaters because home entertainment (VCRs, DVDs) had not yet been invented. Once the movie left the theaters, it was gone for good. Friedkin encouraged the speculations about a "cursed production" and the horrible ordeals the actors were enduring because it both fulfilled Blatty's wish for realistic evil and generated advertising buzz. Friedkin wanted the audience to expect *real* pain, demons, and existential doubt.

Warner Brothers was less sure of the draw of Friedkin's hyperrealism. They had booked a single New York theater to open *The Exorcist* on the day after

Christmas. The plan was to build an audience for what the studio saw as an unpredictable film given its religious subject matter. To Warner Brothers' surprise, the movie drew crowds of people who waited hours for a seat, lining up around several blocks. Warner Brothers should not have been so surprised. William Peter Blatty's 1971 novel *The Exorcist* had been a bestseller. Ten days after an interview with television host Dick Cavett, the book shot up to number 4 on the bestseller list and a week later it was number 1. It dominated the list for fifty-five weeks.[3] The film drew fans of the book as well as the curious. By mid-January three more Manhattan theaters began to show the movie, easing the crowding, but the lines continued.

The film shocked both the audience and the critics. Some viewers had severe physical reactions. Individuals in the audience vomited, fainted, cried uncontrollably, or felt that they had become possessed while seeing *The Exorcist*. Reports of such events began immediately and fueled a curiosity that added to the crowds standing in line in the cold. A guard at the New York theater where the film opened told a reporter that, besides the vomiting and fainting, there had been several heart attacks and a miscarriage in the first few weeks. The film then opened in other cities. Numerous emergency room admissions of sick *Exorcist* viewers occurred across the country. In Los Angeles, a theater manager estimated that each screening of the film resulted in an average of four customers fainting, six vomiting, and many fleeing in panic. More serious stories of damage included an English teenager found dead, apparently from an epileptic seizure, one day after seeing the film; a German boy who shot himself in the head; a teen who murdered a nine-year-old girl and claimed that he did it while possessed; and a man who became convinced he was possessed, underwent an all-night exorcism in his church, then killed his wife with his bare hands. Psychiatrists in Chicago, Los Angeles, New York, and Toronto reported hospitalizing patients who had been convinced by *The Exorcist* that demons inhabited them or their children. Citing the film's "strange effect on adolescent girls," the British Board of Film Classification refused to allow recordings of *The Exorcist* to be distributed in Great Britain until 1999.[4]

No film since *The Exorcist* has evoked such fear that evil could befall those who saw it. A rumor spread that evangelist Billy Graham preached that evil was embedded in the celluloid of the film itself. The pastor of an Assemblies of God church held a public burning of the novel on which the movie was based.[5] Books about exorcisms as well as actual exorcisms became increasingly popular after the mid-1970s. With the election of Pope John Paul II in 1978, the leadership of the church became increasingly conservative, and some bishops appointed official

exorcists for their dioceses. Ministries of "deliverance" spread among Pentec
and by the 1980s Protestants were increasingly using exorcism as a fo
Christian psychotherapy to rid people of addictions and personality disorders.
Prequels, sequels, and television specials exploited the box-office wonder of *The
Exorcist*. *Exorcist II: The Heretic* (1977) provides an explanation for why the demon
possessed Regan; in *The Exorcist III* (1990) William Peter Blatty tries his hand at
directing, and two directors (Renny Hanlin and Paul Schrader) made prequels
(*Exorcist: The Beginning* [2004]; *Dominion: Prequel to the Exorcist* [2005]). Priests and
Catholic religious articles became de rigueur in horror films. From the family who
called up their parish priest to exorcise their house in *The Amityville Horror* (1979),
to the courtroom drama of *The Exorcism of Emily Rose* (2005), Americans in the
movies often resort to this ancient Catholic rite. William Friedkin and William
Peter Blatty had not only captured horror, they had changed the practices of both
Christian churches and of moviemakers.

Audiences flocked to see *The Exorcist*. During its initial run it grossed $165
million, earning more money than *The Godfather* (1972). The most prestigious
critics, however, were not impressed. Vincent Canby of the *New York Times* and
Pauline Kael of the *New Yorker* accused *The Exorcist* of using religion as a pretext for
making money with sensationalism and sex [6] They both hated *The Exorcist*, and they
hated it with a vehemence not evoked by any religious film until Mel Gibson's *The
Passion of the Christ*.

For them, *The Exorcist*'s most serious flaw was that it had no symbolic message
or purpose. The film was not using demonic possession as a metaphor to explore
relations between mothers and daughters, or generations, or some other real social
issue. Instead, the film was actually *about* demonic possession, which it took literally, and then presented with a "solemnity" and "sensationalism" that revealed a
"basically foolish mind." Canby condemned the film as pornography. Kael saw the
film as an example of "the worst imaginable taste—that is, an utterly unfeeling
movie about miracles." It was no wonder Catholics had not opposed the movie,
since it was "the biggest recruiting poster the Catholic Church has had since the
sunnier days of *Going My Way* and *The Bells of St. Mary's*." After all, *The Exorcist* "says
that the Catholic Church is the true faith, feared by the Devil, and that its rituals
can exorcise demons." Kael begged Catholics not to be "willing to see their faith
turned into a horror show," which left viewers with no sympathy for the tormented
little girl or the dead priests, no "feeling for God or terror of Satan." She ridiculed
Blatty's ambition to do "apostolic" or religious work, calling him the "apostle to the
National Enquirer, and to *Cosmopolitan*, in which the novel was condensed."[7]

Apostle to the National Enquirer

Kael and Canby were typical of reviewers who condemned the film, saying that to see in such graphic detail the embodiment of evil was to make evil banal. It was not the movie's obscene language, violence, or sexual explosiveness, however, that critics rejected. Pauline Kael had written many positive words about Arthur Penn's violent *Bonnie and Clyde* (1967), and in 1971 the profoundly disturbing *A Clockwork Orange* won the coveted New York Film Critics Award. In 1972 *Deep Throat* (about a woman with a clitoris in her throat) had moved pornography closer to the American middle-class mainstream. The bodily focus of *The Exorcist* made re-viewers uncomfortable not because of its violence and sexuality but because of the way it connected the body with spirituality. For Kael, Canby, and other reviewers, the film tricked people with its fancy special effects into thinking that the devil and the world of demonic possession were actually real.

The reality of demonic possession, however, was exactly the point that William Peter Blatty had hoped to convey. In 1949, during his junior year at Georgetown University, Blatty had read a *Washington Post* article about a case of possession and exorcism that had taken place in nearby Maryland. A Lutheran boy of fourteen began to experience poltergeist phenomena in his room soon after the death of an aunt from St. Louis, who had played with him with a Ouija board. Sounds were heard in the wall; desks and chairs would move. The boy's bed glided across the room. After having the child for one night in his home, the family's Lutheran pastor told the family that they "have to see a Catholic priest" because "the Catholics know about things like this."[8] The family saw a local priest, and the boy was eventually admitted to Georgetown Hospital. Following hints that emerged in the exorcism, the family moved to St. Louis and, after a month of exorcisms conducted by Jesuit priests, the boy was healed. In the midst of the process, he was baptized a Catholic and given first communion. One of the Jesuits involved in the case, Father Albert Hughes, spoke at Georgetown about his experience in 1950, during Blatty's senior year.

As with many people who search for religious truth, Blatty looked to the 1949 exorcism for evidence of the reality of what he had been taught by his family and in his schools. William Peter Blatty was born into poverty in 1928, the fifth and youngest child of Lebanese Catholic immigrants. After his father abandoned the family in 1934, his mother, Mary Blatty, supported them by selling quince jelly near the Plaza Hotel and Radio City Music Hall, bringing the son she called "Baby Jesus" along with her. The resourceful mother exploited all the charities she could find and moved the family (often after eviction) when she couldn't pay the rent.

Son and mother became extremely close, and their relationship was filled with conflicting emotions. Shortly after the release of the film *The Exorcist*, Blatty published a loving yet revealing memoir of his life with his mother. *I'll Tell Them I Remember You* (1973) details her indefatigable spirit, quirky character, and profound faith in God. "Not the God who gives rest after toil," Blatty explained, "but the God of Joshua and of Lazarus, the God who, for a friend, would reverse the dynamics of the cosmos."[9] *I'll Tell Them I Remember You* also recounts Blatty's encounters with the uncanny, often in connection with his mother.

A Lebanese American with "a deep year-round tan," Blatty was teased by his schoolmates. "So your old man's a sheik," they joked, "So wotta you, a camel?" "I wished that I were Irish so that I could blend [in]," he later lamented as an adult. "I would have given eighty million dollars for just one crummy freckle."[10] Unlike other immigrant children, who asserted their American identities by playing sports, Blatty never joined in.[11] Blatty's mother encouraged him to apply to an elite Jesuit high school, where as a scholarship boy he never felt comfortable. "A new insecurity cycle began," he explained. "[I]n the school cafeteria...none of the

9.2. Trying to be the dutiful son, Damien Karras (Jason Miller) attends to his mother (Vasiliki Maliaros), just as William Peter Blatty cared for his own mother, who was also named Mary. *Courtesy of the Academy of Motion Picture Arts and Sciences*

other boys made any noise when they chewed their food." So Blatty tried to learn how to eat and drink without a sound, like a polite, middle-class American. Like Father Karras, Blatty was a Mediterranean outsider who had made it, and he appreciated the priests who "managed to restore the faith of an eighth-grade atheist, albeit an unwilling one." Another scholarship won him admission to a second notable Jesuit institution, Georgetown University, where he was awakened at five every morning for mandatory mass.

At Georgetown Blatty had to take the required theology classes, and in a course on the New Testament his instructor mentioned the Maryland exorcism.[12] Blatty then did a senior paper on the Maryland possession and entered an oratorical contest with a speech on the subject. The *Washington Post* article had became a touchstone in the life of a young man unsure about his place in the world. Before reading about that exorcism, "I had trust in my Catholic beliefs, but it was then more of a hope than a true conviction." Like the centurion of the Gospels, "who cries out, 'I have faith, but not enough; *help me!*'" the exorcism case provided "corroboration—though not proof—of the life of the spirit."[13] His adult life brought new tests of his spiritual strength. When Blatty married in 1950, his mother "grew hysterical, weeping and bereft," sobbing, "I can't help it. I love him. I can't help it." Blatty joined the air force and then the U.S. Information Agency, which stationed him in Beirut. While working in Lebanon, Blatty perfected his Arabic and eventually published a book on his experiences called *Which Way to Mecca, Jack?* (1960). Blatty knew what it meant to chant *Allāhu Akbar, Allāhu Akbar.*

Blatty's interest in possession and exorcism continued after he returned to the United States and went to work in Hollywood as a comedy writer, penning a script for the Inspector Clouseau movie *A Shot in the Dark* (1964). When Mary Blatty died in 1967, the event threw her son into a search for something more serious to do than write comedies. The absence of his mother was wrenching. Blatty dreamed of her and tried a medium and a Ouija board to contact her, but the spiritualist sessions "proved ludicrous."[14] Comedy writing was also drying up, so Blatty decided to pursue his exorcist idea. He sold the idea to Bantam Books and received a $10,000 advance on publishing royalties. In July 1969 he sequestered himself in a cabin near Lake Tahoe to work. Nine months later, the novel was finished. It went on to sell thirteen million copies in two years.[15]

For William Peter Blatty, *The Exorcist* was not an exploration of the social upheavals of the late 1960s nor an exercise in telling spooky ghost stories. The energy behind *The Exorcist* came from one man's conflicted feelings about the death of his mother filtered through the lens of his upbringing in Jesuit schools. Blatty produced a realistic book and let Friedkin make a hyperrealistic horror film because he wanted to share his *real* experiences with his audience. Because he was intimately connected with the story, he wove his own personality and life into the plot and characters. The filmed version had to clearly reflect *his* sense of exorcism's history and *his* feelings about doubt, death, and mothers. Blatty thus created a surrogate experience for the audience—both of the exorcism and of his own spiritual struggles—through the production of a documentary-like feature film.

Religion Representing Religion

What so infuriated professional movie critics like Pauline Kael and Vincent Canby was the very thing that Blatty and Friedkin intended to do in *The Exorcist*—to blur the boundaries between reality and representation. There is no question that Blatty, in particular, wanted to make a movie in which one could experience the reality of the devil. On this point, Kael was correct. *The Exorcist* was not a mere movie; it was a spiritual movie. Kael also was correct in observing that *The Exorcist* was "the biggest recruiting poster the Catholic Church has had since the sunnier days of *Going My Way* and *The Bells of St. Mary's*." However, for film critics, movies are not supposed to be recruiting posters. Big questions, existential questions, value questions can be raised—and even answered—in film but not in a direct way. Critics look for subtlety and complexity in movies, and films with religious motivations tend to be too heavy-handed in their treatment of spiritual issues. In addition, film critics who have no personal commitments to organized faith communities often see institutional religion as standing in the way of values like freedom, personal expression, individuality, love, honesty, and charity. For Kael and most mainstream media critics, if spiritual values or beliefs are to be explored through film, the film must stay far away from images of organized religion. They join with Hollywood moviemakers who tend to represent "authentic" Christian values—such as redemption or forgiveness—by characters who have no connection with religion and in settings that do not say "church." While crime can be explored by representing criminals or "the frontier" by those living in "the West," religion cannot be represented by religious people.

Some critics, however, appreciated the *Catholic* nature of the film. When the film came out, a few Jesuits noticed that this horror movie was different from Roman Polanski's *Rosemary's Baby* (1968) or Ken Russell's *The Devils* (1971). Early in the spring after the film's release, the Jesuit weekly magazine *America* tried to make sense of *The Exorcist*. After all, the movie is about two priests who are members of the Jesuit order, and Jesuits were called upon as consultants for the film. Father

Robert Boyle, a member of the English Department at Marquette University, rejected Pauline Kael's assertion that the movie is utterly unfeeling. He cited Ellen Burstyn's portrayal of Chris MacNeil as "a triumph of good acting" that conveyed "an agony of suffering." Father Boyle also found feeling in Max von Sydow's "fearless confrontation of evil" and in Jason Miller's sense for the "extremely mixed motives" of Father Karras. Boyle especially appreciated *The Exorcist* for its depiction of the Jesuit community, which Kael had dismissed as "the jocular bonhomie of the Jesuits." Arguing that Kael knew nothing about Jesuit life, Boyle found "the pains and frustrations…the brotherly concern…the quiet effort to help others" of the Jesuits in the movie convincing and familiar.[16]

Most revealingly, in answer to Kael's rhetorical question, "Are American Catholics willing to see their faith turned into a horror show?" this Jesuit professor answered yes. "My faith," Boyle explained, "does include the elements of which horror shows are made—human evil, fear, pain, superhuman evil and malice, and retribution." He rejected *Going My Way* but affirmed *The Exorcist* as an expression of the Catholic world view. Both Father Boyle and Moira Walsh (the regular film critic of *America*) speculated that what secular critics really found objectionable about *The Exorcist* was that "it posited the existence of otherworldly, diabolical evil."[17] In other words, unlike the clearly fictional Dracula movies and *Rosemary's Baby*, *The Exorcist* is a horror movie that believes in its villain and, even worse, recruits its villain as a witness to Catholic truth.

Jesuits Representing Jesuitness

Long before William Peter Blatty read about the 1949 exorcism in Maryland, he was being schooled by Jesuits. Blatty—perhaps unwittingly—articulated in his novel and film themes what he had been taught during his eight years of Jesuit education, which was noticed by Jesuits like Robert Boyle. *The Exorcist* is not merely a proof of God by proving the existence of the devil. It is incorrect to read the film in such binary terms: as the struggle of a powerful evil against a powerful good, as the triumph of religious faith over secular science. Blatty's training in Catholicism would not have motivated him to look at the world in the same way as many contemporary evangelical Protestants do—as the battleground between the two clearly opposing sides of good and evil. Rather, Blatty would have been taught how to see the world differently. A more fruitful way of exploring *The Exorcist* is to look at it as an expression not of Christian dualism but rather of a complicated Jesuit spirituality.

There are two types of Roman Catholic priests: those who work in churches within a geographical area called a diocese and those who join religious orders that take vows of poverty, chastity, and obedience and have specific missions to accomplish throughout the world. Religious orders for men include the well-known Dominicans, Franciscans, and the Society of Jesus (Jesuits) and less well-known orders like the Divine Word Fathers, the Little Brothers of Jesus, and the Missionary Oblates of Mary Immaculate. Each order cultivates its own version of Catholic spirituality that is derived from its specific history and mission. The Society of Jesus was created between 1521 and 1540 by a Spanish nobleman, Iñigo Lopez de Loyola, who later took the name "Ignatius." As with all founders of orders, his personality shaped how he looked at the world and what he thought would remedy its problems. His insights were expressed in a series of meditations called the *Spiritual Exercises*. Ignatius left a spiritual heritage which would form a distinct part of the Catholic world.

As early as the sixteenth century, Jesuits stressed the importance of education, and the schools they set up for boys and young men became famous around the world. In 1969 as *The Exorcist* was being written, they ran twenty-eight colleges and fifty-four high schools in the United States. Even with a declining number of men entering the priesthood, there were 7,775 Jesuits in the United States, of which 2,400 were "scholastics" (men studying to be Jesuits).[18] The Jesuits who taught William Peter Blatty would have had at least fifteen years of education *after* graduating from high school. Their studies would have included secular and religious subjects. At that time, Jesuits studied theology in Latin, with their textbooks, lectures, and classroom conversations entirely in that language. When the German Jesuit theologian Karl Rahner visited Georgetown shortly after *The Exorcist*'s opening, he discussed the film with his English-speaking fellow Jesuits in Latin.[19] The Jesuit stress on education also means they are famous for producing "hyphenated priests." *The Exorcist*'s Father Karras is a priest-psychiatrist, but Jesuits are also priest-professors, priest-engineers, and priest-poets. Blatty has frequently explained that he thought about Jesuit priest-philosopher-paleontologist Pierre Teilhard de Chardin (1881–1955) when creating the character of Father Lankester Merrin. Besides spending years in China on archaeological digs, Teilhard de Chardin taught physics and chemistry at a Jesuit college in Egypt.

The Jesuits were not merely interested in instilling secular education and Catholic teachings. They were interested in influencing the way that the world was set up, and so they concentrated their educational efforts on men who would have the power to change society. Here they could shape the future of the Catholic community. Other orders could do vocational training; Jesuits focused on classical education that would prepare men for careers in law, medicine, diplomacy, and government. The Jesuit style became associated with a rigorous, intellectual Catholicism. Blatty felt uncomfortable in his Jesuit high school at least partly because his fellow students came from the Catholic elite.

Since early Jesuits trained noblemen, many of whom would follow military careers, they cultivated not only the mind and spirit but also the body. They used theater as a venue for cultivating the whole person. As early as 1565, Jesuits put on plays so that their students would develop proper diction, appropriate gestures, and noble carriage. Jesuits not only wrote the plays, they also produced dramas dominated by special effects and sophisticated set designs. "On every conceivable occasion," one theater historian observed, "Jesuit producers made divinities appear in the clouds, ghosts rise up and eagles fly over the heavens, and the effect of these stage tricks was further enhanced by machines producing thunder and the noise of the winds."[20] Dance was also included, and ballet masters traveled from Jesuit school to Jesuit school. Since this dance was performed on magnificent Jesuit sets, ballet became equated with both dazzling movements and stage settings. Jesuit theater and ballet sought to be flashier than the secular theater of the day in order to lure influential people into considering Christian virtues. If biblical drama did not move and motivate, what good was it? Who would be persuaded to be pious by cheap special effects? The creators of Jesuit theater, William Peter Blatty, and William Friedkin all understood that theater must engage the emotions.

The explicit imagery that gives *The Exorcist* much of its power grew from the same Jesuit heritage. As a standard history of American cinema has observed, *The Exorcist* features "acts that had never before appeared in a mainstream film," specifically "urination, vomiting, and masturbation with a crucifix." Such images had been excluded from movies "not only because the Production Code forbade them but presumably because they went beyond the pale of public decency."[21] The physicality of the film is not solely the result of Friedkin's fondness for hyperrealism. The early Jesuit style was also sensual and tactile. Where many schools of meditation teach people to clear the mind of images, Jesuit meditation calls upon the realism of the physical world. The *Spiritual Exercises* of Ignatius told Jesuits to focus on the corporeal details of sin and suffering by recalling, for example, exactly what had happened in rooms where they had lived and by holding imagined conversations with Christ as he died on the cross. The mother church of the Society of Jesus in Rome, the Gesù, is indicative of the expressive Jesuit style of sculpture and painting, which went beyond the classicism of the Renaissance. Begun in 1568, it features dramatic ceiling paintings of full-bodied saints and angels as well as the skeletal right forearm of missionary Jesuit St. Francis Xavier with blood still visible on the bone. Its vivid baroque details still astonish visitors today.

Jesuit theater declined after the temporary suppression of the Society of Jesus in the mid-eighteenth century and the rise of secular forms of entertainment. The Enlightenment valued authenticity over artifice, and the French Revolution executed the nobility. The tradition of drama later returned in Jesuit institutions through a stress on the seriousness of literature and theater. Jesuit Daniel Lord—the author of the Production Code—was interested in the quality of America's movies not simply because he was a Catholic prude. Jesuits understand the power of entertainment. Consequently, it is not surprising that Jesuits were willing to perform as actors in *The Exorcist*, that many gave the film a "thumbs up" in their reviews, that Chris MacNeil (Regan's mother) is an actress, that the reason the family is in Washington is to make a movie, that Detective William Kinderman (Lee J. Cobb) has a fondness for film, and that the Georgetown setting reeks of upper middle-class affluence. Paulist priests might make straightforward movies like *Romero* (1989), in which Catholic heroes fight for social justice, but Blatty—who had considered joining the Society of Jesus—indulges in "Jesuit theater."[22]

The Exorcist not only looks like a Jesuit space, it takes place in a Jesuit space. The movie is not set in a generic Washington, D.C.—filled with government buildings and national monuments—but rather in a neighborhood defined by a Jesuit institution, Georgetown University. As the oldest Catholic university in the country, Georgetown has a physical beauty and elegance that speaks of gentility. Camera crews filmed hallways lined with paintings and wood paneling. Blatty, who moved from tenement to tenement as a child, loved his life on the campus, which was "clean and it was regular and normal and secure."[23] Characters in *The Exorcist* wear sweatshirts with "Georgetown" emblazoned across the chest or monogrammed on shirts. The campus chapel serves as the background for three distinct scenes, although the desecrated statue of the Virgin Mary was filmed elsewhere. When Father Karras speaks with his bishop in order to get permission to do the exorcism, they actually are in the office of the university's president. Even a scene which was not filmed at Georgetown, that of the residence hall where Father Karras lives, was shot at another Jesuit college, Fordham University in the Bronx.

While much of *The Exorcist* takes place—both in actual filming and in imaginary movie space—on campus, it is still a neighborhood drama, not unlike *Going My Way*. The old neighborhood has undergone urban renewal, but it is still a neighborhood. Chris MacNeil walks home from work, and priests move between where they live and the MacNeil house without getting into a car. People work, sleep, exercise, pray, party, and die in a well-defined Catholic and Jesuit neighborhood. The "Georgetown" of *The Exorcist* is stereotypically Jesuit—cosmopolitan, urbane, elite, intellectual, tolerant, versatile, and social. The philosophical and theological problems that are worked out in this neighborhood are decidedly different from those talked about in *Going My Way*.

At the same time, the neighborhood is filled with non-Catholics and even nonbelievers. Agnostics like Chris MacNeil are not only accepted as part of the community, they are helped out by their clerical neighbors when they get into trouble. Although the movie downplays his ethnicity, in the novel Detective Kinderman is explicitly Jewish. This is only hinted at in the film when he compares Father Karras to "John Garfield in *Body and Soul*. Exactly, John Garfield. People tell you that, Father?" In the late 1930s, when Jacob Julius Garfinkle (1913–1952) signed a contract to work for Warner Brothers (the same studio that produced *The Exorcist*), he was asked to change his name. Garfinkle became "John Garfield" to downplay his Jewish identity. Like Blatty and Father Karras, Garfield had been brought up in poverty by a single, immigrant parent in New York City. And, like Karras, he died at a young thirty-nine, after being blacklisted during the Hollywood anticommunist scare.

The Georgetown neighborhood in *The Exorcist* was not merely a 1970s version of 1990s multiculturalism. An integral part of Jesuit spirituality is an understanding of the divine that places God among all things. God is not separated from the everyday workings of the world but rather is mirrored in the details of life and nature. Just as Jesus is an integrated entity, fully human and fully divine, the Jesuits stress the need to see Christ as present and active in all creatures. Ignatius of Loyola, the community's founder, broke with a monastic tradition that separated monks from the world. Instead, he argued that his society should interact with all kinds of people and adapt to the audience to which they were preaching. Jesuit missionaries are known for their tolerance of (and sometimes appropriation of) foreign cultures. Since they are not required to recite the Divine Office in common as other monks do nor to eat together at set times, they are more able to see the presence of God in unlikely individuals—in foreigners, in students, in actresses, in twelve-year-old girls possessed by the devil. God is not held captive in a realm of the pure and holy but is infinitely beyond any categories.

Jesuits elaborate on a Catholic notion of the sacred and the profane that presents them not as isolated categories but rather as differing expressions of the same God-created universe. In this Jesuit spirit, *The Exorcist* became more than a battle between distinct representations of good and evil. Throughout the film, Blatty and Friedkin attempt to blur the distinctions between secular and religious, science and faith, technology and ritual, professional and priest, career woman and mother. Chris MacNeil is a single mother and a celebrity, but she also has an intimate and loving relationship with her daughter. She stands up to both doctor and priest in order to fight for the health of her child—and she does so with wit, intelligence, and spunk. The most terrifying scene of *The Exorcist* happens when Regan is subjected to medical procedures, one of which takes up a grueling three minutes of screen time. Later, it is a medical doctor who suggests exorcism. Father Karras uses his stethoscope to check on Regan's heart during the exorcism, and he tells us he underwent medical and psychiatric training at Harvard and Johns Hopkins. When Chris asks him, "How did a shrink ever get to be a priest?" he corrects her, reversing the order: "It's the other way around. The Society sent me through medical school." The simple binaries that are the staple of other horror films are downplayed in *The Exorcist*.

Seeking his own healing, Karras says mass as well as also working out in a boxing ring and running on the Georgetown track. Unlike Father Chuck of *Going My Way*, who enjoyed a chatty game of golf, Karras follows the lead of Ignatius of Loyola and prefers his sports physical and intense. Karras prays, smokes, drinks Chivas Regal scotch, and ignores the pleas of a subway bum. He shows less doubt about exorcism and more doubt about his own religious commitments and filial behavior. From the Jesuit spiritual perspective, doubt is not erased by faith, nor must the profane be transformed into the religious. God is sought within the world. No one in the movie converts to Catholicism because of their experience of the supernatural (unlike in the original exorcism). Chris even returns Karras's medal to Father Dyer. Indeed, in Blatty's original screenplay he has Father Merrin explain, "Perhaps evil is the crucible of goodness. And perhaps even Satan... Satan, in spite of himself... somehow serves to work out the will of God."[24]

If proving the existence of God by proving the reality of the devil is not the main theme of *The Exorcist*, what does the film seek to say about faith? Ignatius of Loyola had been a courtier, a conquistador, a musketeer. He gambled, chased women, and was quick to pull out his sword. After his leg was shattered in a battle, he began a process of trying to figure out what he should do with his life. He concluded that he should dedicate it to God, *Ad Majorem Dei Gloriam*, to the greater glory of God. This decision, however, did not come easily. The process of discernment is long and complicated. Doubt and change are natural to the human condition. Seeking to understand the will of God was to become a central Jesuit concern. Rather than assuming that his inability to sort his life out indicated spiritual weakness or moral laxity, Ignatius decided that seeing what God would have one do is a lifelong project. Discernment is an active, continual process, and

Ignatius designed a month-long set of meditations, to be repeated each year, to help the members of his society to reflect on their lives. These *Spiritual Exercises* allow the Jesuits to direct a quiet attentiveness to God. Jesuits assume that our natural state is one of insecurity and confusion, but if we use reason enlightened by faith we will discover that God is ever present and working in our lives to draw us into the fullness of the spirit. The key to Jesuit spirituality is constantly asking: is my will God's will?

Neither Father Merrin nor Father Karras debates the existence of God or the devil. For them, as for other Jesuits of Blatty's generation, these are givens. What torments Father Karras is not a cognitive disbelief in the supernatural but rather a crisis of proper behavior. Over and over in the film, Karras's mother—with her own voice and then through the voice of the devil—asks: "Dimmy, why you do dis, Dimmy, why?" Karras faces a challenge to his faith not because he has met a child possessed by the devil, but because he is not sure that becoming a priest and a psychiatrist was such a good idea. As his uncle points out while his mother is suffering in a mental institution, "You know, it's funny. If you wasn't a priest, you be famous psychiatrist now, Park Avenue. Your mother, she'd be living in a penthouse instead of this." When he pushes his way past the demented women on the ward, his mother says, "Dimmy...why you did this to me, Dimmy? Why?" Karras took a vow of poverty to free himself to help others, and a vow of obedience that directed him into medicine, and a vow of chastity to focus his love on all—but in doing so, did he condemn his mother to a lonely death? Damien Karras is in a hell of questioning, guilt, and doubt.

Yet, we know that Dimmy Karras was trying to do what his mother wanted. In a brilliant scene that inverts the old neighborhood of *Going My Way*, Karras attempts to be the good son that William Peter Blatty had tried to be. Karras has learned that a problem with his mother's leg has trapped her in her apartment. Taking a train from his posh Georgetown neighborhood, he ends up "walking despondently along a New York street studded with decrepit tenement buildings."[25] Long gone are the clean and animated spaces of *Going My Way*, sidewalks filled with nosy neighbors and streets where boys play baseball (see figures 1.3 and 5.2). In their place are garbage cans, graffiti, and "ragged, grimy, foul-mouthed street urchins" jumping on an abandoned car. Like Father Chuck O'Malley, Father Damien Karras comes by himself to the neighborhood, but here the resemblance ends. Karras climbs up steps not into a rectory warmed by Victorian furniture and a crusty Irish priest but into a "railroad flat kitchen" outfitted with "sparse and ancient furniture" and "painful reminders of his past." Karras's mother has a bandage on her leg, like Blatty's mother when she "abruptly took ill: an edema, bloating, swelled up through her leg and knocked loud at the doors of her tired heart."[26] Karras tries to convince his mother that he should take her "somewhere where you'd be safe." But, with the spirit of Blatty's mama, she replies first in her native Greek (not unlike Mary Blatty's Lebanese Arabic) and then in English: "You understand me? This is my house and I'm not going no place." Unlike Father Fitzgibbon, who eventually accepts the modernizing ways of Father Chuck in *Going My Way*, this immigrant woman—Mary Blatty or Mary Karras—sets up the problem of discernment: what should a good son do?

While Father Karras's questioning is directed to his own personal life, the fears that he harbors have a cultural dimension as well. The mood of the country during the winter of 1974, when the movie hit most theaters, was bleak. Was a "demon" making a shambles of the social fabric of American life? The United States' involvement in Vietnam had turned into a debacle. The OPEC oil boycott had raised gas prices to new highs. Students in Europe and the United States had demonstrated for more influence over their education, but then they wandered off into sex, drugs, and rock 'n' roll. Blacks, women, Chicanos, gays, and Indians

9.3. By 1973 the old neighborhood, once filled with Catholic immigrants and their children, had turned into an urban slum. Father Karras (Jason Miller), isolated from those who now live there, hurries to his mother's apartment. *Courtesy of the Academy of Motion Picture Arts and Sciences*

threatened traditional power arrangements by demanding direct access to employment, education, and politics, as well as greater cultural acceptance. The Pentagon Papers, the Watergate affair, and the resignation of President Richard Nixon in August had shown the country that lying was the norm at the very highest level of government. The Second Vatican Council had transformed the language of the mass and altered the designs of Catholic churches. Like Karras, many in the nation were wondering if they had done the right thing—in moving to the suburbs, in protesting the war, in desegregating schools, in developing a career in addition to being a mother, in supporting the state of Israel and angering Muslims, in accepting open marriage and divorce, in leaving the priesthood.

For Father Karras, and perhaps for William Peter Blatty, Jesuit spirituality presented a plan for ascertaining whether or not one had done the right thing. Societal changes were profoundly wrenching but could be understood and accommodated. It was not enough to reassure individuals that life is never secure, that change is inevitable, or that doubt is a fixed part of the human condition. This was merely describing reality, not addressing the sense that, as Karras admits, "There's not a day in my life that I don't feel like a fraud." For the Jesuits, the way to end such suffering is to embrace God's love given to humanity through the sacraments of the church and to lose oneself in working for others. This brings the soul internal healing and eternal salvation. While much attention has been paid to the fact that the movie revels in the Catholic ritual of exorcism, what has been overlooked is the central role that the ritual of the Eucharist plays in *The Exorcist*. For Father Karras, it is the sacrifice of the mass—not the exorcism—that heals.

Spiritual Nourishment

The Jesuits are particularly committed to the Eucharist as spiritual nourishment. During the time in Catholic history when most people received this sacrament only once or twice a year, the Jesuits encouraged frequent communion among the laity as well as the clergy. The Eucharist, as the body and blood of Christ, is not simply a way to gain heavenly rewards. Rather, it is spiritual food, Christ's gift of his own flesh and blood. The Jesuit focus on the Eucharist made them keenly interested in the revisions of the Second Vatican Council (1962–1965). Blatty had attended daily mass at Georgetown, and the trend after the council was to encourage Catholics to actively participate in the mass. Rather than say the rosary or focus on devotions to the saints during the mass, Catholics were to concentrate on the priest, who now faced them. The language of the mass was no longer to be in Latin but in the language of the people. Laymen and laywomen became "Eucharistic ministers" and distributed communion at mass and to the sick. Jesuits enthusiastically embraced the changes of Vatican II that connected the laity with the mass because they believed that the modifications reinforced the importance of the Eucharist. Father Karras, like other American priests of 1973, speaks the mass in English, faces the people of his congregation, and recites (mostly) the new liturgy of 1970.

Twice in the film, Karras is shown saying mass. The scenes are brief, but they come at critical times in the movie. The first mass occurs after the death of Karras's mother, and after a depressed Karras has the same nightmare that Blatty reported having about his own mother. In the next scene, which lasts only a few seconds, Regan fights against getting an injection. She spits in the doctor's face and screams, "You fuckin' bastard!" Then comes a quick cut to Karras saying mass. Karras's anguish over the death of his mother and Regan's extreme aggression in the clinic are conflated and then abruptly halted. The problem of the movie now is clear: a child who is seriously disturbed and a man who is in acute mourning. "Remember

9.4. Father William O'Malley, in his role as clerical advisor, explains to Jason Miller the proper gestures for saying mass. Authenticity was valued in the depiction both of the horror and of Catholicism. *Courtesy of the Academy of Motion Picture Arts and Sciences*

also, O Lord, Thy servant, Mary Karras," her son recites with outstretched arms, "who has gone before us with the sign of faith, and sleeps the sleep of peace." Karras does not wear black vestments, as Blatty had intended in the original screenplay, but instead wears a white chasuble—a symbol of the hope of the resurrection of the dead. The film's Jesuit advisors would have pointed out that for authenticity's sake the scene had to conform to the new liturgical practices, which stressed the reality of eternal life rather than the sorrow of human loss.

Still, Blatty did not fully accept the new liturgy. The first half of the scene has Father Karras using the pre–Vatican II wording ("sleeps the sleep of peace"), which is more lyrical and dramatic. But then, Karras moves to the 1970, post–Vatican II liturgy, praying "Lord, I am not worthy to receive you, but only say the word, and I shall be healed." Immediately before eating the host, he requests, "May the body of Christ bring me to everlasting life."[27] This text describes both the problem and the remedy explored in *The Exorcist*: we all think we are unworthy, but through accepting God's love we can achieve peace and everlasting life.

With those words, there is another quick cut to Chris MacNeil standing alone in a corridor outside a doctor's office. Her isolation underscores the doctor's report: there is a "disturbance in the chemico-electrical activity of the brain" of her daughter, requiring a medical procedure to "remove the scar." The scenes of an arteriogram are graphic and all the more horrific because of their realism. This is not the horror of a werewolf lurking in the dark forest; this is the hell that we all fear, that of technology meant for our benefit reducing us to passivity and pain. That which we trust to heal us is invested with the potential to render us debased and in shock. Friedkin and Blatty have placed the mass between the death of a beloved (but challenging) mother and a medical horror. They position the mass as an oasis between death and torture. It is the mass, and not the exorcism, that promises not merely a relief from suffering but "everlasting life."

The second mass scene also comes at a critical point in *The Exorcist*. During a conversation, Regan/Demon tells Karras, "Your mother's in here with us, Karras. Would you like to leave a message? I'll see that she gets it." Regan did not know about the death of the priest's mother. It is this uncanny reminder of his mother's death, and not Chris's tales of bouncing beds, that wins over Karras. Now he is ready to seriously consider the possibility of possession. There is an editing cut to the hands of Father Karras breaking the host in two. "He broke the bread and gave it to His disciples and said: 'Take this, all of you, and eat it. For this is My Body,'" Karras prays. Concluding the consecration, Karras recites, "'This is the cup of my blood, the blood of the new and everlasting covenant'..." But instead of ending with the appropriate 1970 text ("It will be shed for you and for all so that sins may be forgiven"), Karras continues with the pre–Vatican II words: "the mystery of faith." Then the scene cuts to the scarred face of Regan/Demon: "What an excellent day for an exorcism," it growls.

Karras begins to set up a tape recorder, and we assume that he now has decided to collect proof of the demonic procession. Through the ritual of the mass, we are told not about the reality of the devil but rather about "the mystery of faith." The masses of *The Exorcist* are intimate prayers rather than dramatic performances (compare to figure 10.2). Karras's facial expression shows intense concentration on the liturgical words, and the words reflect both his sense of unworthiness and the sacrificial nature of the mass. Christ's body is broken, his blood is shed. This is the mystery of faith that promises eternal life.

The Sacrifice

The mass, as understood in Catholic theology, is not merely a symbolic remembrance of Jesus' last meal with his apostles. The mass connects people to the sacrifice of Christ, who died a brutal death because of his love for humankind. Especially in the Jesuit schools of William Peter Blatty's day, students would have been taught that because Jesus suffered an ignoble death on Calvary, they too should sacrifice their own selfish needs. A key element of Jesuit spirituality, perhaps the most critical one, is the notion of ordering one's life toward loving service. Love of Christ is to be expressed through doing. Love should be "effective," expressed in deeds, rather than merely "affective" or rooted in emotions. The point is not simply to *feel* the love of Jesus but to *respond* to that feeling through concrete deeds. The Jesuits are to orient themselves wholly toward serving God through service to humanity. This service will liberate them from being enclosed in the self, trapped in self-reflection. "The true lover of the crucified Christ," Karl Rahner wrote, "has leaped out of self, and has left self completely; he no longer returns to self and reflects on himself—he remains standing under the cross of Christ."[28] It is not enough to seek God through prayer and meditation, like the monastic orders do. The Society of Jesus is to carry out the service of God through good works like feeding the poor, relieving suffering, educating the ignorant.

Jesuits expect that in their expression of selfless love they will suffer humiliation and contempt as Jesus did. The New Testament Gospel of John states it succinctly: "Greater love than this no one has, that one lay down his life for his friends" (15:13). Martyrdom, the "consummated sacrifice of one's life for Christ" thus becomes "the highest summit to which Christian life could mount, the very perfection of the Christian profession."[29] In countless inspirational stories as well as in later movies like *The Mission* (1986) and *Black Robe* (1991), Jesuits suffer and die. In the religious world in which William Peter Blatty grew up, there could be only one end to a story about a heroic priest—a good death.

Father Damien Karras heals his guilt and doubting not merely through participation in the Eucharist, but through his acting out of love to the point where his commitment demands the sacrifice of his own life. Blatty explained in an interview that the name "Karras" evokes the Latin word *caritas*, which may be translated as "charitable love."[30] Karras's first name, "Damien," also underscores the character he plays. St. Damian and St. Cosmos were twin brothers well known in Mediterranean lands for their ability to heal. Tradition has it that in 287 they were brutally tortured and killed for their Christian beliefs and buried in Syria (where Blatty's mother was born). The twins became the patron saints of doctors, surgeons, and pharmacists (and also of barbers, the first surgeons). In addition, Father Damien (Blessed Joseph de Veuster, 1840–1889) was a Belgian who volunteered to be the resident priest on the Hawaiian island of Molokai. He ministered to 600 lepers, saying mass and treating their wounds, which included (like Blatty/Karras) dressing their ulcerous legs. After twelve years of serving, he too contracted what we now call Hansen's disease and four years later died at the age of forty-nine.

Like the tortured healers named Damien, Damien Karras is spat upon, cursed at, taunted with his dead mother's voice, hurled to the ground, and then thrown down seventy-five steps before he receives the martyr's crown. While Father Merrin also dies, it is Damien Karras's questioning of his vocation that is resolved through acting out the ultimate sacrifice asked of a Jesuit. Whether Karras is killed by the devil or by his own volition is inconsequential. The point is that he willingly dies in order to end the suffering of an innocent child. "Take me," the priest shouts, "come into me." Like Jesus, who forced demons out of a tormented man into pigs and sent them over a "steep place" into a lake where they drowned, the devil moves from the stricken girl, to a man who is then hurled to his death. It is this loving self-sacrifice, and not the words concerning exorcism spoken from the Roman Ritual, that conquers evil. Ritual only becomes "precious," explains Karl Rahner, when "it also contains the selfless, faithful, dedicated life of the priest in addition to the sacramental species."[31] Karras believes (or Blatty believes) that if the demon enters him, it will free the child from possession. Although the exorcism ritual certainly begins this process, the film is quite clear in indicating that Regan is only liberated from the demon after it enters Karras.

Karras, on the other hand, wrestles with the devil. As with other Catholic holy men—St. Jerome, St. Francis of Assisi, St. Padre Pio—the priest does this in a literal, physical manner. The devil has done to Karras what St. Ignatius of Loyola described in the *Spiritual Exercises*: "it is characteristic of the evil spirit to harass with anxiety, to afflict with sadness, to raise obstacles backed by fallacious reasonings that disturb the soul." And in that way, "he seeks to prevent the soul from advancing." "The action of the evil spirit upon such souls," Ignatius wrote, "is violent, noisy, and disturbing. It may be compared to a drop of water falling upon a stone." The mysterious medal that appears in Iraq, then in a dream, and then ripped from around Karras's neck now begins to make sense: it is a medal of St. Joseph, the patron of "happy death" because legend has it that he died in the arms of Jesus and Mary.[32] Karras dies the "good death," vanquishing the devil. He not only dispassionately gives his life for another, he receives from his brother priest absolution for his sins, *ego te absolve*. His eternal life is assured.

A Millennial Hope

The debate over whether the movie is a theological commercial or merely an entertaining horror film was addressed again, over twenty-five years after the original appeared in theaters. Blatty and Friedkin reedited the film, added eleven minutes of new footage, and in 2000 released *The Exorcist*, promoted as "The Version You've Never Seen." Blatty convinced Friedkin to add two explanatory and theologically uplifting scenes that were excluded from the original version. The scene at the staircase during the first failed exorcism was expanded. When Father Karras asks, "Why this girl? It doesn't make sense," Father Merrin replies, "I think the point is to make us despair. It wants us to see ourselves as animal and ugly. To reject the possibility that God could love us." The devil wants us to give up, to allow our doubts to overcome us so that we stop trying to discern God's will and feel God's love.

The ending was reworked to be more hopeful. In medieval Catholicism, encounters with the devil necessitated a transformation, and the original *Exorcist* did not make this clear enough for Blatty. In the 2000 version, Regan not only recognizes the symbolism of Father Dyer's Roman collar with an affectionate kiss, she smiles and waves at him as the car drives away. She has undergone some kind of transformation. Rather than giving Karras's medal to Father Dyer as she does in the original, Chris MacNeil keeps it. Blatty explained that this gesture meant that "she is now open to faith."

William Peter Blatty wanted people at the end of *The Exorcist* to feel glad about its outcome, so he altered Friedkin's ending to provide "a lift."[33] Rather than stopping with a silhouette of Father Dyer, the movie now shows the priest walking back toward the neighborhood. He meets Detective Kinderman, and the two engage in some banter about movies, then walk off arm in arm. The friendship between a Jew and one priest continues with another. Now the sound that began the film returns. As the men cross the street, we hear *Allāhu Akbar* twice repeated against a background of *Tubular Bells*. The last words of the millennial *Exorcist* are "God is most great."

Blatty's final success in transforming *The Exorcist* into a positive statement about the power of the divine over the demonic must have provided him with some long-overdue closure about the film. In the process of promoting the new version, Blatty was able to tell again his story of *The Exorcist* and thus to rearticulate his religious intentions. Now, in the new millennium, when Americans were more comfortable talking about religion, even William Friedkin was willing to acknowledge the importance of the spiritual power of the film. And yet, embedded throughout the 1973 version of *The Exorcist* are poignant reminders of the Catholic nature of this horror film. These elements have been overlooked because of the attention paid to the film's innovative special effects and its exploration of the demonic. Director Friedkin, however, correctly sensed that Blatty's intentions were being realized throughout the first film. On a profound level, the "agnostic Jewish" Friedkin understood the Catholic and Jesuit sensibilities of Blatty better than Blatty himself did.

NOTES

I would like to thank Peter Gardella and Jared Anderson for their important contributions to this chapter. Jason Bivins, Michael Blum, Suju Vijian, and Peggy Fletcher Stack put their two cents in. A special thanks goes to Father William O'Malley, who read through the draft and e-mailed it to William Peter Blatty, who pointed out some errors and sent compliments back to a very nervous author.

1. In October 1973, the Arab oil cartel established an oil embargo as a result of the Yom Kippur War. Later, both the Council on American-Islamic Relations and the American-Arab Anti-Discrimination Committee accused William Friedkin's *Rules of Engagement* (2000) of being racist because of its caricaturing of Yemeni Arabs. See also Tim Jon Semmerling, *"Evil" Arabs in American Popular Film: Orientalist Fear* (Austin: University of Texas Press), 167–201. Semmerling includes a chapter on *The Exorcist* (30–59) that supports Friedkin's rather than Blatty's understanding of the *adhān*.

2. William Peter Blatty, *The Exorcist: From Novel to Film* (New York: Bantam, 1974), 35 and 275–81 (quote at 278).

3. Mark Savlov, "The Horror, the Horror," *Austin Chronicle*, 24 March 2000, available at http://www.austinchronicle.com/gyrobase/Issue/story?oid=oid%3A76550.

4. Mikita Brottman, *Hollywood Hex: Death and Destiny in the Dream Factory* (London: Creation Books International, 1999), 95–99; Judy Klemesrud, "They Wait Hours—to Be Shocked," *New York Times*, 27 January 1974; Los Angeles manager quoted in *Time*, 11 February 1974.

5. Billy Graham's reaction is described in Mark Kermode, *The Exorcist* (London: British Film Institute, 1997), 10, with reference to "embodied evil" in note 2 on page 91; and the burning of the novel is in Brottman, *Hollywood Hex*, 95.

6. Pauline Kael, "Back to the Ouija Board," *New Yorker*, 7 January 1974, reprinted in Pauline Kael, *Reeling* (New York: Atlantic Monthly Press, 1976), 247–51; Vincent Canby, "Why the Devil Do They Dig 'The Exorcist'?" *New York Times*, 13 January 1974.

7. Kael, "Back to the Ouija Board."

8. The description of the exorcism comes from William Peter Blatty, *I'll Tell Them I Remember You* (New York: Norton, 1973), 116–120.

9. Ibid., 63.

10. Ibid., 73.

11. Ibid., 74.

12. Steve Head, "Interview with *The Exorcist* Writer/Producer William Peter Blatty" (September 2000), available at http://movies.ign.com/articles/035/035914p1.html.

13. Blatty, *I'll Tell Them*, 119.

14. Ibid., 151.

15. Interview with Steve Head.

16. Robert Boyle, "Can Catholics Accept 'The Exorcist'?" *America*, 2 February 1974, 71.

17. Ibid.; Moira Walsh, "Skeptical and Ironic Detachment," *America*, 2 February 1974, 73.

18. George Riemer, *The New Jesuits* (Boston: Little, Brown, 1971), xiii.

19. Leo J. O' Donovan, "Losing Oneself and Finding God," *America*, 8 November 2004, available at http://www.americamagazine.org/gettext.cfm?textID=3852&articleTypeID=1&issueID=504.

20. René Fülöp-Miller, *The Power and the Secret of the Jesuits* (New York: Viking, 1930), 416, as quoted in Joseph F. MacDonnell, *Companions of Jesuits: A Tradition of Collaboration*, chapter 4, "The Play's the Thing," available at http://www.faculty.fairfield.edu/jmac/sj/cj/cj4drama.html.

21. David A. Cook, *The History of American Cinema*: vol. 9, *Lost Illusions: American Cinema in the Shadow of Watergate and Vietnam, 1970–1979* (Berkeley: University of California Press, 2000), 226.

22. Blatty writes in *The Exorcist: From Novel to Film*, "In my youth I thought about entering the priesthood; at Georgetown had considered becoming a Jesuit. The notion of course was unattainable and ludicrous in the extreme" (6).

23. Blatty, *I'll Tell Them*, 115.

24. Blatty, *The Exorcist: From Novel to Film*, 240.

25. Ibid., 297.

26. Blatty, *I'll Tell Them*, 139f.

27. The 1962, pre–Vatican II text would have been: "Lord, I am not worthy that Thou shouldst enter under my roof; but only say the word, and my soul shall be healed. May the Body of Our Lord Jesus Christ preserve my soul unto life everlasting. Amen."

28. Karl Rahner, *Spiritual Exercises*, trans. Kenneth Baker (New York: Herder and Herder, 1965), 200.

29. Joseph de Guibert, *The Jesuits: Their Spiritual Doctrine and Practice: A Historical Study*, trans. William J. Young (Chicago, IL: Institute of Jesuit Sources, 1964), 588.

30. Lucy A. Snyder, "A Chat with William Peter Blatty" (26 July 1999), available at http://darkplanet.basespace.net/nonfict/Blatty.html.

31. Both the Douay-Rheims translation used by Catholics before the Second Vatican Council and the Protestant King James version describe a "steep place" in Matthew 8:31–32: "And the devils besought him, saying: If thou cast us out hence, send us into the herd of swine. And he said to them: Go. But they going out went into the swine, and behold the whole herd ran violently down a steep place into the sea: and they perished in the waters." See also Luke 8:29–33. These passages also have Jesus asking of the possessed: "What is thy name? But he said: Legion; because many devils were entered into him" (30–31). *Legion* is the name of a sequel to *The Exorcist*, which Blatty published in 1983. I would like to thank Stephen Foerster for drawing my attention to these biblical passages. Rahner, *Spiritual Exercises*, 215.

32. Rahner, *Spiritual Exercises*, 315 and 335. The notion of a "happy death" is no longer stressed in Catholicism but was up until Vatican II. Critics of *The Exorcist* have tried to understand the appearance of the medal in the film. The medal's uncanny movement may also be linked to Blatty's personal biography. Blatty explains in *I'll Tell Them I Remember You* that Mary Blatty wore two medals around her neck. At her death, the mortician retrieved both from her body. Her son kept the silver one of the Madonna and child Jesus and had the other one—a coppery round one of the Immaculate Conception (probably a "miraculous medal" of St. Catherine Labouré)—buried with his mother. As he was finishing writing *The Exorcist*, he unwittingly picked up a medal in a sauna, which was just like the one buried with his mother (147, 151–52). The image in the film is not a standard iconographic portrayal of St. Joseph, as he is typically represented in a standing position. Having Jesus draped across a lap is, however, a typical pose for the Madonna and child— Blatty's silver medal. It is also interesting to note that neither Mary Blatty nor Mary Karras had a "Joseph" in the household, and perhaps the medal indicates the absent father. St. Joseph was made the patron of the universal church in 1870

during a period of Catholic militant certitude, but there is a more ancient tradition of Joseph's doubt that expands on Matthew 1:18–25. The famous seventh-century Orthodox hymn to Mary, the "Akathist," explains: "Filled with a storm of contradictory thoughts, the wise Joseph was greatly disturbed: until then, he had seen you a virgin, and now he suspected you of secret guilt, all-blameless one! Learning that your conception was of the Holy Spirit, he cried out: 'Alleluia!' " Like Karras, Joseph was freed from disturbing doubt through contact with a supernatural force. I would like to thank Matthew Bezzant for bringing the significance of St. Joseph to my attention.

33. Blatty, *The Exorcist: From Novel to Film*, 277. This sentiment was repeated in many of the interviews Blatty gave to promote the rerelease.

FURTHER READING

Clover, Carol J. *Men, Women, and Chain Saws: Gender in the Modern Horror Film*. Princeton, NJ: Princeton University Press, 1992.

Cuneo, Michael W. *American Exorcism: Expelling Demons in the Land of Plenty*. Garden City, NY: Doubleday, 2001.

Decloux, Simon. *The Ignatian Way*, trans. Cornelius M. Buckley. Chicago, IL: Loyola University Press, 1991.

Fraser, Peter. *Images of the Passion: The Sacramental Mode in Film*. Westport, CT: Praeger, 1998.

Jones, Darryl. *Horror: A Thematic History in Fiction and Film*. London: Arnold, 2003.

Kermode, Mark. *The Exorcist*. London: British Film Institute, 1997.

Legget, Paul, *Terence Fisher: Horror, Myth and Religion*. Jefferson, NC: McFarland, 2002.

Lonsdale, David. *Eyes to See, Ears to Hear: An Introduction to Ignatian Spirituality*. Chicago, IL: Loyola University Press, 1990.

McDonough, Peter. *Men Astutely Trained: A History of the Jesuits in the American Century*. New York: Free Press, 1992.

Prince, Stephen. *The Horror Film*. New Brunswick, NJ: Rutgers University Press, 2004.

Riemer, George. *The New Jesuits*. Boston: Little, Brown, 1971.

Travers, Peter, and Stephanie Reiff. *The Story behind the Exorcist*. New York: Crown, 1974.

10

COPS, PRIESTS, AND THE DECLINE OF IRISH AMERICA

True Confessions (1981)

Timothy J. Meagher

Tom Spellacy was attentive, courteous, kind. He brought them coffee, sat, smiled, and nodded. It was not his nature to be so patient, so accommodating, but what could you do? These people had just lost their daughter—raped, murdered, chopped in half, and left like so much garbage on a vacant lot in a rundown Los Angeles neighborhood. And so he listened as the parents talked wistfully of their dead daughter, Lois Fazenda. Lois loved the movies; Mrs. Fazenda sighed, "*Going My Way* was her favorite picture."

Tom Spellacy blinked and said nothing, but he knew. *Going My Way*? He was the cop investigating their daughter's case and the men he was chasing for Lois's murder were all prominent Catholic laymen. One, Jack Amsterdam, would soon be honored as Catholic Layman of the Year. Tom had worked for Jack as a police bagman when Amsterdam ran a prostitution ring. Tom's brother Desmond was a monsignor, the chancellor of the Archdiocese of Los Angeles, but he also was a friend, a partner, a coconspirator in construction kickbacks and lottery fixes with all of these men. *Going My Way*? That fantasy of the church and its people? Tom knew better.

We know better as well because this scene is from a movie. *True Confessions*, a neo-noir crime drama made in 1981 but set in postwar Los Angeles, stars Robert

Duvall as Tom Spellacy and Robert De Niro as his brother Desmond ("Des"). The movie follows Tom Spellacy's dogged pursuit of Lois Fazenda's killer, climaxing in his exposure of the seamy network of Catholic corruption that surrounds his brother Des, the monsignor. The breaking scandal ruins Des, dragging him down from his post as chancellor of the Los Angeles Archdiocese and forcing him into exile to a small parish in the desert. Nearly twenty years later Tom finds him there, and in the movie's final scenes, visits with his brother one last time before Des dies.

Based on a novel by John Gregory Dunne, *True Confessions* relentlessly, mercilessly, and self-consciously exposes and repudiates the older Irish Catholic America depicted in its iconic forerunner *Going My Way*. The repudiation is both specific and general: specific because *True Confessions* neatly tailors and then starkly reverses some of *Going My Way*'s plot twists, themes, stock characters, and scenes; general in its fundamental reimagining of mid-twentieth-century Irish Catholic America from *Going My Way*'s innocence and self-confidence to *True Confessions*' corruption, perversion, and cynicism.

That reimagining makes *True Confessions* an icon of sorts in its own right. Despite two stars who were then reaching the high point of their careers, the

10.1. Detective Tom Spellacy (Robert Duvall) and his brother, Monsignor Desmond "Des" Spellacy (Robert De Niro), experience their fraught relationship during the investigation of a brutal murder. *Courtesy of the Academy of Motion Picture Arts and Sciences*

movie was in no way as successful as *Going My Way*. It won no Academy Awards nor even any nominations, and it earned but a little over $1 million at the box office. The reviews were mixed. *Newsweek*'s Jack Kroll called the movie a "brilliant brother act," and the *New York Times*'s Vincent Canby lauded the film: "Quite simply, it's one of the most entertaining, most intelligent and most thoroughly satisfying commercial American films in a very long time." Others, like Stanley Kauffman of the *New Republic*, praised the actors but argued that the confusing plot lacked suspense. Pauline Kael of the *New Yorker* found even less to like, suggesting that "the movie is in a stupor. You have to put up a struggle to get anything out of it." William Buckley of the *National Review* perhaps predictably judged it simply "awful."[1]

Nevertheless, *True Confessions* reflects as well as any film has a revolution in the representation of Irish Catholic America on film and in television since the 1960s. That revolution began when the decade's cultural and social revolutions trans-formed American perceptions of Irish Catholic America and thus the film and television representations of those perceptions. Depicted for thirty or forty years as pictures of innocence, guardians of morality, and/or exemplars of patriotism in movies like *Going My Way*, Irish American Catholics were now showing up largely as cynical cops, corrupt politicians, nationalist zealots, or hypocritical priests.

Yet the turmoil of the 1960s did more than transform how most Americans saw Irish American Catholics. The revolutions of the 1960s provoked a crisis in how Irish Americans saw themselves. *True Confessions* also speaks to this crisis of identity within Irish America. John Gregory Dunne, the third-generation Irish American author of the novel upon which the movie was based as well as the film's screenplay, did not try to destroy Irish American ethnicity through the film so much as redefine it. Dunne suggested a new meaning of Irish American. Analyzing *True Confessions* thus provides an opportunity to explore two fundamental changes in Irish American Catholic life since the mid-twentieth century: how American film imagined Irish American Catholics and how Irish American Catholics imagined themselves. Furthermore, because Irish Americans have long dominated and continue to dominate the Catholic church in America, *True Confessions* stands at a critical point in movie representations of the American Catholic church.

Fall, Rise, and Fall Again

Cultural representations of Irish and Irish American Catholics had, of course, been harsh and nasty long before *True Confessions*. For centuries, negative stereotypes of

Irish Catholics had been the norm in the Anglo American world, making the Irish the first and longest lasting "other." The traits of industry, sobriety, and rationality that Anglo Saxons felt marked the English and Anglo American Protestants as the rightful masters of civilization were inverted into the Irish stereotypes of laziness, drunkenness, and emotionalism. This representation of the Irish and Irish Americans as naturally inferior began to change in America in the middle of the nineteenth century as significant numbers of Irish American Catholics emerged as actors, comedians, and playwrights and thus gained some power over the making of their own image in popular culture. Still, negative stereotypes persisted. It would not be until nearly the middle of the twentieth century that popular-culture images of Irish Catholics would tip conclusively toward celebration. As we saw earlier in this volume, Owen Conway, the Irish American slum tough in Raoul Walsh's *Regeneration* (1915), still needs to be tamed by Protestant-dominated social service agencies. By the time it was produced, however, *Regeneration* did imply that once Conway's Irish primitive power was properly controlled and directed, it could offer rich promise for American life.

That secured control is evident in *Angels with Dirty Faces* (1938), where Irish American primitive power is personified by Rocky Sullivan, played by James Cagney. The powerful and charismatic (and, in the end, knowing) outlaw Sullivan sacrifices himself for the greater good. Gone is any sense of a moralizing Protestant establishment and in its place is the Catholic church mediated through his fellow Irishman and long-time friend Father Jerry Connolly (Pat O'Brien). After the appearance of *Angels*, the triumph of the Irish American on-screen was in full swing, affirmed in numerous popular films that celebrated Irish Americans' moral rectitude, "regular guy" toughness, and/or selfless patriotism. Those movies included *Boys Town* (1938), *Yankee Doodle Dandy* (1942), *The Fighting Sullivans* (1944), and, of course, *Going My Way* (1944), Hollywood's most popular and fulsome paean to Irish American Catholics.

From the late 1930s through the 1950s, then, Irish American Catholics reigned as Hollywood's favorite ethnic group. There were several reasons for this. Throughout this period Irish American Catholics only rarely made movies. There were, of course, Irish American directors of note (Raoul Walsh, John Ford, Leo McCarey) and a multitude of actors and actresses. But the men who owned the studios that made the movies were, more often than not, Jewish not Irish. Irish American Catholics, however, did make and enforce the moral standards that moviemakers had to honor. Irish Catholics Daniel Lord and Martin Quigley wrote the Motion Picture Production Code, which laid out rules of decent behavior for what movies should or should not include, and Irish Catholic Joseph

Breen enforced the code. Behind them stood the Irish American–led Legion of Decency that backed the code with threats of ruinous boycotts in the moviemakers' most precious market, the heavily Catholic cities.

Moviemakers found Irish American Catholic characters attractive for other reasons as well. In the first half of the twentieth century, Irish Americans occupied a unique position in American life. They claimed a median position—"the closest to being 'in' while still being 'out.'"[2] Most of them lived in or near big northeastern and midwestern urban centers. To the millions of second-generation Italians, Poles, and others growing up in those lucrative urban markets, Irish Americans were familiar and recognizable as fellow ethnics. They had been in America longer than the new immigrant Italians and Poles, true, but Irish American Catholics still were a people distinct from the WASPs in America's mainstream. The Irish were more than just fellow outsiders: they claimed to be the leaders of the outs as they dominated pan-ethnic labor, religious, and political coalitions. New immigrant Americans (Italians, Poles) were at best ambivalent about such Celtic presumption. They only grudgingly acknowledged that the Irish led the way for outs like them to eventually get in. Nevertheless, Italian, Polish, and even Jewish Americans often recognized Irish Americans—English speakers, long versed in American popular culture, and American superpatriots—as models of Americanism. Hollywood made over forty films pairing Irish Catholics and Jews between 1910 and the early 1930s, for example, and almost all of them taught the same lesson: the easiest way for Jews or any other new immigrant people to become Americanized was to marry, enter into partnership with, or even adopt an Irish Catholic.[3]

This celebration of Irish Catholics in American film did not survive the 1960s. The convulsions roiling America in that decade pushed Irish American Catholics off their favored perch in American films and transformed their image on-screen. Irish American Catholic power over the movie industry collapsed as the Legion of Decency, the church's arm for organizing Catholic movie audiences, shriveled and the Motion Picture Production Code disappeared. Broad social changes sparked or accelerated by World War II—the increase in working wives, the spread of mass university education, the growing middle class, rising African American prosperity and ambitions—laid the groundwork for profound social transformation. Amid the clash of movements and countermovements, Americans grew distrustful of authority. Established institutions, especially the government and church, became suspect. Simultaneously, Americans began to prize self-realization more than self-control and emotional authenticity more than correct behavior.

The effect of all this on the representation of American ethnic groups in American movies, and to a lesser extent on television, was revolutionary. As we saw earlier in this volume, during the 1970s Italian Americans became Holly-wood's favorite ethnic group and remained so for decades. Perceived as authen-tically emotional and passionate, naturally suspicious of government and institu-tions, and physically tough enough to fend off any nonwhite challenger, Italian Americans became the ethnics of the ethnic revival. In the 1970s alone, three films about Italian Americans won the Academy Award for best picture: *The Godfather* (1972), *The Godfather: Part II* (1974), and *Rocky* (1976). Two of the three (*The Godfather* and *Rocky*) and another film focusing on Italian Americans, *Saturday Night Fever* (1977), ranked among the top money-making films in American history by the end of their theater runs.

As Italian American Catholics became a pervasive, powerful presence in Amer-ican film, the Irish American Catholic image shattered.[4] This trend began with *Joe* (1970), a movie about a crazed, chauvinist, and reactionary construction worker named Joe Curran (Peter Boyle). A stream of movies and television shows then followed that depicted Irish Catholic men as racist, repressive, and corrupt. Often overweight and almost always coarse, they masked their sins behind a rabid jingoism and a hypocritical religiosity. Once tough-talking but true-blue defenders of the people against predatory criminals, Irish American police officers and firefighters were now portrayed as corrupt and racist in *Serpico* (1973), *Ragtime* (1981), *The Pope of Greenwich Village* (1984), *Q and A* (1990), and *L.A. Confidential* (1997). Television had its own corrupt cops and reactionaries in dramas like *Homicide: Life on the Street* (1993–1999); in sitcoms like *The Fighting Fitzgeralds* (2001) and *It's All Relative* (2003–2004); and even in cartoons such as *Family Guy* (1999–present).

Militant and Corrupt

True Confessions stands as the near-perfect representation of the dark image of Irish American Catholics that was generated after the 1960s. At the same time it differs from most films or television shows that treat Irish American corruption, racism, or repression in the prominence it gives to *both* the Irish cop and the Irish priest. Though corrupt Irish clerics have hardly been unknown in American films, they have been far less visible than the Irish American policeman on the take. The occasional Archbishop Gilday in *The Godfather: Part III* (1990) and a few thin-lipped or puffed-up church bureaucrats on television shows like *Michael Hayes* (1997) seem lost in a sea of snarling, scheming, racist, and repressive Irish cops on the large and small screens. *True Confessions* takes on the Catholic church because the author of both the novel on which it was based and its screenplay was an Irish

American Catholic, who believed that religion is the key to understanding Irish America. In *True Confessions* we can see how one Irish American struggled to express the transformations taking place within his community and to articulate in the book and on the screen a renewed sense of Irish American Catholic identity. As much as William Peter Blatty is key to understanding *The Exorcist*, Dunne provides the power behind *True Confessions*.

John Gregory Dunne and his wife, writer Joan Didion, were well connected in Hollywood and aware of the power of the movies. "I can say without equivocation that the movies have supported us for the past 29 years," he told an interviewer. "We've written 23 books between us and the movies have financed 19 of them." Even more screenplays were written and bought but never filmed. Dunne also was an astute observer of the inner workings of Hollywood, exploring that world in the books *The Studio* (1969) and *Monster* (1997). While the movie *True Confessions* does not perfectly reflect Dunne's novel and certainly felt the hand of director Ulu Grosbard, the power of *True Confessions* originated in Dunne's imagination. From the small details, including setting much of the dialogue in a whorehouse ("a brothel is a good place for exposition," he once stated), to the almost all–Irish American cast of characters, to the pervasive dwelling on Catholic church corruption, to the climactic redemption of Monsignor Desmond Spellacy—*True Confessions* is writer Dunne's exploration of ethnic and religious identity.[5]

The grandson of an Irish immigrant from County Roscommon, John Gregory Dunne was born into a well-to-do, respectable Irish American family in West Hartford, Connecticut. He attended an exclusive Catholic prep school and Princeton University. Had he not been drafted, he recalled later, he believed he would have almost certainly remained a "Princeton prig." By serving as an enlisted man in the army, however, he "experienced what it was like to be a have-not with the have-nots." There he developed an almost palpable distrust of the haves and discovered the "hardscrabble patch" of the "culturally and economically stateless." This was a discovery not only of the importance of class but also of his own, once largely working-class, Irish American ethnic group. This discovery, critics noted, "provided material for some of his most successful work." Working-class and ethnic identity was the source not only for his novel *True Confessions* (1977) but also for *Dutch Shea, Jr.* (1982) and even more obviously for an autobiography entitled *Harp* (1989)—the title coming from a derogatory term for an Irishman or, more often, an Irish American. Dunne called Irish Americanness the "mother lode for his creativity."[6] Because of Dunne's central role in making *True Confessions*, therefore, the movie not only reflects Hollywood's reimagining of Irish Americans as corrupt and reactionary in films from *Joe* to *L.A. Confidential*, but it also stands as the only major cinematic example before *The Brothers McMullen* in 1995 of the broad effort by Irish Americans to redefine themselves in the wake of the 1960s.

In *True Confessions* Dunne proposes that the Catholic church, not politics nor even the police department, is the root of Irish American corruption and repression. Indeed, Vincent Canby of the *New York Times* stated simply: "This is a film about American Catholicism."[7] Of course his point is an exaggeration of sorts. The movie is also a police drama and a murder mystery, but the oversimplification is basically correct. Few films have ever been so fastidiously attentive to the display of Catholic ritual and sacramentalism as *True Confessions*. The ritual of the Catholic mass and the sacraments are absent from *Going My Way*. On the other hand, *True Confessions* opens with an extended scene depicting Monsignor Des Spellacy presiding at a solemn high mass and includes several long confessional scenes that underline the film's title and critically advance the plot.

The film thus captures as no other major motion picture of the post-1960s era the kind of Irish American Catholicism that had dominated the lives of Dunne's generation of Irish Americans in the 1940s and 1950s. That version of Irish American Catholicism was born in the early twentieth century, as the new American-born Irish generation matured and Protestant-Catholic divisions hardened. At the same time, new Catholic immigrants began to arrive in the United States. A key strategy that the Irish used to move themselves from being outs to being ins was to exploit their religious prominence and power. In order to assert their position within the Protestant nation, the Irish constructed a militant American Catholicism that stressed first and foremost their Americanism but also their difference. This extreme patriotism and piety proved useful in consolidating their power over non-Irish, white immigrants in both the Catholic church and in urban politics. An uncompromising and proud Catholicism was used as the basis for drawing Poles, Italians, French Canadians, and others into a larger American Catholic group. Yet, even as they used religious identity to mobilize all Catholic ethnics as American Catholics, Irish Americans insisted on their own leadership of that Catholic America.

This militant identity flourished through the first half of the twentieth century even as Irish Catholics moved up the occupational ladder and became a politically and culturally powerful force in America. It held even in the postwar world as the GI Bill and other New Deal and Fair Deal policies accelerated Irish and other Catholic ethnics into the middle class. There Irish Catholics emerged as vocal leaders of a vigorous postwar anticommunist nationalism. Indeed, Irish Americans' McCarthyite version of American patriotism provoked as much suspicion among their Protestant and Jewish neighbors as it allayed, thus reinforcing the boundaries of the Irish-led Catholic ghetto. Meanwhile the new wealth of Irish and other Catholics seemed to strengthen the ghetto. Middle-class Catholics were attracted to Catholicism's strict code of bourgeois respectability, and their donations permitted the church to expand its network of institutions. The intense and pervasive power of Irish America's militant American Catholic identity, like the size of the network of Catholic schools, hospitals, and orphanages that was its institutional manifestation, peaked in the 1950s and collapsed in the next decade.

Catholic militancy functioned to secure the Irish in postwar America but at what many Irish Americans came to believe was too high a cost in intellectual and personal repression. Many young Irish American writers relished the liberating revolutions of the 1960s and the crumbling of the old Catholic ghetto. Jimmy Breslin and James Carroll exposed Irish Americans' blind patriotism and shrill anticommunism, which had contributed to the Vietnam debacle and which often masked racist and anti-Semitic hatreds. Young Irish American writers also laid into the starchy and soulless respectability and stunted intellectualism that had come to characterize Irish American suburban life. For almost all members of the new generation of Irish American Catholic writers, the Catholic church lay at the root of all the repression, hypocritical pieties, deadened thought, and narrow ethnocentrism that plagued Irish Catholic America. John Gregory Dunne joined writers like Breslin, Carroll, Tom McHale, Maureen Howard, and above all Mary Gordon who pointed to Catholicism as the source of what stifled Irish American life.

Thus Dunne focuses not just on corrupt cops in *True Confessions* but even more on a corrupt church in a broad denunciation of the Irish America of his youth. Some reviewers felt that denunciation was too shrill, arguing that the film laid on the corruption far too thickly. Stanley Kauffman and Pauline Kael found the movie's exposure of corruption so incessant that they thought the film seemed almost naïvely indignant. Robert Hatch observed in the *Nation* that "the motif of the picture is corruption and it comes close to saying…that everyone is corrupt." Yet whatever case the movie made about the moral nature of humankind in general, the novel and the movie clearly had something specific to say about Irish American Catholics' moral failings. An exasperated Andrew Greeley, commenting angrily on Dunne's work, contended that the "Irish characters in it, civil and ecclesiastical, are without exception, venal, corrupt, obsessed, sick, hypocritical and disgusting."[8]

Goodbye, Father Chuck

True Confessions, then, depicts a very different mid-twentieth-century Irish American Catholicism than the one in *Going My Way*. It does this, of course, in a general way by replacing lighthearted, buoyant optimism with omnipresent and dark cynicism. But it also moves more systematically to dismantle the conceit of Father Chuck's Catholicism. Both *Going My Way* and *True Confessions*, for example, revolve around the staples of Catholic ecclesiastical life in America: building construction and debt. In *Going My Way* the need to raise money drives the plot; it is why the bishop sends Father O'Malley to St. Dominic's parish in the first place and accounts for many of his actions thereafter. A fire in the church and its near-destruction, not a death in the family nor a failed love, provides the principal moment of tragedy in the picture. More important, the film consistently depicts sedulous fundraising for the church and constant fussing over buildings as heroic and uplifting. Though *Going My Way* celebrates the rebuilding of a small, inner-city parish, it also reflects an unquestioning conviction that building up the Catholic institutional network is an end in itself.

This is the same conviction that in real life seemed to animate and sanctify the massive building efforts like those made by Cardinal James McIntyre of Los Angeles. That Dunne sets *True Confessions* in Los Angeles is no accident. Few cities in the country seemed to better reflect postwar trends in Catholicism. Though Irish Americans were few in number in Los Angeles and played little role in the city's politics, they dominated the Catholic church in the city. James Francis McIntyre, the son of an Irish immigrant mother and a second-generation Irish American father, ruled the Los Angeles diocese from 1948 to 1970. Stridently conservative politically and theologically, McIntyre's passion was church finance and construction. A former stockbroker, he often returned to his old haunts on Wall Street as an archbishop to shop for financing for his vast expansion of the diocese's institutional infrastructure. McIntyre often was accompanied by his chancellor, Monsignor Benjamin Hawkes, not unlike the cardinal in *True Confessions* who is aided by his chancellor, Monsignor Des Spellacy. In his more than two decades as head of the Archdiocese of Los Angeles, McIntyre built over 190 new churches and over 180 new schools, while firmly retaining control of the sprawling archdiocese through his chancery's centralized grip.[9]

True Confessions takes dead aim at "bricks-and-mortar Catholicism." Rather than the church's glory, institutional expansion with its focus on construction and finances is its downfall. Church building is the source of its corruption, a Faustian bargain that leads to the criminal underworld. Cardinal Danaher (Cyril Cusack) and his chancellor, Monsignor Des Spellacy, are, like the priests of *Going My Way*, obsessed with money and expansion. They also find no accomplishments more important than lifting the diocese out of debt and building new churches. Yet, for Danaher and Spellacy, this obsession leads them into corrupt alliances with former pimp Jack Amsterdam (Charles Durning) and his pals. Des and the cardinal save on construction costs by working with Amsterdam, but they also do him favors like enhancing the value of his new real estate developments with churches and schools. In the end, the two clerics drop Amsterdam not because of his lurid past but because he commits a graver sin—he goes bankrupt.

Sexual repression rivals obsession with finance and construction as a hallmark of corrupt Catholicism for Dunne and his generation of critics. In *Going My Way* sexuality is treated lightly, with innocence and at times even with romantic flare. Sexual attraction is never dangerous in the film; indeed, it is harnessed for fundraising when Father Chuck convinces a former girlfriend (the opera star) to support his building goals.

Innocent romance is absent in *True Confessions*, and sex plays a vital part in building the movie's indictment of the mid-twentieth-century church. Critic Pauline Kael said of the movie that sex is depicted "completely" in old-fashioned Catholic terms: it is "dirty" throughout.[10] Very early in the film, for example, Tom Spellacy and Frank Crotty (Kenneth McMillan) are called to a whorehouse where they discover the naked, dead body of Monsignor Mickey Gagnon ("Whiz at bingo," Crotty remarks offhandedly. "Pain in the ass for penance."). Gagnon has died of a heart attack after a particularly strenuous night with an African American prostitute. The dead monsignor in the whorehouse is only the first in the movie's many exposures of the Catholic elite's philandering and hypocrisy. All of the married Catholic lay leaders have girlfriends or whores on the side, and the former pimp Jack Amsterdam is to be named Catholic Layman of the Year. No one is safe from sex's corruption. Monsignor Des's brother, the cop Tom Spellacy, has a former girlfriend who is a whore, and he too has been implicated in prostitution. Even the young newlyweds at the center of the movie's grand opening wedding mass have a dirty secret. The bride is already pregnant and has been forced to marry. That her revelation comes so quickly in the movie after the solemnity of the opening liturgy tells the audience that Des Spellacy, the mass's celebrant, knew of her predicament. That the priest urges her to marry despite her own qualms, effectively undercuts the church's moral pretension from the outset of the film.

Yet it is in the sad story of Lois Fazenda, the murder victim, that the harshest inversion of *Going My Way* appears. Here *True Confessions* most clearly and almost self-consciously repudiates the sexual innocence of the earlier movie. Recall Carol James, the perky blonde of *Going My Way* who runs away from a stuffy home to New York City where she is rescued by parish priests, taught to sing properly, and then set up with a reputable young man. Like Carol James, Lois Fazenda also comes to the city to pursue a career in show business, but she finds no happy ending. She meets a priest,

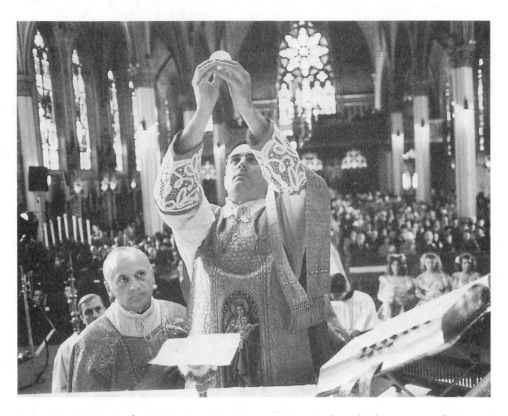

10.2. While *True Confessions* opens with Monsignor Des Spellacy (Robert De Niro) presiding at a solemn high mass, hypocrisy and the abuse of power are not far behind. *Courtesy of the Academy of Motion Picture Arts and Sciences*

Monsignor Spellacy, while she is hitchhiking but only because he is in the car with his cronies, the archdiocese's most prestigious laymen. He promptly forgets her, but the laymen with him in the car do not. They eventually make her their plaything and "pass her around like Christmas candy." Soon she is sent off to the maker of pornographic movies who eventually cuts her in half. In *True Confessions*, Hollywood and Los Angeles really do become what Catholic bishops like Cardinal McIntyre and others had long decried: the pornographic capital of the world and a threat to the innocent. The irony is that, in the movie, respectable Catholics themselves have gleefully helped to make it a modern Sodom.

In *True Confessions* the Irish American Catholic church of the 1940s has sunk into financial corruption and sexual depravity because of the very Americanization of the church lauded in *Going My Way*. The new Catholicism, supposedly at home everywhere in America, has proved to be a middle-class nightmare rather than the fulfillment of an immigrant dream. American born priests like Father O'Malley—savvy about popular culture, financially adept, smooth, moral but with an understanding of young people, modern but respectful—have become heartless organization men. In

True Confessions such men are evil, and so it is an older, immigrant priest, the Father Fitzgibbon analogue named Father Seamus Fargo (Burgess Meredith), who provides the moral edge. Like Father Fitzgibbon, Father Fargo may be a little cranky and cantankerous, but he is the only character in the film free from corruption. His prophetic jeremiads, if a bit whiney ("Everyday I feel less like a priest and more like an employee in a construction company"), are the only call to Monsignor Spellacy and his boss, Cardinal Danaher, to repent. His is the voice that calls them to end their obsession with power and money and to rediscover their spiritual vocation. The cardinal, with the perfect, clipped presumption of authority, banishes Father Fargo to the desert and announces to Monsignor Spellacy: "I'm afraid he'll have to go.... We need younger pastors. Men who will do what they are told." The younger priests here, American born and thoroughly Americanized and modern, are not the church's salvation but its downfall.

The favorite sport of the young priests, golf, appears only briefly in each movie, but the stark contrasts between the golf scenes in the two films powerfully underline their diverging visions of mid-twentieth-century Irish American Catholicism. A priest's ease with sports for much of the nineteenth century was not really important and, indeed, was frowned upon by the hierarchy. In the twentieth century, athletics became essential to the Catholic clerical image. Ease with sports seemed to be proof that the celibate, sexless priest was still a male who was comfortable with American culture. Novelist Edwin O'Connor in *The Edge of Sadness* (1961) wryly summarized the stereotype of the modern American priest: "the quaint, pipe smoking sportsman, but for the unfortunate fact of his ordination might well have become a second baseman." Playing second base (at least regularly) is something of a problem for busy adults, but golf offered an opportunity to be athletic (insofar as golf is athletic at all) well into middle age. Moreover, golf denoted a certain class position that befitted the priest. He was not only masculine and fashionable; he was an educated professional, a manager. Golf marked the Catholic clergy as the equal of other professionals and businessmen. Novelists of American Catholicism and other observers of the church over the last half-century (none more perceptively than J. F. Powers's *Morte D'Urban* [1962]) have thus been very attentive to golf's place in Catholic clerical culture.[11]

In *Going My Way*, Father O'Malley takes his friend Father O'Dowd (Frank McHugh) and his pastor, Father Fitzgibbon (Barry Fitzgerald), to the golf course for an afternoon of play. The movie self-consciously eschews any of golf's class implications or associations with big business. There is no clubhouse, there are no caddies, and there is not even much of a golf course. The priests even use repainted golf balls that they have bought for the princely sum of fifty cents. Father

Fitzgibbon underlines the common-man nature of the game when he calls a golf course "nothing but a poolroom moved outdoors." Yet the priests' golf outing does make a powerful point about generational differences. O'Malley's skill at the game offers further evidence of his American savvy, his comfortable ease with American culture. Conversely, an afternoon on the golf course is a lesson in acculturation for the Irish-born Fitzgibbon, which he later gratefully acknowledges: "You have to manage those old fussbudgets," he says to O'Malley. "Take 'em out to the golf course. Give 'em fresh air." The golf outing is thus another triumph for Father Chuck O'Malley and the American-born generation of priests, graphic proof that they are the happy future of the American church. Even the most traditional, hidebound immigrants could recognize that.

In *True Confessions* golf is clearly the game of the powerful not the proletarian. Golf greens are where the successful businessman plays and, more to the point, works. It is where Monsignor Des Spellacy meets his lay cronies and does the dirty work of the archdiocese. It is on the course during a match with Dan Campion (Ed Flanders) and Sonny McDonough (Pat Corley) that Des and they decide to ditch their mutual friend, Jack Amsterdam. Later, in the locker room, they all agree to mask the dirty deed by honoring him with a banquet, a sash, and the phony title of Catholic Layman of the Year.

Yet it is clear that golf is not merely instrumental for Des Spellacy, not just an opportunity to do business. It is his passion and serves as a metaphor in the movie for his obsession with power, an obsession that prevents him from being truly human. Monsignor Des not only loves golf and is very good at it, but the film-makers set up golf's sinister attractions to parallel the evil temptations of ambition. In one tragic little scene with his brother, Tom, this becomes all too clear. While they are driving back from visiting their mother in a nursing home, Tom makes an awkward, tentative overture to Des, suggesting that the two brothers get together that Saturday. Des hesitates and then blurts out that the meeting would conflict with his regular golf game. By the time he realizes what he has sacrificed, an opportunity to revive the only really human relationship in his life, his relationship with his brother, the moment has passed. In exchange for another afternoon with his corrupt golfing buddies, Des has chosen power and status over his brother, over love.

Searching for a New Irish American Identity

For all of its raking up of Celtic muck, *True Confessions* holds out some hope for Des, Tom, and, in a larger sense, for all Irish Americans. This hope is what separates *True*

Confessions from other film representations of the decline of Irish America. In a post-1960s era of ethnic revival and multiculturalism, a repressive ethnic culture and identity seemed only a little worse than having no ethnicity at all to many Irish American writers. Thus, having demolished the old Irish American identity by exposing it as corrupt and hypocritical, they looked for new anchors for their ethnicity in Ireland's folk culture, modern literature, history, nationalist struggles, or in their own Irish American gritty past. John Gregory Dunne shared this desire to redefine Irish American ethnicity, finding his own new meaning for Irish Americans in fraternal love, the renunciation of power and privilege, and the return to an older Irish American role as populist outsiders, what he called the "harp." Yet Dunne differed from others who attempted such reconstructions of their Irish identity and culture in a crucial respect: he was a Hollywood player. He would find the opportunity to put his vision of the fall and redemption of Irish Catholic America on film; other Irish American writers of his generation would not.

Monsignor Des, then, eventually finds his redemption in *True Confessions*, though only and necessarily after his fall from status and power. As his brother the cop relentlessly pushes his investigation into Lois Fazenda's death, the links between the Catholic lay leaders and prostitution are exposed. At the same time Des's links to Fazenda and those leaders are revealed, and the scandal topples him from his office as chancellor of the archdiocese. By then, however, Des is ready to go. In an ironic reversal of roles, Des the priest and once-confessor uses the dark confessional to confess to his brother, the once-penitent. The cardinal ultimately banishes Des to a poor parish in the desert where he finds his vocation as a simple parish priest. It is there Des finds peace and redemption.

Like many of the other Irish American writers of his generation, Dunne, therefore, offers new ways to be faithful and Irish American in the future. He finds such hope, in part, in family, in fraternal bonds, not married ones. Though generational tension is significant in the movie, the relationship between the two brothers, Tom the cop and Des the priest, is the center of the film. The movie goes to great lengths to suggest the importance of Des and Tom Spellacy's relationship as a kind of island sanctuary of human connection in a sea of corruption and cynicism. Whenever the two brothers appear together on the screen, a version of the well-known tragic Irish love song "Carrickfergus" (*Do bhi Bean Uasal*) is played by a single harp. No lyrics are sung, though to those who know them, the words would resonate:

> *I would swim over the deepest ocean,*
> *for my love to be with me,*

But the sea is wide and I cannot swim over,
  Nor have I wings to fly.
I wish I had a handsome boatman,
To ferry me over,
  my love and I.

Yet even without such words, the sweet melancholy of the tune alone is enough to reveal that these fraternal moments should be considered especially tender and meaningful.

It is not just the brothers' relationship that is important, however, it is also the common ground the two men seek and only occasionally find: an ironic, comic skepticism, challenging pretension and hypocrisy. Des is most human in this film when he jokes with his brother, the two poking fun at their father ("he never missed a wake") and mother (she ate cereal with her hands, Des remarks, because she believed the early Christians in the catacombs had no spoons) or the comic foibles of the holy mother church, including a nun who wants to quit her order to become a professional bowler (Des: "I didn't even know they had alleys in the convents").

10.3. The goodness of Irish American ethnicity is expressed in *True Confessions* through music, dance, and family as well as an attitude of ironic and comic skepticism that challenges pretension and hypocrisy. *Courtesy of the Academy of Motion Picture Arts and Sciences*

For Tom, this skepticism is expressed in more than wry comments about the family or the church. It rises to an angry defiance of power and privilege laced with ironic bitterness that ultimately becomes the engine of the movie as it sets in motion the events that topple his brother. Des is more passive and less sure than his brother, but he also begins to revolt against status and power, becoming aware that his ambition for both is killing him. When he confesses to Tom: "Somebody's got to change my life," he realizes why: "I'm tired of fixing things." Long after, when Des is exiled to the desert for his implication in the scandal of Lois's death and is about to die, Tom comes to see him for the last time. Des thanks him: "You were my salvation actually. You made me remember things I had forgotten. I thought I was someone that I wasn't." Here is *True Confessions'* effort to reconstruct Irish American Catholicism. John Gregory Dunne is calling his people to remember.

An angry, ironic defiance of power and privilege seems a pretty thin frame on which to build the definition of a people. But for Dunne, this does indeed seem to be his definition. For Dunne, being Irish or Irish American has little to do with Ireland or Irish culture. In his autobiography, *Harp*, Dunne reports that his first visit to Ireland as a man in late middle age turned out to be a desultory, meaningless trip. "What the fuck am I doing here?" he asks at one point. Then he stops in a bar in Roscommon and hears the barman deride an English politician caught in a scandal: "The Fook," the barman says, "has a taste for luxury." Dunne finally feels at home: "It was a voice I instantly recognized." It is the voice he celebrates in *Harp*, the voice of the "harp," the Irish American. It is the skeptical, ironic scourge of hypocrisy and pretension that Dunne claims as his own voice. It is the voice he first identified at parochial school in West Hartford, where some of his Irish American classmates evoked "the suspicion of all authority of anyone who would speak for me." He forgot it at Princeton in a self-hating search for assimilation but rediscovered it again in the army. He would always thereafter, he claimed, "be drawn to outsiders."[12]

Comic, populist skepticism has a long tradition in the representation of Irish and Irish Americans in American popular culture. In the middle and late nineteenth century, Irish American vaudevillians and popular playwrights worked hard to turn the degrading and derisive Irish stereotype of Paddy into the urban ethnic version of the American common man. This man (emphasis on the man, as this was a very gendered image) celebrated his roots in old communities and neighborhoods and disdained the company or affectations of distant and cold WASP elites. Ned Harrigan and Tony Hart's Dan Mulligan from their cycle of *Mulligan Guard* plays, George McManus's Jiggs from the *Bringing Up Father* comic strip, Finley Peter Dunne's Mr. Dooley from his popular newspaper columns, and a host of other male figures shared this populist disdain for ambition, pretension, and elite status. In the middle decades of the twentieth century, this representation of the Irishman as the American urban populist evolved into, to use the phrase of historian James Fisher, the image of the Irish American Catholic "regular guy." In the heady celebration of common men in the 1930s and 1940s, the Irish American regular guy became a powerful presence in American political and popular culture.[13]

What Des and Tom miss in *True Confessions*, however, is the old neighborhood. Almost all earlier Irish American common men or regular guys lived in such a place. The old neighborhood stands for the community of "plain folks" to which true Irish American men hold, forsaking ambition and status. Dunne's Mr. Dooley had his Archey Road, Dan Mulligan his Lower East Side, and Jiggs his Dinty Moore's saloon. Dan Mulligan, for example, complained to his wife after she forced him to move "uptown": "I know you're trying to elevate me, but I can't forget me neighbors. There's no one up here to sit out on the front stoop and have a glass of beer wid me."[14] Even in the mid-1950s, Irish American characters, such as Father Kennedy in Edwin O'Connor's novel *The Edge of Sadness*, found redemption in a return, of sorts, to roots in the inner city, a place that contrasts sharply with the shallowness of the suburbs.

There is no old neighborhood to which the Los Angeles Irish Catholics of *True Confessions* can return. When Des is broken, he is transferred not to some inner-city parish but to the desert. A skeptical Tom makes this clear when Des suggests that they both be buried next to the desert church: "Out here in all this sand?" Tom says. "I don't know. I don't know." Setting the location of the film in Los Angeles, not New York or Boston, Chicago or even San Francisco, precludes an old Irish neighborhood, at least in part. Yet the absence of the old neighborhood has as much to do with time as with place. Though the movie is set in the 1940s, it speaks to an Irish America of the late 1970s and early 1980s, when Dunne wrote the book and screenplay. By then the old Irish American neighborhoods had disappeared in almost all parts of the country. *Going My Way* reflected a people still emerging from the immigrant inner city; indeed, it is set in downtown New York. The old neighborhood, like Father Fitzgibbons, is still present—indeed, too present and inhibiting. As we saw in the discussion of *The Exorcist*, in that movie the old neighborhood is a decrepit slum and Catholics now live in the upscale, multireligious Georgetown. That would be true for the post-1960s generation of Irish Americans and is reflected in the world of *True Confessions*. The suburban world of golf courses and the housing construction boom of postwar Los Angeles prefigure the change that is coming.

So, Des Spellacy cannot find salvation in some return to the old ethnic neighborhood: the Acre in Lowell, South Boston in Boston, Hell's Kitchen in New York City, or the Back of Yards in Chicago. He must be exiled to the desert. Having learned humility ("I thought I was someone I wasn't"), Des finds useful honest work in a desert parish. Not unlike Homer Smith and the nuns in *Lilies of the Field*, the desert is the empty space where new relationships can be constructed. This ending suggests a meaning that transcends the specifics of an Irish American Catholic search for identity. Finding humility and salvation in the desert makes Des's story instantly universal, linking it to the religious traditions not just of Catholics nor even just Christians, but of Muslims, Jews, and others. Such an age-old story of faith, broadly and fundamentally religious, might seem surprising given the relentless attack on religion that the movie has already made. As Pauline Kael observes, however, "Implicit in the film's conception is that there is a pure Catholicism tucked away somewhere waiting for Des to return to it."[15] Dunne's muckraking of Catholicism grew out of indignation and not cynicism. Several eulogies noted after his death in 2003 that he remained something of a skeptical believer to the end of his life.

True Confessions suggests the satisfaction of repentance and a return to God for all—Catholics and non-Catholics, Irish and non-Irish Americans alike. Des's salvation, however, has a special ethnic dimension as well. Dunne may have set his ending in the desert, but he still seems to be writing in the tradition of older Irish American writers, most notably Edwin O'Connor. Though Des Spellacy's new parish is in the desert and Father Kennedy's in *The Edge of Sadness* is in the decaying downtown of some New England city (presumably Boston), the two stories have much in common. Dunne read *The Edge of Sadness* and reviewed it for the *National Review*. He claimed to not like it much: "nothing happens."[16] Yet O'Connor's book and Dunne's book and subsequent movie are very similar: a "successful" priest finds that his success destroys him. He then goes on to find a new vocation in apparent disgrace and exile at a run-down parish. In a small but telling similarity, both priests in the O'Connor and Dunne novels find curates of new immigrant ethnicity in their parishes of exile. In *The Edge of Sadness*, the Polish American Father Danowski serves with Father Kennedy and in *True Confessions* the Mexican American Father Duarte supports the ailing Des Spellacy. Both young curates have as yet uncompromised dreams of material success for their churches, hoping to raise money and begin new construction, and such ambitions only serve to remind us of the lessons the older Irish American priests have already painfully learned. "The new St. Mary's is going to be the flower of the desert," exclaims Father Duarte to Tom Spellacy when the policeman comes to visit his brother.

More important, the film makes clear that Des Spellacy never really needed a return to an old neighborhood to find his Irish American ethnic roots, for he has had a brother close at hand who is a constant and visible reminder of them. Tom Spellacy plays many roles in this movie. He drives the plot by investigating the Fazenda killing and by eventually forcing Des's exile. Moreover, the movie makes its moral issues more accessible to viewers by personalizing them through the two brothers' conflict and reconciliation. Yet Tom performs another role as well. As Des says in the closing scene in the desert: "You made me remember things I had forgotten."

It is Tom's assault on Des's corrupt friends that Des seems to be talking about in the movie's final scene. But Tom's very existence is a living, walking reminder to Des of his true, Irish American self, the self he must reclaim. Des and he have shared not just a common populist pose or skeptical attitude but a common history as Irish American working-class kids long before Des's ascent to status and power. The soulful playing of "Carrickfergus" has invoked their Irishness at every one of their meetings and does so again at this last one. Tom, for good measure, offers another reminder of the ethnic cast to their fraternal bond in that final scene. After Des has told him he is going to die, Tom says: "I'll sing an Irish song at your wake," and then laughs, "[with] my voice, I'll wake you up again." Finally and critically, simply pairing tough-talking Irish American brothers evokes—as many critics' reviews of the movie suggested—images of earlier movies in a Hollywood tradition of tough-talking, working-class Irish American brothers. In this way, *True Confessions* invokes *Angels with Dirty Faces*, the classic film pairing of Irish American "brothers" (not literally of the same blood but linked since birth). Both films continue to confound our expectations of who should save whom. In *Angels with Dirty Faces* the savior is the man of the street, Rocky Sullivan the gangster. In *True Confessions* it is a cop but one who is snarling, streetwise, and dirty, a former bag man in a prostitution ring.

And of what does Tom remind Des that saves him? In the movie, Des says simply, "You made me remember things I had forgotten. I thought I was someone I wasn't." In the film, Des Spellacy's renunciation of the ambition and power that had corrupted him seems a kind of generic, universal lesson in humility. Yet in the novel, Dunne worded Des's response differently: "You made me remember something I forgot." And Des continues, "Or tried to forget is more like it. You and me, we were always just a couple of Harps."[17] Like the referencing of themes and characters from earlier Irish American novelists and from earlier films about Irish American brothers, that line reveals that Dunne thought his story had special meaning for Irish Americans. As the movie suggests (even without the line),

Dunne found a redefinition of Irish American in the harp who—even without an old neighborhood—knows he was not born for riches and social status, the harp who remains the chippy outsider, the populist scourge of elite pretension and privilege.

Through Des Spellacy's rise and fall, Dunne tried to trace a path in *True Confessions* out of the moral corruption and personal confusion to which mid-twentieth-century Irish America's scrambling for power and status had inevitably led. It was, in fact, his own path. Dunne thought a writer "only has one character and that is himself or herself. In my case, me, so at the risk of being glib, I am the priest in *True Confessions*." That path led to religious redemption in the desert but not to Irish American assimilation into an American mainstream. Des finds a kind of spirituality and a different meaning for being Irish American than the old militant American Catholicism, a spirituality and ethnic meaning that requires a rejection of status and power and an embrace of the role of a perpetual, skeptical outsider. Trying to be someone they were not was the problem for all Irish Americans, Dunne suggests. It was a problem not just for Des, the cardinal's powerful chancellor, but for Dunne himself, the Princeton WASP wannabe. The solution is repentance but in Irish American fashion: a return to earlier origins and an embrace of the long-time Irish American role as outsider—explicit in the book, implicit in the film—as "just a couple of Harps."[18]

NOTES

1. Jack Kroll, "Brilliant Brother Act," *Newsweek*, 28 September 1981, 87; Vincent Canby, "Film: True Confessions with De Niro and Duvall, Abundant with Life," *New York Times*, 25 September 1981; Stanley Kauffman, "Waiting for Grosbard," *New Republic*, 30 September 1981, 24–25; Pauline Kael, "Three Pairs," *New Yorker*, 26 October 1981, 176; William F. Buckley, Jr., "Hollywood Piety," *National Review*, 18 September 1981.

2. William V. Shannon, *The American Irish: A Political and Social Portrait* (New York: Collier, 1974), p. 132.

3. On "outness," see William Shannon, *The American Irish* (New York: Collier, 1964), 132; Lester Friedman, *Hollywood and the Image of the Jew* (New York: Unger, 1982), 33.

4. A few movies still feature Irish Catholic characters standing in as the American Everyman. Irish American Ray Kinsella (Kevin Costner) is the heroic, iconic lead in *Field of Dreams* (1989), a film celebrating baseball as the heart of America. Everyone recognized *Field of Dreams* as a sentimental paean to America but few realized that it was probably the most clearly Catholic, or at least Irish American Catholic, film of the last three decades. In the movie Kinsella hears voices asking

him to build a shrine, a baseball diamond, in his corn field. Soon a "communion of saints"—dead baseball stars—visit it. He then makes a pilgrimage to another shrine, Fenway Park in Boston, and eventually is rewarded with a miraculous familial reconciliation as well as thousands of worshipful (and paying) pilgrims to his baseball-field shrine.

5. Dunne and Didion's Hollywood support is described in "The Paris Review Interview," in John Gregory Dunne, *Regards: The Selected Nonfiction of John Gregory Dunne* (New York: Thunder Mouth, 2006), 399; and the "brothel" comment comes from "Tinsel" (21) in the same volume.

6. John Gregory Dunne, *Harp* (New York: Simon and Schuster, 1989), 166; for critics who commented on Dunne's ethnic and class identity, see Mark Feeney, "John Dunne: Wrote of Hollywood, Irish Experience," *Boston Globe*, 1 January 2004; and Andrew Rosenheim, "Obituary: John Gregory Dunne," *Independent*, 12 January 2004.

7. Vincent Canby, "Third Quarter Report: Movie Magic Is Back," *New York Times*, 4 October 1981.

8. Stanley Kauffman, "Stanley Kauffman on Film," *New Republic*, 30 September 1981, 24; Kael, "Three Pairs"; Robert Hatch, "Films," *Nation*, 5 October 1981, 452; Andrew Greeley quoted in Francis J. Weber, *His Eminence of Los Angeles: James Francis Cardinal McIntyre* (Mission Hills, CA: St. Francis Historical Society, 1997), 2:452.

9. Weber, *His Eminence of Los Angeles*, 2:673–84.

10. Kael, "Three Pairs," 175.

11. Hugh Rank, "O'Connor's Image of the Priest," *New England Quarterly* 41 (March 1968): 10.

12. Dunne, *Harp*, 200, 47, 66. Dunne's understanding was shared by others who knew him; see David Guy, "Dunne's Monsignor: His Roots as a Writer," *USA Today*, 25 August 1989; Richard Schickel, "Obituary," *Time*, 12 January 2004, 23, who reported that Dunne's "hatred of hypocrisy was legendary"; David Halberstam says he "hated fraud and duplicity," in *Boston Globe*, 1 January 2004; Andrew Rosenheim, in the *Independent* (London), 12 January 2004, concluded, "he could be remarkably bad tempered especially with people he considered pretentious and phony."

13. James Fisher, "Alternative Sources of Catholic Intellectual Vitality," *U.S. Catholic Historian* 13 (Winter 1995): 83–88.

14. William Williams, *'Twas Only an Irishman's Dream: The Image of Ireland and the Irish in American Popular Song Lyrics, 1800–1920* (Urbana: University of Illinois Press, 1996), 168.

15. Kael, "Three Pairs," 175.

16. John Gregory Dunne, "Edge of Sadness," *National Review*, 7 October 1961, 239.

17. John Gregory Dunne, *True Confessions* (New York: Dutton, 1977), 340.

18. "The Paris Review Interview," in Dunne, *Regards*, 384.

FURTHER READING

Curran, Joseph M. *Hibernian Green on the Silver Screen: The Irish and American Movies.* Westport, CT: Greenwood, 1989.

Dunne, John Gregory. *The Studio.* New York: Farrar, Straus and Giroux, 1969.

———. *Monster: Living Off the Big Screen.* New York: Random House, 1997.

Ferraro, Thomas J., ed. *Catholic Lives, Contemporary America.* Durham, NC: Duke University Press, 1997.

King, Neal. *Heroes in Hard Times: Cop Action Movies in the U.S.* Philadelphia: Temple University Press, 1999.

Lourdeaux, Lee. *Italian and Irish Filmmakers in America: Ford, Capra, Coppola, and Scorsese.* Philadelphia: Temple University Press, 1990.

McCaffrey, Lawrence John. *The Irish Catholic Diaspora in America.* Washington, DC: Catholic University of America Press, 1997.

Meagher, Timothy. *The Columbia Guide to Irish American History.* New York: Columbia University Press, 2005.

Negra, Diane. *The Irish in Us: Irishness, Performativity, and Popular Culture.* Durham, NC: Duke University Press, 2006.

Rafter, Nicole. *Shots in the Mirror: Crime Films and Society.* New York: Oxford University Press, 2006.

WORLDLY MADONNA

Entertaining Angels: The Dorothy
Day Story (1996)

Tracy Fessenden

One *finds* in many cities a kind of make-believe newspaper sold by the homeless for a dollar a copy, an alternative to begging. The paper might have recycled news and cheerful stories of uplift, but it is printed and sold not so much to be read as to camouflage acts of charity as transactions between producers and consumers in a capitalist economy. Some part of the proceeds go into social services, the rest into the pockets of those who hawk the paper to passersby and to passengers in cars idled in traffic. Those who bother to read the paper are likely to *find* no explanation for why homelessness exists and nothing to trouble the conscience of the busy person who's just thrown a dollar at someone down on his luck.

Unsuspecting viewers of *Entertaining Angels: The Dorothy Day Story* may be forgiven for seeing the *Catholic Worker* as one such newspaper. In the words of an evangelical Christian movie guide, which awarded the film its highest, four-star rating, it was by "[b]eginning the 'Catholic Worker,' a political and spiritual newspaper which today resources over 100 homes for the poor," that Dorothy Day's "life transcended any smaller purpose she may have chosen." One wouldn't know from the film that the *Catholic Worker* was and remains a radical force for justice and nonviolent social change, a rallying point for the Catholic Left, and a reproach to a nation that grows rich on the neglect of its poor. One learns instead that the newspaper was the inspired answer to a nettlesome personal dilemma. "How does a young, idealistic, intelligent and talented woman find a cause worthy of her abilities? Is it to be found in the women's movement? In political agendas? In investigative journalism? In sexual relationships? In motherhood? Or is she created for such a far greater purpose than any of these that only a transcendent purpose is great enough to challenge and fulfill her?"[1]

Dorothy Day in fact began the *Catholic Worker* not to fulfill a personal quest but instead, as she wrote in the inaugural issue she sold for a penny a copy, "to protest, to expose, to complain, to point out abuses and demand reforms," to hold the Catholic church to its own neglected teachings on social justice and the "recon-reconstruction of the social order."[2] The paper's revolutionary agenda is one of the casualties of *Entertaining Angels*, whose rendering of Dorothy Day's story subordi-nates the causes for which Day stood fast—including economic justice and an end to war making—to a hackneyed narrative of a wayward woman who finds re-demption in surrender to Christ.

In the film's version of Day's life, the radical intellectual who managed to integrate Catholic piety with her fierce desire for social justice becomes a cheerful charity worker whose devotion to the poor testifies to the depth of her repentance for a sorry, stumbling past. The film follows Dorothy Day between the ages of twenty and forty. We watch as she cavorts with poets and radicals in Greenwich Village, writes a bit, and stumbles from one love affair to the next. Wounded in love, disenchanted with politics, Dorothy Day leaves the wicked city for a quieter life by the ocean, converts to Catholicism under the tutelage of a gentle nun, then returns to New York at the height of the Depression to spend the rest of her life helping the poor. "It's been a very lonely life," she announces in a final soliloquy. "I've been looking to fill the emptiness. Now I see that it begins with these people, the ones that nobody else wants.... They are my meeting place with God. And if I will give them a chance, I know that God will fill me with love, fill me through these people." It's a bad movie. In the bigger picture, it gets worse.

There's much at stake in the saccharine portrayal of Dorothy Day in *Entertaining Angels*, and not simply because people are now likely to learn about Day from the schmaltzy film rather than from her own writings. According to its producer, Paulist Father Ellwood "Bud" Kieser, *Entertaining Angels* was intended as a contri-bution to the campaign to have Dorothy Day declared a saint by the Catholic church. The church insists that it doesn't "make" saints, it simply recognizes persons of exceptional holiness and virtue who join God at their deaths and intercede for the faithful in heaven. Canonization is in this sense a project of fact finding, not the inventing of a saint, but presenting the facts of Day's sanctity has required some ingenuity from the parties involved. The canonization process moves through several institutional steps. At the behest of petitioners who wish to see a person declared a saint, a diocesan tribunal may elect to open a canonization cause by making a case for the candidate's exceptional virtue to the Congregation for the Causes of Saints at the Vatican. If the congregation finds the case convincing, it bestows the title of "venerable" on the candidate and moves the process to the College of Cardinals or the pope. (The pope, of course, is free to speed the process along, as John Paul II did in the case of Mother Theresa and Benedict XVI has done in the case of John Paul.) Day has been declared venerable, which means that the Congregation for the Causes of Saints has reviewed the evidence of Day's "virtuousness" and declared her to be of "heroic virtue." To move from venerable to "blessed," Day would need either to have died a martyr, which she did not, or to have one miracle attributed to her; to move from "blessed" to "saint," she needs a miracle more.

These layers of bureaucracy make sainthood a pricey proposition: the costs, running into the hundreds of thousands of dollars, are born solely by petitioners, for whom the Vatican reportedly runs training courses and provides an itemized price list for canonization. The current canonization procedure reflects changes made in 1983 by Pope John Paul II, who streamlined an older, more cumbersome process in his zeal to declare more saints than any previous pontiff—close to 500, in addition to more than 1,000 additional people who made it to the beatification stage before the pope's death in 2005. John Paul's desire to make the saints more widely known, together with his far-flung travels and his special mission to youth, are often cited by those who credit him with maintaining the church's relevance in the modern world. At the same time, however, John Paul II staunchly reaffirmed the church's opposition to contraception, abortion (which he compared to the Holocaust), homosexuality, gay marriage (which he called evil), and all sex outside of marriage. He also supported ultraconservative lay Catholic organizations like Opus Dei. The many hundreds of new names he added to the rolls of the saints were supplied in part, therefore, to give contemporary Catholics more and more orthodox models to live by as they confront relational possibilities in a changing world.

While evidence suggests that U.S. Catholics use birth control, resort to abortion, and take part in extramarital and same-sex relations as much or more than anyone else, they do so in defiance of Vatican pronouncements that some Catholic theologians regard as infallible. According to *Lumen Gentium* (Dogmatic Constitution on the Church), a key document of Vatican II, the pope exercises "infallibility in virtue of his office when, as supreme pastor and teacher of the faithful . . . he proclaims in an absolute decision a doctrine pertaining to faith or morals."[3] *Lumen Gentium* aimed to clarify the doctrine of papal infallibility as it was first pronounced in the First Vatican Council of 1869, when the church faced (or refused to face) the waning of its power in the revolutions of the eighteenth and nineteenth centuries. The words "faith" and "morals" in *Lumen Gentium* represent a shift in the territory over which the church claims absolute authority: rather than continuing to assert its sovereignty over all of human life in its social, political, and spiritual arenas, as it had in the past, the church understands its power as belonging now to the arena of "faith and morals." Of these two, faith—that is, faithful membership in the one true church—is understood to be obligatory for Catholics only, and beyond the power of democratic states to enforce. Morals, however, because they allegedly inhere in natural law rather than in Catholic teaching, remain binding on all, Catholic and non-Catholic, without regard for democratic norms.

Trading the presumption of unimpeachable temporal power for charismatic authority in the realm of faith and morals, the church since 1965 has come increasingly to pronounce on questions of morality, *and* to define morality almost entirely in terms of sexuality and gender. In his 1968 encyclical *Humanae vitae*, for example, Pope Paul VI reiterated the church's condemnation of all forms of artificial birth control, even though the commission he'd established four years earlier to examine the issue had endorsed the use of contraception on both theological and social justice grounds. Since then, the church's commitment to regulating sexuality—a way of consolidating its authority in an era of secularism and religious pluralism—has strengthened its alliances with conservative forces in the United States and worldwide. In this way, the ostensibly progressive reforms of Vatican II in fact gave rise to a new ideological hierarchy in which, as the sociologist Gene Burns puts it, morals—the church's teachings on sexuality and gender, understood to be universal and absolute—occupy the highest position, Catholic faith and doctrine the middle ground, and Catholic social teaching, often weakly interpreted and seldom enforced, the lowest rung.[4]

This new distribution of emphasis sheds light on a number of developments in American religion and politics, in addition to clarifying the narrative arc of *Entertaining Angels*. In the 2004 elections in the United States, for example, the church's opposition to the war in Iraq, though clearly articulated and powerfully urged by John Paul II, went largely ignored as Catholic bishops threatened to excommunicate Catholic candidates who supported the right to abortion, and a majority of Catholic voters sided with the self-proclaimed evangelical George W. Bush over the prochoice Catholic presidential candidate, John Kerry. In the new pontificate of Benedict XVI, meanwhile, the Vatican's response to the U.S. clergy's sexual abuse scandals, far from confronting an ecclesiastical culture of sexual dishonesty, has instead been to pronounce on the unfitness of homosexual men for the priesthood. And as AIDS continues to orphan millions of children each year, ravaging Third World communities and crippling development for generations to come, the church has yet to alter its prohibition of the use of condoms under any circumstances—a position with deadly policy implications for poor and struggling people worldwide.

"Don't Call Me a Saint"

Poor and marginalized people have had few more devoted champions among American Catholics than Dorothy Day, who died in 1980 at the age of eighty-three. Day was an ardent convert to Catholicism, a fearless writer and journalist who moved among intellectual luminaries, an anarchist and stubborn pacifist, and a single mother who lived most of her life in the slums of New York's Lower East Side. Together with the French peasant-philosopher Peter Maurin, her friend and mentor, Day began publishing the *Catholic Worker* in 1933. With tens of thousands of people who have since identified themselves as Catholic Workers, Day and Maurin elected to live in poverty among the poor, all the while challenging militarism, racism, and economic injustice. Day did so in blistering editorials in the newspaper she published, in the Houses of Hospitality she established to shelter, feed, clothe, affirm, and advocate for the poor, and in acts of civil disobedience for which she was repeatedly jailed. Her followers continue to do so in the pages of the *Catholic Worker*, still priced at a penny a copy, and in more than 175 Catholic Worker organizations now in operation in America and around the world. For her insistence on an acutely literal interpretation of the Sermon on the Mount, Dorothy Day has been called the conscience of American Catholicism.

Day would seem to be an improbable candidate for sainthood in an era when American Catholics returned George W. Bush to the White House, not only because of her uncompromising antiwar stance and her rebuke of corporate America, but because as a young woman, prior to becoming a Catholic, she had an abortion. While the Catholic church has long stood fast against abortion in all circumstances—audiences might recall *The Cardinal* (1963), where a priest refuses to grant the dispensation that would save his own sister from fatal complications in pregnancy—opposition to abortion has become *the* symbol of the post–Vatican II church's authority in the area of faith and morals. It is also the issue that has come more than any other to draw conservative Catholics and Protestants together under the banner of the Religious Right and to anchor a political platform that favors precisely the targets of Day's radical social critique.

Nevertheless, the socially conservative Cardinal John J. O'Connor of New York officially opened Day's cause for sainthood in 2000. "It has long been my contention," O'Connor wrote in that year to the Congregation for the Causes of Saints in Rome, "that Dorothy Day is a saint—not a 'gingerbread' saint or a 'holy card' saint, but a modern day devoted daughter of the Church." While he noted Day's pacifism and her commitment to social justice, O'Connor made the strongest case for her canonization in the language of faith and morals:

> [Day's] life is a model for all in the third millennium, but especially for women who have had or are considering abortions. It is a well-known fact that Dorothy Day procured an abortion before her conversion to the faith. She regretted it every day of her life. After her conversion from a life akin to that of the pre-converted Augustine of Hippo, she proved a stout defender of human life. The conversion of mind and heart that she exemplified speaks volumes to all women today on two fronts. First, it demonstrates the mercy of God, mercy in that a woman who sinned so gravely could find such unity with God upon conversion. Second, it demonstrates that one may turn from the ultimate act of violence against innocent life in the womb to a position of total holiness and pacifism. In short, I contend that her abortion should not preclude her cause, but intensifies it.[5]

By putting her abortion front and center, O'Connor's case for Day's sainthood recast her life in the image of the new ideological hierarchy of the post–Vatican II church: morals (read: Catholic teachings on sex and gender) come first, faith second, and social teaching a distant third. In O'Connor's retelling, Day's life became a story of sexual sin, anguished remorse, and divine forgiveness. Her conversion to Catholicism and her work with the poor became significant less in themselves than as testimony to the transformative power of grace in the life of a woman who committed the gravest of sins, the sin of abortion. In O'Connor's account, the grace of conversion cured this most abject of sinners of the radicalism that landed her under FBI surveillance for much of her life. O'Connor continued:

> It has also been noted that Dorothy Day often seemed friendly to political groups hostile to the Church, for example, communists, socialists, and anarchists. It is necessary to divide her political stances in two spheres: pre- and post-conversion. After her conversion, she was neither a member of such political groupings nor did she approve of their tactics. . . . Moreover, her complete commitment to pacifism

in imitation of Christ often separated her from these political ideologies. She rejected all military force; she rejected aid to force in any way in a most idealistic manner. So much were her "politics" based on an ideology of nonviolence that they may be said to be apolitical. Like so many saints of days gone by, she was an idealist in a non-ideal world.[6]

O'Connor's shrewd repackaging of Dorothy Day won praise for its diplomacy in circumventing myriad objections to Day's canonization, including her own. "Don't call me a saint," Day famously admonished her admirers. "I don't want to be dismissed that easily." (O'Connor's letter to the Holy See cites this as evidence that Day wanted no more after her conversion than to be "a simple woman living the Gospel," whatever her airy idealism.) But can it accurately be said that Day, who mentions her own abortion not once in her many candid and finely aware autobiographical writings, "regretted it every day of her life"? Did she, who fasted in repentance for the U.S. bombing of Hiroshima and Nagasaki, who refused to pay taxes to a war-making government, and who went willingly to jail for her protests of the nuclear arms race, consider the ending of fetal life the "ultimate act of violence"? And if Day becomes the patron saint of all women who have had or are considering abortions, what happens to the much larger part of her story a story about economic justice, nonviolence, and solidarity with the poorest of the poor? None of these are popular causes among the conservative forces, Protestant or Catholic, who forge alliances with the Vatican on the issues of sexual regulation.

Good Intentions

"Dorothy Day made many mistakes in her life," granted Father Bud Kieser, the film's producer, "but I have no doubt that she is now a saint! After all, she surrendered her life to God and gave God a chance to work in her. And that's what makes one a saint." Even though she had an abortion, Kieser reflected, "this woman made the necessary decisions to turn her life over to Christ. She entered the Church and spent the last 50 years of her life serving the poor and homeless in New York City."[7] Again, we see the ideological hierarchy: morals (sex/gender ideology) first, faith second, social justice third.

That Kieser would tell Day's story through the lens of her abortion and the heavy weight of guilt that presumably led her to the church shows the power of this ideological framing even for Catholics with sterling progressive credentials. Father Kieser belonged to the Paulist order of priests, who describe their mission as one of promoting justice and dignity for all persons, regardless of where they find themselves in relation to the institutional church. Their goal of "giving the Word of God a voice" made them focus on mass media—pulpits and print, radio, television, and film. The Paulist Press originally published the *Catholic Worker*. As a young Paulist priest, Kieser took his mission to Hollywood and founded Paulist Productions/Paulist Pictures, pausing to write a doctoral dissertation at Berkeley on "Cinema as a Religious Experience." In 1989 Kieser produced his most acclaimed film, *Romero*, about the Salvadoran archbishop assassinated for his campaigns against the landowner- and military-supported death squads that operated with impunity during the Reagan years. Less successful but just as charged politically was *We Are the Children*, a 1987 television drama set in famine-stricken Ethiopia. But Kieser's pet project had always been a film about Dorothy Day. While making *Romero* Kieser told an interviewer that if the film were successful it would foot the bill for the movie he'd wanted to make for decades. "Dorothy and I met in Rome during the fourth session of the Second Vatican Council in the mid 60's," Kieser recalled. "I asked her one day if I could put her story on film—to which she quipped rather brusquely: 'Wait 'til I'm dead!'"[8]

In the meantime Kieser produced the weekly television program *Insight*. Begun in 1960, the series ran for twenty-three years and experimented (sometimes wildly) with a range of genres to spur audiences to moral and spiritual reflection. Fans recall a decidedly 1960s, countercultural flavor to the show; in one episode a group of young people hold a trial to impeach God. (Martin Sheen was a veteran of many episodes, twice playing God on *Insight* long before his run as the president in the television show *The West Wing*.) Another episode recalls cinema verité in its depiction of an alcoholic housewife ruminating drunkenly on the different life she might have had; in other episodes, characters make their way through postapocalyptic rubble to deliver before-it's-too-late lessons to viewers at home. *Insight* usually aired early on Sunday mornings (sometimes very early, just before the station went off the air on Saturday night) to fill programming gaps at odd hours and to help stations meet the community service obligations of their licenses.[9] Though each episode was produced on a shoestring budget and for a nebulous audience cohort, *Insight* won several Emmys in the course of its run and managed to enlist the talents of such well-known actors (and Hollywood liberals) as Carol Burnett, Walter Matthau, Flip Wilson, and Ed Asner, in addition to Sheen, who would go on to play Peter Maurin in *Entertaining Angels*.

Both Moira Kelly (who plays Day) and Martin Sheen described their participation in the film as motivated by their own deeply held Catholic faith. Kelly claimed—at least during interviews to promote this movie—that her childhood dream was to become a nun, but that she'd settled on becoming a Hollywood actress when a priest convinced her that she might do God's work on the screen. Martin Sheen, born Ramón Gerardo Antonio Estévez, took the surname of Bishop Fulton Sheen as a young actor. He spent time in Catholic Worker houses and was nurtured in Day's and Maurin's brand of social protest (he has been arrested more than sixty times for civil disobedience). The film was directed by Michael Ray Rhodes, an *Insight* veteran and a seminary-trained Presbyterian. Its writer, John Wells, is the son of an Episcopal priest. As on the set of *Insight*, the cast and crew ended each day's shooting of *Entertaining Angels* with a celebration of mass.

In the charitable estimation of the *National Catholic Reporter*, however, "good intentions don't necessarily make good movies." The production sags with heavy-handed cues, like the thunder and lightning in the scene where Day, temporarily cast out of the House of Hospitality business by disgruntled coworkers, hurls angry questions at a statue of Jesus, or the choir that sings from nowhere when she embraces a violent resident. Day's unlikely conversion to Catholicism goes largely unelaborated; her devotion to the poor and homeless is conveyed in wincingly obvious gestures (as when Day joins Maurin in washing the feet of the derelict men who come to sleep on her floor) and scored to schmaltzy music. To the *New York Times*'s Stephen Holden, such bumbling portrayals of faith make "what could have been a compelling film seem pat, manipulative and shallow." A few positive reviews came from conservative Protestants who applauded *Entertaining Angels* as the story of an individual's rocky but triumphant road to redemption. For the most part, however, Kieser's portrait of Day as an "American Mother Theresa—but a Mother Theresa with a past!" found few champions among the critics. Even *TV Guide* judged the film to be shallow.[10]

In fairness, subtlety is not what *Insight*'s early Sunday morning demographic of toddlers, insomniacs, and collapsed Saturday night revelers best prepared its producer to deliver. "The interaction of contraries is the engine that drives a story," Kieser explained of his made-for-TV morality plays. "The more evenly matched the adversaries are, and the more uncertain the outcome, the more compelling is the drama."[11] *Entertaining Angels* tells its story as a conflict of opposites, albeit within a single person: Dorothy Day the sexy Jazz Age bohemian and Day the Mother Theresa of the Lower East Side. The problem is not that these portraits are exaggerated: Day really did drink until dawn with poets and anarchists, work as a dime-a-dance girl and an artist's model, give her bed to drug addicts and prostitutes, study the lives of the saints, go daily to mass, and command the respectful attention, not to say reverence, of the Catholic hierarchy all the way to the top. The problem is that the bad-girl-gone-good schema reduces a journey of ever-deepening faith to a simple U-turn, and the textured narrative of Day's life to a before-and-after story.

History and Selective Memory

The "before" is certainly colorful: *Entertaining Angels* leans heavily on the Greenwich Village milieu of its protagonist's preconversion years ("it was like free love in the 1960s!" Moira Kelly enthuses in a bonus feature on the DVD) and ends its story soon after Day has taken to wearing shapeless housedresses and allowed her hair to go grey. Except for a pair of brief, bookending scenes of a New York City jail cell in 1963, *Entertaining Angels* is set entirely between 1917 and 1937, the period, Kieser explained, in which Day "faced the great crises of her life and made the decisions which shaped all else." The great crises include a disappointing love affair, an out-of-wedlock birth (Day described her relationship to Forster Batterham, her daughter's father, as a common-law marriage), and most sensationally, a tenement abortion. In this way the crux of Kieser's film—given as the story of "a woman who overcame many obstacles in her life," "a woman who went through many personal struggles to find her calling"—becomes an episode about which Day herself was notoriously circumspect, and the struggle against war and systemic injustice that so occupied her both before *and* after her conversion all but disappears from view.[12]

The jail scenes that begin and end the movie, for example, seem awkwardly to telescope parts of Day's life that would otherwise be lost to the film. *Entertaining Angels* opens on the scene of a drug-addled African American woman being dragged screaming to a prison cell, where a match held to a cigarette illuminates the elderly Day sitting Buddha-like in a corner. (Day had stopped smoking by 1963, though she reportedly became so prickly in withdrawal that her fellow Catholic Workers would beg her to light up.) The disturbed woman shakes, retches, and claws the floor; the soft-spoken Day explains that she is in jail for protesting the hydrogen bomb, then embraces and miraculously calms her companion. The episode is missing from the scene-by-scene synopsis included in a promotional release for the film, suggesting a hasty postproduction shoot, and the granny glasses and Halloweenish grey wig worn by Kelly to evoke the sixty-six-year-old Day give the impression that the makeup and wardrobe crews were nowhere on the set. *Insight* fans might feel a rush of nostalgia at the low production values and clunky staging of the 1960s, but the scene's problems go beyond the bad makeup and sensationalism: when Kelly sings "Amazing Grace" and the camera

11.1. At both the beginning and the end of *Entertaining Angels*, the camera focuses on Dorothy Day's (Moira Kelly) face, lit with a saintly glow. The grey wig and granny glasses worn by the young actress to evoke the aged Day suggest a hasty post-production shoot, with makeup and wardrobe crews nowhere on the scene.

pans to her beatific, unlined face on "saved a wretch like me," we realize that the manacled black woman is a period detail like the talcum-powder wig, a prop in service of a story emphatically not her own.

Neither is the story Dorothy Day's: Day is honored here not for her relentlessness in calling the military-industrial complex to account but rather for her ability to calm a prisoner. (Note that the year is 1963: Alabama governor George Wallace declares "segregation now, segregation tomorrow, and segregation forever"; Martin Luther King, Jr., pens his "Letter from Birmingham Jail"; and Dorothy Day—the white-washed, movie-version Dorothy Day—quiets an excitable black woman.) But for the briefest shot of a second African American woman marching in a suffragette parade, we will see no more nonwhite faces in the film. Nor will we see any of Day's civil rights work, her antiwar activities, or the civil disobedience for which she went to worse jails than the one shown on-screen. In condescending to its poor and marginalized characters, the film condescends to Dorothy Day, sized up even before the opening credits not as the conscience of

American Catholicism but instead, as the words of the old Protestant hymn would have it, the "wretch" who now is saved.

By limiting its story to the years 1917–1937, *Entertaining Angels* slights the commitments Day pursued in the last four decades of her life, among them commitments that socially conservative American Catholics might well find unpalatable. But the truncated time frame of the film also suggests that nothing to which Day devoted herself as a young woman in the movie's first half quite mattered after her conversion. The women's movement, journalism, socialism, her relationships with those she counted as lovers and friends—all are represented as transient and superficial. The before-and-after structure imposed on Day's life requires that the before amount to nothing, or less than nothing; not only must there be an abrupt break with the past, the past must be shown to be fundamentally flawed.

In the 1917 women's rights march to which the film cuts immediately from the 1963 prison scene, for example, the twenty-year-old Day and Maggie Bowen (Heather Graham) bring to the cause of women's suffrage all of the seriousness of Mrs. Banks in *Mary Poppins*. The two become fast friends in the uproarious aftermath of Day's pelting of a police officer. The fictional Maggie, Day's "soulmate" in the film and a bit of a floozy even before her descent into alcoholism and street life, seems an all-purpose stand-in for the many women friends Day includes in her autobiographical writings. In particular Maggie seems to be a composite of the beautiful and fiery Rayna Prohme, the fellow radical and "dearly loved" companion with whom Day lived in both Chicago and New York, and Peggy Baird, whom Day actually did meet while picketing for women's rights in front of Woodrow Wilson's White House in 1917. It was Baird who introduced Day to a Greenwich Village literary milieu that included the likes of Malcolm Cowley (to whom Baird was for a time married), Eugene O'Neill, and Kenneth Burke. What we don't learn from the film is how crucial such friends were to Day's development both before and after her conversion. In the movie, Maggie's lack of spiritual moorings makes her the lost sheep Day will save in the end. "I'm not religious," Maggie tipsily responds to the barroom Marxists who pronounce on the emptiness of faith, "but I feel empty all the same." By contrast, Rayna Prohme, who died an atheist and a communist at the age of twenty-nine, always belonged, in Day's mind, to "the invisible unity of the Church." "When I think of Rayna," Day wrote, "I think of Mauriac's statement in his life of Christ that those who serve the cause of the masses, the poor, working for truth and justice, have worked for Christ even while denying him."[13]

Nor do we learn that when Day and Peggy Baird picketed for women's suffrage in 1917 they were on no silly female adventure. The two were among forty women protestors arrested on the White House lawn and taken to a rural workhouse where they were roughly handled, which spurred them to respond with a hunger strike. Only after President Wilson issued an executive order were they released. During this time, Day found strength in reading the psalms. The violence of incarceration, the solidarity with her fellow protestors, and the comfort of the Bible were all experiences that would leave their lasting impression on the Catholic Worker movement. In the giddy hijinks of the suffragette march we see on film, we learn nothing of how formative were Day's intellectual milieu, her friendships, and her experience of injustice at the hands of government. We learn instead that feminism was one of the misguided causes in which Dorothy Day dabbled before finding the church.

So too with her journalism. *Entertaining Angels* portrays Day as a sexy girl-reporter for the socialist daily the *Call*, but her writing, like her feminism, clearly comes to naught: when a fire destroys an occupied tenement whose unscrupulous landlord Day had criticized in print, we see her shaking her head over the news and concluding tearfully that her reporting had "just made it worse." After leaving Greenwich Village for a quieter life on Staten Island, Day occasionally taps at her typewriter to pass the time, but she had never worked much even before then: so elegantly groomed is Day in these early scenes, so attractively artsy her living quarters, that one reviewer could reasonably (but mistakenly) infer that "Dorothy's journey begins in the pampered wealth of a New England heritage." The reality was something else again: Day sprang from modest roots in the Midwest, attended the University of Illinois until her scholarship ran out, and rented unheated rooms in the slums of New York where she held a number of jobs (including twelve-hour nursing shifts at a charity hospital) in addition to her newspaper work. As a journalist, Day wrote muckraking articles, interviewed Trotsky in exile, and was deeply immersed in labor history and Marxist theory. And it was as a journalist first and foremost that she founded the Catholic Worker movement. As she wrote in 1943, "We are called, we have a vocation, we have a talent. It is up to us to develop that. Mine, for instance, is journalism writing and it is only because of the paper, the *Catholic Worker*, that Houses of Hospitality" and the rest of the movement "came into being."[14]

An abiding mystery is why *Entertaining Angels* gives this most compelling of American writers almost none of her own lines. But Day is not the only one to whose literary brilliance the film remains deaf; even Eugene O'Neill is made to utter such banalities as "Eat, drink, make love, that's what it's all about!" ("Not enough for me, Gene!" is Day's sparkling retort.) The two are stumbling drunkenly home from a Lower East Side dive called the Hell Hole—which really was the

11.2. Dorothy Day's (Moira Kelly) pride over her story making the front page is quickly deflated when her friend and sister suffragette Maggie announces, "I've broken my damn shoe."

bar's name and not one of the film's ham-fisted touches, and the heavy drinking that went on there is amply attested in Day's memoirs and others'. But what Day remembered of such outings were O'Neill's recitations of "The Hound of Heaven," not tomorrow-we-die platitudes, and when she didn't go home with O'Neill she often went to 5 a.m. mass. Some have criticized *Entertaining Angels* for devoting too much time to the preconversion Dorothy, but Day herself dwells lovingly on these years in her memoirs. As she vividly recounts in *The Long Loneliness* (1952) and *From Union Square to Rome* (1938), these were years of growing self-knowledge and of restless spiritual seeking, of deep intellectual and political commitments nurtured in prayer, in work, and in a circle of brilliant and beloved friends. It was a period of ferment that Day's conversion to Catholicism would build upon, not renounce.

In the film version of Day's Greenwich Village years she sings torchy cabaret songs, smokes like a supermodel, and seduces her way into print, sometimes all in the space of a few frames. Lest this life look too appealing to count as wretched (as the hymn the aged Day croons in prison insists), we soon learn that her wildness

11.3. In a fury after her abortion and desertion by her lover, Day smashes a mirror and concludes, "I can't believe how stupid I was."

comes home to roost in an unwanted pregnancy and in her abandonment by her sometime-lover Lionel Moise (a journalist and compatriot of Ernest Hemingway's) at the abortionist's doorstep. After allegedly being forced by Moise into ending the pregnancy, Day smashes a mirror in grief and remorse.

"Prolife" Revisionism

From here the film follows what has emerged, quite independently of Day's own writings, as the familiar narrative of secret guilt and lifelong expiation on which the case for her canonization relies. In the words of one biographer, for example, the "reason for Dorothy's resistance to admiration was that she believed people would think quite differently about her if they knew the whole truth of her pre-Catholic life and the fact that she had caused the death of her own unborn child"; or again, "[n]othing horrified Dorothy more about her own past than the abortion. This memory was so painful to her that the event was only implied in the vaguest way in her later, Catholic autobiographical writing." "Guilt-ridden about the

abortion," a competent viewer of *Entertaining Angels* observes, "the God-haunted young woman feels that God has given her a second chance."[15] Her lover Forster Batterham (Lenny von Dohlen), meanwhile, can't abide her growing absorption with religion and refuses (as the film has it) to "be caged" by a rite performed by church or state. Day's renunciation of an unsanctified relationship to Batterham then fits easily into this narrative as belonging to the penitential offering that becoming a Catholic would entail for a marked woman (scarlet A for abortion) like Dorothy Day.

In skipping directly from Day's abortion to what was allegedly a needed period of healing on a then-bucolic Staten Island, *Entertaining Angels* passes over Day's brief marriage to a literary agent, Barkeley Tobey, which was apparently of so little consequence that even Day herself neglects to mention it in *The Long Loneliness*. Day does recount that after returning from a year in Europe (she went with Tobey but apparently returned alone), she lived in New Orleans, where she worked as a taxi dancer in a Canal Street bar and attended benediction daily at the St. Louis Cathedral. While in New Orleans Day reported "being filled with an immense sense of gratitude to God and a desire to make some return"; she also published a purportedly racy novel, *The Eleventh Virgin* (1924), which brought $5,000 in film rights from Hollywood, and in this way she financed the time she spent on Staten Island.[16]

Although never mentioned in the film, *The Eleventh Virgin* is crucial to the story that Kieser and Day's other hagiographers tell in that it offers what is widely taken to be a disguised account of her own abortion in the trials of the novel's free-spirited protagonist. Later in her life Day admitted wanting to burn every copy of *The Eleventh Virgin*. This wish together with her failure ever to remark on her abortion in her memoirs are routinely taken up by those who would canonize Day as evidence that the unspeakable memory haunted her every moment of her life. No one suggests that Day excluded her time with Tobey from her reminiscences because it was impossibly painful for her to recall, or that she feared people would think quite differently of her if they knew she'd abandoned a failing marriage. Nor that she may have wanted *The Eleventh Virgin* destroyed because it was simply a very bad book, one that fell far short of the standards she would set for herself as a writer. "[I]f having an abortion changed [Day's] own life," the editor and critic Paul Elie observes, "she never said so in print. In two memoirs, five other books, and some fifteen hundred articles and columns, all grounded in her conviction that firsthand experience and the art of recording it in prose are vital to religious insight," Day never once mentions her abortion; among her biographers, even those who knew her well and prized her candor "treat [*The Eleventh Virgin*] as the most reliable account of the experience, indeed the only one."[17]

Day was not entirely silent on the question of abortion. She made her most expansive statement on the issue as a signatory to the 1974 Catholic Peace Fellowship Statement on Abortion. While objecting in strong terms to the Supreme Court's 1973 decision in *Roe v. Wade*, this letter also refused to pass judgment on "any individual for a tragic decision she or he may have felt forced to make." It urges church leaders to steer the discussion of abortion away from sexual morality and instead to promote the "inter-relatedness of the life issues: war, capital punishment, abortion, euthanasia and economic exploitation," to address "the underlying social problems which turn many people to these deadly alternatives," and finally "to condemn all forms of social and economic injustice and to work for their elimination and the establishment of a social order in which all may find it easier to be 'fully human.'"[18] In this way Day made abortion first and foremost a political issue, an issue of social justice, and not simply a question of sexual morality on which the church might infallibly pronounce.

The film nevertheless portrays Day's post-abortion life on Staten Island as a period of "self-imposed exile from the political causes of the day," a penitential retreat from the sexual adventurousness that had brought her so low, and a time of growing disenchantment with the coterie of jaded radicals who gather on the beach to drink whiskey from hip flasks and sneer at religion as the opiate of the masses. To this portion of the story *Entertaining Angels* adds the largely fictional character of Sister Aloysius (Melinda Dillon), whom the film struggles mightily to depict as both Day's equal and her salvation. On one hand, the film relies on the visual shorthand of a pre–Vatican II nun in a flowing habit to code the path she represents as a Catholic one, and to represent this Catholicism as a nostalgic and morally purified alternative to Day's ostentatiously modern and messy bohemianism. On the other hand, *Entertaining Angels* portrays Sister Aloysius as a decidedly post–Vatican II nun, enlightened, feminist, and street-savvy, who runs a homeless shelter and urges Day to read the kinds of books that honor her God-given intelligence. In fact, the real Sister Aloysia whom Day met during this period was hardly the inspiration for her work among the poor; the nun's spiritual tutelage consisted of holding Day to the perfect memorization of the Baltimore Catechism. "You're a smart woman, make up your own mind," says Sister Aloysius to Day in the film; in *The Long Loneliness*, Sister Aloysia upbraids Day for her slowness in learning the catechism: "And you think you are intelligent.... My fourth-grade pupils know more than you do!"[19]

As the film would have it, the chance encounter with the compassionate nun moves Day from the emptiness of her atheist comrades and their revolutionary chatter to the fullness of serving the poor. But in fact this period of her life was one of ever-deepening love and aliveness that in Day's own account culminated inevitably in her turn to the church. Staten Island was the setting for the chapters of her autobiography that Day titled "Man Is Meant for Happiness," "Having a Baby," and "Love Overflows." For Day, her radical circle and her life with Batterham and their baby were intricately bound to her development as a Catholic. As she wrote later, "I have said, sometimes flippantly, that the mass of bourgeois, smug Christians who denied Christ in his poor made me turn to communism, and that it was the communists and working with them that made me turn to God." Day explained that she chose to have her daughter, Tamar, baptized a Catholic and then to become a Catholic herself because she understood Catholicism as the religion of the masses, the poor. Hours after giving birth Day asked for cigarettes and a typewriter to be brought to her in bed and proceeded to write for the *New Masses* about the miraculous power of childbirth "no matter what [a mother's] grief at poverty, unemployment, or class war." "The article so appealed to all my Marxist friends," Day wrote, "that the account was reprinted all over the world in workers' papers.... I had rubles awaiting me in Moscow."[20]

In showing her resolve to follow the nun's example rather than to chase after the live-for-today Batterham, *Entertaining Angels* implies that *this* time Day will get it right; *this* time the answer to her yearnings for a larger life will come not in her own silly scribbles, her sexual escapades and shallow causes, but in "the words, love and power of Jesus Christ." The film makes what must have been an extraordinarily complicated decision look easy; though he lacks Moise's malevolent glint, Batterham is finally a cad who can't commit, and the sadder-but-wiser Day moves on. But as Day tells her story, it was Batterham, not Sister Aloysia, who led her to God; the love of Christ—wanly embodied in the kindhearted nun, so much more vividly conveyed in Day's rendering of her happiness—was not the alternative to her love for Batterham, but rather, she comes gradually to discover, its ground. "I loved him in every way," Day recalled of Batterham. "I loved his lean cold body as he got into bed smelling of the sea, and I loved his integrity and stubborn pride." And: "It was killing me to think of leaving him." It seems Day concluded that she could not be baptized a Catholic and continue to live with the man she loved outside of marriage. Members of her family say that Batterham would gladly have married her, but not in the church, while for Day a civil union would have had no different status than the common-law arrangement they already had.[21] There was also the issue of her marriage to Tobey, which would have needed to be annulled.

Day had little interest in marrying when she and Batterham began to live together, nor after she became pregnant, because it did not occur to her to dissemble in the service of a propriety she did not respect. ("Who says I'm not honest?" asks Day in the film, which this time gets it right.) Surely then she understood Batterham's unwillingness to dissemble in the service of a faith he did not share. One wouldn't guess from the film that after their common-law partnership ended, Batterham and Day remained close until her death; at her funeral mass, Cardinal Terence Cooke shook his hand.

Viewers who object that the movie gets bogged down in Day's preconversion years will find no pulse-quickening change of tempo when the scene shifts to Depression era New York City and the origins of the *Catholic Worker*. Even as *Entertaining Angels* makes the winsome Sister Aloysius the unlikely champion of Day's intelligence, it strangely mutes the intellectual synthesis of Day and Peter Maurin, who arrives at Day's doorstep after she prays for guidance in bringing her newly embraced Catholicism to bear on the problems of the day. Day described Maurin (whom there has been no comparable move to canonize) as "a genius, a saint, an agitator, a writer, a lecturer, a poor man, and a shabby tramp, all in one."[22] Here the tramp is very much in evidence, and something of the agitator, but whatever mix of faith, discernment, talent, and fortitude allowed Day and Maurin to persevere in their revolutionary undertaking is lost in the film. The two of them started the *Catholic Worker* quite literally to change the world, and to do so by holding Catholicism to its own teachings on justice and the dignity of all. Houses of Hospitality came later, as those who worked on the paper endeavored to live as they wrote. In the film's version of events, the first House of Hospitality comes into being when Day allows Maurin to stay at the apartment she shares with her brother and his family, and Maurin, genial tramp, starts bringing his Bowery chums along. The newspaper comes along after the fact, a way of making ends meet and expanding the operations of the flophouse/soup kitchen Day's home has become.

From this point on in the film nothing much happens, beyond the trials that might beset any shelter for the poor—troublesome residents, a shortage of funds—so the makers of *Entertaining Angels* manufacture a few crises to move the action along. In the first, the unnamed Cardinal of New York (Brian Keith) visits Day to voice suspicions of her communist leanings; Day deflects the Cardinal's request that she dissociate the paper from the Catholic church with the improbable (and insufferable) "I thought we were *being* church." A second crisis erupts when the *Catholic Worker* staff members move to shut down the House of Hospitality and devote themselves to the more important work of putting out the newspaper. (The episode is fictional—Catholic Workers attest that hospitality has been the one value the movement never debated—but Day's principled dissent seals the relative unimportance of journalism to the film's version of her post-conversion life.)

After running into a church to yell existential questions at a statue of Jesus, Day returns to the scene of the attempted coup to confront a final crisis, the now-depraved Maggie attempting to steal from the house's common fund and soon threatening Day with a wooden cane. Nothing like a catfight to spice up a hagiography: Day wrestles Maggie to the ground and manages to seize the weapon, Maggie begs Day to kill her ("I'm a drunk! I'm a slut!"), but just as the saint-in-the-making seems ready to vanquish her bad-girl doppelgänger once and for all, compassion miraculously stays her hand. The erring Maggie's gentleness returns, and the mutinous Catholic Workers are hushed and appeased, reconfirmed in their admiration of the hardheaded but large-hearted Day. It is, after all, in ministering to the wretched likes of Maggie that Day, in words one fully expects to hear spoken before the credits roll, has "found herself." The film ends in a flash-forward to the 1963 prison scene we saw at the beginning, with Day singing once more of the salvation the film has ostensibly dramatized: "Amazing grace, how sweet the sound, that saved a wretch like *me*." Prostitutes, addicts, and the homeless may reap the benefits of Dorothy Day's conversion, but they're the window dressing. Whatever social-justice Catholics like Father Kieser and Martin Sheen may have brought to the film, *Entertaining Angels* ends up as the story of a penitent sinner's redemption from worldliness, a fitting symbol for the faith-and-morals emphasis of the post–Vatican II hierarchy.

Matters of Faith and Morals

The Wesleyan hymn that opens and closes the film is presumably meant also to underscore the ecumenical (not merely Catholic) appeal of its protagonist. "We *are* Catholic," Day insists when she feistily stands up to the Cardinal, who asks that she remove the word "Catholic" from her newspaper's name, but viewers may come away wondering precisely where Catholicism fits into this story. Day rarely appears inside a church and never at mass; the word "Catholic" is never heard in the film's trailer. Interviews with the principals suggest a deliberate omission. Moira Kelly told the *St. Anthony Messenger* that the role of Dorothy Day is "definitely spiritual—and it is a Catholic film—but the message is universal." Kieser described Day not merely as Catholic but as "quintessentially American," a woman who struggled heroically with "the live-nerve issues of contemporary American society: feminism and women's rights, sexuality and commitment, abortion, single motherhood." Moira Kelly makes the point more plainly: "We see Dorothy as human. We see her reach the lowest of lows. We see her make the mistakes that anyone can make—whether he or she be Catholic, Jewish, Buddhist, you name it. We are all human and capable of choosing the wrong path." As Kelly glossed her role, Day's early "mistakes" were key to her journey insofar as Day discovers on turning to God that "she does not need to rely on the relationship of a man to make her feel whole." Kelly's own Catholic faith, she reported, helped her to guard against the "temptations" she encountered in the movie business; the role of Dorothy Day afforded Kelly a source of "inner strength that I can tune in to when I really need that extra help."[23]

The uncomfortable conclusion is that Dorothy Day's story is Everywoman's story insofar as the burden of sexual temptation falls on women—all women. While this message is at least as old as Christianity—"Do you not know," the second-century bishop Tertullian reminded a group of women converts, "that you are each an Eve?"—it tallies particularly well with the binding-on-all quality of Catholic teachings on sexual morality. It is this binding-on-all quality, moreover, that has enabled sexual morality to trump the Catholic social teachings to which Day sought to return the church. In her view, Catholics had come mistakenly to emphasize private morality over social justice. Her commitment to calling her fellow Catholics on these misplaced priorities, and not some vapid notion of "being church," lay behind Day's insistence on the "Catholic" in the *Catholic Worker*. "Many times we have been asked why we spoke of *Catholic* workers," she wrote:

> and so named the paper. Of course it was not only because we who were in charge of the work, who edited the paper, were all Catholics, but also because we wished to influence Catholics. They were our own, and we reacted sharply to the accusation that when it came to private morality the Catholics shone, but when it came to social and political morality they were often conscienceless.[24]

In her objection to the prospect of being made a saint surely Day had some notion of what it would mean to have her life's work "dismissed," as she put it, on the way to canonization. Like the pulp novel she regretted having written, the emerging narrative of St. Dorothy would mark her as a woman with an unseemly sexual past, now gloriously redeemed. And this, indeed, is the irresistible plot line that Cardinal O'Connor's successor, Cardinal Archbishop Edward Egan, took up in his 2005 announcement that a Dorothy Day Guild was being formed in order to finance the canonization campaign. "Before she made her way to the Lord and His Church," Egan reflected:

[Day] pursued a, let us say, "Bohemian" lifestyle, full of excesses of all kinds. She lived with men in common law arrangements. She had a child in her womb killed by an abortionist. She consorted with communists and anarchists. She was jailed for controversial demonstrations on behalf of workers, women's suffrage, and the rights of the imprisoned. She preached a pacifism that knew no limit, and she wrote at least one book which in her later years she regretted so much that she declared she would do anything if she could have every copy of it destroyed. In brief, she was anything but saintly in her early years.

Sexual agency, pacifism, support for labor, feminism, a commitment to side with the poor and despised, the arc of a literary life: how vast the repertoire of sin, how dazzling the scale of redemption. "Once she discovered the Lord and His Church in 1918," Egan continued:

Dorothy Day was "re-born." ... She went to Mass and Communion every day. She confessed her sins to a priest every week. She meditated on the Scriptures whenever she had a free moment. She prayed the Rosary with never-failing delight. And all the while, she handed herself over totally to the humble and courageous service of the poorest of the poor by fighting for their causes in her newspaper.

Once more, we see the familiar hierarchy of emphasis: morals (sex and gender ideology) first, faith (Catholic observance) second, social justice a distant third. If her commitment to this last made Day a tad outspoken, Egan conceded, if she "told Church leaders in no uncertain terms when she thought they were mistaken in matters of social policy," he made a point of insisting that she nevertheless "stood foursquare with them in matters of faith and morals." Egan ended with a plea for donations to the Dorothy Day Guild from all who share his conviction that Day is indeed a saint, one to be invoked alongside "the saint who anointed the feet of the Savior with perfume and wiped them with her hair."[25]

The movie version of Day's *The Eleventh Virgin* was never made, perhaps because the novel lacked the Hollywood ending that might have given the film a place among Jazz Age melodramas like *The Worldly Madonna* (1922). As Judith Weisenfeld notes in chapter 2 in this volume, *The Worldly Madonna* tells the story of twin sisters who follow opposite paths, one into the convent and the other into drugs and cabaret life; in a no-surprise ending, the would-be nun abandons the novitiate and her worldly twin takes the veil. On the strength of her screenplay for *The Eleventh Virgin* Day was offered a stint in a Hollywood studio, where her job was to help producers to churn out such fare. "Occasionally a group of us," she recalled:

were summoned into a most comfortable lounging room, where we sat in chairs with ash trays at our sides and viewed some stupid production (I can remember none of them now) and were invited to give our views on it. I remember one most inane office conference where we were supposed to discuss the plot of some such typical story as *The Grand Duchess and the Waiter* [1926], and of course the waiter turns out to be a grand duke or prince. There was no thought. There was no discussion of ideas or attempt to portray ideas.[26]

Surely there would have been no more ruthless critic of *Entertaining Angels* than Dorothy Day herself. Had she previewed the film in such a studio setting she would have seen a Hollywood version of *The Eleventh Virgin*, with a saintly "after" tacked onto the steamy before. In this way *Entertaining Angels* brings the hackneyed familiarity of an old-time matinee to a life that stubbornly refused to be scripted. In doing so, it lends all the power and glitz of the movies to the conservative framing of Day's canonization by Cardinals O'Connor and Egan. Against the complexity and enduring provocation of Day's own life and writings, the church-sanctioned narrative offers simplicity, even closure, the B-movie happy ending. The story goes something like this: Dorothy Day had a wild streak. This brought her low, even under the abortionist's knife. Yet she repented, humbled herself, and did many good works in the end. *Entertaining Angels* offers a TV-ready version of this Dorothy Day, the penitent whore. The story of Dorothy Day the revolutionary will not, one suspects, be televised.

NOTES

1. Hal Conklin and Denny Wayman, "*Entertaining Angels*: Four Stars (Inspirational)," *Cinema in Focus: A Social and Spiritual Commentary*, available at www.cinemainfocus .com/Entertaining%20Angels_4.htm.

2. Dorothy Day, "To Our Readers," *Catholic Worker*, May 1933, 4. All texts from the *Catholic Worker* are available from the Dorothy Day Library on the Web at http:// www.catholicworker.org/dorothyday.

3. The text of *Lumen Gentium* may be found at http://www.vatican.va/archive/hist_ councils/ii_vatican_council/documents/vat-ii_const_19641121_lumen-gentium_ en.html.

4. Gene Burns, *The Frontiers of Catholicism: The Politics of Ideology in a Liberal World* (Berkeley: University of California Press, 1992), 201–2. My thanks to Marian Ronan for introducing me to this discussion and for framing it in a way I draw on here.

5. Cardinal John O'Connor, "Dorothy Day's Sainthood Cause Begins," 16 March 2000, available at http://www.catholicworker.org/dorothyday/canonizationtext. cfm?Number=82.

6. Ibid.

7. Father Ellwood Kieser quoted by Jack Wintz, "The Dorothy Day Story: Father Kieser's New Film," *St. Anthony Messenger*, September 1996, available at www .americancatholic.org/Messenger/Sep1996/feature1.asp. Kieser's own view on abortion is a familiar one; it grants women near-total autonomy until the possibility of conception arises and none thereafter. Characterizing as "nonsense" the claim that women have the right to "control their own bodies and terminate a pregnancy if they choose," Kieser insisted, "Except for rape, if a woman is pregnant, it's because she chose to do those things that got her pregnant." Ellwood E. Kieser, *Hollywood Priest: A Spiritual Struggle* (Garden City, NY: Doubleday, 1991), 130.

8. Kieser quoted in Wintz, "The Dorothy Day Story."

9. I owe much of this description of *Insight* to the appreciative Kieser obituary at Suck.com (www.suck.mirror.theinfo.org/daily/2000/10/05/1.html); Kieser also discusses *Insight* at length in *Hollywood Priest*.

10. Joseph Cunneen, "*Entertaining Angels*: Movie Review," *National Catholic Reporter*, 27 September 1996; Stephen Holden, "A Crusader for the Faith, Both Saintly and Sexy," *New York Times*, 27 September 1996; Kieser quoted in Wintz, "The Dorothy Day Story."

11. Kieser, *Hollywood Priest*, 237.

12. Kieser quoted in Wintz, "The Dorothy Day Story"; "Commentary by Moira Kelly," *Entertaining Angels* (DVD, Vision Video, 1997).

13. Dorothy Day, *The Long Loneliness* (New York: Harper and Brothers, 1952), 71.

14. Conklin and Wayman, "*Entertaining Angels*"; Dorothy Day, "Day after Day," *Catholic Worker*, February 1943, 1, 4.

15. Jim Forest, "The Living Legacy of Dorothy Day," reprinted by Claretian Publications, available at http://claretianpubs.org/issues/Dorothyday/legacy.html. The Claretians, an order of priests with a strong progressive record, were among the first to call for Day's canonization in 1983. Forest was a close associate of Day and, with her, a signatory to the Catholic Peace Fellowship Statement on Abortion, discussed below. Dean Peerman, "*Entertaining Angels: The Dorothy Day Story*," *Christian Century*, 26 February 1997.

16. Day, *The Long Loneliness*, 108.

17. Dorothy Day, *The Eleventh Virgin* (New York: Boni, 1924). Day's desire to burn every copy of *The Eleventh Virgin* is attested to by nearly all of her biographers. She nearly succeeded: just twelve copies of the book are to be found in libraries worldwide, according to www.worldcat.org. Paul Elie, *The Life You Save May Be Your Own: An American Pilgrimage* (New York: Farrar, Straus and Giroux, 2004), 39.

18. The Catholic Peace Fellowship Statement on Abortion, 28 June 1974, signed by Dorothy Day, Eileen Egan, Hermene Evans, Joseph Evans, M.D., Thomas C. Cornell, James H. Forest, and Gordon C. Zahn, is available at www.cjd.org/paper/cathpeac.html. For a forceful rearticulation of this position, see the 2006 statement of Sister Helen Prejean, http://dpdiscourse.typepad.com/sisterhelen.

19. Day, *The Long Loneliness*, 143.

20. Dorothy Day, *From Union Square to Rome* (1938; reprint, New York: Arno, 1978), 10; Day, *The Long Loneliness*, 137.

21. Day, *The Long Loneliness*, 137, 148. On Day's relationship with Batterham, see Kellyann Day, "Dorothy Day," 2002, Papers of the Nancy A. Humphreys Institute for Political Social Work, University of Connecticut School of Social Work, available at http://politicalinstitute.uconn.edu/papers/Day.pdf.

22. Dorothy Day, "Background for Peter Maurin," *Catholic Worker*, October 1944, 3, 6.

23. Moira Kelly quoted by Wintz, "The Dorothy Day Story."

24. Tertullian, *On the Apparel of Women*, available at http://www.earlychristianwritings.com/text/tertullian27.html; Day, *The Long Loneliness*, 210.

25. Cardinal Edward Egan, "Saint Dorothy?" *Newsletter of the Archdiocese of New York*, 7 July 2005, available at http://www.archny.org/news-events/columns-and-blogs/cardinals-monthly-column/index.cfm?i=1698.

26. Day, *The Long Loneliness*, 157.

FURTHER READING

Burns, Gene. *The Frontiers of Catholicism: The Politics of Ideology in a Liberal World*. Berkeley: University of California Press, 1992.

Byrnes, Timothy A., and Mary C. Segers, eds. *The Catholic Church and the Politics of Abortion: A View from the States*. Boulder, CO: Westview, 1992.

Carmody, Denise Lardner. *The Double Cross: Ordination, Abortion, and Catholic Feminism*. New York: Crossroad, 1986.

Coles, Robert. *Dorothy Day: A Radical Devotion*. Reading, MA: Addison-Wesley, 1987.

Curran, Charles E. American. *Catholic Social Ethics: Twentieth-Century Approaches*. Notre Dame, IN: University of Notre Dame Press, 1982.

Day, Dorothy. *From Union Square to Rome*. Silver Spring, MD: Preservation of the Faith Press, 1938.

———. *Loaves and Fishes*. San Francisco, CA: Harper and Row, 1963.

———. *The Long Loneliness*. New York: Harper, 1952.

Elie, Paul. *The Life You Save May Be Your Own: An American Pilgrimage*. New York: Farrar, Straus and Giroux, 2004.

Fisher, James Terence. *The Catholic Counterculture in America, 1933–1962*. Chapel Hill: University of North Carolina Press, 1989.

Kaplan, E. Ann. *Feminism and Film*. New York: Oxford University Press, 2000.

Kieser, Ellwood E. *Hollywood Priest: A Spiritual Struggle*. Garden City, NY: Doubleday, 1991.

Miller, William D. *Dorothy Day: A Biography*. San Francisco, CA: Harper and Row, 1982.

Piehl, Mel. *Breaking Bread: The Catholic Worker and the Origin of Catholic Radicalism in America*. Philadelphia: Temple University Press, 1982.

Riegle, Rosalie G. *Dorothy Day: Portraits by Those Who Knew Her*. Maryknoll, NY: Orbis, 2003.

Roberts, Nancy L. *Dorothy Day and the Catholic Worker*. Albany: State University of New York Press, 1984.

Zwick, Mark, and Louise Zwick. *The Catholic Worker Movement: Intellectual and Spiritual Origins*. New York: Paulist, 2005.

12

BORDER SAINTS

Santitos (1999)

Darryl V. Caterine

In the year 2000, consumers of mainstream American cinema received their *first* exposure to a movie about Mexican Catholic devotionalism. Directed by Alejandro Springall, the 1999 Mexican *film Santitos* depicts a young widow named Esperanza Díaz (Dolores Heredia) who undertakes an outrageous journey through the brothels of Veracruz, Tijuana, and Los Angeles in search of her late daughter Blanca (Maya Zapata) who died mysteriously during a tonsillectomy. Esperanza has received a series of visions from St. Jude, whose plaster statue regularly appears in her home oven with the news that Blanca still lives. Puzzling over the mystery with Padre Salvador, the local priest (Fernando Torre Laphame), she deduces that Blanca has been kidnapped into prostitution and sets off to find her, becoming a prostitute herself in the process. In search of a pink house mentioned during one of the apparitions, Esperanza is eventually led over the international border to a particular brothel in Los Angeles.

During her sojourn in the city, Esperanza meets and falls in love with the Angel of Justice (Alberto Estrella), a Mexican-born professional wrestler whom she had mistaken for a supernatural being in an earlier vision. Beginning to doubt her interpretations of St. Jude's apparitions and disgusted by her life in the brothels, she decides to return home after an unexpected encounter and conversation with the Virgin of Guadalupe at a public shrine. In the final scenes of the movie, the Angel of Justice tracks her down in Veracruz and swears his love to her. Esperanza receives a vision of Blanca by her bathroom mirror, and at last accepts the fact that her daughter is dead. Together the two lovers paint Blanca's grave a bright pink and drive off in his pickup truck into a new life with Esperanza's bathroom mirror—still attached to a section of the wall.

Santitos is based on a short story by María Amparo Escandón, who was born in Mexico City and moved to Los Angeles at the age of twenty-four. Escandón narrated her tale as both a novel and a screenplay. The novel was published in Spanish as *Santitos* in 1998 and in English as *Esperanza's Box of Saints* in 1999. Escandón had earlier converted the story into a screenplay at the Sundance Screenwriters Lab in Utah, where she met the film's future director, Alejandro Springall. The differences between the novel and screenplay are slight. In the novel, the local Catholic priest is attracted to Esperanza and vents his sexual frustrations in prayers to God. In the movie, he plays a more paternal role. Blanca appears to Esperanza in the novel through a rust stain underneath the bathroom sink, while in the film she appears next to the bathroom mirror. Finally, the novel does not identify Blanca's grave as the pink house. At the end of the story, Esperanza realizes that Blanca has become a saint, and the painting of her grave site is left to the Angel of Justice. Despite these differences, however, both novel and screenplay tell the same tale of a woman healing from her grief by undertaking a pilgrimage through Mexican and American brothels, guided by the saints and the Virgin of Guadalupe.

In 1999 *Santitos* was released as a movie in Mexican theaters, and it premiered during the same year at the Sundance Film Festival, the largest independent cinema festival in the United States. In the year 2000, it was released in mainstream American theaters by Latin Universe, an independent distributor. Historically, independent producers and distributors have filled marketing niches passed over by major media studios, which cater predominantly to white, middle-class audiences. Latin Universe was founded in order to create a new market of Latino filmgoers by providing Spanish-language films to multiplex theaters.[1] *Santitos* was the first film released by the company, which had already created a stir in Hollywood by outbidding Twentieth Century Fox for the distribution rights to the Mexican blockbuster *Sex, Shame, and Tears* (1999). Unfortunately, Latin Universe debuted *Santitos* simultaneously in 155 theaters in nine states after only one week of advertising rather than releasing it gradually to create a word-of-mouth buzz. It opened during Super Bowl weekend when movie attendance was low. Further, the company had shunned English-language advertising venues, bypassing native-born Americans as well as the many Latinos who do not speak Spanish.

Santitos thus failed to attract viewers' attention at the movie theaters. A frustrated Springall bought back the distribution rights, and the enthusiastic plans of Latin Universe ground to a halt after its one and only theater release to date.

While *Santitos* received fourteen awards at international film festivals, it has remained a sleeper in American cinema. Its relative obscurity can be attributed only in part to the mishandling of its initial marketing. As a movie about Mexican Catholic devotion, *Santitos* has faced deeper, conceptual challenges to its popular reception in the United States. The story is a product of the Mexican-American borderlands, a geocultural region spanning the political divide between the two nations. It is a social tale about Chicanos/Mexicans living betwixt and between Mexico and the United States, and also a religious tale for those Catholics who turn to their tradition as an aid for enduring personal and social experiences of suffering. Many American viewers have ignored or misunderstood the political and religious messages of the film.

Magical Realism

Latin American and Spanish reviews of *Santitos* drew attention to both its artistic style and its religious content. Stylistically, *Santitos* stands in the tradition of magical realism, a genre of literature and film that playfully blurs the borders between conventional cultural categories. Magical realism has a long history in Latin American arts and literature. In 1949 the Cuban novelist and musicologist Alejo Carpentier used the term *lo real maravilloso americano*—American magical realism—to describe the blurring of social borders in the Spanish New World as Europeans, Africans, and Native Americans came together to create a mestizo or hybrid culture. Expressions of this Latin American *mestizaje* can be found in the interracial marriage patterns of its peoples. It can also be found in various cultural expressions, like Afro Caribbean music or religions like Mexican *curanderismo* (a folk healing tradition) that combine indigenous and European elements. Famous Latin American writers like Jorge Luis Borges from Argentina and Gabriel García Márquez from Colombia have similarly mixed the realism of modern European literature with dream realities—reminiscent of indigenous and African world views—in their novels. *Santitos* extends the genre of magical realism into its exploration of Catholic devotionalism by blurring the boundaries between sensory experience and the religious imagination.

Viewers outside the United States also recognized Springall's movie as a Catholic allegory. Esperanza's name, which means "hope" in Spanish, was readily

12.1. In keeping with the sensibilities of Latin American magical realism, St. Jude's miraculous appearance in Esperanza's (Dolores Heredia) oven blurs the boundaries between the everyday and supernatural worlds.

understood as signaling an allegory of religious faith. It is especially significant that her primary devotion is to St. Jude, the Roman Catholic church's patron saint of desperate or lost causes. Jude or Judas—not to be confused with Judas Iscariot, who betrayed Jesus—is identified in the Gospels as one of the original twelve apostles. As the brother of James the Just, he has been identified by tradition as Jesus' half brother or his cousin. Tradition has it that Jude was martyred in the first century, and his relics were transferred to Italy and France. The saint's association with desperate causes stems in part from his alleged authorship of the New Testament's Letter of Jude, which exhorts Christians to persevere in faith through their difficulties. Jude's devotional cult began to grow in popularity during the early nineteenth century in Spain and Italy. From there it quickly spread to South America and then moved north through Mexico and into the United States. In *Santitos*, St. Jude guides Esperanza's, or Hope's, spiritual journey, which is a passage from desperation to renewed faith. By the end of the story, she is united in supernatural love with her deceased daughter Blanca and with her newfound love, the Angel of Justice.

Within the United States, *Santitos* was reviewed almost exclusively for its stylistic dimension, and its religious content was sidestepped altogether. Critics readily identified *Santitos* with *Like Water for Chocolate* (1992), a Mexican film about the erotic and spiritual powers of food, which had introduced the term "magical realism" into American pop-culture vernacular. For the *Los Angeles Times*'s reviewer,

Santitos had "the same kind of humor, charm, and sensuality that made *Like Water for Chocolate* the most popular foreign-language film until *Life Is Beautiful* [1997] came along." *The Village Voice* summarized: "Aspiring toward magic[al] realism, Alejandro Springall's first feature is in essence a formulaic heal-thyself inspirational, a feel better fantasy that, for all its gaudy Catholic flourishes, seems touched mainly by the hand of Oprah." The Web site *Spirituality & Practice* declared, "Alejandro Springall directs this phantasmagorical Mexican drama that brings to mind the magic, the lyricism, and the comedy of *Like Water for Chocolate*. Only here the focus is not food but the strange ways God speaks to us and surprises us with grace-filled moments of mystery."[2]

The connotation of magical realism in these reviews differed significantly from its meaning in a Latin American context. As we have seen, Alejo Carpentier used the term to describe the fluidity of biological, cultural, and religious boundaries in the Spanish New World. In contrast, for U.S. critics, the Catholic devotionalism of *Santitos* was equated with "fantasy" and "the phantasmagorical"—as opposed to and separate from commonsense notions of reality. Consequently, Esperanza's interactions with the saints or the Virgin of Guadalupe were not taken seriously as the subject matter for these reviewers. In the words of the *Village Voice*, they were "gaudy flourishes" to a movie about a woman's healing. Or at best they were charming, as the reviewer for the *Los Angeles Times* expressed. These sharp distinctions between the unreal world of practicing Catholics and the real world of commonsense experience distorted the true meaning of magical realism, which revels in the ambiguity of borders. The reviews also deflected attention away from the religious dimension of *Santitos*—a film whose title means "dear beloved saints"—by subsuming the content of the film into a vague discussion about its style.

Considered alongside mainstream American films about Latin American Catholicism, these reviews become more intelligible. The dominant secular orientation of U.S. culture imposes strict limits on how seriously visionary experiences and miracles can be taken. In American-made films, the possibility of miraculous intervention is commonly portrayed as paranormal or delusional. *Household Saints* (1993) begins with a realistic portrayal of girlhood piety but then ends in fantasy. In *Stigmata* (1999), Catholic devotions are associated with forces of terror, which even scientifically trained doctors are powerless to thwart. In this film a young white woman succumbs to possession after her mother mails her a spiritually contaminated rosary from Brazil. In *The Maldonado Miracle* (2003), Catholic devotion is lampooned. In this made-for-TV movie a Mexican immigrant mistakes ordinary human blood for Christ's bleeding wounds on a statue, bringing new economic and cultural vitality to a remote border town in the form of misguided Catholic pilgrims. *Santitos*, in contrast, defies conventional secular categories. Here, devotionalism is neither paranormal nor the product of ignorance.

Santitos thus raised daunting interpretive questions for U.S. critics. Was it a film about religion or a film about fantasy? Did Springall want his viewers to believe in the saints, or was the movie a Catholic spoof? The *Seattle Post-Intelligencer* went so far as to conclude that Springall's "cheerfully absurd" film "stays just this side of lampooning the veneration of saints and heeding the call of questionable visions."[3] When *Like Water for Chocolate* first ran in American theaters, viewers had no problem suspending their commonsense notions of food to enter into a world of culinary and alimentary magic. Faced with apparitions of saints in *Santitos*, however, they were befuddled. As we saw in the discussion of *The Exorcist* earlier in this volume, film critics have a difficult time accepting the miraculous aspects of Catholicism as authentically religious. The sophisticated exploration of Mexican Catholic devotionalism in *Santitos* was thus rendered invisible to non-Latino moviegoers.

Another obstacle to understanding Catholic devotionalism on its own terms can be found in the often-unacknowledged Protestant orientation of U.S. culture. This orientation persists unchanged even amid the growing denominational diversity within the country. Protestants do cross the boundaries between the extraordinary and the ordinary, heaven and earth, divine and human, but with great caution. *Santitos*, in contrast, is replete with crossings-over between the ordinary and extraordinary worlds, which are never presented as strange. Esperanza takes the apparition of Jude standing behind her grimy oven door as a matter of course, worrying only that future applications of Easy-Off oven cleaner will obstruct further visitations by her saint. The appearance of Blanca's ghost by her bathroom mirror is also taken in stride, creating cognitive dissonance for many U.S. viewers. Such crossings-over are closely connected to the history of American occultism where the weird, the primitive, and the uncanny are conjured up without recourse to traditional Christian notions of the supernatural.

The gap between traditional Protestantism and Catholicism has historically contributed to the tensions and misunderstandings between Anglo Americans and Chicanos/Mexicans. While Mexican culture admits to a wide variety of religious communities, beliefs, and practices—including Pentecostalism, *espiritualismo*, and *curanderismo*—its dominant tradition remains Catholicism. As we have seen throughout *Catholics in the Movies*, Catholics have been frequently singled out for ridicule and denigration in the United States. Despite the modernizations effected in Mexico and elsewhere by Vatican II, many Catholics continue devotions promulgated by the Council of Trent or ones that even pre-date the Counter-

Reformation. This devotionalism centers on the Virgin Mary and the saints. It shaped the contours of Spanish Catholicism and was introduced in the sixteenth century by conquistadors and missionaries to the indigenous peoples of Mexico. In Mexican Catholicism the extraordinary (the more-than-human powers to which people orient themselves) is varied. These extraordinary powers include many saints as well as more centrally the Virgin of Guadalupe, the national patron of Mexico, whose identity is ambiguously Catholic and indigenous. In this world view, artistic and ritual expressions of the supernatural world are themselves conduits for grace. Statues and images of the Virgin and the saints pervade the physical landscape of Mexico and the U.S.–Mexican borderlands, not only in churches and chapels, but also on home altars, on public murals, and in handmade portraits of saints and their miracles.

Fear and contempt of Catholicism in the United States remained an integral part of the predominantly Protestant nation throughout the nineteenth century, continuing an anti-Catholicism that dated back to the Puritan foundations of American culture. Sixteenth-century Protestant Reformers saw Catholicism as "paganopapism"—a hybrid of demonic religious customs and a soul-crushing religious hierarchy. The Reformers castigated Catholic devotionalism to Mary and the saints both as unbiblical and as idolatrous. They painted the institutional church as an unnecessary obstacle to the individual believer's relationship with God. Many Protestants feared that Catholics did not support the separation of church and state as laid out in the U.S. Constitution. To the older theological arguments of the Protestant Reformers were added new political fears that Catholic citizens would not be loyal to the democratic principles or the sovereignty of the United States. For their part, descendants of European Catholic immigrants strove to disprove these negative assumptions by accommodating their religion to liberalized Protestant creeds and practices, a process that accelerated in the immediate wake of Vatican II.

This fear of Catholicism not only fueled discrimination against European immigrants; it also stimulated distrust of the vanquished Mexicans who resided in the United States after the Mexican War. In 1848, after fighting a series of competing claims over Texas, the United States and Mexico signed the Treaty of Guadalupe Hidalgo, which ceded a large portion of the Southwest to the United States. Mexicans who were living in what are now the states of Texas, California, New Mexico, Nevada, and Utah found themselves as residents of the United States, without moving an inch. This increase of mostly Spanish-speaking Catholics in what was understood to be a Protestant America caused considerable concern and stimulated anti-Catholicism in the nation. Would the West embrace the spirit of democracy and freedom of the Yankee East, or would it maintain the "superstitions" of Mexican Catholicism? Politicians and businessmen urged native-born Protestant Americans to move west to secure this newly occupied land.

Mexico itself eventually underwent significant political and social changes that altered how average Mexicans understood Catholicism. In 1910 Mexico became embroiled in a revolution that lasted for almost ten years. The revolutionaries condemned the influence that priests and the Catholic hierarchy played in the secular sphere. When a new constitution was signed in 1917, it severely limited the role of the Catholic church in the political life of the nation. Education came under the control of the state and not the Catholic church. Worship had to stay within churches and not spill onto the streets. Property ownership by religious groups was strictly limited. Most important, no clergyman could comment publicly on political affairs or even vote. One of the results of these restrictions was that Mexican Catholicism turned inward and developed a more involved devotional focus. If religion was prohibited from influencing the public life of Mexico, then it would influence the private, spiritual lives of Mexicans.

Throughout the twentieth century, Mexicans moved back and forth across their country's northern borders. This movement increased in 1965 after the United States changed its immigration laws. With immigration from Mexico and other Latin American countries on the rise, U.S. Catholicism increasingly became two churches in one. On the one hand, the Euro American church since the Second Vatican Council has striven to embrace the varieties of Catholicism celebrated throughout the world as expressions of the "inculturated gospel." One of the changes of the council was to permit the partial adaptation of Catholic myth and ritual to fit the beliefs, practices, and values of local cultures and non-Christian religions. The term was again popularized in 1990 by Pope John Paul II in his encyclical *Redemptoris mission* (Mission of the Redeemer) as one way to renew missionary activities by being open to local customs. The inculturated gospel permits such things as guitars being used during mass or a priest's blessing of a girl's initiation rite, called a *quinceañera*.

On the other hand, Catholic leaders have continued since Vatican II to guide the church on a course toward modernization. The council stressed that Catholic Christianity was firmly rooted in the Bible and that popular devotions to Mary and the saints should never overshadow the centrality of the message of Jesus. Local traditions and customs should support rather than contrast with the saving message of Christ. How to interpret and regulate the cult of the saints—especially when the cult involves miraculous healing—has become a continual problem for the clergy. The U.S. church wants to accommodate Catholic sensibilities different from its own, but it certainly does not want to resuscitate pre–Vatican II stereotypes of Catholicism as a religious community at variance with dominant Anglo Protestant values or biblical sentiments.

Borderlands

Compounding the confusion for American-born viewers of *Santitos* are the manifold crossings-over of "ordinary" or cultural boundaries, including Esperanza's forays into brothels and her illegal crossing of the U.S.–Mexico border. *Santitos* came to the United States in 1999 as tensions smoldered along the U.S.–Mexico border. Five years earlier, the United States, Canada, and Mexico had passed the North American Free Trade Agreement (NAFTA), a liberalization of economic regulations aimed at facilitating international investment and trade. However, the plan had conspicuously omitted any changes to restrictions on the international movement of labor, raising fears in the southwestern United States of an increase in illegal Mexican immigration. In 1994, soon after NAFTA had been enacted into law, Californians launched a popular political movement known as the Save Our State initiative, whose primary purpose was to keep undocumented immigrants on the other side of the border. The campaign culminated in the passage of Proposition 187, a law that denied basic human services to illegal workers and their children. Anxieties about the international border, discrimination against Mexican laborers, and related tensions between Euro Americans and Chicanos were hardly new developments in southwestern history. Since the U.S. annexation of northern Mexico in 1848, both Mexicans and Chicanos had endured cultural and socioeconomic hardships stemming from American racism and xenophobia. NAFTA and its aftermath were simply the latest chapter in this troubled history.

Esperanza's search for Blanca follows a circular course from Veracruz to Los Angeles and back again, marking out the transnational space of the U.S.–Mexican borderlands. Relative to both nation-states, this space is a no-man's land, a world of outlaws and social outcasts where all roads lead to Tijuana. In her search for the Pink House, a brothel rumored to keep teenage girls, Esperanza travels first to the northern Mexican border town and from there to Los Angeles. This in-between, liminal space is populated by the monstrous and the unpredictable. On her bus ride from Veracruz, she sits beside a homeless teenage prostitute, who steals her money, and across from an adult midget, who suckles at a woman's breast. Before Esperanza has even left the Tijuana bus station, a thief has stolen one of her bags, and by the time she leaves for Los Angeles, she has worked as a prostitute in a

brothel called the Quagmire run by a man named Cacomixtle ("Weasel," played by
Demián Bichir) and in another whorehouse run by a flamboyantly gay man and a
transvestite in love with a cow. Mexicans are not the only outcasts in this wilderness. Tijuana is also the destination for U.S. citizens transgressing the law, like
Scott Haines (Roger Cudney), a prominent San Diego judge who becomes
Esperanza's exclusive john. It is he who smuggles Esperanza across the border in
the trunk of his car. He then directs her to an androgynous travel agent in Los
Angeles for daytime employment. Once in Los Angeles, Esperanza continues to
search for Blanca, working in a brothel where voyeurs peek at women through a
kaleidoscopic "sex-o-scope."

The myths and rituals of Catholicism, however, transform the borderlands
from a space of danger to a place of safety. Throughout her perilous journey,
Esperanza travels with a full set of devotional paraphernalia, including holy cards
and small plaster statues. In all of the brothels Esperanza sets up her elaborate
altarcito (home altar), and in one she performs a *limpia*, a spiritual cleansing ritual in
curanderismo. She prays to the appropriate saints in times of danger and need:
Michael and Raphael for protection in her travels, Juan Soldado for safe passage
across the border, and Anthony for help in locating Blanca. Esperanza even wields
the saints as weapons, using St. Jude's plaster statue to whack two pimps when she
finally breaks free from the Los Angeles brothel before leaving for Veracruz.

Esperanza's devotions deal with universal problems of meaning, such as suffering,
injustice, and death, by placing the human condition within a more-than-human
cosmology. In Catholic theology, problems of meaning are subsumed under the
theological category of sin and solved by Christ's crucifixion and resurrection. For
Christians, God incarnated in the material world where he identified with human
suffering and underwent a sacrifice. Christ's death overcomes the divide between
the human and divine worlds, bringing blessings to earth and eventual eternal life to
the dead. The martyrdom and self-sacrifice of Jesus is replicated in the lives of the
Catholic holy men and women, who after their deaths become saints mediating
between heaven and earth. The Virgin Mary, as the most holy of all Christ's followers, is an exemplar of endurance in suffering. She witnessed on a profound and
intimate level the torture and death of her son. As the mother of God, she is an
influential mediator between the divine and human realms and a model of Christian
piety. Catholic gestures and rituals call up these stories, thus providing ways that the
suffering might seek divine grace when human help is not forthcoming.

Further, Catholic devotionalism as portrayed in *Santitos* redresses the experiences of pain, loss, and injustice suffered by the Mexican people as a whole.
Esperanza must come to terms not only with the death of her daughter but also

with the suffering of her compatriots whose hardships are enmeshed in the economic, cultural, and political realities of the borderlands. Mexicans are uprooted and drawn north by the push-and-pull economics of transnational capitalism. At the same time, citizens of the United States look south for their cheap labor, drugs, and teenage hookers. *Santitos* exposes how the American hemispheres are joined in a symbiotic relationship of exploitation and vice. As the search for her daughter unfolds, Esperanza becomes both an illegal immigrant and a participant/victim in the international underworld economy. At the outset of her journey, she pleads with St. Michael the Archangel, "I've always prayed to you for the victims of the drug lords, but now I pray for my own daughter with all my strength." Her personal pilgrimage subsequently leads her into the world of the drug lords, a transnational outlaw space populated by hookers and thieves.

Catholic myths and rituals have also been used in Chicano/Mexican history to subvert the political meaning of borders, reaffirming the humanity of outlaws and illegal migrants. *Santitos* is not simply a film that portrays devotion to the saints. More fundamentally it is a depiction of life in the borderlands through a devotional perspective. Esperanza's identity, both in her own imagination and through the lens of the camera, is constructed in and through her devotion to Saints Jude and Anthony rather than in relation to the nation-states of either Mexico or the United States. Even when she is working in a Mexican brothel or crossing the border without a passport, she is not depicted as wanton or criminal. While the transgressive nature of these acts cannot be erased entirely, they are nevertheless subsumed under Catholicism. Chicano/Mexican religions—both Catholic and non-Catholic—provide their communities with strategic resources to remake the inherited social and political realities that oppress them.

The Catholicism portrayed in *Santitos* is clearly laid out in Esperanza's devotion to Juan Soldado and the Virgin of Guadalupe. As she is smuggled across the border in the trunk of Scott Haines's car, Esperanza tightly clutches a plaster statue of Juan Soldado. "This is your land," she prays. "You have helped so many immigrants. Please hold our hand." In this short scene, Springall memorializes a devotion well known to Mexican Catholics but not recognized by the institutional Catholic church. Juan Soldado ("John the Soldier"), a Mexican variant of GI Joe, was born Juan Castillo Morales in Tijuana in 1913/1914. While serving as a private in the Mexican army, Morales was tried, convicted, and executed for the rape and murder of an eight-year-old girl, Olga Consuela Comacho. Shortly after his death in 1938, local legends began to circulate that he had been falsely accused and that the guilty party was his military superior. A devotional cult spontaneously formed around his grave, with Juan Soldado emerging as one of several "victim intercessors" of the U.S.–Mexican borderlands. Today he is the patron saint—by popular acclaim, not by the Vatican—of undocumented immigrants. With several shrines on both sides of the border, his legend poignantly discloses the subversive power of Mexican Catholicism: the nation-state might unjustly accuse and execute; it might arrest and deport border crossers; however, people can draw on Catholic ideas of the saints to claim power for their own needs. For Mexicans, devotion to Juan Soldado erases the political reality of the international border by the Catholic practice of appealing to a saint for a miracle.

In her veneration of the Virgin of Guadalupe, Esperanza continues a devotion dating back to the origins of Mexican Catholicism itself. The devotion to Guadalupe is also founded on the religious erasure of national spaces. As the Mexican legend recounts, the Virgin made three special appearances to the Indian Catholic convert Juan Diego in 1531, on the hill Tepeyac outside of Mexico City. Prior to the Spanish colonization, Tepeyac had been the center of devotion to Tonantzin, a goddess of the indigenous Mexican pantheon. During her third visitation, Guadalupe is said to have emblazoned her image onto Diego's poncho and caused roses to bloom in the dead of winter. These miracles convinced the local bishop to build a shrine to her at the site and catalyzed widespread devotion to Guadalupe among indigenous and mestizo Mexicans. Originally introduced to the native Nahua peoples of Mexico as a Spanish Catholic devotion, Guadalupe lacked popular appeal in the earliest years of colonialism.

12.2. In Los Angeles a mural painting of the Virgin of Guadalupe, spiritual mother of the Mexican people, reminds Esperanza (Dolores Heredia) of her maternal and domestic responsibilities during her sojourn through the U.S.–Mexican borderlands.

Eventually, devotion to the Virgin of Guadalupe became more popular as she came to combine certain features of both the Catholic Mary and the Mexican goddess. Like the legend of Juan Soldado, the Virgin mediates between two cultures. She is no longer solely the apocalyptic Mary of the Book of Revelation come to Christianize the demonic Indians as the Spanish conquistadors had originally understood her. For Mexicans, Guadalupe was not an import but an indigenous Virgin and the quintessential image of Mexican/Spanish Catholic *mestizaje.* Her presence helped to create Mexico not as an extension of Spain but as a blended New World culture unto itself. Devotion to Guadalupe symbolically worked to wrest Mexico from Spanish Catholic control.

The Virgin of Guadalupe has been appropriated in manifold ways throughout the centuries but always she remains the Mother of the Mexican and Chicano/Mexican people. Her presence, be it at a shrine or through an apparition or even on a tattoo, signifies that a place has been "Mexicanized," oriented toward a sacred center that is at once religious and national. The Virgin was the symbol of an independent Mexico during the Wars of Independence from Spain in the early nineteenth century and the emblem of a modern Mexican nation during the revolution of 1910–1920. In *Santitos* Esperanza's transnational wanderings come to an end when she inadvertently comes across a public shrine/mural to Guadalupe in Los Angeles shortly after breaking out of the brothel. Looking up at the Virgin she exclaims, "So you've ended all the way up here too? It's amazing what we do out of love for our children!" Alongside its conflation of Esperanza with the Virgin, this scene depicts the intimate association between Guadalupe and the Mexican people: she goes where they go. Between the devotions to Juan Soldado and to the Virgin of Guadalupe, the reconceptualization of the borderlands is complete. Juan Soldado sanctifies illegal border crossings, and the Virgin of Guadalupe consecrates the borderlands as a continuous Mexican and Chicano/Mexican space. Its meaning is not derived in relation to either the United States or Mexico. It belongs to the Virgin of Guadalupe and hence to her "children."

Juan Soldado and the Virgin of Guadalupe, while playing important roles in *Santitos*, are by no means the only Mexican Catholic symbols that subvert the political meanings of international boundaries. To their devotions could be added a wide range of myths and rituals found along the Arizona-Sonora borderlands. Moving east from California to the Arizona-Sonora border, one finds the Pimeria Alta, a transnational space dedicated by both Catholics and Native Americans to its local patron, St. Francis Xavier. Between the mission church of San Xavier del Bac—south of Tucson, Arizona—and a church dedicated to him in Magdalena de Kino in Sonora, Mexico, thousands of Catholics conduct pilgrimages each year, marking and sustaining a social and cultural space much older than either the Mexican or the U.S. nation. Similarly, Santa Muerte (or La Santisima Muerte)—Saint Death—is understood by her believers to side, like Juan Soldado, with social outcasts. Today her devotion is gaining popularity among those Mexicans who have been driven into the social and economic underworld by the forces of transnational capitalism. We can also reflect upon the self-conscious use of religious symbols, including the Virgin of Guadalupe and the rituals of pilgrimage, by Cesar Chavez in mobilizing the United Farm Workers (UFW) movement in the American Southwest. An integral part of the civil rights movement, Chavez and the UFW championed the rights and dignity of exploited agricultural laborers, among whom are undocumented Mexican immigrants. Like Esperanza, he appealed to moral laws that transcend those of capitalism and the nation-state. It is within this context of devotional creativity that *Santitos* must be viewed.

Although *Santitos* is a Mexican film, its extensive exploration of the borderlands aligns it with the central themes of Chicano/Mexican cinema popular in the United States as well as Mexico. The subversion of the U.S.–Mexico border and the creation of a distinctive borderlands identity have figured as distinguishing motifs of Chicano cinema since Luis Valdez's visual adaptation of *I Am Joaquín* (1969), a seminal text of the Chicano movement. *Zoot Suit* (1981), *La Bamba* (1987), *Born in East L.A.* (1987), and *Quinceañera* (2006) also expand the idea of a fluid culture fashioned by influences from both sides of the international border. Chicano/a identities are *mestizaje*, betwixt and between the defining limitations of class, gender, nationality, and religion. *Santitos* explores but one possible formation of borderlands consciousness in its narration of Esperanza's circular journey, an identity forged in the liminal spaces between nation-states and between Mexican Catholicism and modernity.

Esperanza's identification with the Virgin of Guadalupe at the shrine in Los Angeles brings together two important meanings of Catholic devotionalism in modern Mexican and Chicano/Mexican culture. As noted above, Guadalupe symbolizes Mexican space, meaning a public expression of collective social and/or political identity. Equally significant is Guadalupe's symbolic association with motherhood and, in traditional Mexican/Chicano culture, the home. Esperanza's remarks to the Virgin elegantly combine these public/political and private/domestic meanings. She notes that Guadalupe, like a mother, has followed her children from Mexico to the United States, transforming the borderlands into a home. At the shrine in Los Angeles, Esperanza bids farewell to St. Jude and St. Anthony and leaves the dangerous borderlands. She decides to continue her search for Blanca in the domestic world, returning home to her apartment in Veracruz.

A New Family

Many reviewers interpreted *Santitos* as a kind of self-help film, the story of one woman's recovery from grief. But the film portrays more than an individual's quest. For viewers familiar with Mexican popular culture, its focus on the Mexican family—and not merely the individual—is undeniable. *Santitos* culminates not only in the union of a man and a woman but also in the union of two Mexican cultural icons. While Esperanza's character identifies with the Virgin of Guadalupe, her lover, the Angel of Justice, bears a striking resemblance to El Santo, the Saint. The legendary masked wrestler of Mexican professional wrestling, El Santo was born Rodolfo Guzman Huerta. El Santo not only dominated Mexican professional wrestling from his debut in the 1930s until his death in 1984, but he also inspired a bestselling comic book in the 1940s and 1950s and a subgenre of horror films. Starring regularly in both the ring and the movies as a fighter against evil and injustice, his persona paralleled various superheroes in the United States. Most famously, Guzman never removed his silver mask in public, except on one occasion

12.3. Bearing an uncanny resemblance to El Santo, the legendary masked fighter of Mexican professional wrestling, the Angel of Justice (Alberto Estrella), restores unity to Esperanza's (Dolores Heredia) fragmented family life.

during a televised talk show only a few days before he died. Today his grave site in Mexico City draws thousands of pilgrims every year. Another cinematic *homage* to Mexican professional wrestling, *Nacho Líbre* (2006) has actor Jack Black putting on a mask in order to compete in secret.

In *Santitos*, Esperanza meets the Angel of Justice at a live wrestling match in Los Angeles where he is battling against the archenemy of the Mexican and Chicano spectators: La Migra, the Border Patrol. After the match she and the masked wrestler proceed to a dance club and then to Esperanza's apartment where he wears his mask even while making love. When the fully suited Angel of Justice tracks down Esperanza in her Veracruz church (where she is praying to the Virgin of Guadalupe), the story comes to its end. They and Esperanza's sister come together as a new family over Blanca's grave, which they transform into a pink house with a can of paint. Esperanza now sees that her search for Blanca in the underworld of prostitution was misguided. Her personal grief is resolved and a new family is reconstituted through the love between two characters, both of whom are identified with icons of popular devotion. Esperanza, the self-sacrificing mother, is a living embodiment of Guadalupe's love, while the Angel of Justice is a legendary "saint" of Mexican mass culture.

In its exploration of both familial and women's issues, *Santitos* stands squarely in the tradition of the Mexican melodramatic genre, which "intersects with the three master narratives of Mexican society: religion, nationalism, and modernization."[4] In the history of Mexican cinema, melodrama was inaugurated by *Santa* (1932), an adaptation of a novel by Federico Gamboa. Directed by Antonio Moreno, the film is about a young woman forced into a life of prostitution. In addition to being the first Mexican film to use synchronized sound, *Santa* also served as the prototype for the so-called *cabaretera* films of the 1940s, which developed the theme of urban women driven by economic hardship into lives of prostitution. Melodrama has also long dominated Mexican and Latin American television in the form of its widely popular *telenovelas*, serialized stories of romance and the family, akin to U.S. soap operas. *Santitos* makes several self-referential allusions to *telenovelas*—both Soledad (Ana Bertha Espín) and the parish priest Padre Salvador (Laphame) are addicted to them. In addition, the prostitution narrative is strikingly similar to the story of *Santa*. In the Mexican film classic, the protagonist (Lupita Tovar) flees her rural community to become a prostitute in Mexico City, where she falls in love with a famous bullfighter named Jaremeño (Juan José Martínez Casado). Her name, Santa—"Saint"—identifies her with the Virgin. In *Santitos*, Esperanza-as-mother is also identified with the Virgin and, like Santa, flees into a life of prostitution where she falls in love with a famous professional wrestler.

The genre of Mexican melodrama emerged in film as a means to explore the difficulties of integrating women and the traditional female-centered family into a modern industrial society beset with new economic pressures and cultural up-heavals. A recurring motif in melodrama is women caught between two allegiances. They have their familial and maternal duties, modeled by the Virgin of Guadalupe, and also their sexual desires, associated in Mexican culture with La Malinche, Hernando Cortés's mistress. In the prototypical movie *Santa* the wages of wantonness are death. The erring protagonist is ostracized from her family and rural community after being seduced and abandoned by a soldier. Her bull-fighting lover also abandons her, and Santa is left to die a destitute alcoholic. As one commentator summarily noted, "Santa has to die, because she cannot be both virgin and whore."[5]

Santitos stands in marked contrast to the traditional film melodrama, because it subverts the Virgin-Malinche dichotomy. Esperanza does not emerge from her life in the brothels as a destitute alcoholic but as a renewed family woman. Her lover does not abandon her but swears his undying love. Personal and economic trials do not overwhelm the acting woman; she triumphs over them. *Santitos* both resuscitates traditional Mexican notions of gender and modifies them in the light of late twentieth century feminism. Esperanza embraces both maternal love for Blanca and erotic desire for the Angel of Justice. At the same time, prostitution and pornography—epitomizing "the masculine gaze"—are critiqued as a "violation of intimacy."[6]

A Renaissance in Filmmaking

Mexican cinema has closely paralleled the political agenda of the nation because since its emergence as an industry it has been funded and regulated by the Mexican federal government. Movies from the early 1930s through the late 1950s concerned themselves primarily with shaping an imagined community of Mexican nationalism. These films sought to instill normative class, gender, and cultural roles and to articulate *Mexicanidad*, the quintessential Mexican identity. *Santitos*, however, was made during a renaissance in Mexican cinema. Breaking with the national cinema of the past, films of the late 1980s and 1990s reflected the changed politics of the administration of Carlos Salinas de Gortari, who sought to position the nation to enter an increasingly international, globalizing world. Under the directorship of Ignacio Durán Loera (1988–1995), the Mexican Film Institute bolstered the exhibition of Mexican cinema nationally and abroad, even as it aggressively pursued the production of new films reflecting changing cultural attitudes toward women, gender roles, and alternative lifestyles. In its challenges to traditional gender roles, as well as its inclusion of gay, lesbian, and transgendered characters, *Santitos* reflects these broader developments in the themes of Mexican cinema.

Moreover, in its foregrounding of Catholicism, *Santitos* reflects a new era of church-state relationships in Mexico, also inaugurated by the Salinas administration. Approved by the Mexican congress in 1992, new federal laws lifted a number of prohibitions that dated back to the revolutionary Constitution of 1917, which had severely curtailed the church's participation in national politics. The Catholic church is once again officially recognized by the state and diplomatic ties with the Vatican have been renewed. The right to vote has been extended to the clergy, and the church is now permitted to own property and to teach religion in its private schools. While Catholicism had always been featured as a prominent component of Mexican cinema, not until *Santitos* did it receive such sustained attention as the central theme in a Mexican movie.

As we have seen, Springall's movie lost much of its meaning (religious and otherwise) in the United States. American filmgoers—Spanish speaking or not—just did not have the cultural background to appreciate this new creative move in Mexican movies. Having been reviewed by U.S. critics primarily as the latest expression of magical realism south of the border, *Santitos* has remained largely unappreciated as a sophisticated commentary on Mexican Catholic devotion from a Mexican point of view. In the final analysis, *Santitos* neither lampoons nor promotes the devotions of Mexican Catholicism. By ending the film with a prolonged shot of a mirror, Springall points to the illusory dimension of devotionalism without ridiculing it. The reality of Esperanza's visions and the power of her rituals are reflections of her own imagination—but it is her own imagination that finally makes her well. The concerns of Soledad, expressed early in the film, that Esperanza has lost her mind are both vindicated and disproved by subsequent events. The pink house has no reality in the outside world, but Esperanza has to embark on her journey to reconstitute her family and heal from her grief. From a modern psychiatric perspective, she has utilized the various ritual strategies provided by the Catholic tradition to make conscious her inner conflicts and to find a pragmatic resolution to her grief. With the help of the saints, she crosses over the final border separating the conscious mind from the unconscious and returns to sanity as a healed person. Completing her circular journey from Veracruz to Los Angeles and back again, Esperanza emerges as an integrated and empowered woman ready to build a new family.

As another kind of mirror, *Santitos* offers native-born Anglo and Euro Americans an opportunity to better understand how they imagine religious and cultural borders. If it is to avoid both intellectual and political marginalization, the study of Mexican Catholicism and Latino religions more generally must include an examination of how Americans define "normal" religion—including "proper" Catholicism. Lacking this kind of self-examination, the meaning of these traditions remains invisible, just as the meaning of *Santitos* has remained largely hidden from viewers in the United States. Latino Catholicism will soon constitute one-half of the American church, and this changed religious landscape will increasingly challenge the neat borders of American life. *Santitos* affords one glimpse of how political, religious, and social boundaries are imagined outside of modern Protestant America.

NOTES

1. "Latino/a" is used in this chapter to signify U.S. citizens of Latin American descent. It replaces the term "Hispanic" to emphasize political self-determination and descent from the mixed European, indigenous, and African cultures of the Spanish New World. "Hispanic," in contrast, is an imposed ethnic label derived from U.S. census categories and connotes primary descent from Europe. "Chicano/a" is used in this chapter in place of "Mexican American." It denotes a hybrid cultural identity fashioned betwixt and between Mexico and the United States. "Mexican American," in contrast, insinuates primary identification with the United States and only secondary affiliation with Mexican culture.

2. Kevin Thomas "'Santitos': Refreshing Tale of One Woman's Reawakening," *Los Angeles Times*, 31 January 2000; Dennis Lim, "In the Heat of the Moment," *Village Voice*, 2 February 2000; Frederic Brussat and Mary Ann Fisher Brussat, "Santitos: Esperanza's Box of Saints," *Spirituality & Practice* (July 2000), available at http://www.spiritualityandpractice.com/films/films.php?id=2302.

3. Sean Axmaker, "Santitos' Sinful Journey Is Absolved by Zany Jokes," *Seattle Post-Intelligencer*, 6 October 2000.

4. Ana Lopez, "Tears and Desire: Women and Melodrama in the 'Old' Mexican Cinema," in *Feminism and Film*, ed. E. Ann Kaplan (New York: Oxford University Press, 2000), 507.

5. Joanne Hershfield, *Mexican Cinema/Mexican Women, 1940–1950* (Tucson: University of Arizona Press, 1996), 13.

6. Linda Mulvey, "Visual Pleasure and Narrative Cinema," in Kaplan, *Feminism and Film*, 34–47.

Further Reading

Badillo, David A. *Latinos and the New Immigrant Church.* Baltimore, MD: Johns Hopkins University Press, 2006.

Campbell, Russell. *Marked Women: Prostitutes and Prostitution in the Cinema.* Madison: University of Wisconsin Press, 2006.

Caterine, Darryl V. *Conservative Catholicism and the Carmelites: Identity, Ethnicity, and Tradition in the Modern Church.* Bloomington: Indiana University Press, 2001.

Dolan, Jay P., and Gilberto M. Hinojosa, eds. *Mexican Americans and the Catholic Church, 1900–1965.* Notre Dame, IN: University of Notre Dame Press, 1994.

Fischer, Lucy. *Cinematernity: Film, Motherhood, Genre.* Princeton, NJ: Princeton University Press, 1996.

Graziano, Frank. *Cultures of Devotion: Folk Saints of Spanish America.* New York: Oxford University Press, 2006.

Hershfield, Joanne, and David R. Maciel. *Mexico's Cinema: A Century of Film and Filmmakers.* Wilmington, DE: SR Books, 1999.

Limón, José E. *American Encounters: Greater Mexico, the United States, and the Erotics of Culture.* Boston: Beacon, 1998.

Mora, Carl J. *Mexican Cinema: Reflections of a Society.* Berkeley: University of California Press, 1989.

Mora, Sergio de la. *Cinemachismo: Masculinities and Sexuality in Mexican Film.* Austin: University of Texas Press, 2006.

Noriega, Chon A. *Chicanos and Film: Representation and Resistance.* Minneapolis: University of Minnesota Press, 1992.

Sandoval, Moises. *On the Move: A History of the Hispanic Church in the United States.* Maryknoll, NY: Orbis, 1990.

Valdivia, Angharad N. *A Latina in the Land of Hollywood and Other Essays on Media Culture.* Tucson: University of Arizona Press, 2000.

13

CATHOLICISM WOW!

Dogma (1999)

Amy Frykholm

Critics seem to agree on one thing about Kevin Smith's 1999 apocalyptic comedy *Dogma*: it is a Catholic movie. Albert Bergesen and Andrew Greeley wrote that Kevin Smith "may be so possessed by the Catholic imagination that he doesn't have to reflect consciously on what he is telling the audience about God." Michael Atkinson wrote in *Interview* that *Dogma* "might stand as the most forthrightly Catholic movie seen in America since *The Song of Bernadette* (1943)." Writing in *Salon*, Charles Taylor described the violence in *Dogma* as Smith's attempt to "plunge right into the bloody obsessiveness at the heart of Catholicism."[1]

While critics tended to be more vague on *what* makes *Dogma* a Catholic film, perhaps the answer is obvious enough. The protagonist is a Catholic who goes to church; the angels who appear in the film are familiar with Catholic theology; and the problem that generates the action of the film is caused by a golf-playing Catholic cardinal. On a less obvious and more speculative level, the movie engages classic issues in Catholic theology—especially those of free will and an absent God (*Deus absconditus*). It plays with the so-called Catholic imagination and something we might call a Catholic sensibility, perhaps by engaging religion and the grotesque in a baroque, Catholic way.

Even the controversy around the film suggested it was primarily a conversation among Catholics about the representation of the faith in the media. An organization called the Catholic League of America for Religious and Civil Rights stridently objected to the film's mixture of vulgarity and sacred content and dubbed the movie anti-Catholic. A war of words briefly escalated. A few poorly attended protests of the film did take place and Miramax heads Harvey and Bob Weinstein reported receiving threats. The size of the audiences, however, remained the same. On the whole the Catholic League essentially functioned to prove Kevin Smith's point that Catholics take their faith too seriously and ironically to raise publicity and profitability for the film via controversy. Yet the controversy also framed the film within a Catholic discourse. Smith used the opportunity to label himself a "practicing Catholic," discuss his church-going habits and Catholic upbringing, and use his Catholic identity to counter the Catholic League's objections.

Despite the labeling of this film as decidedly Catholic, when I asked audiences that viewed *Dogma* about religion in the film, they showed very little interest in discussing its Catholic identity. Instead they connected the film to a different narrative deeply embedded in the religious context of American life. For many viewers, *Dogma* is a story of the depravity of institutional religion and the benefits of a personal spirituality. This disconnect—among the message that professional critics and scholars received, what Smith himself says about the film, and audience response—raises questions about how the Catholic idiom functions in American popular culture. While Smith himself may have had a particularly Catholic message for audiences, what they heard was that often-repeated refrain in American culture that it is better to be "spiritual but not religious."

The Audience

Most analyses of a film begin and end with the film itself. While critics analyze the script and images of a film and possibly ask questions about those who produced it, they rarely take the time to consider the film's audience. The audience in film criticism is often constructed to look exactly like the critic, and the critic makes an implicit assumption that others view the film in the same way that he or she does. Instead of taking the audience for granted, some scholars have tried to study film audiences as a way to learn something about a film that they cannot learn simply through studying the text and images.

In audience studies, the scholar's own interpretation becomes less important than balancing the multiple interpretations of audiences. One of the greatest benefits of audience studies is the way that the audience can offer surprises by using a film to do significantly different work than the scholar had imagined. The meaning of a film is not fixed by the filmmaker or the critic but is a dynamic process that involves audiences and their responses.

At the same time, audience research raises its own set of difficult questions. Just because a scholar interviews someone and asks her questions does not necessarily mean that the scholar suddenly "knows" and understands something about the audience that she did not know before. Movie watching is complicated. People respond both intellectually and emotionally to a film. Many people cannot explain how or why they like or do not like a film. Beyond their visceral responses, people often do not have a vocabulary for explaining the impact of a film on them, and they are not accustomed to considering their consumption of popular culture critically. It is very difficult for a researcher to move beyond people's response of pleasure or displeasure and even more difficult to draw conclusions from responses given in focus groups and individual interviews. If a question is asked one way, viewers may give a certain kind of response. Ask the same question a different way or on another day, and they may offer a completely different response. The instability of audience research is what convinces many scholars to avoid it altogether. Still if we listen carefully, ask enough questions, and consider the uncertainty present in our conclusions, audience research can lead us to some surprises that at the very least can teach us something new.

Dogma's persistent popularity among young audiences and its controversy in the media situate the film well for an audience study. While, as far as we know, no specific broad surveys of *Dogma*'s audience have been done, we do know that *Dogma* is Kevin Smith's highest-grossing film to date. Tellingly, *Dogma* has been shown repeatedly on Comedy Central, a cable channel that caters to a young, upscale, and educated audience with shows that feature edgy humor and that push at the boundaries of television standards.

In order to gain a richer understanding of *Dogma*'s audience, I did not conduct a general survey but instead used focus groups. I hoped to deepen my understanding of the role of images of Catholicism in popular culture and to understand how viewing audiences interpret the Catholic idiom of the film. My assumption was that the focus groups would generate discussion and that impressions and ideas about the film would emerge in a natural way. Film viewing is typically a collective experience and while I could not replicate movie theater conditions, I knew that most people are comfortable viewing films with other people, including strangers. While appropriate for an audience study of a film, focus groups are still very difficult. People may suppress their thoughts even in a small group. Their feelings about a film may change or develop over a short period of time.

For this study, I employed nine focus groups with a total of fifty-one viewers. That may seem like a very small number, certainly only the tiniest fraction of viewers who have ever seen *Dogma*. In that sense, my study was not representative nor statistically significant. Instead, this study was what is called a qualitative, rather than a quantitative, study. Rather than gathering specific, comparable data as a social scientist or a statistician might do, I was looking for a deeper under-standing of a smaller number of people. This is a research technique developed especially in the field of cultural anthropology, and it yields a kind of scholarship often called "thick description." Viewers in the focus groups ranged in age from fourteen to seventy-three with the majority (65 percent) under twenty-five. The group under twenty-five, Generation Y or the Millennials, as they are called in the media, had typically viewed *Dogma* multiple times, sometimes as many as twenty. Two-thirds of the people under twenty-five in the focus groups had seen the film more than once. One-third had seen it more than five times. Those forty-five and older were less well-acquainted with this film. The vast majority were seeing it for the first time in the focus groups. While the focus groups all took place in a small town in the western United States, the regional composition was far more diverse than that. I had access to groups of young people from all over the country who were participating in an AmeriCorps program, and only one person involved in my study was born and raised in the town where the study was conducted.

At the beginning of each focus group, I gave participants a questionnaire asking whether they had seen the film previously and asking them to identify their reli-gious background and current religious affiliation(s). People with dogmatic in-clinations rarely came voluntarily to see the film. Instead, viewers represented quite a different cross-section of the population. Just over half of the viewers in my study claimed no explicit religious affiliation whatsoever, answering the question about current religious affiliation with the word "none." Protestants of various kinds accounted for the next largest group (20 percent) followed by those who claimed an eclectic form of belief often described as "my own" or naming some more specific combination. Three claimed a current Catholic identity, an equal number current Jewish identity. Two people were members of the Church of Jesus Christ of Latter-day Saints, and one person wrote "science of mind" on the questionnaire.

Far more participants claimed a particular religious heritage than a current religious affiliation. Just under half said that they were raised Protestant and a fifth Catholic. Only 14 percent claimed to have been raised without religious affiliation. Almost 40 percent then had opted out of their religion of origin to claim no religious affiliation. This does not mean that participants were not religious or, as many of them put it, "spiritual." Overall, however, they demonstrated a disinclination toward institutional forms of religion.

Participants in my focus groups were illustrative of a trend that many scholars have noted: American religion is undergoing a significant shift away from religious institutions and doctrines. As people pursue life's meaning outside of institutional structures, they frequently come to describe themselves as "spiritual but not religious." From this designation, people often put together eclectic forms of belief and practice that do not easily correspond to religious labels. These were the people most drawn to my study and the viewing of *Dogma*. The rejection of religious institutions was not found among youth alone. While the vast majority (77 percent) of participants under twenty-five claimed "none" or some eclectic form of religious belief for their own, so did almost half of those in the older group. Very rarely in group discussions did any kind of specific religious controversy emerge. People tended to express their religious and spiritual inclinations in terms that appeared, on the surface at least, to make room for a wide diversity of beliefs and practices. In other words, no one was interested, whatever their religious background or current affiliation, in defending religious dogma.

The Film

Kevin Smith became famous with his 1994 independent film, *Clerks*, which looked at the lives of two young men who worked as clerks at neighboring convenience and video stores. After the success of *Clerks*, Smith went on to make several films drawing on the same set of quirky characters in a variety of settings. *Dogma* is the fourth of these, but it casts Smith's intentions onto a much grander scale, blending low-key, vulgar, slacker humor with sweeping claims about life, God, sin, grace, and the state of humankind. It makes for an odd mix, and *Dogma* makes for strange viewing. All of the pieces of the complex plot do not quite add up, and the dialogue is thick and rapid-fire. Even after multiple viewings, I sometimes lost my footing in the convoluted plot lines. At the same time, *Dogma* has enjoyed broad appeal and is Smith's most popular movie, grossing $30 million at the box office and going on to a long life in home entertainment.

Dogma tells the story of a young woman named Bethany (Linda Fiorentino), who is selected by heavenly beings for a special mission. This mission is to stop two fallen angels, Loki (Matt Damon) and Bartleby (Ben Affleck), from entering a Catholic church in New Jersey. Cardinal Glick (George Carlin) is attempting to create a time of renewal for the Catholic faith by designing a "Buddy Christ" and by allowing anyone who enters the church on a certain day to have their sins forgiven. The action of the film is then based on the following premise: if the two angels are allowed to enter the church, all existence will be erased because the two angels will have defied God's decree and proved God to be fallible. God has said that these two angels can never enter heaven; if they do, God is wrong. As Metatron (Alan Rickman), who acts as the voice of God, says, "Existence in all its form and proven splendor functions solely on one principle: God is infallible." Meanwhile, God has disappeared. Bethany eventually accepts her special mission and is joined by two prophets: Jay (Jason Mewes) and Silent Bob (Kevin Smith) of other Smith films. A thirteenth, black apostle named Rufus (Chris Rock) falls in with the group as does an incarnate muse named Serendipity (Salma Hayek).

At the end of *Dogma*, Bartleby's fury at God over his exile causes a bloody scene outside Cardinal Glick's church. Bartleby has ripped the heads off several corpses and dropped bodies from the top of the church. When Bethany and her party arrive after being held hostage by the demon Azrael (Jason Lee), whose evil plot has caused the disappearance of God, they find blood, mayhem, and destruction on the level of the apocalyptic. Bartleby has been too busy killing people, however, to

13.1. Cardinal Glick announces, "Christ didn't come to Earth to give us the willies.... He came to help us out. He was a booster. I give you... the Buddy Christ."

complete his task. He has not yet entered the church doors. Bethany suddenly remembers John Doe Jersey (Bud Cort, whom the viewer learns is actually God imprisoned in a body), a man being kept on life support at the hospital just across the street from the church. She rushes to the hospital and removes the man from life support just as Bartleby is flinging open the doors of the church. Out from the church comes a blazing white light, followed by the appearance of God (Alanis Morissette) and Metatron. In the final minutes of the film, God forgives and destroys Bartleby, plays in the church garden, cleans up the messy street, and resurrects Bethany, who was killed as she freed God from bondage as a human. Bethany is now told that she is carrying a child who will assume the same holy lineage as her own and that of Christ. God, Metatron, Serendipity, and Rufus return to heaven through the church doors. Bethany, Jay, and Silent Bob sit outside on the church steps on a sunny day and contemplate the future.

Dogma provides through the character of Bethany a version of the spiritual quest. Bethany becomes the Everywoman who moves from malaise and uncertainty to a passionate engagement with faith. The film thus provides a version of what authentic spirituality looks like and also provides commentary on what lies outside the boundary. One place where we see that boundary come into play is when Loki and Bartleby enter a corporate boardroom with the intent of punishing the "idolaters" in the room. Loki carves a voodoo doll out of an onion and places it before the chair of the board. He teases the man with the threat of a voodoo-like spell and then asks, "Do you know much about voodoo? It's a fascinating practice. No real doctrine of faith to speak of, more an arrangement of superstitions." As he is leaving the boardroom to get the gun he will use to kill all but one of those in the room, he says disgustedly, "I don't believe in voodoo." Voodoo thus provides a limit for authentic spirituality. While it is noninstitutional, it is also not spirituality. Loki's commentary cannot be taken without Smith's trademark irony. Loki believes that he is acting with God's approval when he is killing the "idolaters" in the room, but nothing in the film suggests that he is correct. Instead the images the film provides of God suggest that Loki's judgment and fanaticism are as misguided as Cardinal Glick's. Still, Loki's assessment of voodoo as "not religion" goes unchallenged and contrasts to Bethany's discovery of an authentic, open-ended faith.

An important element of *Dogma* is the persistent use of vulgarity and sexual humor. In interviews, Smith calls these "dick and fart jokes" and hints at two seemingly contradictory purposes for them. The first is to add playfulness to religion, something Smith feels is all too often lacking. The second is to reach people outside traditional denominations with a message that religion matters. Smith has been particularly forthright about his intentions with the film. To pious objections by the Catholic League, Smith retorted with an obscenity followed by "I am doing what should be your job!"[2] Smith uses vulgarity and sexual humor to remove any trace of piety, and thus he hopes to attract a young and jaded audience to consider his views.

Using scenarios drawn from Catholic theology and mixing those with a popular-culture idiom, *Dogma* seems poised to offer a distinctly Catholic viewpoint to the discussion of religion and film. Yet in order to fulfill the purposes that writers, directors, and producers have for a film, the film has to enter into a cultural moment ripe for its message.

Viewer Responses

Viewers who participated in my study responded, on the whole, positively to the film. Laughter—sometimes uncomfortable, sometimes hearty—accompanied the viewing in focus groups, and viewers generally said they "liked" the film after seeing it. A majority of viewers saw in the film and affirmed in themselves a spiritual-but-not-religious thesis through which they interpreted the action of the film. When I asked focus groups what religious messages they heard, they pointed to two moments. At one point Serendipity remarks, "It's not about who is right or wrong. No denomination has nailed it yet because they are all too self-righteous to realize that it doesn't matter what you have faith in, just that you have faith." And Rufus, who is perhaps the wisest of the movie's characters, tells Bethany that Jesus Christ is upset by the way that people take a good idea and turn it into a belief, something they are willing to die or kill for. He advocates for a more open-ended faith that does not rely on absolute certainty. Participants tended to resonate and agree with these two statements. A fairly typical comment was like this one from one of the few professed Catholics in the focus groups: "The main point of the film is basically summed up when the muse says, 'It doesn't matter what you believe in, just that you believe in something.'"

When interpreting the religious messages of the film and what the spiritual-but-not-religious thesis meant to them, most young people articulated their spirituality in such a way as to make it distinct from their parents or grandparents. While they had had a crisis of faith, certainly their parents never did. Moving away from institutional religion and critiquing it from a position of spirituality was something they genuinely believed to be unique to young people and something relatively new in American culture. In my study, however, what seemed clearer than the uniqueness of Generation Y is the persistence of the spiritual-but-not-religious thesis across generations. Both those under twenty-five and those over forty-five tended to use this phrase to distinguish themselves from the generations before them. Young people often thought that the phrase distinguished them from their parents, but so did people over forty-five—the "parents." "I could never have shown this film to my grandmother," one sixty-year-old man said. "But I agree with its basic premise." This seems to be a particular cultural strain in America, an available story out of which multiple generations can create their own meanings. In order to maintain its power, spiritual-but-not-religious has to be seen as new and different. As an innovative and corrective tradition, it is constantly in the process of reinvention. Paradoxically, the very aspects that give this tradition strength—its flexibility and its individuality—prevent it from being perceived as a tradition by the very people who engage in and practice it.

The development of American religion tells a different story. A movement away from institutional religion can be seen in American culture at least as early as the nineteenth century. In spite of scholarly focus on those exclusively committed to one particular religious tradition, many Americans have had more open views. Americans—those both within faith communities and without—have embraced the importance of pursuing a personal, spiritual quest. They have constructed beliefs and practices that are eclectic and show open curiosity about other religions. In general, Americans have emphasized that "authentic" and "true" religion should stress positive and unselfish actions.

These are the recurrent themes of what some have called the "spiritual Left" or "seeker spirituality." Some have gone so far as to argue that, as eclectic and spontaneous as this tradition appears, it constitutes a viable, cohesive alternative that has persisted in American culture over many generations. There is nothing "new" about the "new spirituality." Young people find it easy to tell the story of how they 3found their way out of institutional religion precisely because this is a story deeply embedded in American culture that finds a new mode of expression in every generation. The sentiment, however, changes very little. The exact phrase "spiritual but not religious" was used repeatedly and transparently by younger and older people in focus groups to describe their spiritual and religious lives, indicating that it was not recognized as a cliché for them.

Several of the other films discussed in this volume explore the spiritual-but-not-religious thesis and help us to see that it has played a role in Catholic filmmaking over the course of the twentieth century. In *Lilies of the Field* (1963) Homer offers a kind of non-Catholic, lively critique of the nuns' religiosity. Even in a film as Catholic as *The Song of Bernadette* (1943), the institutional church has a difficult time adjusting to Bernadette's spiritual vision. In *True Confessions* (1981) we see the institutional church as thoroughly corrupt. In other words, this way of depicting religious institutions has a long tradition in filmmaking and in films that represent Catholicism. "True" religion, which is fundamentally personal and spiritual in nature, is set against "false" religion, which is overly tied up in institutions.

In order to look more deeply at what spiritual-but-not-religious meant for focus group participants in relationship to *Dogma*, I have identified three modes of interaction with the film. In the most common version, the film modeled a spiritual journey that participants recognized in themselves, and they used their own experiences to reflect on the film. For others, the film served as a kind of spiritual mentor and fed them with ideas about an authentic spiritual life. For a third group, the film was essentially misguided in its interpretation of spirituality, and they used the film as an opportunity to offer corrections. Each of these three ways of interpreting the film suggest that viewers perceived that *Dogma* wanted to lead them somewhere, and they maneuvered themselves accordingly.

Dogma's representation of the religious quest resonated with viewers so clearly that they often used the film as a model in telling their own religious stories. One participant put it this way: "I grew up Catholic.... I don't go to church, but there has been a change where I am more spiritual. It isn't structural for me any more. What my beliefs are, I guess they are a little bit of everything. I don't need the structure or the pressure of the Catholic church." Viewers used the film to explain or defend "spirituality" over and against "religion." They tied religion to conservative and strict forms of belief and practice and asserted their alternative in a broader, more personal, and less confining "spirituality."

Despite the fact that the film clearly makes this point, its perspective seems less straightforward. For example, in the scene in which Serendipity is expounding her view of spirituality, the shit demon, Noman the Golgothan (Ethan Suplee), is rising out of the toilet in the strip joint's bathroom. Serendipity's speech is punctuated by images of the shit demon, and everything she says is then illustrated by what the shit demon does. Who or what is the "shit" in this particular scene? Perhaps the juxtaposition of Serendipity and the Golgothan demon suggests that we are not to take even Serendipity's words as the final meaning of faith. Perhaps Kevin Smith is not so much espousing this view of spiritual-but-not-religious as he is constructing an irony out of the sentiment. If that is the case, such irony was lost on the viewers in my focus groups who found Serendipity's message illustrative of their own beliefs.

Viewers often located the start of their own spiritual quests, like Bethany's, in a confining and irrelevant institutional setting. In an early scene in the film, Bethany attends Sunday mass. As we are led into her church, we see a sign outside with the title of the day's sermon: "The Labored Voice of God." The voice of God truly does labor in that church. The priest drones on in the pulpit while people in the pews sleep, fidget, and stare mindlessly into space. The pews are full of far more young people than might be expected of an average Catholic parish. The camera lingers on no one over forty years old, and I wondered if perhaps Smith's purpose was not to depict real Catholicism in the United States but instead to construct a picture of youthful response to it. As I watched this scene, I was so busy observing those bored expressions that I also had trouble concentrating on what the priest was saying, which I am sure was Smith's point.

After an announcement about a prolife-prochoice softball game, the priest mentions a man on life support in New Jersey (whom we later learn is God) and urges Catholics everywhere to take a stand against euthanasia. Then the priest says, "All rise for the recession of faith." This is of course another joke. Normally this moment is called the "profession" of faith, as people profess what they believe. Here they are "recessing"—not only reciting but also leaving. The scene fades out as Bethany rises and recites without expression or emotion, "We believe in one God, the Father, the Almighty..." Bethany later admits that she has no idea why she still goes to church and that she feels fairly sure that God is dead.

Young people who viewed the film readily identified with the criticism of institutional religion embedded in Bethany's disgust and boredom over church politics and Sunday mass. As one young viewer put it, "Church is just not... it's not where I find my relationship with God." Viewers were eager to tell the negative side of their experiences with institutional churches. They began a good deal of their comments with "I grew up Catholic (or Jewish or Methodist)" and went on from there to tell the stories of their disaffection with the religious organizations that influenced their upbringings.

Audiences further identified with the story Bethany tells about an experience of lost faith. On a train, speaking with Bartleby, Bethany says, "I remember the exact moment [that I lost my faith]." Young people in the focus groups told their own versions of this story, which often began, "When I was a child, I went to church and was fairly religious." It continued with a life-changing event that drew them away from church and from "structural religion." Then the young person had a discovery of "spirituality" or of "what I personally believe." Here is one young man's short version of this story that is unique in its details but whose sentiment was common: "I had all of these questions about the church and when I asked them, no one could tell me anything. I could go to church or I would go and just meditate by myself. But if I went to church with my questions, I just wasn't getting any answers. So I guess I don't worry myself any more about the right way. I guess

I'm 'spiritual,' but…" In focus groups, viewers connected their stories to Bethany's, sometimes even echoing her directly. Like Bethany, more than one participant said, "I remember the exact moment when I lost my faith."

For some participants the film went beyond merely providing an example of a spiritual journey that looked something like their own. One young woman turned the film into an authoritative source. She had seen *Dogma* "more than twenty times" and described herself as having been raised Episcopalian and now practicing her own "mixture of Christianity and Greek mythology." This movie precisely summed up her understanding of religion, and she loved no line better than Serendipity's about faith. When I asked her about the power that this movie had for her, she said, "My religion is my religion. It's something I have put together. When I watch this movie, I get ideas for how things might be. Like the muse saying the Bible is gender-biased or Rufus talking about the fractioning of all religions." She used the film to contribute to a reservoir of ideas and possibilities from which she constructed her religious life. Repeated viewings gave the film an almost iconic power for her. Moments in the film signified not only truths she already accepted but also new teachings that held authority for her. The film thus served as a kind of mentor. Other viewers did not take their viewing as far, but they expressed learning something about Catholicism from the film and gave the film some limited authority in helping them to understand what an invigorated spirituality might look like.

A third kind of response, within the spiritual-but-not-religious realm, was to criticize the film for failing to take eclectic spirituality seriously enough. One older woman who saw *Dogma* for the first time in a focus group was fascinated by the names of the various angels in the film—a group of names as diverse as its multicultural cast. Loki is a Norse trickster god, Azrael has roots in Islam, Metatron derives from the Greek, Bartleby is the name of a scribe in a law office in the writings of nineteenth-century American writer Herman Melville. Several days after the focus group, this woman e-mailed me with citations from various books on angels, demonstrating that Metatron and Azrael were part of a broader angel spirituality than I had known. She wrote, "For me, the fact that 'Azrael' was the name of the little devil guy offended me. I wasn't offended by the profanity or the heads being blown off—but this irritated me. I've had an affectionate connection with Azrael for many years and feel him to be a loving teacher." While she did not show interest in the Islamic origins of the figure of Azrael, she included him in a pantheon of angels that was significant in her own spiritual life. She explained that Azrael's name means "he whom God helps" and that his role is primarily in helping people cross over to heaven after death. He also comforts the grieving and eases the suffering of death. She had an investment in an actual being, Azrael. Both *Dogma*'s depiction of the angel and the use of his name demonstrated in her view a lack of understanding. In other words, the playfulness of the film was not offensive insofar as it critiqued institutional religion but only where it touched on practices and beings that she took seriously. This position within the spiritual-but-not-religious thesis struck me as quite similar to a dogmatic position that nearly all viewers outwardly rejected. This kind of response was rare among participants but still significant for the way that it disrupted and undermined the message viewers frequently cited: "lighten up and don't think you have all the answers, whatever your religion."

Typically this "lighten up" message was effective in quashing dissent in the groups and dismissing any talk about Truth with a capital T. In one group, a young woman tentatively offered that she could not see the point in joking about something as serious as religion and eternity. But when I tried to draw her out to speak more about this view she declined. She appeared clearly uncomfortable with how unpopular that view would be in the group. In another instance, dissent ended before it even began when another young woman who was helping to arrange a showing of the film at the local college suddenly dropped out. She never spoke to me personally about her decision, but through others I learned that people in her church had explained that it was inappropriate for her to be involved in a showing of the film. Both of these tentative objections, marginalized by the groups in which they were offered, suggest that there is an entirely different way of looking at this movie that was not enabled by my focus groups.

I caught another hint of this from an older woman who had seen the film for the first time with her highly religious sister and brother-in-law. The vulgar language made them so uncomfortable that she could hardly stand to watch the movie with them. Now, in another setting, she found the movie provocative and intriguing but not offensive. "I was surprised this time," the woman said, "by how traditional the content is. I was offended the first time I saw it because of all the swearing. And I knew how offended my sister and brother-in-law were by the language, by seeing any God-topic treated with vulgarity. This time I saw it differently, how it could speak to younger people." When she saw through the "screen" of the vulgarity, she saw a very traditional, God-affirming message about the significance of faith.

All of these objections came not from Catholics but from evangelicals. In the contemporary United States, evangelical Protestants tend to be more conservative in their theology, politics, and lifestyles. They take the Bible seriously—sometimes literally—and stress the importance of having a personal relationship with Jesus. Evangelicals more than Catholics had higher stakes in objecting to the film and to seeing it as antithetical to their faith. Evangelical constructions of faith are very often oppositional, constructing the culture as "other" and hostile. *Dogma* provided an opportunity to feed that construction.

Catholic viewers, including those who felt tied to the institutional church, tended to find a reason to connect themselves to the stories in the film or to reason *along* with the film instead of in opposition to it. In one group, two men in their fifties from the local Catholic church came to see the movie and talk about it. This was a mixed group with participants ranging from seventeen to fifty-seven. Neither of them had ever seen the film before, and I confess to feeling a bit anxious about their response to it. But their reaction echoed Kevin Smith's own intentions much more than I could have imagined and more than I saw in other audience members. One man said that while he could clearly see that the movie was not directed at him, he could also see that it was aimed at a generation of Catholics who perhaps might see faith as a more viable option after viewing the film. Like Smith, these two viewers felt that the church needed more youthful spokespeople, and they did not think that Smith had crossed any sacred lines. These participants were not people who found the spiritual-but-not-religious thesis particularly compelling, and they connected to the film in a different way.

Third Option: Spiritual Catholicism?

Perhaps these participants, the committed Catholics who enjoyed the film, were the ones who came closest to understanding Kevin Smith's own purposes. Smith seems to be reaching for a third option—neither an irrelevant institutional faith nor a free-floating spirituality but instead an invigorated, open-minded, spiritual Catholicism. When all is said and done, Catholicism is not erased but rather chastised and remade. This continued hope in the power of Catholicism, however, was not shared by those who were the most committed to the film.

In an early scene in *Dogma*, Bethany's coworker at the Women's Clinic suggests that Bethany's spiritual deprivation is related to the lack of sex in her life:

"You need to get laid, Bethany Sloane. You need a man, if only for ten minutes."
"It's been my experience that the average male is never a man, not even for ten minutes in his entire life span."
"That sounds a little bit militant. Are you thinking of joining the other side?"
"Couldn't do it. Women are insane."
"Well, then you need to go back to church and ask God for a third option."

While the dialogue here is about a third option for sex—neither male nor female—there is a hint that passionate faith also offers a kind of third option. In popular culture, a dichotomy is often set up between a religious figure and a spiritual one. Ministers are often portrayed as hypocritical, while spiritual seekers are depicted as authentic and people of integrity. As we have seen, this dichotomy was familiar to the viewers of *Dogma* who participated in my study, and it seemed to describe something in their own experiences as well. While *Dogma* indeed repeats this dichotomy, it does so with an implicit difference.

Because visual media like film have to rely on a kind of shorthand to make complicated assertions very quickly, "religion" gets represented by a priest in a robe or a clerical collar, a crucifix hanging above a bed, or an ornate sanctuary. Frequently in this shorthand, the media use specifically Catholic images to reference institutional religion more generally. As we have seen throughout this volume, no other religion in American culture is more available for this kind of vivid, visual shorthand than Catholicism. In the case of *Dogma*, Smith uses these images to tell viewers what they already know and are ready to believe: institutional religion is dead.

By the end of the film, Bethany no longer thinks "God is dead." Instead she is "burdened with an overabundance" of faith. Where and when did this transformation happen? All of the scenes of spiritual reinvigoration that mark Bethany's conversion from rote religion to inspiration happen outside the church walls. Metatron meets Bethany in her bedroom and then removes them to a Mexican restaurant; he meets Bethany a second time in the woods. Bethany discovers her spiritual powers, which are a result of her heritage as the "Last Sion," in a bar. In other words, secular and natural locations are chosen to demonstrate spiritual healing and spiritual growth. Those in search of the film's Catholic imagination might suggest that this is part of the way that the film imbues the secular with the spiritual, emphasizing the action and presence of God in the world. But for viewers, particularly those I interviewed, this seemed more strongly to suggest the fact that the church is no place to seek spirituality.

On the other hand, the film occasionally proposes the possibility that church and spirituality can be linked. Without directly questioning the spiritual-but-not-religious premise, the film hints at the possibility that Catholicism itself can be a form of seeker spirituality. At the end of the film, a gruesome scene perpetrated by Bartleby happens just outside a Catholic church. As Bartleby flings open the doors of the church to get the reward he feels he deserves, he is thrown back by a blinding light emanating from the church itself. From this light, God, in the form of Alanis Morissette, emerges. She walks out of the church, through its doors. Again, at the very end of the film, God, Metatron, Rufus, and Serendipity all return to heaven via the church doors. The church is not destroyed, and it continues to stand as the portal into which people—albeit unusual ones—enter what is assumed to be a better (or at least more desirable) world. These scenes provide a sense of the Catholic church as containing an unexplored mystery, a realm that may very well lead to the holy. My viewers responded well to this final scene and to the depiction of a playful, benevolent God. While they were not entirely sure about the fate of Bartleby when he meets God and God kisses him before she blows his head off, they were certain that this representation of God had significant appeal. No one objected to God emerging out of and returning into the church.

In the scene in the Mooby boardroom, we learn that Mooby is a doll shaped like a cow. It is also a cartoon franchise, a chain of fast-food restaurants, and a dominant symbol of American popular culture. The figure of Mooby hints not only specifically at Disney and McDonald's but also more broadly at corporate America. When Loki and Bartleby arrive at the Mooby corporate headquarters, a figure of a golden cow—Mooby—is on the boardroom table. The camera frames the golden Mooby in a window. Through the window, we see a church. I had thought that viewers might read that scene ironically, implicating the church in the petty idolatry of worldly goods that Mooby represents, i.e. the Golden Calf of *The Ten Commandments* (1956) fame. Instead they seemed to read it as a quite sincere pictorial representation: people put money before God. Thus in this scene, viewers in my focus groups were willing to conflate God and the church instead of insisting, as they did in their personal stories, that God or spiritual meaning are best sought outside of organized religion.

The difficulty in communicating this possible third option—that the institutional church so easily rejected by viewers can also serve as a location where spiritual meaning can be sought—comes from the fact that audiences did not have a ready vocabulary to describe it. If Smith is successful in his attempt to convey this message, he does so by conceding what viewers already believe and then subtly proposing an alternative. Several film critics have pointed to Smith's own similarity to Cardinal Glick in the opening scene of the movie: a religious man on a mission to update and reform the Catholic church, to make it more appealing and more palatable. Smith himself acknowledges this in self-mockery. He sees himself as a salesman of a sort, advertising for a more contemporary, less dogma-bound church. His audiences, however, at least in my small study, are not buying exactly that product. Even enthusiastic and repeat viewers hear another, somewhat louder, cultural message that is also available to them in the film: church is dispensable and faith is better when it is not attached to specific, hardened beliefs or practices.

13.2. Audiences read movies in many different ways. How should one interpret the Mooby corporate logo framed by a church? As people putting money before God? As the petty idolatry of worldly goods?

While participants described faith as a private and personal journey for many of the people in the focus groups, they did not seem opposed to the possibility of faith communities. The film depicts a sort of ad hoc faith community in the collection of people who join Bethany on her mission. The old neighborhood depicted in earlier films like *Angels with Dirty Faces* (1938) or *Going My Way* (1944) becomes in *Dogma* a far more eclectic grouping where the shared material for identification is not ethnic or religious identity but rather the idiom of popular culture and the ability to reference a wide range of media. The space has been deemphasized and the residents highlighted. Young viewers responded to conversation about religious and spiritual communities by suggesting that they were something they would perhaps seek out when they were older, while some older viewers lamented the loss of faith communities they once had. Very few articulated a present faith community.

Perhaps Catholicism is indeed reinvigorated by the film, as it takes place within a spirituality marked by both a personal, spiritual quest and the creation of a kind of faith community. Smith renders Catholicism as a viable possibility of the spiritual life, as long as it remains open and not overly attached to its dogma. He

13.3. Behind a defeated Bartleby (Ben Affleck), the "Catholicism WOW!" banner now reads "Catholicism OW!"

does not exactly urge his readers to embrace Catholicism but rather suggests that it be allowed a place within the discourse of authenticity that contemporary American culture demands of its religious (read: spiritual) forms.

Smith himself does not seem so sure of his success and undermines this possibility as much as he affirms it. In his own unrelenting irony, he shows the state of Cardinal Glick's Catholicism WOW! campaign at the end of the film, after Bartleby's revenge-filled destruction. Instead of "Catholicism WOW!" the banner now reads "Catholicism OW!" When God comes to do the final cleanup at the very end of the film, the banner disappears altogether.

NOTES

1. Albert J. Bergesen and Andrew M. Greeley, *God in the Movies* (New Brunswick, NJ: Transaction, 2000), 174; Michael Atkinson, "Kevin Smith Stirs It Up," *Interview* (1 October 1999), available at www.newsaskew.com/dogmarc/article63.html; Charles Taylor, "Dogma," *Salon*, 12 November 1999, available at www.salon.com/ent/movies/review/1999/11/12/dogma/index.html.
2. Quoted in Atkinson, "Kevin Smith Stirs It Up."

Further Reading

Clark, Lynn Schofield. *From Angels to Aliens: Teenagers, the Media, and the Supernatural.* New York: Oxford University Press, 2003.

Hardwick, Lorna. *Reception Studies.* New York: Oxford University Press, 2003.

Holmlund, Chris, and Justin Wyatt. *Contemporary American Independent Film: From the Margins to the Mainstream.* New York: Routledge, 2005.

Holtz, Geoffrey T. *Welcome to the Jungle: The Why of "Generation X."* New York: St. Martin's, 1995.

Levy, Emanuel. *Cinema of Outsiders: The Rise of American Independent Film.* New York: New York University Press, 2001.

Lewis, Jon. *The End of Cinema as We Know It: American Film in the Nineties.* New York: New York University Press, 2002.

Muir, John Kenneth. *Askew View: The Films of Kevin Smith.* New York: Applause Theatre, 2002.

Nightingale, Virginia. *Studying Audiences: The Shock of the Real.* New York: Routledge, 1996.

Ruddock, Andy. *Understanding Audiences: Theory and Method.* Thousand Oaks, CA: Sage, 2001.

Smith, Christian, with Melinda Lundquist. *Soul Searching: The Religious and Spiritual Lives of American Teenagers.* New York: Oxford University Press, 2005.

Staiger, Janet. *Media Reception Studies.* New York: New York University Press, 2005.

Tzioumakis, Yannis. *American Independent Cinema: An Introduction.* New Brunswick, NJ: Rutgers University Press, 2006.

14

VOTIVE OFFERING

The Passion of the Christ (2004)

Colleen McDannell

The year 2004 was a *defining* moment in American religious history. The two most controversial movies of the year—Mel Gibson's *The Passion of the Christ* and Michael Moore's *Fahrenheit 9/11*—were both made by men who name themselves "Catholic." A third 2004 film, the multiple Academy Award–winner *Million Dollar Baby*, featured an Irish American boxing coach struggling with his Catholic conscience. Gibson's film in particular drew considerable media and scholarly attention. Everyone, it seemed, was talking about how religious stories should be represented, marketed, and received. Catholics, either within the movie frame or behind the camera, had generated a national discussion about biblical history, moral values, ethical choices, political decisions, and artistic sensibilities. These movies hit American theaters during a presidential election year when emotions and rhetoric were running high. The Republican candidate, George W. Bush, was thought by some to have "stolen" his last election. Would he have a more solid victory this time around? An evangelical Protestant, Bush spoke for many conservative Christians. The Democratic candidate, John Kerry, was a moderate Catholic whose prochoice position had estranged him from many in his own church. Religious identity—who could claim "I'm Catholic" and what that might mean—was a hot topic. That year it was nearly impossible to avoid a discussion of politics, religion, and the movies.

The Passion of the Christ was cowritten, financed, and directed by the Oscar-winning director and popular actor Mel Gibson. The movie depicts the last hours of Jesus' life, as he is brutally tortured and crucified. Only the last few minutes of the film celebrate the risen Christ. Gibson released the film on Ash Wednesday, the first day of Lenten preparation for Easter. Long before it opened, however, Mel Gibson and his movie were making news. A group of scholars and religious leaders had publicized their concerns that the movie's violence and its representation of Jewish leaders departed significantly from the messages contained in the New Testament Gospels. A journalist who interviewed Gibson's father published reports of the senior Gibson's fondness for conspiracy theories and his denial of the extent of the Holocaust. Mel Gibson fought back, also through the press. He previewed cuts of the film to those he thought would be more open to his cinematic and spiritual intentions. Those audiences responded enthusiastically by denying its anti-Semitism and proclaiming its faithfulness to the Passion narrative.

Once the film opened, the language used to describe Gibson and his film became even more fiery. Leon Wieseltier, a reviewer for the New Republic, called it a "sacred snuff film," and Harvard religion professor Robert Orsi described it as "deeply sadistic." On the other hand, film critic Roger Ebert reported, "I was moved by the depth of feeling, by the skill of the actors and technicians, by their desire to see this project through no matter what." After its first weekend, The Passion of the Christ had earned $126.2 million. Only three other films in the history of moviemaking had made more money in their first week in theaters. At the end of its first year, The Passion of the Christ had grossed the astonishing amount of $370.3 million domestically and $611.9 worldwide. When a DVD was released the following summer, it made $4.1 million the first day. For a film estimated as costing between $25 and $30 million, The Passion of the Christ far exceeded anyone's financial expectations.[1]

News reporters covered Gibson's film as a conflict story that pitted one group of Americans against another. They easily exploited fissures within America's religious communities as they covered responses to Gibson and his movie. On the liberal team were Bible and religion scholars from secular universities, major newspapers such as the New York Times and the Los Angeles Times, and a host of newsstand magazines. Gibson and his family were portrayed as wacky Catholics who do not accept the English mass or the authority of the current pope. On the conservative team were Bible scholars from evangelical theological seminaries, interviewers who worked for Fox News and the religion-focused EWTN, and faith-based magazines. For them, Gibson was a true Christian and a devout Catholic. Each team called up various rabbis and Jewish leaders to support their side with non-Christian opinions. Caught up in election-year hype, the controversy over *The Passion of the Christ* was presented as one more battle in the culture wars.

Given the heat of the battle, it was difficult at the time to see the significance of *The Passion of the Christ* for American religious history. *The Passion of the Christ* is a cinematic devotional gesture by a Hollywood celebrity that became wildly popular. Most movies are communal productions with no clear-cut "author" and yet, as we saw with *The Exorcist* (1973), sometimes they can become very personal expressions. Icon Productions, the company that made *The Passion*, was founded in 1989 by Mel Gibson, who also directed the film and cowrote the screenplay. His creative control over the film is undeniable and so by acknowledging the highly personal nature of the film, we can better understand the energy behind its production and distribution. In the past, independent filmmakers have made movies that speak to their political or spiritual commitments, but none—I would argue—sought to make a film that in itself is a personal prayer. *The Passion of the Christ* is unique because it calls on the world of Hollywood to produce a piece of Christian material culture, an ex-voto. *The Passion of the Christ* is Mel Gibson's votive offering to his God.

While many who saw the film found it boring and gross, many more agreed with this teenage girl and her classmates: "We liked it. We liked it a lot."[2] Mel Gibson not only used an unusual medium for his expression of devotion—a movie—he also echoed the political and theological concerns of many Catholics and Protestants of post-9/11 America. *The Passion* came during a particular period in American religious and political history. Those who liked the film brought with them an understanding both of the world of Jesus and of the world around them. Understanding what the audience members may have brought with them to the theater helps to explain why many Americans responded (and continue to respond) so positively to a film about torture. Thus, to understand the significance of the film in American religious history, we must try to understand what kind of religious expression it is and then speculate as to why it makes sense to so many people.

A few hours after midnight on 28 July 2006, Mel Gibson was pulled over for speeding. Drunk and angry, he shouted obscenities at the arresting officers, bragging that he owned Malibu and would get even for the insult. A key element of his tirade was a barrage of anti-Semitic statements that included accusing the Jews of being "responsible for all the wars in the world." The arrest rekindled the debate over *The Passion* and drew media attention back to Gibson. Bloggers who had found Gibson unacceptable before gloated that their suspicions were confirmed. Those who approved of the film and the faith of the filmmaker condemned his behavior but admired his eventual apology. Those critical of Gibson now damned him for being a hypocritical, intolerant drunk. Sympathizers reflected on the pernicious character of alcoholism, the inevitability of sin, and the need for forgiveness. By December of that year, Gibson's film *Apocalypto* (2006) was opening across the country, and the inevitable references to *The Passion* put it back in the news again. To promote *Apocalypto* and to illustrate his steps toward sobriety, the celebrity appeared on the *Tonight Show*. The conversation over Mel Gibson and *The Passion of the Christ* was renewed as the nation reflected on its own sacrifices in the violent war in Iraq.

Ex-voto

The Passion of the Christ follows in a long line of Hollywood movies about biblical characters. From the earliest days of filmmaking, cinematic versions of the story of Jesus have drawn appreciative audiences. Directors like Cecil B. DeMille looked to biblical texts, European art, and popular hymnody to construct stories that would uplift and inspire moviegoers. Filmmakers followed in the footsteps of writers like Lew Wallace and Bruce Barton, who supplemented the Gospels with their own interpretations of what Jesus' world looked like. DeMille's *The King of Kings* (1927), for instance, starts in the luxurious estate of Mary Magdalene (Jacqueline Logan), who eventually dashes off in a chariot pulled by zebras to see the town's newest prophet. While DeMille had wanted to develop a love interest between Judas (Joseph Schildkraut) and the Magdalene, he decided to stick to the biblical text. A practicing Episcopalian, but not above making racy movies, DeMille made sure his cast acted respectfully during the shooting, and he invited representatives of the world's religions to participate in prayer services. Jesuit priest Daniel Lord, who later went on to write the Production Code, was the official Catholic advisor and said mass on *The King of Kings'* set.

While DeMille stuck to the biblical story in *The King of Kings*, other "Bible" movies, like *Spartacus* (1960) or *Barabbas* (1962), moved far from the text in order to create exciting plots and characters. Jesus was merely the starting point for them. In the early 1970s, successful stage musicals were adapted for film with *Godspell* (1973) and *Jesus Christ Superstar* (1973), shaping the Gospel stories into counter-culture tales. These movie musicals raised the ire of some Christians, but it would be a film about Jesus made by an Italian American Catholic that would provoke both Catholics and Protestants to rise up in protest. Martin Scorsese's *The Last*

Temptation of Christ (1988) not only contained a level of biblical violence that Gibson would perfect, it indulged in speculation about the fantasy life of the Savior. Scorsese, who was raised as a Catholic and considered becoming a priest, read Nikos Kazantzakis's 1953 novel in 1972 and was immediately enchanted. He bought the motion picture rights from Kazantzakis's widow in 1977 because, as he later explained, "I've always wanted to do a spiritual movie but religion gets in the way." The movie was difficult both to produce and to film, but Scorsese interpreted such struggles spiritually: "the more suffering the better." Scorsese insisted that *The Last Temptation* did not seek to restate the Gospels but rather to "tear away all the old Hollywood films…and create a Jesus you could talk to and get to know." The film, however, came at a time of increased media scrutiny by conservative Protestants and Catholics, who found Scorsese's representations to be offensive. Religious groups picketed and boycotted the film, thus publicizing their role as a media watchdog. The more they attacked the film, the more Scorsese defended it as his own exploration of faith and art.

That *The Last Temptation of Christ* had personal, theological meaning for Martin Scorsese was overshadowed at the time by threats to free artistic expression. The year the film was released, British Indian novelist Salman Rushdie published *Satanic Verses*. Shortly after, in 1989, the political and spiritual leader of Iran, Ayatollah Ruhollah Khomeini, called on zealous Muslims to kill Rushdie and his publishers because the book profaned the Prophet Muhammad. Rushdie went into hiding and writers and artists around the world condemned this attack on artistic freedom. In the United States, conservative Christians found support in the Reagan White House and forced art museums that received government funding to censor their exhibits. At the very time that independent filmmaking was growing and becoming financially more stable, artists worried that their vision of the world would be attacked and distorted (and, most important, left unfunded) by a powerful coalition of politicians and ministers. Fear of reprisals made museum curators and movie studios nervous about representations of religion. Cultural attention shifted away from how individuals explore and assert religious expressions through the visual arts to how the faithful muzzled the arts.

While many filmmakers have reported exploring faith through film, Mel Gibson is a major Hollywood celebrity who insists that his movie reflects his own personal Christian convictions. Unlike Martin Scorsese, whose movies in the 1970s and 1980s appealed mostly to the art-house crowd, Gibson is an action hero whose films were never praised for their subtle symbolism. The controversy surrounding *The Passion of the Christ* easily drowned out Gibson's repeated comments that his film is not merely an edifying story geared to teach people about the life of

Jesus. Unique in both film and religious history, *The Passion of the Christ* is a specific pious gesture of *one* man, who calls on certain devotional tropes of popular Catholicism.

The film went on to find acceptance among both Catholics and Protestants. If we take Mel Gibson seriously when he describes his movie as a devotional expression, what kind of prayer is it? Rather than analyzing the film as a true (or not true) representation of the Gospels, it is more profitable to think of Gibson's movie as a cinematic ex-voto, a personal "thank you" to God for a miraculous healing. Unlike Scorsese, who sought to represent Jesus in a way that engendered reflection and conversation, Gibson portrays the Passion in a way that intimately and directly speaks to his need for healing.

The term "ex-voto" is the shortening of the Latin phrase *ex-voto suscepto*, "from the vow made." It refers to an expression of gratitude that one makes after moving through a period of crisis. Ex-votos are ways that people say "thanks for the blessing." Believers craft physical symbols and then offer them to God. The impulse to thank God or the gods is ancient and widespread. The Romans carved out of wood or stone small representations of eyes, breasts, internal organs, arms, and legs. These carvings symbolized the parts of the body that had been healed (or that one hoped would be healed). The objects were then thrown into sacred wells or streams. Christians expanded the tradition. In addition to making small metal parts of the body, they represented other ways that God graced their lives. A small fish could be made if there had been an exceptionally good catch or if someone had survived a boating accident while fishing. These objects would be placed in a church or a shrine. European Catholics elaborated on these simple ex-votos and placed in their chapels highly decorative silver hearts. The hearts were reminders of the human heart given to Jesus in thanks as well as the heart of Jesus burning in love for his children.

In the fifteenth century, these symbols of "prayers answered" began to take the form of painted narratives. Wealthy patrons commissioned paintings where they themselves appeared in the scene, and these were placed in churches, shrines, and chapels. The expense of the piece simultaneously spoke of the piety and the prominence of the family. The practice of commissioning paintings also spread to the less wealthy, who hired local artisans to make smaller paintings to be hung behind the altars of churches. Small, painted ex-votos of miraculous events became popular throughout Europe, and Catholics traveled great lengths to hang their stories of divine intervention on the walls of churches. Pilgrimage churches often became filled with the small paintings of unknown craftspeople, which narrated the miracles of ordinary men and women.

11 Votivtafel mit Skapuliermadonna
Österreich, 1787

14.1. In this 1787 Austrian ex-voto we see the core elements of votive offerings: the disaster of a boy falling in a well is averted through the intercession of divine figures: the Virgin Mary, the baby Jesus, and St. Simon Stock.

The painted ex-voto tradition traveled with European colonists to the New World. The Spanish brought the tradition to Mexico, where it flourished. During the nineteenth century, artisans learned how to fix paint on tin, producing ex-votos quickly and cheaply. As the number of ex-votos proliferated, the wealthy abandoned the tradition, leaving the devotion to the average Mexican, who paid a local artisan to make an ex-voto based on his or her miraculous story. In the late nineteenth century, words describing the event came to be painted at the base of the ex-voto. Making ex-voto paintings declined in Europe but remain popular in Latin America. Europeans, however, still leave votive offerings at healing centers such as Lourdes or Fatima. In the contemporary United States where literacy is the norm, ex-votos are typically written. People who believe a miracle has touched their lives write a letter and either mail it to a shrine or publicize the event with a brief thank you in a newspaper or magazine.

All ex-votos—whether painted or written, New World or Old, contemporary or antique—have four characteristics. First, they illustrate a problem that was overcome, a disaster experienced and survived. Either in paint or through words, ex-votos represent the donor sick, struggling with a difficult childbirth, drowning, enduring a fall, being attacked by animals, or coping with war. Some ex-votos, like the *milagros* (miracles) of Mexico or the objects left behind at Lourdes, are mere traces of the tragic story. Others, like the paintings placed in pilgrimage churches or the letters sent to the patron saint of the impossible, St. Jude, are detailed retellings of the event. The key is that an ex-voto needs a crisis and a person who has survived a crisis. Sometimes only the crisis is represented, sometimes only the saved donor, and sometimes both the event and the individual.

The second characteristic of ex-votos is that they represent the one who came to the rescue. Ex-votos do not merely thank a generalized God. Ex-votos thank the specific divine character who performed the miraculous intervention: the Virgin of Guadalupe, St. Anthony of Padua, Christ of the Column (Jesus being scourged at the pillar), the Infant of Prague. Holy figures represented on ex-votos typically follow Catholic iconographic traditions. While believers often thank Jesus or the saints in the privacy of their own hearts, it is the third characteristic of the ex-voto tradition that the holy person is thanked through a *public* gesture. Making ex-votos is a devotional tradition that moves from the private and individual to the public and communal. Ex-votos are placed in churches, often covering the walls. *Milagros* are attached to statues in churches. Letters expressing gratitude are published in the devotional magazines of shrines. Open up a newspaper and look in the personals column and you will see thank yous to St. Jude or to the Sacred Heart. Those who have survived a crisis, through what they understand to be divine grace, are eager to testify to others about the power of God, Mary, and the saints.

And finally, the ex-voto tradition is a lay devotion not under the control of the clergy. One of the reasons people tuck their ex-votos in out-of-the-way places is because in recent years the guardians of major Catholic shrines have found ex-votos to be a nuisance. Bits of paper and metal not only clutter up the churches, their physicality is thought to border on superstition. Why does God need a material reminder of what is in a person's heart? People, however, continually seek to translate their religious experiences into visual and physical representations. They narrate their troubles and recoveries in ways that make sense to them. Clergymen and religious experts do not bless or control the production of ex-votos. Since ex-votos are not attached to Catholic sacramental life, priests have no authority to judge their authenticity against theological norms. Artisans use a set of traditional images and people have common social problems, but at their heart, ex-votos illustrate the endurance of a creative folk Catholicism.

The Problem Survived

In what ways, then, does *The Passion of the Christ* fulfill these four characteristics of the ex-voto? Why should we think of a movie as a votive offering? Mel Gibson did not merely make a film and let his marketing staff promote it through the usual media outlets. The movie was closely accompanied by the stories that Gibson told about why he made it, what it meant to him, what happened during the filming, and what he hoped people would take from the theater. Gibson expressed his thoughts to media interviewers as well as at arranged previews before the movie's opening. This is not merely a movie about Jesus. This is a movie about Jesus accompanied by a story about Mel Gibson. The story, which Gibson told over and over, is about his personal crisis and his eventual healing. Both in the narrative surrounding the film and in the film itself, Gibson paints a picture of pain and suffering relieved only through divine intercession. As with all ex-votos, *The Passion of the Christ* represents a disaster and the one who survived the disaster.

In perhaps his most famous *Passion* interview, with *Primetime* television reporter Diane Sawyer, Gibson laid out why he made the film. Sawyer told her viewing audience that Gibson explained how "the seed of the film was planted thirteen years ago in his personal struggle, self-destruction, and despair." Then, in a colorful raconteur style, Gibson elaborated: "Let's face it, I've been to the pinnacle of what secular utopia has to offer. . . . I've got money, fame, this, that and the other. . . . And when I was younger, I got my proboscis out and I dipped it into the fountain and sucked it up." But living the high life was "not good enough. It leaves you empty. The more you eat, the emptier you get." Gibson then revealed that he had what psychologists might call an addictive personality. "I would get addicted to anything," he admitted, "drugs, booze, anything. You name it. Coffee, cigarettes, anything. . . . I'm just one of these guys who is like that. That's my flaw." This life drove him to "the height of spiritual bankruptcy," to the point that he considered suicide. People had told him for years that "you know, bud, you got a problem" but to no avail. Then, "I think I just hit my knees. I said, help. And then I began to meditate on it. . . . I read all those [Gospels] again. I remember reading bits of them when I was younger. Pain is the precursor to change, which is great. That's the good news." For Gibson, his personal suffering became meaningful when it was connected to the suffering of Christ as expressed in the Bible. "He was beaten for our iniquities. He was wounded for our transgressions," Gibson paraphrased Isaiah 53:5. "And by his wounds we are healed. That's the point of the film."[3]

Critics of the film wondered why Gibson spent almost all of his efforts documenting the brutal beating and crucifixion while including only brief glimpses of Jesus' message and final resurrection. If we think of the film as an ex-voto, then it makes sense that the movie is about suffering. The miracle—the redemption—is the fact that one can make the ex-voto at all. In ex-votos, it is the crisis of the donor that is painted or described in detail. Ex-votos do not only show the person healed, or with the healthy new baby, or standing on safe and dry land. Ex-votos show how the building was shaking, how the bull was pawing the ground, and how the sick person lay in her bed. By remembering the previous pain, the person who has been saved enters into the story and makes sense out of the world-shattering event. When outsiders see ex-votos, they are engaged by the drama of the story. It is through the depiction of troubles that we enter into the religious story. The drama that draws us to look at the ex-voto is the drama of suffering. We look at the suffering with concern and wonder, but we know how the story ends. The suffering does not make us despair or fill us with unrelenting pain because the ex-voto was made. We know the ending is happy.

A year before his film premiered, Gibson explained to a reporter that he was trying to "access the story on a very personal level and trying to be very real about it. I'm doing it in a realistic manner so that it doesn't suffer from the traps of a lot of biblical epics, which quite frankly, suffer from either being too corny, or laughable, or have bad hair or really bad music."[4] The blood and the violence that shocked many viewers have resonances in Mel Gibson's life, as a man, an actor, and a director. *The Passion of the Christ* is not a modern version of medieval piety and anti-Semitism, it is a visual exploration of Gibson's own biography. The emotions and aggression expressed in the film are directly related to how Gibson narrates and performs his own life.

Born in 1956, Mel Columcille Gerard Gibson was the sixth of eleven children. His father, Hutton Gibson, was one of many Irish Americans who earned his living in New York state working on the railroads. His mother, Ann, was also of Irish ancestry, only her family had settled in Australia and then moved to America. Gibson was named after a series of holy men, including St. Columcille (Columba) who along with Saints Patrick and Brigid are the three patron saints of Ireland. Columcille was known for his arrogance and pride. A warrior monk, Columcille waged a battle that, legend has it, succeeded in destroying 3,000 soldiers. The church initially excommunicated him for his action and in 563 exiled him. As a penance for his support of violence, he left Ireland forever and established a monastery on the island of Iona. There he was allowed back into the church and redeemed himself by converting Scotland to Christianity.

The displacement of exile also played out in the Gibson family. After being injured in a railroad accident and successfully winning compensation (as well as some prize money from a quiz show), Hutton Gibson moved his family to Australia. At the age of twelve—no longer a little boy but not yet a man—Gibson was sent to a private Catholic boys' school in a Sydney suburb. A relatively small boy with a Yank accent, Gibson was targeted for teasing and hazing. Rebelling against the Christian brothers who ran the school and trying to hold his own in a hypermasculine Australian culture, Gibson recalls he got "whacked around for smoking, fighting, not following their stupid rules."[5] His family eventually put him in a public school where he learned how to be a proper Aussie "bloke"—to drink and to fight, to lose his American accent, to rely on his wits, and to reject the piety preached by the Christian brothers. Mel Gibson was well acquainted with displacement, beatings, and blood.

In the mid-1970s Gibson's sister Mary filled out his application for the National Institute of Dramatic Arts at the University of New South Wales. When asked by the auditioning committee why he wanted to become an actor, he said, "I've been goofing off all my life. I thought I might as well get paid for that." A shy man whom friends describe as a dreamer, he found that drinking emboldened him. The night before the interview that would win him the lead role in what would become the profoundly violent Mad Max series, Gibson got in a drunken brawl with three other men. "I was a mess," he told an interviewer for Playboy. "I had stitches in my head. I was peeing blood. I couldn't see."[6] His wild look, however, was just what was needed. Mad Max eventually became a hit in Australia and around the world. Even after Gibson's marriage in 1980 to Robyn Moore, the births of their children, and his success in the United States as a movie star, the drinking and sparring continued. In 1984 he was arrested and fined in Canada for drunk driving. Three years later, overworked and frustrated with the burdens of celebrity, he moved his family to a ranch in Australia and began to reconsider his life.

Gibson's struggles are closely tied to a male code of drinking and fighting. It is a code with which men in Catholic countries, where drinking is the social lubricant for liturgical celebrations and saints' festivals, are familiar. There is a profound feeling of helplessness expressed in *The Passion of the Christ* that parallels the alcoholic's sense of slowly being destroyed by an outside, uncontrollable force. Jesus, like a man struggling with drink, cannot avoid the blows and the humiliations. By eliminating all but a few brief scenes of Jesus' life, the film represents the Savior as a passive recipient of the decision of the Sanhedrin, the betrayal of Judas, the taunts of the crowd, and the viciousness of the Romans. This irrational world causes the hero to be beaten and bloodied. As an ex-voto, the movie represents the suffering that Gibson felt as his life was breaking apart under the pressures of celebrity and addiction. "I've been angry all my life," Gibson told Diane Sawyer in a second interview, after his 2006 arrest for drunk driving.[7]

The Passion of the Christ expresses suffering in ways that aficionados of Gibson's movies find familiar. Writing for *Vanity Fair* in 1989, Stephen Schriff observed the celebrity's "passionate masochism" and recited Gibson's litany of pain:

> In *Mad Max* pictures, [Gibson] is regularly pummeled to a pulp and then pummeled again; in *Mrs. Soffel*, he's shot to smithereens and left to crawl in the snow; in *The Year of Living Dangerously*, his very eyes are attacked, so that he's forced to conceal them from our sight in his humid Indonesian bungalow; in *The River*, he's crushed by tractors and spat upon by striking laborers; in *Lethal Weapon*, he's strung up and tortured until he shrieks.

Over a decade before *The Passion*, Schriff quipped, "Gibson looks good in blood." If we think about *The Passion* as a narrative both of Gibson's sufferings and of Jesus, Schriff's final reflection on Gibson is curiously prescient: "His physical perfection is continually sacrificed on the altar of derring-do, as though beauty this intense can be made tolerable only by punishing it." In interviews, Gibson said that he always wanted to play the part of the suffering Christ, but he decided that at forty-seven he was too old. As with all ex-votos, Gibson intended to be the protagonist in his own drama. Instead, he had to give that role to actor James Caviezel and claim center stage through writing, producing, directing, and promoting the film. And Gibson let it be known that it was his hand that drove the nail into Jesus' palm. "I went to the wounds of Christ in order to cure my wounds," Gibson reported. "I didn't try to make a religious film.... I tried to make something that was real to me."[8]

The Rescuer

If *The Passion of the Christ* is a votive offering in the style of a visual ex-voto, then who is the supernatural character who rescues the sufferer? Who remakes the world that is on the edge of being obliterated? I suggest that although Jesus is the subject of the film, it is his mother, Mary, who does the divine intervention. In the larger cosmic scheme, Gibson certainly would say that Christ is the redeemer of the sins of the world. However, in Gibson's cinematic ex-voto, it is Jesus' mother and not the suffering Christ, who is the divine rescuer.

The first clue we have of the centrality of a feminine savior in Gibson's narrative comes from his comments about the role that his wife, Robyn, played in his recovery. "I mean the real medal goes to my wife," Gibson told Diane Sawyer, "Who's a wonderful woman, you know." Unique among movie stars whose romantic lives are the stuff of the tabloids, Gibson is justified in being proud of having been married since 1980 to the same woman. By 2004 the couple had seven children together. "She's the best friend I've ever had. She's just great. And would be there completely, 100 percent, 110 percent." It was Robyn Gibson who eventually told her husband to either stop drinking or their marriage was over. In 1993 Mel Gibson went to Alcoholics Anonymous and stopped for a period. "I think when it comes to a lot of decisions, my wife is definitely the boss," he has said with an air of admiration. "She's head office. She's central and everyone revolves around her." Robyn Gibson's perceived saintliness has motivated her husband to take contradictory stands on where non-Catholics will end up in eternity. To a *New Yorker* writer, Gibson took the hard line, "There is no salvation for those outside the Church.... My wife is a saint. She's a much better person than I am. Honestly. She's, like, Episcopalian, Church of England. She prays, she believes in God, she knows Jesus, she believes in that stuff. And it's just not fair if she doesn't make it, she's better than I am." In his *Primetime* interview a few months later, a more ecumenical response was asserted. When asked if the door of heaven is barred to Jews, Protestants, and Muslims, Gibson responded, "It is possible for people who are not even Christian to get into the Kingdom of Heaven." Diane Sawyer, however, was more interested in having Gibson admit that he had a "ticket" to get through the pearly gates, and so his more-inclusive take on eternity

was ignored.[9] Since anti-Semitism is a key element in the "Gibson phenomenon," reporters and scholars often align the son with his father, Hutton Gibson, who is a Holocaust denier. While the eccentric octogenarian has certainly played an important role in Gibson's life, it is Gibson's wife, the Episcopalian, and not his traditionalist Catholic father whom the moviemaker credits with his turnaround.

The importance of "the mother" is clearly laid out in *The Passion of the Christ*. The movie is structured around common and familiar Catholic devotions, like the rosary and the stations of the cross, which explores the Passion drama through the experiences of Mary. The movie follows the five sorrowful mysteries of the rosary, as Jesus moves from praying in the Garden of Gethsemane, through being scourged and crucified, and eventually ending in the arms of his mother. The film is a meditation by Gibson, who as a former Catholic school boy prayed the stations of the cross: "At the cross her station keeping / Stood the mournful Mother weeping / Close to Jesus 'til the end." At the same time, the film draws from less well-known Marian sources. Gibson recalled how at one point in his religious pilgrimage, a book mysteriously fell off a shelf and he read it. *The Dolorous Passion of Our Lord Jesus Christ* (1833) told of the revelations of the mystic Anne Catherine Emmerich (1774–1824). Her series of visions in the early nineteenth century were cast into prose by Clement Brentano. Emmerich's visions put Mary front and center in the Passion, and the nun later expanded on her understanding of Mary in another work, *The Life of the Blessed Virgin Mary* (1832).

While playing the role of Jesus did not challenge the acting skills of James Caviezel, even the harshest critics of the film noted the dramatic talent of Maia Morgenstern. Morgenstern, the stage actress who plays Mary, was absolutely critical to the success of *The Passion of the Christ*. Appearing in almost every scene in the movie, Morgenstern provides its visual continuity. She shows up in the crowd scenes and interacts intently with an increasingly bloodied Jesus. A practicing Jew from Romania whose grandfather died at Auschwitz, Morgenstern has consistently supported the film and Gibson's role in it. She became pregnant with her third child in the middle of the four-month shoot and has told interviewers that she understood her role as "essentially the question of a mother losing a child."[10] Unlike other Jesus movies where the male apostles represent the first followers of Christ, for Gibson in *The Passion* it is the Virgin Mary who is the first Christian.

Gibson solidifies Mary's presence early in the film when she sees Peter (Francesco De Vito) in the crowd and goes to him for reassurance. When Mary Magdalen (Monica Bellucci) demands that the Roman soldiers halt the arrest of Jesus, his mother is nearby. Soon after that early scene—in a flashback—Mary's place in the film is established. Jesus is standing in chains and hears the sound of wood being hammered. The sound sparks a memory of a day in Nazareth when he was a young man completing a carpentry project. In the vignette, Mary is shown to exercise power over Jesus, and he responds with loving, but independent, acceptance. The two are undeniably connected. The film continues in this pattern: any respite from watching the brutal torture on the screen comes in the moments when the camera pauses on Mary.

This is particularly the case in the exceedingly long whipping scene. As Jesus is scourged, the action is interrupted by two parallel movements. In the first, Satan (Rosalinda Celentano) moves among the Romans. In the second, Mary moves among the watching crowd. Mary and Satan wear identical clothing although the mother's face is framed in white. Eventually, the camera comes to rest on Mary's face as the sounds of the beating continue in the background. Fear, pain, and helplessness are expressed. Gibson includes a scene from one of Emmerich's visions as he has Pilate's wife, Claudia (Claudia Gerini), give Mary a piece of white linen to wipe up the shed blood. We feel not merely the sorrow of one mother, but the agony of all women who have helplessly watched their sons, husbands, and fathers being tortured and killed. It is not difficult to imagine Robyn Gibson watching her talented spouse struggle with alcoholism. Maia Morgenstern explained that she understood the film as conveying the message that "a human being with a weapon in his hands turns easily [in]to a beast in front of a harmless...human being with chains on his wrists."[11] Gibson, however, breaks the potential universality of the scene by introducing Satan again, this time carrying a monstrous baby. The beating is motivated by this supernatural evil and not simply by men with weapons in their hands. Asserting his own Christian convictions—creating his own ex-voto—Gibson evokes the Madonna and child, whom he then inverts into the devil with its repulsive and creepy offspring. This is only one of the many places in the film where Gibson visually reminds us that this is a *supernatural* story, not a story about human nature. Mary is a divine character, not a wife leading her husband to Alcoholics Anonymous.

In the final moments of the film, Gibson presents viewers with the clearest reference to feminine divine salvation. After a dramatic death, the bloodied body of Jesus is taken off the cross and laid in the arms of his mother. Mary caresses her son and kisses him on the cheek. The camera then focuses on her face as she looks up, directly at the viewer. Slowly the camera pulls back, as Mary continues to look out at us. For a dramatic twenty-five seconds—a long time in movie time—Mary stares at a point just beyond the viewer. By the end of the pullback, Gibson (through his director of photography, Caleb Deschanel) creates a version of Michelangelo's *Pietà*. Gibson's Mary, however, does not look downward at the

14.2. Jesus' mother, Mary (Maia Morgenstern), is the supernatural being who rescues the troubled Mel Gibson through his cinematic ex-voto, *The Passion of the Christ*.

body of her child as she does in the famous statue. In the movie her gaze is outward at the viewers whom she "involves in the pain and the guilt of this horrific moment."[12] Through Mary the viewers outside of the frame of action are brought into the sacred event. In this traditionalist Catholic construction of redemption, it is Mary who connects sinners to the saving moment of Christ's death. After the fadeout, there are ten seconds of darkness and then the scraping sound of stone against stone. Slowly the music builds, and we see the profile of the face of the risen Christ. As the drums become more pronounced, the music turns into a march and the camera focuses on the pierced hand of Jesus as he walks out of the tomb. And thus the movie quickly ends. Critics are fully justified in seeing this as an afterthought to the main saving moment of the film.

Public Witness

Ex-votos are not merely prayers of thanksgiving to God, Mary, and the saints. In almost every Christian ritual, God is thanked for his mercy and love. Ex-votos create a *public* witness to supernatural intervention during a crisis. In September 2002, Mel Gibson announced at a press conference that he was going to make a film in two dead languages, Aramaic and Latin. From the beginning, Gibson himself promoted his movie in order to lure people into the theater. Incredulous reporters heard that the movie would be self-financed because of the apathy and wariness of the major movie studios. Such early publicity motivated other reporters to dig up the background on Gibson's quirky Catholicism, leading them to his father and to the church that the celebrity was building in Malibu. Their articles motivated more articles, with Gibson then explaining his position in an interview in January 2003 with Bill O'Reilly on Fox News. Eventually the film's screenplay would be leaked (or stolen, depending on whom you believe) and scholars would warn of its anti-Jewishness. In addition to contacting Eugene Fisher, associate director of the Secretariat for Ecumenical and Interreligious Affairs of the United States Conference of Catholic Bishops, Gibson published in June a statement in the movie journal *Daily Variety* defending both his movie and himself against charges of anti-Semitism.

By the summer, a rough cut was ready for screening, and Gibson began to tour it around the country. He previewed the film not to the usual coterie of movie critics but to groups of conservative Protestants and Catholics. These groups are typically ignored by Hollywood, but Gibson himself answered their questions about religion and movies. He showed a four-minute trailer at the annual meeting of the National Association of Evangelicals in Colorado Springs, Colorado, and a longer version in Houston, Texas, to interfaith and civic leaders. At Loyola Marymount University in Los Angeles, 350 Jesuits watched it. Gibson joked to a reporter that he was nervous about their response. "We're Catholics, right? We're scared of the Jesuits. Every good Catholic is."[13] Left out of the loop, reporters seemingly could not stop discussing the film in print and on television. By the fall, bootlegged copies had appeared, and by Christmas the chatter was whether or not Pope John Paul II had really watched the film and said, "it was as it was." By the film's opening on 25 February 2004, it had already received an unprecedented amount of free publicity and had become a public talking point.

While the controversy surrounding *The Passion of the Christ* took unpredictable turns that thrust it into the media limelight, a considered marketing strategy was also devised to convince people to see the movie. A public needed to be created that understood what Gibson was trying to accomplish. Evangelicals, who stress the importance of a personal relationship with Jesus and who take the scriptures very seriously, had to be convinced that a movie made by a Catholic spoke to their sensibilities. In May 2003 Paul Lauer, marketing director for Gibson's Icon Productions, hired A. Larry Ross Communications (ALRC) to promote the film among Christians. Larry Ross, who for over twenty years had been the director of media and public relations for Billy Graham, had set up ALRC in 1994. His company assists "Christian-focused organizations, associations, ministries and churches in telling their stories through the Christian and secular media in the context of traditional news values."[14] The Dallas company is well known in media circles and among evangelical Protestant organizations. It handled the promotion of DreamWorks' *The Prince of Egypt* (1998), Big Idea Productions' *Jonah: A VeggieTales Movie* (2002), and Cloud Ten Pictures' *Left Behind* movies (2000, 2002, 2005) and videos.

ALRC brashly communicated *The Passion*'s relevance to the evangelistic mission and aggressively marketed it to church congregations. Prior to the film's release, ALRC produced a DVD and mailed it to ministers across the country. In it a prominent evangelical pastor promoted the film as "perhaps the best outreach opportunity in 2,000 years." Promotional materials were sent to churches, and pastors were urged to organize groups to attend. Churches around the world rented theaters to make sure that people had an opportunity to see the film. One Texas couple bought 6,000 tickets to give away at their Baptist church. The official Web sites for the movie sold *Passion*-themed material culture that resembled merchandise sold in Christian bookstores—jewelry, T-shirts, coffee mugs, and books of photographs. ALRC coordinated the private preview screenings for evangelical notables like Billy Graham and Robert Schuller and mass previews for the Full Gospel Business Men's Fellowship meeting. Icon Productions also contracted with smaller public relations firms to target other niche religious markets. Guice Communications, for instance, helped to secure the endorsement of popular black minister T. D. Jakes to promote the film among African American churchgoers. The result of both the intended and unintended publicity for *The Passion of the Christ* was that millions of people saw Mel Gibson's ex-voto. Americans learned from experts whom they trusted—often their own pastors—that Gibson's cinematic representation was "Christian."

Folk Catholicism

Those who publicly represent a miraculous intervention through the production of an ex-voto claim religious authority for themselves. They not only assert that the story really happened as they depict it, they claim that *their* understanding of an intervening God or saint is true. A fundamental assumption of ex-voto making is that the sacred readily and frequently breaks into the profane world. All men, women, and children—not only the clergy, the educated scholar, the seminary professor—directly experience the divine and the biblical message. Ex-votos physically recall the promiscuous character of the divine, who speaks whenever and to whomever.

Mel Gibson surprised many when he explained during previews of his film, "The Holy Ghost was working through me on this film, I was just directing traffic." Diane Sawyer on *Primetime Live* jumped to the conclusion that Gibson "seemed to imply that the Holy Ghost had given him the one true version of the story." Ignoring her overstatement, Gibson reiterated his initial claim: "I think that the Holy Ghost is real. I believe that he's looking favorably on this film. And he wanted to help. I could always use a little help." Gibson's statement reflects a common understanding of religious people that the divine speaks to them. God and his holy people address not only those formally trained but also the average man and woman.

Mel Gibson, of course, is not your "average Christian." The last ten films in which he appeared prior to *The Passion* grossed a cumulative $1.27 billion in North American theaters; *Signs* (2002), for example, grossed nearly $400 million worldwide. Gibson typically earns $20 million to star in a film. He is hardly the same as a Mexican woman who hires a local artisan to paint an ex-voto on tin. Although not a common man, Gibson sees himself as one. Although his films cost millions of dollars, they are a part of the world of the "folk."

Gibson consistently chooses roles where he plays an average Joe who has been brutalized by the powerful and then who comes back to overrule their authority. Gibson's later films, especially those in which he both directed and starred, routinely ridicule acknowledged experts and triumph over the powerful. In *The Man without a Face* (1993), a shaggy-haired Yale professor is the ineffectual suitor of the protagonist's mother. In *The Patriot* (2000), a sadistic British officer meets his comeuppance from an enraged South Carolina farmer. The minister who figures in the plot is fully under the inspiration of the farmer. A tagline for *Braveheart* (1995) was "What kind of man would defy a king?" And the answer was the commoner William Wallace (Gibson), who shouted, "Go back to England and tell them Scotland is free." Even the bucolic hero of *Apocalypto* (2006) triumphs over his elaborately headdressed enemies. Likewise, the Jesus of *The Passion of the Christ* resolutely withstands the accusations of the Pharisees, the condemnation of Pilate, and the scourging of the Roman soldiers. Unlike the confused Jesus of Scorsese's *The Last Temptation of Christ*, Gibson's Jesus is a self-confident carpenter. He does not weigh the various options like a thoughtful social reformer, he does what he is destined to do.

Gibson's antiauthoritarianism is echoed in his real-life rejection of the authority of the current pope, the Second Vatican Council, and the advice of biblical historians. After a group of Catholic and Jewish scholars read an early version of the script of *The Passion*, they sent a report detailing the film's historical and theological inaccuracies to Gibson. Gibson in turn directed his lawyers to accuse them of being in possession of stolen property while he reasserted his right to represent the Gospels. "They always dick around with it, you know?" he explained in a *New Yorker* interview:

> Judas is always some kind of friend of some freedom fighter named Barabbas, you know what I mean? It's horseshit. It's revisionist bullshit. And that's what these academics are into. They gave me notes on a stolen script. I couldn't believe it. It was like they were more or less saying I have no right to interpret the Gospels myself, because I don't have a bunch of letters after my name. But they are for children, these Gospels. They're for children, they're for old people, they're for everybody in between. They're not necessarily for academics.

And to make sure he placed himself on the side of the average person, Gibson concluded, "Just get an academic on board if you want to pervert something."[15]

The image of Gibson as "just like us" was only solidified in the minds of his supporters after his DUI arrest. Here was a millionaire celebrity, pulled over in his Lexus, who was drunk and swearing at the police. They carted him off to jail, and he eventually had to apologize to his family, to Jews, to his fans, and to his critics. Gibson was humbled as we all have been—only more so.

Washed in the Blood of the Lamb

Gibson intended to bring the same people who enjoyed *Braveheart* into the theater to watch a film about Jesus. These were not individuals schooled in the various cinematic adaptations of the biblical story or those who were familiar with New Testament scholarship. Gibson's audience was made up of churchgoers and those who enjoyed his action movies. But why would evangelical Protestants, who are known to privilege the word of God over the image of God, flock to Gibson's film? After a private showing of *The Passion of the Christ*, the noted evangelist Billy Graham praised it: "Every time I preach or speak about the Cross," he was widely quoted as saying, "the things I saw on the screen will be on my heart and mind."[16] Why did Bible-believing Protestants pay to see Mel Gibson's Catholic ex-voto? What was the local context for the reception of *The Passion of the Christ* which made this ex-voto meaningful to many evangelicals, especially to young male evangelicals? The reception of the film indicates that the devotional orientation of many Catholics and Protestants is converging and that the post-9/11 political environment is speeding up that process.

Protestants have their own versions of ex-votos, which tell stories of disasters and salvations. A critical dimension of evangelical Protestantism is the conversion experience—the movement from sinfulness into acceptance of Jesus and a Christian lifestyle. Beginning in the eighteenth century, Protestants took advantage of new printing technologies to publish their narratives of how they—and their communities—were delivered out of the dark worlds of bitterness, bondage, and despair. Cut off from having an intimate relationship with God, they were engulfed by guilt and misery. Conversion stories, like Jonathan Edwards's *The Faithful Narrative of the Surprising Work of God* (1737) and John Newton's *An Authentic Narrative* (1764), provide detailed descriptions of the inner turmoil that people went through before they were "delivered out of an horrible pit, and from the miry clay, and set upon a rock, with a new song of praise to God in their mouths."[17] These narratives contributed to the new style of "evangelical" Protestantism by establishing the oral (and written) confession as a religious practice. When Mel Gibson went before groups of Protestants and told his "once was lost, now am found" story, he was participating in a long-standing evangelical tradition of witnessing.

If Gibson had merely spoken about his life, he would have resembled the revivalist preacher who calls on his own struggles as proof of the Lord's abiding care for humanity. Gibson, however, did not merely publicly speak or write about his conversion experience. He made a *visual* testimony that conflated his own struggles with those of Jesus. Why would Protestants respond to his highly imaginative, theatrical portrayal of suffering? While scholars have remarked that Gibson's masculine Christ reflects a trend in Protestantism to turn away from the feminized Victorian Jesus, what they have missed is the long-standing focus on blood and pain in evangelical popular piety. Gibson and others might be correct in accusing Hollywood of portraying Jesus as sanitized and soft, but this is not to say that this is the only representation of the Savior. One does not have to return to medieval Europe or baroque Mexico to find powerful images of the redemptive power of blood and sacrifice.

Since the eighteenth century, Protestants have been singing about the "blood of the lamb," which is shed for them and their sins. In the poem that became the famous "Rock of Ages" (1776), the first stanza summarizes what many hymnists have said in more or less vivid terms:

> *Rock of Ages, cleft for me,*
> *Let me hide myself in Thee;*
> *Let the water and the blood,*

> From Thy wounded side which flowed,
> Be of sin the double cure,
> Save from wrath and make me pure.[18]

William Cowper, another British evangelical, suffered from suicidal bouts of depression and wrote in 1772 that "There is a Fountain Filled with Blood." His concluding verse claimed the blood image for Protestants:

> E'er since, by faith, I saw the stream
> Thy flowing wounds supply,
> Redeeming love has been my theme,
> And Shall be till I die.

Jesus was not merely an example to Christians, he was a sacrificial offering whose shed blood enabled their salvation. "Lay aside the garments that are stained with sin," wrote Elisha Hoffman in 1878, "And be washed in the blood of the lamb." Hymn writers have drawn from Hebrews 9:22: "everything is cleansed by blood and without the shedding of blood there is no forgiveness." Such blood images were combined with texts about a purifying fountain from Zechariah 13:1, thus inspiring Protestants to sing:

> That crimson stream flows from Thy side,
> O fountain great, so deep and wide
> My sins are gone, it reaches me
> That precious blood of Calvary. (Barney Warner, 1911)

By the late twentieth century, contemporary Christian rock musician Carman recited in his song *This Blood*:

> Violently they grabbed his arms,
> As they tightly strapped each wrist,
> With a hellish look stood a strong armed soldier,
> Whip clenched in his fist,
> Laced with chips of bone they beat him hard,
> From his shoulders to his feet,
> And it sliced right through his olive skin,
> Just like razors through a sheet.

Evangelicals are no strangers to blood imagery. Carman frequently sings to large audiences of college students the traditional hymn "Oh, the Blood of Jesus" with its refrain "What can make me whole again? / Nothing but the blood of Jesus."

It is not only the blood of Jesus that is shed. Generations of Protestants have been reared on martyr stories that dramatically describe suffering, torture, and death. From Foxe's *The Book of Martyrs* (1563) with its woodcuttings, to the heroic tales of frontier missionaries, to the sufferings of evangelicals in communist China, to the brutal murders of the Columbine High school teens, Protestants have produced and consumed stories of violence. Martyrdom narratives are designed to outrage and to inspire. They join conversion stories as verifiable examples of the strength of believers. Readers explore worlds of pain and suffering translated into redemptive sacrifice. In recent years, the bestselling *Left Behind* novels by Tim LaHaye and Jerry B. Jenkins have added the genre of apocalyptic fiction to such Christian crisis literature. Loosely based on the biblical Book of Revelation, the novels are filled with scenes of murder and mayhem. Violence is a critical aspect of popular Christian fiction, and evangelical Protestants are routinely exposed to the shed blood of believers as they battle Satan's minions.

By the late twentieth century, conservative Protestants were not merely singing and reading about blood, they were looking at violence and pain in evangelical cinema and church dramas. In 1970 a movie version of the popular memoir *The Cross and the Switchblade* (1963) was released. The film tells the story of converted New York gang member Nicky Cruz (Erik Estrada). Although the bulk of the film focuses on street minister David Wilkerson (Pat Boone), the movie is more than a pious version of *West Side Story* (1961). Savage beatings, gritty scenes of stabbings, and explicit renditions of a prostitute shooting up heroin shocked and fascinated young viewers. The film became a classic youth-group movie. *The Cross and the Switchblade*'s author, David Wilkerson, claims the film has been dubbed into thirty languages, shown in 150 countries, and watched by over fifty million people.

The Cross and the Switchblade began a trend of evangelical movies that did not shy away from faith cultivated in a context of violence, pain, and blood. Most were hopelessly corny and rarely moved beyond the fundamentalist southern subculture. In 1971, former B-movie director Ron Ormond made *If Footmen Tire You, What Will Horses Do?* Based on the sermons of Baptist preacher Estus W. Pirkle, the movie dramatizes what happens when communists take over the United States and begin to execute Christians. Ormond fills the movie with blood: a father is impaled on a pitchfork over and over by his own son, a boy has his ear pierced with bamboo sticks for listening to the Gospels being read, and another has his head lopped off by a communist goon, who tosses it in a driveway. A more widely circulated movie is the end-times tale *A Distant Thunder* (1978), where a woman is executed by guillotine at the movie's end.

These early movies now seem outrageously cheesy, but Christian violence is consistently being upgraded by special effects experts. Cloud Ten Pictures' productions of the *Left Behind* novels (2000, 2002, 2005) and Trinity Broadcasting Network's popular *Omega Code* films (1999, 2001) include technically sophisticated representations of explosions and bloodshed. And when the singer Carman decided to move into acting, he starred in *The Champion* (2001), a movie that ends with a former boxer reentering the ring for one last bloody match. Christian filmmakers see themselves as producing movies that are not filled with violence and sexuality, but at the same time they know that all moviegoers are used to sophisticated visual excitement and will not pay attention unless the action is gripping. In particular, men, who are not easily drawn into church culture, can be courted by providing stories that parallel the excitement of secular entertainment. Films that include redemptive violence are often directed toward teenage boys who have been raised on a diet of video games, reality TV shows, and heavy metal rock music. They know that a movie made by Mel Gibson has high production values with none of the soft, Sunday school sentimentality that colors most family-friendly films. The financial success of *The Passion* will continue this trend of action-packed Christian cinema as non-Christian distribution companies, like FoxFaith, seek to capture the dollars of the churchgoing audience. How to achieve just the right amount of bloodshed within family-friendly plots will be the moviemakers' difficult task.

Watching Christian movies is one part of a flourishing evangelical subculture that includes wearing T-shirts with an outstretched crucified arm, sending Christmas cards that look like three drops of blood were spilled on them, and building seasonal Halloween "hell houses" where sinners have "died" from abortions and suicides. Christian companies exploit the conflation of pop culture and faith. To teenagers familiar with rap music and goth fashions, they market T-shirts with slogans like "My Posse's Ready for Spiritual Warfare" or "Body Piercing Saved My Life." Computer games like "Catechumen" enable players to use swords to convert Roman soldiers to Christianity. While Mel Gibson certainly ratcheted up the level of violence, his preference for the blood of Jesus is not alien to evangelicals. Even believers who recoil from the poor writing of the *Left Behind* series or the ridiculousness of having Michael York play the Antichrist see images projected on movie screens during Sunday worship services in their suburban megachurches. The modern megachurch—a large, Bible-based Protestant church—often has spacious lobbies designed to look like a food court or a multiplex movie theater entry area. The division between worship and entertainment is not precise.

Conservative Protestants developed a highly visual and tactile religious culture after the Second World War. By the 1980s, material culture and the media were called up as aids in waging "spiritual battles" against an increasingly "secular" America. Representations of Christian suffering—both in written and visual forms—play into a widespread conservative claim that our ordered society is breaking apart. While the crisis that Gibson addresses in this film might be his personal struggle with alcoholism and anger, on a cultural level the film echoes the oft-stated notion that "forces" are destroying our civilization, not unlike the Romans destroyed the body of Jesus. It does no good to try to address these forces with reason or understanding as they are motivated by supernatural powers. Like the androgynous devil who haunts *The Passion of the Christ*, this kind of evil is not simply generated by disordered thought or faulty interpretations. For Gibson and many of his fans, there is a metaphysical reality to evil that justifies the need for extreme violence. Those who destroyed the World Trade Towers must not be reasoned with, they must be eradicated. The visceral suffering that the good endure in this process—the trials of Jesus in *The Passion*, of Benjamin Martin in *The Patriot*, or of William Wallace in *Braveheart*—parallel the struggles of those who sacrifice for their highest ideals. When Jesus' blood is shed with such profusion during a presidential election year, it raises the political questions of who defines "sin" and who are the "redeemed." For Republicans, who ran an evangelical Christian candidate and claimed the support of the "values voter," *The Passion of the Christ* aided in the establishment of a sacred authority that could justify a war in Iraq and Afghanistan and the curbing of civil liberties. Just as there could be no compromises with the Roman guards, there must be no negotiation with terrorists. Normal patterns of social interaction—talk, dissent, compromise—are rendered impossible by the need for redemptive vengeance.[19]

That social scientists will tell us that postwar Americans still go to church and synagogue far more than their European cousins is of no comfort to those who see their world being unmade by unseen beings. Likewise, the very successful political and religious alliances that have solidified the Republican party base never seem to make the nation secure and moral enough. Indeed, the repetition of what one scholar has termed "the religion of fear" functions to keep believers always on the alert for new threats to what is perceived to be their precarious Christian hold over public and private morality.[20] Mel Gibson's drunken tirades are indicative of what can happen when one is not vigilant—against the disease/sin of alcoholism, against Muslim terrorists, against homosexual claims to marriage, against an activist Supreme Court.

Today, evangelicals—much more than those in liberal Protestant denominations—are comfortable using modern technology, music, and material culture to stimulate religious sentiments. Evangelicals believe that running a Christian bookstore or designing a video game can promote the kingdom of God. Indeed, many younger evangelicals would argue that the entertainment world of movies and games are more effective in spreading the gospel than are sermons and tracts. Media are used to arouse religious passion, which then can be closely aligned to patriotism in general and to a Republican political agenda in particular. The heightened emotional state that Catholic Mel Gibson creates in a darkened theater is no longer considered that frightening by evangelicals because they produce similar environments for their religious and political causes. *The Passion of the Christ* makes sense to many Protestants because of the devotional and ideological practices cultivated within their own religious communities.

The highly visual and sensual nature of contemporary evangelical piety means that traditional Catholic devotionalism with its images of Mary and the Passion are no longer alien in the United States. The financial success of *The Passion*, for instance, motivated the commercial studio New Line Cinema to produce *The Nativity Story* (2006). Filmed partly in the same Italian town of Matera as *The Passion* and Pier Paolo Pasolini's *The Gospel According to St. Matthew* (1964), *The Nativity Story* centers on a sixteen-year-old Mary's (Keisha Castle-Hughes) reaction to her arranged marriage, pregnancy, and birth. The film was first premiered to 7,000 invited guests at a hall next to St. Peter's basilica in the Vatican. Although its young star had become pregnant by her boyfriend during its filming, evangelical leaders praised the film and encouraged attendance. Spiritual emotions stimulated by sight—characteristics once ascribed to idolatrous immigrant Catholics—now have a secure place in Protestant America. Movies encourage the conflation of the biblical word and the biblical image.

At the same time, for Catholics, the changes of the Second Vatican Council have made them more open to Protestantism. Vatican II firmly established the right of both democracy and religious pluralism to exist. This permitted American Catholics to associate more closely with Protestants—of all theological orientations. Catholics are encouraged to do what Protestants have long valued: read the Bible more intently and cultivate a personal relationship with Jesus. Protestants and Catholics have drawn together both socially and theologically. At the same time, the popes who came after the council have insisted that there is a fixed moral and supernatural system. The Vatican's stance on sexuality, women's rights, the importance of the scriptures, and the magnitude of the mysteries of faith resonate with Protestant conservatives. Even though Gibson does not believe that the current pope is a legitimate Catholic authority, he does share a common moral system with the Vatican. Evangelicals and conservative Catholics agree that they must reject the idea of a disenchanted, secular world. Catholics can embrace Mel Gibson's stress on blood atonement and his public evangelizing without threat to their faith. While Gibson's own Catholic identity is complicated by the fact that he does not recognize the authority of the Second Vatican Council, he has forged a more powerful identity as a "Christian," which embraces Protestants and Catholics.

During the presidential election year of 2004, campaign strategists for George W. Bush realized that the boundaries between Protestants and Catholics had changed. They knew that capturing the Catholic vote for the Republican candidate was critical, especially in swing states like Ohio. Campaigners targeted church-going Catholics, convincing over half of them not to vote for their fellow Catholic, John Kerry. Just as Catholic Mel Gibson engaged evangelicals in his visual votive offering, evangelical Bush persuaded Catholics that he represented their Christian values. *The Passion of the Christ*, like the reelection of George Bush, is emblematic of a new form of conservative ecumenicism. Words and images can be gathered from many Christian traditions and assembled into imaginative stories that speak to individual hopes and collective spiritual longings.

NOTES

1. Leon Wieseltier, "The Worship of Blood," in *On* The Passion of the Christ: *Exploring Issues Raised by the Controversial Movie,* ed. Paula Fredriksen (Berkeley: University of California Press, 2006), 256, originally published in the *New Republic* (8 March 2004); Robert Orsi quoted by Beth Poitier in "At the Divinity School Passionate Talk of *The Passion of the Christ,*" *Harvard University Gazette,* 25 March 2004, available at http://www.news.harvard.edu/gazette; Roger Ebert, "The Passion of the Christ," 24 February 2004, available at http://rogerebert.suntimes.com; box office figures are grosses not adjusted for inflation. The three films that had earned more were *Spiderman* (2002), *Matrix Reloaded* (2003), and *Lord of the Rings: The Return of the King* (2003), all summer releases. *The Passion* had the highest gross for a winter weekend (http://boxofficemojo.com). For DVD sales, see http://www.the-numbers.com/movies/2004/pason.php.

2. George M. Smiga, "The Good News of Mel Gibson's *Passion,*" in *Mel Gibson's Bible: Religion, Popular Culture, and* The Passion of the Christ, ed. Timothy K. Beal and Tod Linafelt (Chicago, IL: University of Chicago Press, 2006).

3. *Primetime Live: Mel Gibson's Passion: Interview with Diane Sawyer,* aired 16 February 2004.

4. *New York Daily News,* 26 January 2003.

5. Quoted on http://www.tiscali.co.uk/entertainment/film/biographies/mel_gibson_biog.html. Such biographical information on Mel Gibson can be found on many

fan pages and movie sites on the Internet that summarize popular biographies of Gibson such as David Ragan, *Mel Gibson* (London: Allen, 1986), and Wensley Clarkson, *Mel Gibson: Living Dangerously* (New York: Thunder's Mouth, 1999).

6. There are many versions of Gibson's comment about being paid for goofing off; see his 1999 interview at Harvard, available at http://www.news.harvard.edu/gazette/1996/11.14/LearningfromPer.html; Lawrence Grobel, "Interview with Mel Gibson," *Playboy*, July 1995.

7. Mel Gibson interview with Diane Sawyer, *Good Morning America*, 13 October 2006.

8. Stephen Schriff, "Mel Gibson: Jack of Hearts," *Vanity Fair*, July 1989. According to *Christianity Today*, "Mel Gibson the director grabbed the mallet and spikes from the actor who was supposed to be nailing Jesus to the cross. The cameras kept rolling as Gibson wielded the hammer to show how he wanted the nails driven. The close-up cameo of Gibson's hands became part of *The Passion*." Gibson repeated this comment about not making a religious film at the previews of *The Passion*, including when it was shown at Willow Creek Community Church, a megachurch outside of Chicago. For both comments see *Christianity Today*, 24 March 2004, available at http://www.christianitytoday.com/movies/commentaries/passion-passionofmel.html.

9. *Primetime* interview; Peter J. Boyer, "Reporter at Large," *New Yorker*, 15 September 2003.

10. Naomi Pfefferman, "Actress Defends Gibson's Jesus Film," *Jewish Journal* (10 October 2003), available at http://www.jewishjournal.com/home/searchview.php?id=11135.

11. Ibid.

12. Diane Apostolos-Cappadona, "On Seeing *The Passion*: Is There a Painting in This Film? Or Is This Film a Painting?" in *Re-Viewing* The Passion, ed. S. Brent Plate (New York: Palgrave, 2004), 106.

13. Boyer, "Reporter at Large."

14. See http://www.alarryross.com/homepage.aspx.

15. Boyer, "Reporter at Large."

16. Cited at http://www.thepassionoutreach.com/quotes.asp.

17. Jonathan Edwards, *The Faithful Narrative of the Surprising Work of God* (1737), section I, is available at http://members.aol.com/jonathanedw/Narrative.html.

18. Full lyrics for all hymns are found on Internet sites such as lyricsdownload.com and hymnsite.com.

19. I'd like to thank Bob Orsi for helping me sort out the political ramifications of the film.

20. Jason Bivins, *The Religion of Fear*, forthcoming from Oxford University Press.

FURTHER READING

Bartov, Omer. *The "Jew" in Cinema: From the Golem to Don't Touch My Holocaust.* Bloomington: Indiana University Press, 2005.

Beal, Timothy K., and Tod Linafelt, eds. *Mel Gibson's Bible: Religion, Popular Culture, and* The Passion of the Christ. Chicago, IL: University of Chicago Press, 2006.

Corley, Kathleen E., and Robert L. Webb, eds. *Jesus and Mel Gibson's* The Passion of the Christ: *The Film, the Gospels, and the Claims of History.* New York: Continuum, 2004.

Cuneo, Michael W. *The Smoke of Satan: Conservative and Traditionalist Dissent in Contemporary American Catholicism.* New York: Oxford University Press, 1997.

Fox, Richard W. *Jesus in America: Personal Savior, Cultural Hero, National Obsession.* San Francisco, CA: HarperSanFrancisco, 2005.

Landres, J. Shawn, and Michael Berenbaum. *After* The Passion *Is Gone: American Religious Consequences.* Lanham, MD: AltaMira, 2004.

Levy, Emanuel. *Cinema of Outsiders: The Rise of American Independent Film.* New York: New York University Press, 2001.

McDannell, Colleen. *Material Christianity: Religion and Popular Culture in America.* New Haven, CT: Yale University Press, 1995.

Orsi, Robert A. *Thank You, St. Jude: Women's Devotion to the Patron Saint of Hopeless Causes.* New Haven, CT: Yale University Press, 1996.

Perspectives on The Passion of the Christ: *Religious Thinkers and Writers Explore the Issues Raised by the Controversial Movie.* New York: Miramax, 2004.

Plate, S. Brent, ed. *Re-Viewing* The Passion: *Mel Gibson's Film and Its Critics.* New York: Palgrave, 2004.

Prothero, Stephen. *American Jesus: How the Son of God Became a National Icon.* New York: Farrar, Straus and Giroux, 2004.

Riley, Robin. *Film, Faith, and Cultural Conflict: The Case of Martin Scorsese's* The Last Temptation of Christ. Westport, CT: Praeger, 2003.

Tatum, W. Barnes. *Jesus at the Movies.* Santa Rosa, CA: Polebridge, 1997.

Weaver, Mary Jo, and R. Scott Appleby, eds. *Being Right: Conservative Catholics in America.* Bloomington: Indiana University Press, 1995.

Due to the large number of titles in the index, initial articles have been dropped to avoid confusion.